Mathieu Bourgois

HAZEL ROWLEY was born in London and educated in England and Australia. She is the author of three previous biographies: *Christina Stead: A Biography*, a *New York Times* Best Book of the Year; *Richard Wright: The Life and Times*, a *Washington Post* Best Book of the Year; and *Tête-à-Tête: Simone de Beauvoir and Jean-Paul Sartre*, which has been translated into twelve languages. She received fellowships from the Radcliffe Institute and the Rockefeller Foundation. She died in New York City on March 1, 2011.

ALSO BY HAZEL ROWLEY

Christina Stead: A Biography

Richard Wright: The Life and Times

Tête-à-Tête: Simone de Beauvoir and Jean-Paul Sartre

Additional Praise for *Franklin and Eleanor*

"A compelling history with first-rate character portraits of the Roosevelts and their closest friends." —*The Christian Science Monitor*

"Hazel Rowley has gone beyond the gossip and gives us a book of real insight and a tale that is as sympathetic as it is cautionary." —*The Washington Times*

"Vivid and deft." —*The Cleveland Plain Dealer*

"An incisive portrait of a new kind of marriage . . . The author turns a familiar story into a page-turner, bringing out the nuances of this marriage and of their relationships with others around them." —*Library Journal*

"History with an attitude." —*The Buffalo News*

"A focused account of a complex marriage that continues to fascinate." —*Kirkus Reviews*

"An engrossing account of an unusual pairing of two extraordinary people." —*Publishers Weekly*

"*Franklin and Eleanor* is a fascinating read, rich with insight and detail. Here is a political marriage that rose above politics; a partnership that was driven as much by idealism as by ambition; and a friendship that survived despite it all. Hazel Rowley is a wonderful writer with a gift—rare among historians—for entertaining her readers."
—Amanda Foreman, author of *Georgiana: Duchess of Devonshire*

Franklin and Eleanor

Franklin and Eleanor

AN EXTRAORDINARY MARRIAGE

Hazel Rowley

PICADOR

FARRAR, STRAUS AND GIROUX
NEW YORK

www.picadorusa.com
www.twitter.com/picadorusa • www.facebook.com/picadorusa

Picador® is a U.S. registered trademark and is used by Farrar,
Straus and Giroux under license from Pan Books Limited.

For book club information, please visit www.facebook.com/picadorbookclub
or e-mail marketing@picadorusa.com.

Grateful acknowledgment is made to Nancy Roosevelt Ireland for permission to reprint excerpts from Eleanor Roosevelt's memoirs *This Is My Story* © 1939 and *This I Remember* © 1949, as well as her "My Day" columns.

Grateful acknowledgment is made to the Boston Medical Library in the Francis A. Countway Library of Medicine for permission to reprint the following material: Excerpts from a letter written by Dr. Eben Bennet to Dr. Robert Lovett, August 31, 1921. Excerpts from a letter written by Dr. Robert Lovett to Dr. Eben Bennet, September 3, 1921. Excerpts from a letter written by Dr. George Draper to Dr. Robert Lovett, September 24, 1921. Excerpts from a letter written by Kathleen Lake to Dr. Robert Lovett, December 17, 1921. Excerpts from a letter written by Dr. George Draper to Dr. Robert Lovett, June 9, 1922. Excerpts from a letter written by Kathleen Lake to Dr. Robert Lovett, May 24, 1923, and March 17, 1922. Excerpts from a letter written from Dr. Robert Lovett to Franklin D. Roosevelt, August 14, 1922.

Grateful acknowledgment is made to the Estate of Daisy Suckley for permission to reprint excerpts from Daisy Suckley's diary, published in *Closest Companion,* Geoffrey Ward, ed., Boston and New York, Houghton Mifflin Company, 1995. Courtesy of Wilderstein Preservation.

Grateful acknowledgment is made to the following to reprint material: Reprinted from Lorena A. Hickok, *Eleanor Roosevelt: Reluctant First Lady* (New York: Dodd, Mead & Company, 1962).

Designed by Jonathan D. Lippincott

The Library of Congress has cataloged the Farrar, Straus and Giroux edition as follows:

Rowley, Hazel.
    Franklin and Eleanor : an extraordinary marriage / Hazel Rowley.— 1st ed.
      p. cm.
    Includes index.
    ISBN 978-0-374-15857-6
    1. Roosevelt, Franklin D. (Franklin Delano), 1882–1945.　2. Roosevelt, Eleanor, 1884–1962.　3. Presidents—United States—Biography.　4. Presidents' spouses—United States—Biography.　5. Married people—United States—Biography.
I. Title.
    E807.R763 2010
    973.917092—dc22
    [B]

        2010005678

Picador ISBN 978-0-312-61063-0

First published in the United States by Farrar, Straus and Giroux

First Picador Edition: October 2011

10　9　8　7　6　5　4　3　2　1

CONTENTS

Preface • *xiii*

ONE: Cousins in Love, 1902–1905 • 3

TWO: A Victorian Marriage, March 1905–March 1913 • 39

THREE: Somewhat at Sea, March 1913–February 1920 • 63

FOUR: Tragedy at Campobello, June 1920–March 1922 • 91

FIVE: The Wilderness Years, March 1922–November 1928 • 119

SIX: In the Governor's Mansion, November 1928–
    March 1933 • 153

SEVEN: Grand Hotel, March 1933–November 1936 • 179

EIGHT: Embattled, November 1936–November 1940 • 211

NINE: "I am a bit exhausted . . ." December 1940–
    March 1945 • 241

TEN: The Rose Garden, March 1945–November 1962 • 275

Notes • *303*
Acknowledgments • *329*
Index • *333*

PREFACE

I can honestly say—though I'll be thought biased—that the best museum I've ever visited, anywhere in the world, is the Franklin D. Roosevelt Presidential Library and Museum in Hyde Park, two hours north of New York City by train or car, in the beautiful Hudson valley. It's a large country estate, with several different dwellings, and it takes a whole day to go through it properly.

There's the Big House, where FDR was born in an upstairs bedroom in 1882, and where he brought his bride, Eleanor, for the first week of their honeymoon in 1905. Although it belonged to his mother, Sara Delano Roosevelt, FDR always regarded it as his true home. The house has been preserved as it was at the time of his mother's death in September 1941. In the front entrance you see a glass cabinet with some of the birds Franklin shot and stuffed in his adolescence. Scattered throughout the house are ornaments from China, where Sara Delano spent several years in her childhood, while her father made a fortune from the opium trade. There are naval prints and paintings of ships everywhere. The most imposing room in the house is the library, with its handsome wooden panels, vast bookcases, fireplaces, and magnificent views of the Catskill Mountains across the Hudson River. Not far from the house, near the stables, is the rose garden where FDR and Eleanor are buried, side by side.

A short walk away is the museum, a Dutch fieldstone building, which contains absorbing photos, letters, recordings, historical film footage, FDR's and Eleanor's private studies, and FDR's 1936 Ford Phaeton, outfitted with hand controls. Eleanor Roosevelt's cottage, Val-Kill, two miles through the woods in a minibus, looks from the outside like the factory it once was. Inside it is humbly cozy, a maze of guest rooms, looking out onto forest, the stream, and a pond. It was here that Eleanor entertained people from all walks of life—from annual picnics for underprivileged "Negro" boys from the Wiltwyck School for Boys to some of the most important world leaders of the time, including John F. Kennedy, Pandit Nehru, Marshal Tito, and Haile Selassie. The same guided tour takes you over rough winding roads to Top Cottage, one of the highest points in Dutchess County (inaccessible in winter because of the ice), where FDR liked to take tea with friends on the porch, enjoying the rustle of leaves in the breeze.

When I first went to Hyde Park, the summer after I moved to New York, I thought I already knew a lot about the Roosevelts. But as our cheerful little group drove from Sara's gloomy cluttered Victorian mansion to FDR's simple stone dwelling among the dogwoods and pines, I became freshly fascinated by this couple and their remarkable lives. So, it seemed, was everyone else, since there were lots of questions, particularly about the Roosevelts' relationship.

One person asked if there was a good book on the Roosevelt marriage. "Nothing recent," the guide replied. She mentioned *Eleanor and Franklin* (1971) by Joseph Lash, a close friend of Eleanor's; and Doris Kearns Goodwin's *No Ordinary Time: Franklin and Eleanor Roosevelt: The Home Front in World War II* (1994), which focuses on the final five years in the Roosevelts' forty-year marriage. There were plenty of books in the New Deal Store, she said, next to Mrs. Nesbitt's Café in the Welcome Center. It was sunset by the time I drove back to Manhattan, with the seed of my next book in my head.

This is the story of the Roosevelt marriage—its evolution from a conventional Victorian family into the bold and radical partnership that made Franklin and Eleanor Roosevelt go down in history as one of the most inspiring couples of all time. In the face of trials that would test any marriage—FDR's domineering mother, the onset of FDR's polio, the strains of twelve years in the White House, the burden of leading the American people through the twentieth century's most traumatic catastrophes—FDR and Eleanor emerged triumphant. As president and first lady, they commanded respect at home and abroad. In the eyes of the free world, their partnership came to represent the ideals of Western liberal democracy. Were they not a model of equality, openness, and freedom of speech?

When I told the chief archivist at the FDR Library that I was researching the Roosevelt marriage, he remarked, "A touchy subject." The marriage raised eyebrows in the Roosevelts' lifetimes, and since Eleanor's death details have emerged which makes it more controversial than ever. Was it a good relationship, or was it "flawed," as most Roosevelt scholars seem to think? Did Franklin and Eleanor have affairs? Was Eleanor a lesbian?

It is astounding, when you think about it, that the Roosevelts' marriage is still shrouded in mystery and secrecy. From March 1905, when the bride was given away by her father's brother, President Theodore Roosevelt, until the death of Franklin Roosevelt in April 1945, at the beginning of his fourth term as president, this marriage was played out in the public gaze. FDR was the longest-serving president in American history, and yet even as the most famous couple in the nation, living under relentless scrutiny, the Roosevelts managed to maintain their unorthodox private lives, keeping major details hidden from the public and sometimes from each other.

Surprisingly, the fresh material that has come our way in the past few years has had little impact on what I call "the standard narrative"— by which I mean the story most of us think we know. According to this version, Eleanor's discovery of FDR's affair with Lucy Mercer in 1918 was a dramatic turning point, after which the marriage degenerated, with Franklin and Eleanor keeping up a gracious façade, all the while finding their escape in politics and close friends.

This, at least, is the basic plot, and beyond this, everyone takes sides. Some see Franklin as the long-suffering partner, while others claim it was Eleanor. FDR's partisans (usually male) paint a picture of Eleanor that is one-dimensional to the point of misogyny. Eleanor Roosevelt's supporters (usually female) paint FDR as a slippery egotist. Just after Eleanor's death, Martha Gellhorn, who as a young left-wing journalist was a frequent guest at the White House in the late 1930s, told Adlai Stevenson:

All the weeping for Mrs. R should have been done years ago, starting seventy years ago . . . I always thought she was the loneliest human being I ever knew in my life; and so used to bad treatment, beginning with her mother . . . and going right on that it did not occur to her to ask for anything for herself. Not ever . . .

I never liked the President, nor trusted him as a man, because of how he treated her.

Bizarre though this sounds coming from Gellhorn (who had been married to the famously macho Ernest Hemingway), the ferocious taking of sides, as well as this view of the marriage as a kind of tragic compromise patched together by two "lonely" people, has lasted almost half a century.

I find this an absurdly conventional and condescending interpretation of one of the most interesting and radical marriages in history. In my view, the Roosevelts' bond was political in every sense of the word: they were two politically astute people, very tough underneath their vulnerabilities, who knew exactly what they needed in order to do their best work. They were real radicals, in their different ways. Their courage and boldness—in their public and private lives—was remarkable. Their marriage did not evolve by itself; they consciously shaped the way it changed. It was a joint endeavor, a partnership that made it possible for the Roosevelts to become the spectacular and influential individuals they became. The extended family of close companions were not there to paper over the holes in the marriage; they were embraced as part of it. Both FDR and Eleanor had other intimate companions, other loves. They accepted this about each other. It was part of their generous spirit.

I do not want to idealize the marriage. Of course it was a shock for Eleanor to come across Lucy Mercer's love letters to Franklin. And of course the marriage was not without problems. But it was precisely the troubles, trials, and conflicts that brought out the strength, courage, and radicalism of these two people. Their bond was strong enough to withstand betrayal, polio, and the White House. Their affection and tenderness for each other shines through their correspondence. In the months after the Lucy Mercer affair, FDR still called his wife "Dearest Babs." She called him "Dearest Honey."

It was the tragedy that occurred on Campobello island in the summer of 1921 that dramatically transformed the Roosevelt marriage. At the age of thirty-nine, FDR was stricken with polio. Never again would he be able to stand up without help; never again would he be able to take a single step on his own. He needed constant attendance. His mother wanted him to retire to Hyde Park, which would have meant sinking into gentrified invalidism. Eleanor urged him—despite the immense obstacles—to keep up his political career. From then on she played a crucial role as his partner.

She could not have done it without Louis Howe. The "Little Man" had been FDR's closest adviser since FDR entered politics, in 1911. During the anguished vigil by FDR's bedside and in the following years, when FDR was struggling to come to terms with the changed circumstances of his life, Howe entered the marriage in a major way. For months at a time, while Franklin was in the South with his secretary, Missy LeHand, doing his utmost to find himself again, Louis Howe lived with Eleanor and the children in the Roosevelt family home, looking after FDR's work and political interests. For seven years, Howe collaborated with Eleanor almost as much as with FDR. Their combined talents, along with their deliberate cover-up of the extent of FDR's disability, resulted in a spectacular triumph. In 1928, FDR was elected governor of New York. In November 1932, at the age of fifty, FDR was elected president of the United States.

In the meantime, the Roosevelt marriage had become a community. There had always been more than two in this union (Sara Delano Roosevelt loomed large from the beginning), and after polio several close companions entered the picture. The Roosevelts believed in "community," "neighbors," and "friends." These would become key words in FDR's speeches over the years. Their houses were like residential hotels, with family and close friends staying for weeks or months at a time.

The question of extramarital relationships has been a thorny subject in Roosevelt scholarship over the years. FDR was an intensely private man, who was a master of concealment. He never began the autobiography he intended to write in his Hyde Park retirement years. His letters (all but the most private dictated to secretaries) were written with the knowledge that they would one day go to the FDR Library at Hyde Park. Eleanor Roosevelt's three-volume autobiography is a study in evasion. Even with her closest friends, Eleanor said what she felt she *ought* to feel, rather than what she felt.

The Roosevelt companions were admirably discreet. In contrast with today's kiss-and-tell indiscretions, most took the view that their secrets should go with them to the grave. The gaps in the record, the silences, evasions, and distortions provide a challenge to Roosevelt biographers. But enough has survived to give us a sense of the Roosevelts' intimate world. As with all politicians, we need to read between the lines.

FDR could not have faced a more challenging presidency. He entered the White House in March 1933, at the depth of the Depression, and six weeks after Hitler became chancellor in Germany. In his inaugural address, FDR told the American people: "The only thing we have to fear is fear itself." From his very first day in the White House he introduced major reforms. Conservatives hated him. Vested-interest groups despised him. FDR did not give in. "I welcome their hatred," he said.

In September 1939, war broke out in Europe, and in December 1941 the United States joined the war. Throughout the war—indeed, throughout his years in the presidency—FDR radiated sublime confidence. The uncomplaining way he surmounted his physical handicap, his handsome face, ready smile, and soaring eloquence went straight to people's hearts.

Eleanor Roosevelt became the most outspoken first lady this country has known—the most active, the most independent, the most courageous, the most admired, the most controversial, the most savagely mocked. She dealt, as a woman in the political arena, with constant condescension. "Any woman in public life needs to develop skin as tough as rhinoceros hide," she said.

Throughout the world, FDR and Eleanor were widely viewed as embodying the best of the American character. In their personal and political lives, they were idealistic, energetic, hardworking, courageous, and deeply democratic. Eleanor put FDR in contact with the people more than any other president's wife has ever done. To their dinner table, to their picnics, she brought the world.

FDR, the man at the helm, knew what he owed to Eleanor. She was not the "woman behind the scenes"; she was the woman *on* the scene, the woman the press liked to joke was "ubiquitous." Eleanor Roosevelt could not have been the woman she was without Franklin, but nor could Franklin Roosevelt have been the man he was without Eleanor. Together they made possible what to most people would have seemed impossible. Eleanor Roosevelt once said, "You must do the things you think you cannot do." She did. He did. As a couple, they both did.

Franklin and Eleanor

ONE

Cousins in Love

1902–1905

They were cousins, fifth-generation, once removed. Their common ancestor, Claes van Rosenvelt, had emigrated from Holland around 1650 and settled in New Amsterdam, as New York City was still called at that time. On American shores the family name, which meant "field of roses," had been changed to "Roosevelt," but the descendants still pronounced the first syllable "rose," in deference to their Dutch heritage. However the name was pronounced, there was no ambiguity about its standing: "Roosevelt" was a pedigree name among the New York aristocracy. Indeed, when Franklin and Eleanor happened to find themselves on the same train, in the summer of 1902, it was the most famous name in the country.

The cousins were on the New York Central, traveling north from New York City, along the east bank of the Hudson River. Franklin was strolling through the coach car when he spotted Eleanor, sitting with her maid. They had not seen each other for three and a half years.

The last occasion had been a family Christmas party, held in Orange, New Jersey, at the grand country home of Corinne Roosevelt Robinson—the "little sister" of Anna, Theodore, and Elliott Roosevelt. At fourteen, Eleanor looked gangly and awkward in a short white dress with blue bows on each shoulder—a hand-me-down from one of her maternal aunts. Seeing her looking lost on the sidelines, Franklin went up and asked her to dance. "I still remember my gratitude," Eleanor wrote years later, in *This Is My Story*.

At that Christmas party in 1898, the family had been celebrating Theodore Roosevelt's latest triumphs. In August, he had returned from the Spanish-American War covered in glory for his exploits as commander of the cavalry regiment, the Rough Riders. Theodore Roosevelt had become a popular hero, the man everyone talked about. In November he had been elected governor of New York. That Christmas, he was about to move his family to Albany.

Since then, Theodore Roosevelt's rise had been meteoric. A progressive Republican, he was governor of New York for two years and then was elected vice president, under President William McKinley. In September 1901, when McKinley was shot by an anarchist in Buffalo, New York, Theodore Roosevelt became the youngest president in American history, at the age of forty-two.

To Eleanor, Uncle Ted might be the most famous man in the land, but above all he was the elder brother of the man she would idealize to her dying day—her father, Elliott, who had died when she was nine. Uncle Ted, a sentimental man, often told her that he loved her like a daughter. Eleanor found him a little overpowering. During her adolescence, when she made her annual summer visit to the Roosevelt cousins at Oyster Bay, Long Island, he used to give her such bear hugs that her clothes once tore. "Eleanor, my darling Eleanor!" he greeted her. With alarming boisterousness, he would chase the tribe of children through the haystacks in the barn, or down the hill to the waterfront. Although Eleanor had never learned to swim, Uncle Ted told her to jump off the dock and have a go. She had come up spluttering and panicked. Uncle Ted took her in his lap and explained to her that he had formerly been afraid of many things—grizzly bears, mean horses, and men with guns—but he had found that if you acted fearless, after a while you became fearless. It was important, he said, never to fear the challenges life threw in your path.

To Franklin, cousin Theodore was quite simply a hero. Everyone in the family knew that Theodore had been a sickly, puny boy, who suffered terribly from asthma, and seemed far less promising than his handsome younger brother, Elliott. But whereas Elliott had led a dissipated life and drank himself to an early death, Theodore excelled at Harvard, wrote books, and entered politics, eager to give his life to "public service." Calling himself a "Lincoln Republican" (Abraham Lincoln was his hero), the young president was promising to bring back the virtues of the old Republican Party—social justice and reform.

Franklin saw himself as a Democrat, just as his father had been. It was a political allegiance that set them apart in the aristocratic circles in which they moved. But it was not out of family loyalty that Franklin intended to vote Republican in the next presidential election. He considered Theodore Roosevelt more progressive than the Democrats. The new president promised a "square deal" for every man, favored suffrage for women, spoke out against lynching, defended the right of labor to organize, and believed in strict regulation of big business.

Franklin had felt privileged to have a couple of personal conversations with the president earlier that year, when Theodore's eldest daughter, Alice, had her coming-out ball at the White House. It was too bad Eleanor had been unable to attend, he told her. He had had a glorious few days in Washington. Alice was creating a sensation these days. The press was calling her "Princess Alice." The ball, held in the East Room, had made front-page news. Franklin did not add that he had been one of Alice's most eager dance partners.

Eleanor, who had been out of the country for three years, in England, had not felt tempted to come home—not even for a glamorous White House event. Her time at Allenswood, a girls' finishing school in Wimbledon, outside London, had been the happiest years of her life, she told Franklin. Her aunt Bye (Anna Roosevelt) had attended Marie Souvestre's school twenty years earlier, and had recommended that Eleanor go there. Mlle. Souvestre's classes, held in French, were wonderfully stimulating. The Frenchwoman liked Americans, whom she thought more open and less class-bound than the British. Eleanor had become her favorite protégée. During vacations, Eleanor had even traveled with Mlle. Souvestre on the Continent.

Franklin grinned. He had heard the scandalous news that his Hyde Park neighbors, the Newboldts, had come across Eleanor in the Luxembourg Gardens in Paris, wandering around without a chaperone. The family elders had been horrified.

Eleanor blushed. Mlle. Souvestre was seventy now, and not in the best of health, she explained. Some afternoons, she had wanted to rest and sent Eleanor out by herself, with a guidebook. Moreover, the headmistress, a sophisticated European, did not hide her impatience with the staid conventions of New York society. Eleanor would have given anything to stay at Allenswood another year, but her grandmother would not hear of it. Eleanor was turning eighteen in October, and it was time to come out.

Franklin was about to begin his third year at Harvard. He enjoyed his courses in history, economics, and government, he told Eleanor, but he was happiest in the office of *The Harvard Crimson*, the campus newspaper. He hoped to be made an assistant managing editor this year. The *Crimson* played an important role in bringing together the Harvard community, and could exert quite a bit of influence.

His mother had been lonely since his father's death, but she was keeping herself busy. She managed their estate at Hyde Park, in the Hudson valley, to which they were now returning. For the past two winters she had rented an apartment in Boston, to be closer to Franklin. Last summer, they had traveled together to Europe. They were on the ship home when they heard the news—by megaphone from a passing vessel—that President McKinley was dead.

His mother would be wondering where he was. Would Eleanor like to accompany him to the Pullman car to see her? Eleanor stood up. Only now did Franklin see how tall she had grown. She was five-eleven, just two inches shorter than he was. Her thick golden hair came to her waist, and in her fashionable Paris clothing she looked willowy and graceful. He had been noticing her gentle blue eyes, which had a new sparkle to them. While she was abroad, cousin Eleanor had turned into a lovely young lady.

Eighteen months after her husband's death, Sara Delano Roosevelt was still wearing a black gown and mourning veil that went from her hat to her ankles. She had become a widow at the age of forty-six. For the rest of her life she would look back nostalgically to those twenty years of happy marriage to James Roosevelt.

It was her friend Anna Roosevelt—known as "Bye"—who had introduced them. Everyone in the family owed so much to Bye. The eldest of the four siblings (Bye, Theodore, Elliott, and Corinne), Bye had severe physical problems—her spine was deformed, and she was almost hunchbacked—but she looked after everybody, was interested in everything, her mind was razor-sharp, she was the stalwart of the family. The life of the party wherever she went, Bye had a frenetic social schedule. It was because she was always running off to another engagement that the family, who once called her "Bamie," renamed her "Bye."

In April 1880, Sara Delano and Bye Roosevelt were twenty-five and still single. Sara did not relish the prospect of spinsterhood, but she had little interest in young men her own age, who could not hold a candle to the father she adored. Bye, who everyone said was too busy for marriage, had just turned down a proposal from her cousin James Roosevelt, a fifty-two-year-old widower. But Bye was nevertheless fond of her cousin, and she invited him to a family dinner. Among the guests was Sara Delano—or "Sallie," as she was known to family and friends.

Most of the evening, James Roosevelt had talked to *her*. Soon after, he invited Bye, Corinne, and their mother, Martha, to visit his Hyde Park estate, Springwood, adding that he would be delighted if Miss Sallie would accompany them. The women had gone there in early May and stayed a week. During that time, James ventured another proposal.

He was luckier this time. It had not taken Sara long to warm to her suitor. She was flattered by the older man's interest in her. He was a handsome man, and with his muttonchop whiskers and Old World chivalry, he reminded her of her father. James Roosevelt was wealthy, sufficiently so for it to be clear that he was not pursuing her for her own large fortune. And despite the twenty-seven-year age difference, they had a great deal in common. They both belonged to the Hudson valley landed gentry, who modeled themselves on the British aristocracy, spoke with English-sounding accents, hired French and German governesses and tutors for their children, wintered in Manhattan (two hours away by train), and made annual trips to Europe. The Delano family estate, Algonac, comprised sixty acres of land on the west bank of the river, at Newburgh. Springwood, twenty miles to the north, was set among thirteen hundred acres of meadows, woods, vineyards, and orchards on the east bank, at Hyde Park. Sara's family descended from French Huguenot nobility (her ancestor, Philippe de Lannoy, was one of the earliest settlers in the Plymouth Colony); James hailed from an illustrious mix of Dutch Roosevelts and Yankee Aspinwalls. His son from his first marriage, James Roosevelt Jr. ("Rosy"), who was just six months younger than Sara, had recently married Helen Schermerhorn Astor, from the fabulously wealthy Astor family.

At first Sara's father, Warren Delano, was taken aback by the whirlwind romance. But he liked James Roosevelt, a graduate of Harvard Law School, a director of the Delaware and Hudson Railroad, and a respected leader within the Hyde Park community, and was soon telling the family, "James Roosevelt is the first person who has made me realize that a Democrat can be a gentleman."

The wedding was held at Algonac, on a sunny October day, amid the fall foliage. The couple spent a blissful month at Hyde Park, then sailed off on their European honeymoon. They were away ten months, and when they returned, Sara was four months pregnant. "We have had such happy days," she wrote in her journal.

Eleanor had always found cousin Sallie intimidating, and on the train that day her mourning attire made her seem even more formidable than usual. She was a handsome, tall woman, with an aloof, regal manner, and a prominent, square jaw that suggested obstinacy. She sat bolt upright, and had a habit of lifting her chin and looking down her nose at people, which made Eleanor feel she was being appraised. "Mrs. James Roosevelt . . . was sorry for me, I think," she wrote in her autobiography.

Sara Delano Roosevelt had good reason to feel sorry for Eleanor. She had not seen much of the girl's family over the years, but she was well aware of their tragedies, one after another. Bye Roosevelt had often confided her worries about her brother, Elliott.

Sara first met Elliott Roosevelt soon after her marriage. In November 1880, she and James were crossing the Atlantic on their honeymoon. Among their fellow passengers on the new White Star liner, the *Germanic*, was twenty-year-old Elliott, on his way to India, where he was going to hunt big game—elephants and tigers. Like everyone else, Sara and James had found the handsome young man irresistibly charming. When Franklin was born, fourteen months later, they asked Elliott to be a godfather.

At the christening, in March 1882, Elliott, just back from India, cut a dashing figure. With his name, wealth, and good looks, he was one of the most eligible bachelors in New York City. Before long he was courting Anna Livingston Ludlow Hall, an exquisitely beautiful nineteen-year-old from Tivoli on the Hudson, whose family was among the famous "Four Hundred" who constituted the elite of New York Knickerbocker society. When the engagement was announced a year later, Elliott's siblings were relieved that the "dear old boy" was settling down at last, "with a definite purpose in life." The wedding, in December 1883, was hailed in the press as "one of the most brilliant social events of the season."

Ten months later, on October 11, 1884, Anna Eleanor (known as "Eleanor") came into the world. Sadly, the girl did not appear to have inherited her parents' good looks, and Anna seemed embarrassed by her. Sara remembered the family coming to Springwood when Eleanor was two. The little girl stood around sucking her thumb, looking solemn and anxious. Anna taunted her, calling her "Granny." Sara had felt grateful to young Franklin, who crawled around the nursery with his cousin on his back, making her laugh.

All too soon, Sara was hearing troubling stories about Elliott. He had suffered seizures since he was fourteen. The doctors called it "hysteria." His family called it "Elliott's weakness." Because of ill health, he had left school at sixteen. His father sent him to a frontier post in Texas to toughen him up, and Elliott spent a year hunting buffalo. But now another weakness, more serious, was coming to light. Sara supposed it began among the cowboys in the Wild West and grew worse in India, where Elliott fraternized with hard-drinking young aristocrats from Europe and America. There was no longer any hiding the fact that Elliott was an alcoholic.

Elliott could not settle down to married life, or, it seemed, to anything else. He talked about writing up his India stories (his elder brother had already written several books); he talked about entering Republican politics, like Theodore. Instead he spent whole days drinking with friends at the exclusive Knickerbocker Club, on Fifth Avenue. He was often away—riding to the hounds, playing polo, and partying with friends. When he broke his leg in a riding accident, he took morphine and laudanum for the pain, and after that he was addicted to opiates.

In March 1889, Anna gave birth to a son. They named the boy after his father, calling him "Ellie." But it was around this time that the family started to worry about Elliott's sanity. His moods fluctuated wildly. He told Anna that he wanted to leave America; Theodore made him feel a failure. Difficult though it was with the young children, Anna agreed to go to Europe. Once there, Elliott went to this and that sanatorium, spending all his trust money and writing home for more.

Around Christmas 1890, Anna found herself pregnant a third time. Her husband's behavior was alarming her, and she begged Bye to come over and help. Bye arrived in Paris in February 1891, and was appalled, she wrote home, by the scene that greeted her. Elliott oscillated between depression, violence, and contrition. His drunken ranting was that of a mad man. He even accused Anna of infidelity, and demanded to know whether the baby was really his. Anna still loved her husband and longed to help him, but she was suffering from chronic headaches, and occasionally became hysterical herself under the strain. With Elliott at home, Bye feared for the safety of Anna and the children.

Theodore wrote back that a young woman named Katy Mann, a former servant of Elliott's at their summer house on Long Island, had given birth to a child she claimed was Elliott's. She was asking the family for $10,000—an enormous sum.

In Paris, Elliott denied any truth to the story. But he was now threatening suicide. Meanwhile, Theodore sent an investigator to see the servant's baby son. "He came back convinced from the likeness that Katy Mann's story was true," Theodore wrote to Bye. Dreading public scandal, Theodore arranged an out-of-court settlement. Elliott was nothing more than a "flagrant man-swine," he railed to his sisters.

In June 1891, Anna gave birth to another son, Hall. In August, as soon as they could travel, Anna, Bye, and the three children sailed for home, leaving Elliott behind. The American newspapers blazoned the news to the world: "Elliott Roosevelt Demented by Excesses . . . Wrecked by Liquor and Folly, He Is Now Confined in an Asylum for the Insane near Paris."

That winter, Theodore sailed to France to confront his brother and make financial arrangements for Elliott's family. He found Elliott surrounded by empty bottles, looked after by a devoted American mistress. Theodore bullied his younger brother for a week, then reported that Elliott had "surrendered." "He was in a mood that was terribly touching," he wrote to Bye. "How long it will last of course no one can say."

For a while it looked as if Elliott might have mended his ways. He returned to the United States, undertook a cure at a rehabilitation center in Illinois, then went to Abingdon, Virginia, where Corinne's husband, Douglas Robinson, had arranged a managerial position for him on the Robinson estate. From Abingdon, Elliott wrote pleading letters to his mother-in-law, assuring her that he had reformed himself. Mary Hall wrote back: "Do not come."

In November 1892, Anna contracted diphtheria or scarlet fever—or both. Elliott's letters grew increasingly desperate. He had proven himself trustworthy, he pleaded with his mother-in-law. "Can I not win forgiveness?" He wanted to see his wife. "I ought to be with her unless my presence is actually distasteful to her . . . It is my place and my right." In early December, Anna died. She was twenty-nine.

Mary Hall, who had four adolescents of her own still at home (Anna's younger brothers and sisters) took in Anna's three children—Eleanor, Ellie, and Hall. She rarely permitted Elliott to see the children, and never on his own. Spring came around, and Ellie, just four, died of scarlet fever. He was buried at Tivoli, next to his mother.

Elliott Roosevelt moved to Manhattan, where he lived incognito. The patrons of his local club knew him as "Mr. Elliott." According to his valet, the master hallucinated a great deal and tried to throw himself out of the window. In the summer of 1894 he drove his carriage into a lamppost and was hurled onto the street. He never recovered, and a month later, his valet found him dead. "Many people will be pained by this news," *The World* reported on August 16. "There was a time when there were not many more popular young persons in society than Mr. and Mrs. Elliott Roosevelt."

Elliott's mistress turned up at the cemetery and stood weeping by the grave. Poor little Eleanor, not yet ten, was not allowed to go.

This Is My Story, the first volume of Eleanor Roosevelt's autobiography, published in 1937, when she was in the White House, carried the dedication: "To the memory of my father who fired a child's imagination, and to the few other people who have meant the same inspiration throughout my life."

Inspiration was a strange word to use about a man who destroyed his life and the happiness of all those around him, but when it came to her father, Eleanor was willfully blind. For her mother, she had surprisingly little sympathy. Her father was "loved by all who came in contact with him, high or low," she wrote, whereas her mother was a snob, preoccupied by "Society."

In November 1932, soon after Franklin had been elected president, Eleanor Roosevelt read her father's letters—to his mother, siblings, wife, mother-in-law, and daughter—and published a carefully culled selection in a volume entitled *Hunting Big Game in the Eighties*. As she delved into her father's past, she must have understood how much her mother had suffered in her marriage. And yet she continued to see her father, the black sheep among the Roosevelt men, in the rosiest possible light.

The irony is that Eleanor experienced her father mostly as an aching absence. She admitted that her mother did her best to compensate.

"My mother made a great effort for me, she would read to me and have me read to her, she would have me recite my poems, she would keep me after the boys had gone to bed, and still I can remember standing in the door, very often with my finger in my mouth—which was, of course, forbidden—and I can see the look in her eyes and hear the tone of her voice as she said: 'Come in, Granny.'"

Eleanor Roosevelt's biographer, Blanche Wiesen Cook, points out that it is to Anna Roosevelt's credit that she never tried to turn the little girl against her father, and never burdened Eleanor with her anxieties. But to Eleanor, even as an adult, all that counted was that her father loved her ("to him I was a miracle from Heaven") and her mother did not. Or so it seemed to her. "With my father I was perfectly happy," she wrote in her autobiography. "I loved his voice . . . Above all, I loved the way he treated me."

The reality was a long way from this idyll. Her father was impatient with what he saw as her lack of physical courage, and as a young girl Eleanor learned to hide her terror so as not to incur his wrath. Early on, she understood that her father did foolhardy things, and that he made lots of promises but could never be relied upon. In *This Is My Story*, she did not mention the occasion—she was eight—when her father asked her to wait for him in the lobby of the Knickerbocker Club, and she waited, holding his three fox terriers on their leashes, until six hours later the doorman sent her home in a carriage.

When their mother died, Eleanor and her two brothers went to live with their grandmother and Eleanor took refuge in a dream world in which her father was the hero and she was his companion:

After we were installed, my father came to see me . . . He was dressed all in black, looking very sad. He held out his arms and gathered me to him. In a little while he began to talk, to explain to me that my mother was gone, that she had been all the world to him, and now he only had my brothers and myself, that my brothers were very young, and that he and I must keep close together. Some day I would make a home for him again, we would travel together and do many things.

Somehow it was always he and I. I did not understand whether my brothers were to be our children . . . He told me to write to him often, to be a good girl, not to give any trouble, to study hard, to grow up into a woman he could be proud of, and he would come to see me whenever it was possible.

It was a confusing scenario for a little girl. Later in life, having had six children of her own, Eleanor wrote: "I do not think that I am a natural born mother . . . If I ever wanted to mother anyone, it was my father."

She wholeheartedly assumed the role of her father's angelic little woman. After her brother Ellie died, eight-year-old Eleanor wrote to her father: "We must remember Ellie is going to be safe in heaven and to be with Mother who is waiting there and our Lord wants Ellie boy with him now, we must be happy and do God's will and we must cheer others."

Her father sent her presents—books, puppies, a pony to ride at Tivoli, white violets ("which you can put in your Prayer book at the XXIII Psalm")—and wrote letters full of loving admonitions, which whispered the promise of a cozy future together. "Father's Own Little Nell," he called her. She should learn to ride her pony, he wrote, "for it will please me so and we can have such fun riding together after you come to the city next fall." She must stop biting her fingernails, and take "good care of those cunning wee hands that Father loves so to be petted by." It was important for her to work on "all those *little* things that will make my dear Girl so much more attractive if she attends to them, not forgetting the big ones. Unselfishness, generosity, loving tenderness and cheerfulness."

In early July 1894, Eleanor wrote that she and her brother Hall ("Brudie") were going to Bar Harbor, in Maine:

Dear Father,
    I would have written before but I went to Cousin Susie. We are starting today for Bar Harbor we are in a great flurry and hurry I am in Uncle Eddies room. The men are just going to take the trunks away. We are to have lunch at 15 minutes before twelve. We are going to Boston in the one o'clock train. Brudie wears pants now.
    Good-by I hope you are well *dear Father.*
    With a great deal of love to everybody and you especially I am your little daughter,
                                                        Nell

From Bar Harbor she wrote that she was enjoying herself: they had visited an Indian encampment, she had walked to the top of the nearby mountain, she had caught six fish ("don't you think I did well for the first time"), and she was taking daily lessons with Grandma.

Elliott wrote back: "I hope my little girl is well . . . Kiss Baby Brudie for me and *never forget* I love you." The gaps between his letters caused him to feel bursts of contrition. "What must you think of your Father who has not written in so long," he wrote on August 13, 1894. "I have after all been *very* busy, quite ill, at intervals not able to move from my bed for days . . . Give my love to Grandma and Brudie, and *all*."

Two days later, Eleanor was told that her father was dead. Her reaction, her grandmother wrote to Corinne Robinson, was subdued. "Poor child has had so much sorrow crowded into her short life she now takes everything very quietly, the only remark she made was 'I did want to see father once more.'"

If Eleanor's childhood comes over like fiction, so much it resembles the unrelentingly grim, tearjerker Victorian novels that were popular at the time, Franklin's is like a painting—one of those idealized landscapes of the sleepy Hudson on a serene summer day.

Franklin Delano Roosevelt was a golden boy growing up in a golden world. This was the late nineteenth century. The automobile and telephone had not yet been invented, and the village of Hyde Park, seventy-five miles up the Hudson River from New York City, was a close-knit rural community. The Albany Post Road, which ran in front of Springwood, linking New York City to Albany, was a horse-and-cart route. James Roosevelt and his family knew everyone in the village of Hyde Park. On Sunday, they greeted their neighbors at St. James Episcopal Church, where James was a vestryman.

The "River families," as the locals called the fifty or so families whose magnificent country estates dotted the banks of the Hudson, visited one another regularly, went to one anothers' houses for parties and dances, and met one another on their travels in Europe. Their lifestyle was luxurious, but not ostentatious. (The Roosevelts looked down on their nouveau riche neighbors, the Vanderbilts, and refused to visit their meretricious mansion.) James Roosevelt, who believed that privilege came with responsibility toward the less fortunate, was actively involved in the village school and local affairs. Franklin would always look back to his Hudson valley childhood as an idyllic community of friends and neighbors.

Franklin Delano Roosevelt was born on January 30, 1882, in his parents' second-story bedroom at Springwood, Hyde Park. It was a difficult birth, and the doctor probably told Sara that she should not risk another child. To her, he was always "my precious Franklin." Most aristocratic families employed a wet nurse to feed their babies, but Sara breast-fed her son herself, for a year.

In the fashion of the time, Sara dressed Franklin in short skirts until he was five. In the old photographs, with his long blond ringlets and little boots, he looked like a girl. Until he was nine, his mother dressed him in Scottish kilts, Little Lord Fauntleroy outfits, and sailor suits. Later in life Franklin confessed that he had longed to wear shirts and pants, like other boys his age.

Sara kept everything to do with her beloved son—his blond baby locks, his first teeth, his drawings, scribblings, every letter he ever wrote her. The first one, in neat looping handwriting on carefully ruled pencil lines, was written in May 1888. Franklin was six, and his mother was at Algonquin, looking after her sick father:

> My dear mamma
> I went fishing yesterday after noon with papa we caught a dozen of minnows we left them on the bank papa told me it would frighten the fish to put them in the pond how is dear grandpapa I hope he is better dear mamma I send you a kiss
> your loving son
> Franklin

Franklin was aware that his mother tended to be overprotective. No doubt his father often said so. Franklin was eight when he wrote to his father jubilantly: "Mama left this morning and I am going to take my bath alone. I have jumped from five to six feet today."

Sara Delano admitted in her memoir, *My Boy Franklin*, that her boy was kept under close surveillance:

> We never tried, . . . his father and I, to influence him against his own tastes and inclinations or to shape his life. At least we made

every effort not to and thought we were succeeding pretty well until one day . . . we noticed that he seemed much depressed . . . Finally, a little alarmed, I asked him whether he was unhappy. He did not answer at once and then said very seriously, "Yes I am unhappy."

When I asked him why, he was again silent for a moment or two. Then with a curious little gesture that combined entreaty with a suggestion of impatience, he clasped his hands in front of him and exclaimed, "Oh, for freedom!"

There is no doubt that Sara Delano, in her loving way, was extremely controlling. Nevertheless, Franklin's flashes of rebellion were rare. He was his parents' pride and joy, and he liked it that way. On the whole he was eager to please, and it was not difficult for him to do. He was a handsome, polite lad, with a sunny disposition and keen interest in the world around him. As an adolescent he already had a remarkable knowledge of the trees, birds, history, and architecture of the Hudson valley. When he was ten, Sara gave him her stamp albums, which contained exotic stamps from China, where she had lived for a time as a child, and Franklin became a devoted stamp collector—a passion that would endure for the rest of his life. When he was eleven, he began to keep a bird diary, carefully noting sightings. His father gave him a shotgun, and Franklin began a collection of stuffed Hudson River birds that remains to this day the most comprehensive in existence. He agreed with his father to shoot only one male and one female from each species, and for several months, until it made him ill, he stuffed and mounted the birds himself. On trips to New York City, his favorite excursion was to the American Museum of Natural History, co-founded by cousin Theodore's father, and to which cousin Theodore had donated many of his own bird specimens.

James Roosevelt was old enough to be Franklin's grandfather, but in his fifties he was still a vigorous man, and he enjoyed riding, sailing, iceboating, and shooting with his young son, just as he had done with his first son, Rosy. When Franklin was nine, James bought him a forty-five-foot yacht, with an auxiliary motor, for summers at Campobello. They named it *Half Moon*, after the ship on which Henry Hudson explored the river for the Dutch East India Company. It was to his father that Franklin owed his love of boats and the sea.

Like most boys of his social class, Franklin was initially schooled by tutors, who could speak to him in their native French or German. Private tutoring also had the advantage that the family's travels were not confined by the school year. Franklin and his parents (accompanied by servants and tutors) spent time in New York City, where they had an apartment at the Renaissance Hotel, on West Forty-third Street. In the spring, they sailed to Europe. In the summer they withdrew to the cool air of Campobello, a Canadian island off the coast of Maine, and spent three months in their sprawling house—they called it a "cottage"—on a hill overlooking Passamaquoddy Bay. Throughout the year, they made frequent railroad trips to stay with family members and friends up and down the East Coast. As manager of the Delaware and Hudson Railroad, James Roosevelt had at his disposal a private railroad car, with bedrooms, a sitting room, and a Negro porter and cook.

Franklin was not yet ten when his father had a heart attack. James Roosevelt was sixty-three. Overnight, Sara turned him into an invalid. From now on, she and Franklin had a tacit agreement never to worry Papa unnecessarily. To Franklin, his father became a distant figure. More than ever, it was Mama who ruled the household.

Until Franklin went to Groton, he had rarely been separated from his parents. Because his mother had not been ready to part with him earlier, he started school at fourteen, two years later than the other boys. It made it more difficult for him to make friends. The "new boy" was considered arrogant, with an affected manner. Even his female cousins thought Franklin "prissy," an overprotected young man, who danced attendance on his mother. His cousin Alice teased him about his initials, F.D. "We used to call him 'Feather Duster,'" she said later, "because he pranced around and fluttered."

The Spartan conditions at Groton must have come as a shock to Franklin after his pampered life at Hyde Park. Later, he admitted that he was terribly lonely at boarding school, and always felt an outsider. But he never showed it. For the four years he was at Groton, he wrote home twice a week. What is most striking about these letters, his biographers agree, is the degree to which Franklin perfected the art of amiable chatter, without revealing a thing about his inner self. The emotional register rarely flickered.

The school of Groton, two miles from the village by that name, was an isolated community in rural New England, thirty-five miles northwest of Boston. In the winter, the school was sometimes completely cut off by snow and ice. The headmaster, Reverend Endicott Peabody, born in Salem and educated in England, had founded the institution in 1884, with the elite British public school as its model. Groton was expensive, there were no scholarships, and the boys came exclusively from old WASP families. Following the timeworn British tradition, the boys were to be toughened up for leadership. They were, after all, the American aristocracy, the ruling class.

Peabody used an invidious combination of benevolence and bullying to coerce the boys. The more rebellious fellows bitterly resented him. Most were eager for his approval. Franklin was more eager than most.

The headmaster believed in the Victorian ethic of "muscular Christianity"—the idea that subjecting the body to strenuous exertion promoted moral health and vigorous masculinity, which should be harnessed in service to God and country. Like his friend Theodore Roosevelt, Peabody was a Republican, who nevertheless believed in social justice. He often told the boys that he had great respect for any man who chose politics as a way to bring about reform.

For these 150 "Grotties," as they called themselves, the day began before dawn with a cold shower (no concessions were made to the bitter New England winter), followed by chapel, classes, athletics, prayers, evening meal in stiff white collars, study period, and bed in a bare cubicle, with a curtain instead of a door. The boys were not encouraged to form close friendships, and were not permitted to go for a walk in pairs. But Peabody was not against hazing, which at Groton took the form of "boot-boxing" (being crammed into a footlocker), or "pumping" (head-dunking into a toilet bowl)—practices that occasionally necessitated resuscitation. It discouraged the rebels, those whom Peabody called "undesirable citizens."

Franklin regarded Groton as something of a survival course. "I am getting on very well and I have not been put in the boot-box yet!" he wrote to his parents in his first week. One week later: "The Biddle boy is quite crazy, fresh and stupid, he has been boot-boxed once and threatened to be pumped several times." One year later: "You will be pleased to hear that George Cabot Ward Low . . . has been pumped, &

a pretty sight he was! He left off swaggering immediately!" Franklin was nothing of a rebel.

In his early teens, Franklin was thin and gangly, and showed no prowess at football or baseball. At Groton, athletics were deemed almost more important than academic studies. There were eight football teams, graded from best to worst, and Franklin was placed in the second to worst. In his first months at the school he received no "black marks," whereas most boys were given two or three a week. His performance in class was consistently better than average, and he regularly won a prize for punctuality. As he would discover, these things did not make him popular.

An additional trial was Taddy Roosevelt, the son of Franklin's half brother, Rosy, who was in the form ahead of him. The boys were greatly amused that the nephew was older than the uncle, and Franklin was immediately dubbed "Uncle Frank." Worse, Taddy was a wild young man, with an allowance twice the size of everyone else's, who cared little about his studies and even less about sport. Franklin found him an embarrassment.

At least Franklin could be proud of his name when Theodore Roosevelt came to visit the school, in June 1897. Cousin Theodore, who was assistant secretary of the navy at the time, gave a "splendid talk on his adventures when he was on the Police Board," Franklin told his parents, with "killing stories about policemen and their doings," which "kept the whole room in an uproar for over an hour." When cousin Theodore invited Franklin to his Long Island home for the Fourth of July long weekend, Franklin accepted eagerly. It turned out that his mother had other plans for him, but Franklin stood firm. "I am sorry you didn't want me to go to Oyster Bay for the 4th but I had already accepted Cousin Theodore's invitation & I shall enjoy it very much," he told her. "I wish you had let me make my own plans as you said." A rebuke like this was rare indeed.

Popularity with girls would have helped him, but Franklin hardly knew any. Apart from Mrs. Peabody, the headmaster's wife, who was something of a mother figure within the school community, the only women the boys saw, for months at a time, were visiting relatives and friends. When Franklin, about to turn seventeen, was required to invite a girl to a social event, he asked his mother for help: "I wish you would think up some decent partner for me for the N.Y. dance, so that I can get somebody early, and not get palmed off on some ice-cart." His mother obliged with four suggestions. All were cousins, apart from Mary Newboldt, their neighbors' daughter at Hyde Park, with whom Franklin had played as a child. "As you know very few girls you ought to make haste," she urged him.

Like the British schools on which Groton was modeled, the headmaster chose prefects from the boys in the final year, and conferred on them special authority. Franklin was not selected. When eighteen-year-old Franklin packed up his belongings on June 24, 1900, the evening before his graduation, his letter home gave a rare glimpse of self-doubt: "Tomorrow is Prize-Day and my fate will soon be decided but I don't really expect to get one, so shall not be disappointed . . . In the afternoon everyone will amuse the numerous girls, and I don't think I know one that is coming, but will probably be shelved with a 'pill.'"

By the following evening, Franklin's good cheer was restored, and he was every bit the grateful Grotonian. "My darling Mama and Papa, 'The strife is o'er, the battle won!' What a joyful yet sad day this has been. Never again will we hold recitations in the old School, and scarce a boy but wishes he were a 1st former again." To his relief, he was acquainted with one of the visiting girls, and had proudly shown her over the school. During the awards ceremony, to his delight, his name had been called for the Latin Prize. "I can hardly wait to see you," he told his parents, "but feel awfully to be leaving here for good."

Eleanor embraced the Christian ideal of feminine selflessness with an almost missionary zeal. Everyone was struck by it; her cousin Alice was impatient with it. The cousins were the same age (Alice was a few months older); they looked alike (tall, with fair hair and blue eyes); their fathers (Theodore and Elliott) were brothers; their mothers had died when they were young (Alice Lee, Theodore's first wife, died one day after giving birth to Alice), but the two girls could not have been more different. In an interview later in life, Alice mused:

Whereas she responded to her insecurity by being do-goody and virtuous I did by being boisterous and showing off . . . I didn't do any of the nice and proper things expected of me. Whereas Eleanor certainly did. She always made a tremendous effort to do everything she thought was expected of her . . . I can still see those large blue eyes fixed on one, worrying about one, and wanting you to know that in her you had a friend. She always wanted to discuss things like whether contentment was better than happiness and whether they conflicted with one another. Things like that, which I didn't give a damn about.

As a young child, Eleanor had experienced maternal rejection and paternal abandonment, and was well acquainted with insecurity, self-hatred, and guilt. She had tried to please her mother, tried to please her father, and both had died—deserting her. As an adolescent, she felt grateful to her mother's relatives for taking her in and did her best to be good and make herself useful. She would always feel that she had to *deserve* love.

From the age of nine, she lived most of the year in her grandmother's gloomy brownstone house on West Thirty-seventh Street in Manhattan, along with her uncles, Vallie and Eddie (in their late twenties), her aunts Pussie and Maude (in their early twenties), and her younger brother, Hall. Eleanor's maternal grandfather, Valentine Hall, had died a decade earlier, at forty-six, without a will, so that his widow had only dower rights to his estate. Although the Hall family had the highest Knickerbocker credentials, it was struggling to keep up appearances. Eleanor's uncles were already alcoholics. Her aunts were beautiful, talented, unmarried, and frustrated. Eleanor was acutely aware of the tensions in the house.

She was closest to her aunt Pussie, but Pussie was moody, especially when she was in love. Fourteen-year-old Eleanor wrote in her diary: "Poor Auntie Pussie she is so worried. I am going to try and see if I can't do something for her . . . I've tried to be good & sweet & quiet but have not succeeded. Oh my."

Eleanor was painfully conscious that she was no beauty. Her height and her aunts' hand-me-down dresses did not help. "Poor little soul," Theodore's second wife, Edith, remarked to her mother, "she is very plain. Her mouth and teeth seem to have no future. But the ugly duckling may turn out to be a swan." When Eleanor was seventeen, her aunt Pussie, in one of her vile moods, told Eleanor to her face that she was an "ugly duckling" who would never find an eligible man.

After being too lenient with her own children, Mary Hall was strict with her granddaughter. In Manhattan, Eleanor was never allowed out without a maid. Even at Tivoli, during the summer months, she was closely supervised. "There were hot, breathless days when my fingers stuck to the keys as I practiced on the piano," she wrote. "I would roll my stockings down and then be told that ladies did not show their legs and promptly have to fasten them up again."

In Manhattan, Eleanor was schooled, along with a handful of other girls, by Mr. Roser, a fusty, bewhiskered fellow who had made a name for himself as an educator of wealthy young women. In one of Eleanor's surviving essays—the topic was "Loyalty and Friendship"—we see the thrust of her self-admonitions: "It may seem strange but no matter how plain a woman may be if truth & loyalty are stamped upon her face all will be attracted to her & she will do good to all who come near her & those who know her will always love her for they will feel her loyal spirit & have confidence in her."

In Allenswood, fifteen-year-old Eleanor would discover the truth of those words. It was frightening to sail to England and be left alone at boarding school, but in that small community of thirty-five to forty girls from around the world, she thrived. Within a short time, the hawkeyed headmistress, Mlle. Souvestre, was *very* impressed by Eleanor. "She is full of sympathy for all those who live with her and shows an intelligent interest in everything she comes in contact with," the Frenchwoman wrote to Eleanor's grandmother. "As a pupil she is very satisfactory, but even that is of small account when you compare it with the perfect quality of her soul."

Marie Souvestre was a cultivated, charismatic woman, whose friends included Henry James, Marcel Proust, Sir Leslie Stephen (Virginia Woolf's father), and the socialist reformers Sidney and Beatrice Webb. She believed that young women should develop independent minds, take responsibility for themselves, and participate in the social issues of the day. The school syllabus, with its emphasis on literature, history, and languages, seemed on the surface to be eminently suitable for young Victorian ladies, but Mlle. Souvestre's classes, held in the library among the books, flowers, and risqué sculptures, were surprisingly subversive. If a girl wrote an essay in which she parroted someone else's views, Souvestre tore it up in front of the others. She talked to her students about social justice, the savagery of British imperialism, the plight of the Negro in America, and the importance of the trade union movement. Eleanor often thought to herself that if her grandmother had any inkling of Mlle. Souvestre's views, she would call her home immediately.

Eleanor was seriously shocked to discover that Marie Souvestre was an atheist. Was she also aware that Mlle. Souvestre was a lesbian? It would have been an unusual girls' boarding school if rumors did not fly. If, perchance, Eleanor did not fully grasp the meaning of sapphism when she was at Allenswood, she certainly understood it later. In *This Is My Story*, she hinted that Marie Souvestre's relationship with the school administrator, a tiny Italian woman, was far more intense than the standard collegial rapport. And she did not hide the fact that Souvestre chose favorites from among her students whom she invited for "salon" evenings in her inner sanctum. It was from Mlle. Souvestre that Eleanor learned the art—it became a lifelong practice, which Eleanor did beautifully—of reading aloud to friends.

Eleanor's cautious picture of the school in her autobiography was boldly reinforced in 1949, when Dorothy Strachey Bussy's lesbian novel, *Olivia*, exploded onto the literary scene. Dorothy Strachey, sister of the famous homosexual biographer Lytton Strachey, taught English at Allenswood. She sent Eleanor a copy of her novel, with the dedication: "For Tottie, in memory of old days from D.S." A thinly fictionalized portrait of Mlle. Souvestre, the novel portrayed the fervent emotions "Mlle Julie" aroused among her favored protégées.

By the time Eleanor became her favorite student, Marie Souvestre was seventy, and no longer the flirtatious beauty she once had been. Eleanor ardently admired her, but there is no indication that she fell in love with her mentor. Indeed, Eleanor found it a burden as well as a privilege to be Mlle. Souvestre's chosen protégée. She was expected to sit opposite the headmistress every evening at dinner, directly across from that "eagle eye which penetrated right through to your backbone." It meant having to behave perfectly, take part in the conversation with the invited guests, and eat everything on her plate—including that disgustingly clammy English dish, suet pudding.

As for Mlle. Souvestre, she was enchanted by Eleanor. When they went traveling together, the headmistress wrote to Mrs. Hall, in her flawed English: "It is impossible to wish for myself a more delightful companion traveling. She is never tired, never out of sorts, never without a keen interest in all that she sees . . . She looks always very thin, delicate and often white and just the same I have rarely seen such a power of endurance . . . What a blank her going away will leave in my life."

Eleanor would always feel profoundly grateful to Mlle. Souvestre. As a teacher, Souvestre made her students curious; she encouraged them to think critically. As a Frenchwoman, she told Eleanor frankly what she thought of her dowdy clothes, and insisted that she have some fashionable dresses made up in Paris. As a mentor, she encouraged Eleanor to become more self-reliant and adventurous. On their European travels, she taught Eleanor something about the art of enjoying life. She introduced the girl to the local wines (mixed with water), and to some of her bohemian friends on the Riviera. They were on the train to Pisa when Souvestre, on a whim, decided they would get off at Alassio, so they could look at the stars from the beach. It was the first time Eleanor had ever seen such thrilling spontaneity in an adult. "Never again would I be the rigid little person I had been."

At the beginning of Eleanor's final semester at Allenswood, Corinne Robinson (the daughter of Aunt Corinne) arrived as a student. Corinne could scarcely believe the transformation in her cousin. From being the earnest little orphan, Eleanor had become the most sought-after girl in the school:

> She was beloved by everybody. Saturdays we were allowed a sortie into Putney which had stores where you could buy books, flowers. Young girls have crushes and you bought violets or a book and left them in the room of the girl you were idolizing. Eleanor's room every Saturday would be full of flowers because she was so admired.

"This was the first time in all my life that all my fears left me," Eleanor wrote in her autobiography. But in July 1902, after three years at Allenswood, it was time to sail for home. Not only was Eleanor returning to the old family tensions but she was about to face the ordeal of "coming out," that ritual initiation ceremony every young woman dreaded. And by now Eleanor Roosevelt was not just *any* young woman. She was the niece of the president of the United States.

That summer, the grand old house at Tivoli was sinister. Pussie was hardly ever there, Maude and Eddie had married, and Uncle Vallie had become a violent drunk. Eleanor had two friends from England to stay, and she spent the whole time worrying that her uncle would go on one of his rampages. Her grandmother had put three heavy locks on Eleanor's bedroom door, but that still left the rest of the house.

"When does the big season of social dissipations start in New York?" Marie Souvestre asked. She missed Eleanor every day of her life, she told her. "Ma chère petite, my mind is so divided in respect to you. I should like to know that you are happy, and yet how I fear to hear that you have been unable to defend yourself against all the temptations which surround you; evenings out, pleasure, flirtations. How all this will estrange you from all that I knew you to be!"

Souvestre was the one person who understood Eleanor's conflicts. She knew how insecure Eleanor was, and how much she craved love and admiration. The Eleanor she loved was a serious, intelligent girl, full of curiosity and energy, who genuinely wanted to make a meaningful contribution to the world. Over their evening meals abroad, they had discussed the social pressure that faced Eleanor in New York. "Protect yourself to some extent against it, my dear child," Mlle. Souvestre now urged. "Even when success comes, as I am sure it will, bear in mind that there are more quiet and enviable joys than to be among the most sought-after-women at a ball or the woman best liked by your neighbor at the table, at luncheons and the various fashionable affairs."

Eleanor made her debut at the Assembly Ball, one of New York's most exclusive social occasions, held in the Waldorf-Astoria on December 11, 1902. Four other Roosevelt debutantes shared the limelight that evening, including Alice, who had already made her official White House debut in January. The press dubbed them "the magic Five." "Interesting-looking," *Town Topics* declared, "but they are not pretty."

Eleanor looked elegant in her gown from the famous Paris fashion design house of Callot Soeurs, but she was to discover that she knew only two unmarried men in the entire gathering, and both were much older. The dance card dangling from her wrist had empty spaces on it. "I do not think I quite realized beforehand what utter agony it was going to be or I would never have had the courage to go," she wrote later. "By no stretch of the imagination could I fool myself into thinking that I was a popular debutante! I went home early, thankful to get away."

Eleanor had a name that counted in society, and that winter she did not lack invitations. Once she came out, there were theater parties, dinners, receptions, luncheons, and dances. Acutely conscious that she was too tall, not a good dancer, and not good at small talk, she suffered terrible anxieties. "That first winter nearly brought me to a state of nervous collapse."

One of the two older bachelors at her debutante ball was the tall, dark, lanky Robert Munro Ferguson. Born into an aristocratic Scottish landowning family, he had come to the United States as an eighteen-year-old and became a close friend of Bye and Theodore Roosevelt. Eleanor had first met Bob when she was seven and he was twenty-two. Dashing as a young man, he was now thirty-three, too thin, and often ill. But Bob Ferguson saved Eleanor that winter. When he took her to informal gatherings at the homes of his artist friends, Eleanor actually managed to enjoy herself. Since Ferguson was an older man, Grandmother Hall even allowed him to escort Eleanor home without her maid.

All that ended when Bob Ferguson proposed marriage to Eleanor. She was flattered, but she could not see herself married to this rather dour older man. She liked him a great deal. She did not love him.

When Franklin turned seventeen, on January 30, 1899, his invalid father wrote to him at Groton: "Do you realize that you are approaching manhood and next year, when you begin your university life, you will be away from the safeguards of school and will have to withstand many temptations? . . . But I always feel your character is so well formed and established I have no fear."

Franklin arrived at Harvard in September 1900. He roomed with a Groton friend, Lathrop Brown, and they were proud of their handsome apartment on the luxurious end of Mt. Auburn Street, known to Harvard men as the Gold Coast. At eighteen, Franklin had reached his full height, six-one, and become a singularly handsome young man, with a radiant smile and abundant charm. After four years of being exiled in the male wilderness of Groton, he was looking forward to his new bachelor freedom at Harvard. But he had barely settled into the place when a crisis descended on the family.

Franklin's half nephew, Taddy Roosevelt, who had been the bane of Franklin's existence at Groton, had been at Harvard for a year—at least officially. In fact, he was spending most of his time down in Manhattan, in the notorious red-light meatpacking district known as the Tenderloin. No sooner had he turned twenty-one and come into his late mother's vast Astor legacy than he took his prostitute girlfriend along to City Hall and married her. In mid-October, the scandal hit the press: "Boy millionaire weds: Astor scion's bride won in dancehall." Two days later, James Roosevelt had a heart attack. Mama wrote to Franklin:

> Your father cannot get . . . out of his mind the thought that his grandson has been leading a bad wicked life for months. His marrying the creature brings it before the public, but the sin came first and he has disgraced his good name. Poor Papa suffered so much in the night for breath that he thought he could not live. He talked of you and said "Tell Franklin to be good and never be like Taddy."

Franklin wrote back:

> The disgusting business about Taddy did not come as a very great surprise to me or to anyone in Cambridge. I have heard the rumor ever since I have been here, but in the absence of facts the best course has been silence. I do not wonder that it has upset Papa, but although the disgrace to the name has been the worst part of the affair, one can never again consider him a true Roosevelt. It will be well for him not only to go to parts unknown, but to stay there.

In early December, Franklin was urgently summoned to the family apartment at the Renaissance Hotel, in New York. Franklin, his mother, and his half brother, Rosy, were standing vigilantly by when seventy-two-year-old James Roosevelt took his last breath. Franklin's mother would always blame Taddy.

Franklin remained at Hyde Park until the New Year, then returned to Cambridge, in mourning attire. Melancholy letters arrived from his mother. With his "darling father's spirit flown," she wrote, she now lived for Franklin. Over the years she would constantly tell her son: "You are my life."

Not surprisingly, Franklin kept any interest in other women entirely to himself. He scarcely went out during the six-month mourning period for his father, but after that his sporadic entries in his line-a-day diary refer to at least a dozen girls. He did not mention them to his mother.

By the summer of 1902, twenty-year-old Franklin had a serious love interest. Mama knew Alice Sohier, of course. The Sohiers were a distinguished New England family, with a house in Boston and a large country estate at Beverly, Massachusetts. Alice's father was active in local Republican politics, and a keen yachtsman. Mama knew that Franklin spent time with the Sohier family. She had no idea that Franklin was in love with seventeen-year-old Alice.

At twenty, Franklin was high-spirited and ambitious. Alice Sohier would never forget the evening when he told her family that he planned to be president of the United States one day. The Sohiers laughed. But Alice found herself very attracted to this confident young man. They saw a lot of each other in June. It was summer, and they were cavorting in swimming costumes, and the Sohier family sometimes left them alone together. It seems that Franklin and Alice indulged in some serious petting. Franklin proposed to her. He was in a hurry to marry. As he saw it—especially after the ignominious Taddy affair—marriage was his only chance for sexual fulfillment. It would also mean freedom from his mother. Alice hesitated. She was too young for marriage. Her parents, no doubt wanting her to bide her time, decided to send her to Europe.

In July 1902, Franklin wrote in his diary that he and two friends sailed in the *Half Moon* to Beverly. They took Alice for a "good long sail" to Marblehead. He was invited to the Sohiers for dinner, and afterward he and Alice sat outside. At this point, he resorted to code: "Spend evening on lawn. Alice confides in her doctor." The next morning he and his friends left Beverly at 6 a.m. Franklin wrote, again in code: "Worried over Alice all night."

The code Franklin had devised, which substituted numbers for vowels and deleted the tops or bottoms of consonants, creating the effect of hieroglyphic squiggles, was clearly intended to foil his mother, in case she snooped among his papers when he was home. Cryptologists have cracked the code, but not the meaning.

We will never know what lay behind Franklin's anxious entry, but it is probable that Alice's period had not arrived. Those were times when young women feared that a kiss would lead to pregnancy. In the course of their lusty embraces, Franklin might have accidentally ejaculated. He was clearly terrified. Taddy had done enough damage to the Roosevelt name. Everything was at stake—Franklin's reputation as much as Alice's. Whatever they had done on those hot June nights, neither Franklin nor Alice Sohier would ever tell anyone.

Some fifty years later, Alice Sohier Shaw did tell her granddaughter that Franklin was very forward. "In a day and age when well brought-up young men were expected to keep their hands off the person of young ladies from respectable families, Franklin had to be slapped—*hard*." According to her, Franklin had more than once stepped onto the train in Beverly with a bright red mark on his cheek.

For whatever reason—it could well be that this scare put her off her ardent suitor—Alice decided against marriage to Franklin. In her old age, having been a lifelong Republican voter, Alice would tell her granddaughter how relieved she was to have escaped becoming the wife of Franklin Delano Roosevelt. He had confided in her that his lonely childhood made him want a whole brood of children—at least six. She mused: "I did not wish to be a cow."

On October 8, 1902, Franklin wrote in his diary: "Today Alice Sohier left for Europe & I saw her off on the 'Commonwealth.'" That was it. There was no mention of his mood as he stood waving from the Boston wharf.

In mid-November, six weeks after Alice left for Europe, Franklin saw Eleanor again—the first time since their meeting on the train that summer. Rosy, Franklin's half brother, invited a contingent of Roosevelts to the gala horse show in Madison Square Garden, followed by dinner at Sherry's, New York's most fashionable restaurant.

In December, Franklin asked Eleanor out twice—for lunch and tea in New York. He and Eleanor were invited to the first family's New Year party. Eleanor stayed in the White House, with her cousin Alice. Franklin stayed with the president's sister, Bye Roosevelt, in her house on N Street. On New Year's Day there was a dinner at the White House, at which Franklin chatted with the president, then the group attended the theater. "Sit near Eleanor," Franklin wrote. "Very interesting day."

One of Eleanor's attractions for Franklin was certainly the fact that she was so closely related to Theodore Roosevelt. With her came the whiff of the White House, which held a magical appeal for Franklin. But even without that, she was special. Eleanor had qualities that many people—particularly older people, like Mlle. Souvestre—found deeply appealing. She was open to new experiences, and appreciative. Although she looked fragile, she had quite extraordinary resilience and determination. Despite her name, she never pushed herself forward. Unlike his cousin Alice, with whom Franklin had flirted over the years, Eleanor was warm, selfless, and supportive. Franklin had been with girls who were more beautiful and more fun, but Eleanor cared about others, and cared about the world. With that sixth sense he would show so often in his future life, Franklin was realizing that he *needed* this woman.

Eleanor's grandmother closed her Manhattan townhouse that winter— money no longer flowed as it once did in the Livingston Hall family—and Eleanor and her aunt Pussie were living at the home of their cousin, Mrs. Susan Parish, on East Seventy-sixth Street. Franklin began to make trips to New York to see Eleanor. It was quite a juggling act. His mother must not know what he was up to, and the straitlaced Mrs. Parish thrived on gossip. Franklin and Eleanor were never alone. He accompanied her to church, he took her on drives with her maid, they ate at friends' houses, then he took the midnight train back to Cambridge.

On January 30, 1903, Franklin turned twenty-one. Rosy organized a dinner party, and Franklin invited sixteen guests, including Eleanor. "Very jolly," Franklin wrote in his diary. Soon after, he was elected managing editor of *The Harvard Crimson*. He was graduating in June, but decided to return to Harvard for one more year, officially to attend graduate school, but mostly to run the newspaper.

To celebrate his graduation, he wanted to travel to Europe with a Harvard friend. This required delicate negotiation. Although Franklin was twenty-one, it would be his first vacation away from his mother. He approached her with the skill of a master tactician:

> I really want you to tell [me] what you would want me to do. I have told you what I feel about it: that it would in all probability be good for me, and a delightful experience; but that I don't want to be away from you for four weeks in the summer; also that I don't want to go unless you could make up your mind not to care at all. I feel that really it would be a very thoroughly selfish proceeding on my part.

Two days later, Mama wrote back: "I am perfectly willing for you to go as it is only for a month, and with a nice fellow. I do not think I should feel the same if it were for longer or if it were with several fellows."

Before he left, Franklin spent several weeks at Hyde Park, with his mother. He organized two house parties with a small group of friends and relatives his own age. Eleanor was among them each time. Since she was spending the summer just up the river, at her grandmother's house in Tivoli, Franklin was able to invite her without making his mother suspicious. There were tennis parties, picnics, and dinners with neighbors. On Sunday, June 21, Franklin wrote in his diary: "Dine at Rogers & play blind man's buff." Tuesday June 23: "Took E to early train."

Two weeks later, he invited six cousins. One evening he took his mother and guests on a dinner cruise in the *Half Moon*. His cousin Corinne was particularly struck by him that night. Franklin was "handsome at the tiller . . . a splendid sailor and completely confident," she recalled. Franklin wrote in his diary that the day was "great fun." He added, in code: "E is an Angel."

At the end of July, Mama was on board the *Celtic* to see off Franklin and his friend. When the whistle blew for guests to disembark, she burst into tears. "I *meant* to be very brave," she wrote him the next day. "It is . . . the thought of the ocean between me and my *all* that rather appalls me."

Before he left, Franklin had made Eleanor promise to come to Campobello a few days after his return. Somehow, when he told his mother, he made it sound like a casual invitation to a cousin.

Eleanor arrived at the end of August with her maid and stayed for five days. She must have been nervous. She knew how much Franklin loved Campobello and the outdoor life there. She could not swim, she was scared of rough seas, she was hopeless at tennis, and she could not play golf.

Franklin was not put off. Accompanied by Mama, they went out sailing. With Eleanor's maid, they walked to the village of Welshpool, two miles away. They picnicked with friends at Herring Cove, on the other side of the island. They had dinner at Mrs. Hartman Kuhn's, their neighbor, who said later that she noticed the tenderness between them the first time she met Eleanor, and was sure there was marriage in the air. Mama, it seems, had no such premonition.

That fall, Franklin invited Eleanor twice to Hyde Park. In November, he asked her to the big Harvard-Yale game. She arrived in Boston on Saturday, November 21, chaperoned by Sara Delano's sister, Kassie, and her daughter, Muriel Robbins. Despite Franklin's enthusiastic leadership of the Harvard cheer squad, Yale won sixteen to nothing. Franklin showed the three women the rooms he shared with Lathrop Brown, and in the evening the women took the train to Groton. Eleanor was going to visit her thirteen-year-old brother, Hall, who had been at Groton a year. She visited regularly, along with all the parents. As she told Franklin, she wanted Hall to feel as if he belonged to somebody.

The next morning, Franklin got to Groton at nine, in time for church and the Reverend Peabody's sermon. He had lunch with his aunt Kassie, cousin Muriel, and Eleanor. In the afternoon, he managed to maneuver some time with Eleanor on her own, and took her for a walk by the river. That evening, his diary entry was in code: "After lunch I have a never to be forgotten walk with my darling." He had proposed to her. To his delight, Eleanor accepted.

Franklin and Eleanor were eager to announce their engagement. But Franklin still hesitated to tell his mother. Thursday was Thanksgiving, and he was to join Mama in Fairhaven, Massachusetts, for a celebration in the bosom of the Delano family. He and Eleanor had arranged to meet the following Sunday, November 29, in New York. He now wrote to Eleanor that he would lie to his mother, inventing some other reason for going to New York. Eleanor was dismayed. Couldn't he tell his mother that he was seeing her, even if he did not tell her why? "I never want her to feel that she has been deceived."

Franklin realized that he was going to have to bite the bullet. Either he was serious about this engagement or he was not. After the Thanksgiving dinner and singing around the piano, he took his mother aside. Sara wrote in her journal: "Franklin gave me quite a startling announcement."

Sara apparently had no inkling. Naturally she felt hurt by Franklin's secretiveness, not to mention threatened and betrayed. Franklin was her *all*. And now another woman was making claims on him.

She did not hide her displeasure. She reminded her son that he was only twenty-one, and Eleanor had just turned nineteen. None of his friends had married yet; his father had been thirty-three when he married for the first time. Franklin had only just entered graduate school; next year he was starting law school; he was not established in his career; how on earth did he think he could keep a family in the style to which he and Eleanor were accustomed?

Franklin stuck out his chin. He had made his choice. Eleanor was a fine woman. They had known her since she was born. He had not hidden anything from his mother; there was nothing to hide. He loved Eleanor and he wanted to marry her. That was all there was to it.

Sara bid for time. There was just one thing she asked of him: to keep the romance secret for a year. They were very young, he and Eleanor, and young people were known for changing their minds. Marriage was a commitment for life. This was not a decision to be taken lightly. If he and Eleanor still felt the same way after a year, they could announce their engagement with her blessing.

Franklin was not at all happy with this outcome. A year was a long time. It was going to be extremely awkward to keep their engagement a secret, even with their own friends. He knew Eleanor would be bitterly disappointed. But he could not afford—literally—to fall out with his mother. His trust fund from his father gave him $5,000 a year. That was equivalent to a professional salary, but Franklin liked to travel, and he liked to buy fine clothes, old books, and rare prints. He already relied on his mother's help, and that was without a family. In his will, James Roosevelt had left his fortune to Sara for the duration of her life, along with the statement: "I do hereby appoint my wife sole guardian of my son Franklin D. Roosevelt, and I wish him to be under the influence of his mother."

Franklin had little choice but to agree to his mother's terms. After that, she had little choice but to let him spend Sunday and Monday in New York. He saw as much of Eleanor as they could respectably get away with. On Monday evening he took the train to Cambridge, and Eleanor sat up till after midnight writing to him: "I love you dearest and I hope that I shall always prove worthy of the love which you have given me. I have never known before what it was to be absolutely happy nor have I ever longed for just one glimpse of a pair of eyes."

On Tuesday, December 1, Sara took Eleanor shopping, then sat her down for "a long talk." She told "the dear girl" that she was about to move up to Boston for the winter, and she did not want Franklin coming down to New York during that time. She would invite Eleanor up once or twice. As for their next reunion, Franklin had arranged for the three of them to lunch together in New York on Saturday, December 12. That was fine, Sara said, but she did not want Franklin to stay on in New York on Sunday. People would begin to talk. She wanted Franklin to spend that Sunday at Hyde Park.

Eleanor was distressed by the conversation. "Boy darling, I have rather a hard letter to write to you tonight," she wrote that evening. The first hurdle was Sunday, December 13: "I don't want you to stay if you feel it is your duty to go up & I shall understand, of course . . . Whatever you do I shall know to be right but I don't quite think your Mother quite realizes what a very hard thing she was asking me to do for I am hungry for every moment of your time."

Eleanor had understood the precariousness of her situation. If Franklin's mother did not like her, she risked losing Franklin. The next morning, she wrote to Sara:

> Dearest Cousin Sally:
>
> I must write you & thank you for being so good to me yesterday. I know just how you feel & how hard it must be, but I do so want you to learn to love me a little. You must know that I will always try to do what you wish for I have grown to love you very dearly during the past summer.
>
> It is impossible for me to tell you how I feel toward Franklin, I can only say that my one great wish is always to prove worthy of him.
>
> I am counting the days to the 12th when I hope Franklin & you will both be here again & if there is anything which I can do for you you will write me, won't you?
>
> With my love dear cousin Sally,
> Always devotedly
> Eleanor.

Franklin, meanwhile, was caught between two women. He wrote to his mother on *Harvard Crimson* notepaper, telling her he was very busy, working into the early hours of the morning on the newspaper and various committees. Then came this:

> Dearest Mama— I know what pain I must have caused you and you know I wouldn't do it if I really could have helped it—mais tu sais, me voilà! That's all that could be said—I know my mind,

have known it for a long time, and know that I could never think otherwise: Result: I am the happiest man just now in the world; likewise the luckiest— And for you, dear Mummy, you know that nothing can ever change what we have always been & always will be to each other—only now you have two children to love & to love you—and Eleanor as you know will always be a daughter to you in every true way.

Franklin had done the unthinkable. He had stood up to his mother, squarely and firmly. "My dearest Franklin," came the reply from Hyde Park, "I am so glad to think of my precious son so perfectly happy, you know that and I try not to think of myself. I know that in the future I shall be glad and I shall love Eleanor and adopt her fully when the right time comes. Only have patience dear Franklin, don't let this new happiness make you lose interest in work or home."

Franklin wrote back: "I am so glad, dear Mummy, that you are getting over the strangeness of it all—I knew you would." That left the battle about the following weekend.

I confess that I think it would be poor policy for me to go to H.P. next Sunday—although, as you know and don't have to be told, I always love & try to be there all I can—I have been home twice already this term . . . If I am in N.Y. on Sunday *not a soul* need know I have been there at all as if we go to Church at all we can go to any old one at about 100th St. & the rest of the day w'd be in the house where none c'd see us . . . Now if you really can't see the way clear to my staying in N.Y. of course I will go to H.P. with you, but you know how I feel—and also I think that E. will be terribly disappointed, as I will, if we can't have one of our first Sundays together— It seems a little hard & unnecessary on us both.

He and Eleanor won that round. But there were plenty more battles to come. Franklin was used to his mother, and had long ago chosen his way of dealing with her—lies, evasion, and feigned docility. Eleanor swung between compliance and anger. "You know how grateful I am for every moment which I have with you," she wrote to Franklin, and signed her letter, just as she used to sign letters to her father, "Your devoted

Little Nell." But she did not see why her future mother-in-law should dictate to them when and where they could meet. "It is hard for her to realize that any one can want or need you more than she does," Eleanor told Franklin, "so I suppose I ought not to mind, only I do mind terribly."

Franklin managed to persuade his mother not to move to Boston that winter. He preferred to come down to New York to see her—and Eleanor. As a trade-off, he consented to go on a five-week cruise of the Caribbean with Mama and his best friend, Lathrop Brown. They sailed on February 6. Sara wrote in her diary: "F. is tired and blue." So was Eleanor, who found the separation quite frightening. Would Franklin still love her when he got back? She knew that Sara would be intensely relieved if her son changed his mind.

Fortunately, Eleanor had another interest that winter. She had volunteered her services in the settlement movement, which aimed, through "settlement houses," to provide social services to the urban poor. Eleanor was assigned to University Settlement House, on Rivington Street, where she and a friend taught dance and calisthenics to immigrant girls—mostly Jews and Italians—who lived in the dingy, malodorous slum tenements of the Lower East Side. (Eleanor once went inside one, with Franklin, when they took a sick girl home.) Unlike her friend, who came and went in her carriage, Eleanor preferred to take the elevated train and walk across the Bowery with her maid. It was a glimpse of another world—the streets teeming with foreign-looking people, the pushcart vendors at the curb, the strange food smells. She greatly admired the spirit of her young pupils, who worked long days in a factory or did piecework at home. Her cousin Susie was horrified, convinced that Eleanor would bring tuberculosis back to the household. But Eleanor, for the first time in her life, felt as if she were doing something useful. Her classes, she wrote to Franklin, were "the nicest part of the day."

In late February, Eleanor went to Washington, where she spent two weeks with her aunt Bye, gaining some confidence in that highly sociable house on N Street. On March 10, Sara and Franklin arrived in Washington (they had taken the train up from Miami) and went straight to the Shoreham Hotel, where Bye soon called and invited them to tea. For two hours, while their maid unpacked, Sara marched an impatient Franklin around Washington. Finally, that afternoon, he and Eleanor were reunited. "Franklin's feelings had not changed," Eleanor wrote in her autobiography.

"Darling Franklin," his mother wrote from Hyde Park, "I am feeling pretty blue. You are gone. The journey is over . . . but I must try to be unselfish & of course dear child I *do* rejoice in your happiness . . . Oh how still the house is . . . *Do* write. I am already longing to hear."

Franklin had returned to Harvard, where he relished his job as editor in chief of the *Crimson*. When he was elected chairman of his class committee, Eleanor was thrilled for him. "I know how much it meant to you and I always want you to succeed. Dearest, if you only knew how happy it makes me to think that your love for me is making you try all the harder to do well, and oh! I hope so much that some day I will be more of a help to you."

They were able to see each other more when Franklin entered Columbia Law School, in September 1904. Sara had given up their apartment at the Renaissance Hotel, and rented a house at 200 Madison Avenue. She and Franklin were once again under the same roof.

On October 11, Eleanor's twentieth birthday, Franklin presented her with a diamond engagement ring from Tiffany. The secret was still closely guarded, but Sara had accepted the inevitable. "I pray that my precious Franklin may make you very happy," she wrote to Eleanor, "and thank him for giving me such a loving daughter."

The engagement was announced on December 1, 1904. "President's Niece to Wed her Cousin," the newspapers reported. This made it "one of the most interesting engagements of the season." With that vicious penchant the gossip rags had for comparing women's beauty, *Town Topics* commented: "Miss Roosevelt has more claims to good looks than any of the Roosevelt cousins. This she inherits from her mother, who was the beauty of Mrs. Valentine Hall's four daughters."

From the White House, Theodore Roosevelt sent congratulations to Franklin:

We are greatly rejoiced over the good news. I am as fond of Eleanor as if she were my daughter; and I like you, and trust you, and believe in you. No other success in life—not the Presidency, or anything else—begins to compare with the joy and happiness that come in and from the love of the true man and the true woman . . . Golden years open before you. May all good fortune attend you both, ever.

Her uncle Ted wanted to give Eleanor away, and offered to have the wedding at the White House. Franklin and Eleanor preferred a more modest setting, in New York. Cousin Susie Parish's home on East Seventy-sixth Street, where Eleanor was currently living, was two interconnected houses (Susie's mother lived in the other one), and the second-floor drawing rooms could be opened up to make a spectacular ballroom. Pussie had recently been married there.

It was no easy matter to arrange the date: the president had a full calendar. But he was coming to New York on March 17 for the St. Patrick's Day parade and dinner, and in between, he could give the bride away.

Two weeks before the wedding, Sara, Franklin, and Eleanor traveled to Washington to attend the presidential inauguration. Theodore Roosevelt had won the election by the largest majority in American history. Franklin and Eleanor listened to his speech, watched the parade, and danced at the inaugural ball.

The day before the wedding, there was a great deal of coming and going at 6–8 East Seventy-sixth Street. The drawing room looked splendid. An altar had been set up in front of the mantel, and the cousins were to be married under an exuberant bower of palms and pink roses, symbolizing the "field of roses" in the family name. That evening, Sara wrote in her diary: "This is Franklin's last night at home as a boy."

TWO

A Victorian Marriage

March 1905–March 1913

St. Patrick's Day, March 17, 1905, was unseasonably warm, and midtown Manhattan was filled with exuberant crowds. This was not simply the usual parade up Fifth Avenue. Theodore Roosevelt, the newly inaugurated president, was about to give away his niece at her wedding.

By noon, a large crowd had gathered in front of the twin houses at 6–8 East Seventy-sixth Street. Soon after, seventy-five police officers arrived, and the onlookers were pushed back to the two ends of the block, at Fifth Avenue and Madison.

At 3:30 p.m., Theodore and Edith Roosevelt entered the block in an open landau, surrounded by mounted police and Secret Service. There were loud cheers. People were leaning out of windows up and down the street, flourishing flags and handkerchiefs. The president, who wore a shamrock in his lapel, waved his top hat, beamed, and led his wife into the Parish residence.

It was warm inside the house, and the drawing-room windows were open. When the musicians struck up the wedding march, they found themselves competing with the fiddles and drums on Fifth Avenue. Franklin and his best man, Lathrop Brown, stepped forward to the altar, looking handsome and nervous. Their former headmaster, Reverend Endicott Peabody, had come from Groton to officiate.

The six bridesmaids, dressed in cream taffeta, swept down the stairs from the third floor, crossed the hall at the rear of the drawing room, and made their way slowly up the aisle. Their sleeves were embroidered with silver roses, and in their hair—much to the dismay of Princess

Alice, who led the procession—they wore three silver-tipped ostrich feathers, symbolizing the Roosevelt crest. The six ushers followed, sporting tiepins with three little feathers made of diamonds—Franklin's design.

And then, on the arm of the president, came the bride. Her white satin robe was draped with rose-point Brussels lace that her grandmother and mother had worn at their weddings. Her veil was caught with a diamond crescent that had belonged to her mother. The pearl-and-diamond collar at her neck was a gift from her future mother-in-law. The newspapers declared her "beautiful," "regal," "magnificent."

After the ceremony, the president gave his niece one of his more gentle bear hugs, made the obvious quip that there was nothing like keeping the name in the family, and strode off to partake of refreshments. The bride and groom stood in front of the mantel to receive congratulations, only to discover that most of the guests had flowed after the president into the banquet room, where they were "laughing gaily at his stories." As Alice put it: "My father . . . lived up to his reputation of being the bride at every wedding and the corpse at every funeral and hogged the limelight unashamedly."

Thirty-two years later, on March 17, 1937, the most popular president since Theodore Roosevelt would give a radio address from his favorite spot in the hills of Georgia, where he had first come seeking a miraculous cure for his polio. "I have a particular tenderness for St. Patrick's Day," he told his listeners. "As some of you know, it was on the seventeenth of March, 1905, that a Roosevelt wedding took place in New York City with the accompaniment of bands playing their way up Fifth Avenue to the tune of 'The Wearin' of the Green.' On that occasion New York had two great attractions—the St. Patrick's Day Parade, and President Theodore Roosevelt, who had come from Washington to give the bride away . . . I might add that it was wholly logical and natural that in the spotlight of these two simultaneous attractions, the bride and the bridegroom were almost entirely overlooked." FDR relished that story, which over the years had acquired a delightful irony.

At 5 p.m. the president's carriage departed, turning left toward Fifth Avenue, still jammed with people hoping for a glimpse of the first couple.

Now that "the lion of the afternoon" had left, Franklin and Eleanor changed into traveling clothes and set off, amid a shower of rice, to

Grand Central. On their way, they called in to see Bob Ferguson, who was ill again, and had not been able to attend the wedding. The Scot, despite being rejected himself, had given his hearty approval to Eleanor's marriage.

At Grand Central, the newlyweds took the train to Hyde Park. This was to be their first honeymoon, a week in Franklin's family home, while his mother tactfully stayed away. In early June, they would take a second honeymoon—three months in Europe.

The Roosevelt coachman met them at the little station in Hyde Park. In the Hudson valley, the night air was crisp, and Franklin held his bride close. Their carriage swept up the drive, the windows were sparkling with candles, and they were greeted by Elespie McEachern, the old Scottish housekeeper who had served James Roosevelt's first wife, Rebecca, and who had opened the door to Sara when she first came here as a bride. The new Mrs. Roosevelt was painfully conscious of the housekeeper's appraising gaze.

The choice to spend his wedding night at Hyde Park was a strangely insensitive one for Franklin to make. He was taking his bride to his mother's house—the place where Sara had begun her married life, the place where she had given birth to Franklin. The house was filled with Sara's past: Oriental vases from her childhood years in China (her father, Warren Delano, had made his fortune from the opium trade); portraits of her siblings, alive and dead; endless photographs of Franklin—the blond boy in a kilt, the jaunty young Harvard man in a boater. In the dark entrance hall Franklin's stuffed birds stared out through beaded eyes. The household staff glided in and out of rooms. In eighteen months of courtship, Franklin and Eleanor had been constantly watched, and they were still under surveillance.

The wedding night must have been awkward. Cousin Alice had once attempted, when they were in their early teens, to tell Eleanor the vague details she had gleaned about the facts of life. "I almost came to grief," Alice recalled. "She suddenly leapt on me and tried to sit on my head and smother me with a pillow, saying I was being blasphemous. So I shut up and I think she probably went to her wedding not knowing anything about the subject at all."

Sara was wondering how it had gone. The morning after their wedding night, she wrote: "My precious Franklin & Eleanor, it is a delight to write to you together & to think of you happy at dear Hyde Park, just where my great happiness began. You have a real spring day and I can just see the sun . . . and feel how you two are resting and reveling in your quiet time together."

Later in life, Eleanor would recall her terror on "the dreadful day after I was married." At one point, Franklin handed her one of his rare books to admire, a precious first edition, and when she turned the page, she accidentally tore it. "Cold shivers went up and down my spine." She confessed to Franklin, who was chivalrous about it: "If you had not done it, I probably would."

There was a mean-spirited account of their wedding in *Town Topics*. "The event was characterized by pathetic economy," the gossip rag declared, "and the guests were not overly conservative in discussing it." The food was "supplied by an Italian caterer, not of the first class," the flowers by "a Madison Avenue florist of no particular fame," and "one man said he got only a fleeting glimpse of a bottle of champagne." It was not easy, the young couple was already discovering, to be in the public eye.

One week after their return to New York there came sad news from England. Marie Souvestre had died, at the age of seventy-four. She had sent a telegram to Eleanor on her wedding day, wishing her "bonheur!" Indeed, that had been Mlle. Souvestre's great gift to Eleanor, the glimpse she had given her of happiness. She had shown Eleanor an alternative path: that of an independent, professional woman. She had encouraged Eleanor to think for herself, make her own choices, and aspire to do something meaningful with her life. And now she was gone.

It was early June, and the RMS *Oceanic* was scarcely out of New York harbor when Eleanor sat down to write to her mother-in-law. "Thank you so much dear for everything you did for us. You are always just the sweetest, dearest Mama to your children and I shall look forward to our next long evening together, when I shall want to be kissed all the time!" The parting had been difficult. Mama had never been away from Franklin for so long. Eleanor felt bad about taking him away for three months.

Throughout their European honeymoon, Franklin and Eleanor wrote twice a week to Mama. They often signed off: "Your devoted children." Franklin wrote lighthearted letters, and enjoyed teasing Mama about the wild shopping they were undertaking in London and Paris. "Yesterday a.m. . . . Eleanor ordered a cloak and one dress, a cloth skirt and coat, very dressy. Then we went to Combe & Levy and ordered thousands of dollars worth of linen, 8 doz. tablecloths, 6 napkins, ½ pillow case, and a handkerchief." Eleanor scribbled in the margin: "Don't believe *all* this letter please. I may be extravagant but—!!!" Her own epistles were earnest and reassuring: "Your letters are so nice dear, they are just a breath of home and I wish you could see how we read and reread them when they come."

Franklin told his mother: "We are having a scrumptious time." In *This Is My Life*, written three decades later, Eleanor would hint that their honeymoon was not unmitigated bliss. From the moment they boarded the *Oceanic*, she was apprehensive about disappointing Franklin. "How terrible to be seasick with a husband to take note of your suffering, particularly one who seemed to think that sailing the ocean blue was a joy!" As it turned out, the sea was calm, and she was fine. But one night, Eleanor, startled by strange sounds, found Franklin walking out of their cabin in a trance, apparently bent on escape. While they were away there were several worrying episodes. Neither of them mentioned Franklin's somnambulism in their letters home. Eleanor *did* mention that he had developed severe hives.

Franklin took hundreds of photographs, and afterward, to Eleanor's astonishment, he could remember exactly where each was taken. She would always admire his "photographic memory." Franklin was interested in architecture, politics, history, forestry, farming, conservation— in everything, it seemed to Eleanor. But his favorite pastime was to plunge into bookshops, browsing through rare books, first editions, and prints of ships. He was sending dozens of trunks home, adding to his already vast collection of naval material.

Franklin enjoyed bargaining; Eleanor did not. She worried about their extravagance; he did not. Franklin was casual about spending money— presumably because he knew his mother, with a little cajoling, could be relied upon to come to his aid. When she was in Paris two years later, Mama would discover that Franklin had still not paid all his bills. "I will say nothing, as it will do no good," she wrote to him, "only it *is* a surprise as I am not accustomed to this way of doing business my dear Franklin, and if you love me you will be more careful in the future."

When Franklin climbed mountains, tramped the moors, and played golf, Eleanor stayed behind. In the Italian town of Cortina, in the Dolomites, Franklin got up at dawn to climb Mt. Faloria with a coquettish, slightly older woman, who owned a fashionable hat shop in New York. "It took us nearly four hours up but the view was well worth the pull," Franklin wrote to his mother. "She—Miss G.—was quite nice (smoked all my good cigarettes) and promised me a new ostrich feather hat for next winter. We . . . got back late for lunch."

"My husband climbed the mountains with a charming lady, Miss Kitty Gandy," Eleanor wrote, years later, in her autobiography. "She could climb, and I could not, and though I never said a word I was jealous beyond description." Eleanor was learning about Franklin's flirtatiousness whenever he was around attractive women. Franklin was learning about Eleanor's "Griselda moods," as she called them—those long retreats into self-righteous silence whenever she was hurt or angry. A friend of hers described them as "the most maddening things in the world."

In early July, Mama wrote that friends were wanting to rent out their house on East Thirty-sixth Street, three blocks from where she lived. Should she take it for them? Franklin responded from St. Moritz, in the Swiss Alps. "We are so glad that it is really through you that we get the house—if indeed we are so lucky and it is so good of you to take all the trouble for us . . . Ever your loving infants."

Did Franklin and Eleanor ever discuss, as they gazed across to those icy alpine peaks from their balcony at the Palace Hotel, whether the house might be *too* close to Mama? Eleanor most likely had this thought but did not dare express it. It was difficult for her to bring up the subject with Franklin. He disliked intimate, introspective talk, and had long since learned to deal with emotional problems by ignoring them. Eleanor had to fall in with her role—which was something akin to being the second wife—as best she could. "Franklin and I had tea out on our balcony and mapped out our future plans a little and then went down to dinner," she wrote Mama. "I have been writing this and he has been mending his Kodak and occasionally telling me that I have a wonderful husband, so I suppose he is being successful!"

Two weeks later, they heard that Mama had secured the house, and even negotiated a slightly lower rental fee. "You are an angel to take so much trouble about the house and in all this hot weather too," Eleanor wrote from St. Blasien, in the Black Forest. Mama had also sent money to Franklin's Barings account in London. "It is really too sweet of you,"

Franklin gushed, "and all afternoon we have been talking over what we shall get with it."

They were astounded by a wire announcing that Bob Ferguson had just married Isabella Selmes, one of Eleanor's bridesmaids, in New York. Bob was thirty-seven; Isabella was nineteen. Franklin and Eleanor had not even known of the romance. Bob and Isabella would soon be arriving at the Ferguson estate in the Scottish highlands, and they were hoping that Franklin and Eleanor would visit them there.

In the north of Scotland, it rained constantly. Franklin and Eleanor stayed with Mrs. Ferguson, the family matriarch, and trotted over in an open cart with a Shetland pony to see Bob and Isabella, who were honeymooning at a nearby inn. Franklin went tramping on the moor with Bob's brother, Hector, who wore a kilt. One night, Eleanor was woken by "wild shrieks." She tried to hush him up, but Franklin would not be calmed. He pointed at the ceiling: "Don't you see the revolving beam?" He was angry that she did not see the problem. The thing, with its wild gyrations, was bound to fall on them. Eleanor kept telling him there was no beam. After a long struggle, he finally went back to sleep. The next day he did not remember his nocturnal torment.

In mid-September, Franklin and Eleanor sailed for New York. Included in their vast quantities of luggage was a Scotch terrier, Duffy, acquired in Scotland. "I cannot tell you how delighted we shall both be to get home again," Franklin wrote. "You know how we long to see our Mummy again."

On the ship coming home, Eleanor suffered from nausea. Mama was at the dock to meet them. While Franklin dealt with the luggage, the women went to Mama's. The rented house would not be available for a week or so. That weekend, the three were together at Hyde Park. Sara noted in her diary: "Eleanor very tired so she keeps quiet."

On October 11, Eleanor's twenty-first birthday, she was still pale and tired. Three days later she greeted the doctor's diagnosis with relief. One of her many anxieties was that she might not be able to have children. Now Franklin and his mother would not be disappointed.

They moved into what Franklin jokingly called their "fourteen foot mansion." Mama helped them furnish it, and supplied them with a cook, maid, and butler. During the day, while Franklin was at Columbia

Law School, Eleanor, who was still feeling ill, was taken in hand by Mama. Every morning at ten, they went for a walk. In the afternoons, they went for a drive in Mama's carriage. They usually had either lunch or dinner together. In later years, Eleanor looked back on this time of her life with thinly concealed bitterness. "I was growing very dependent on my mother-in-law, requiring her help on almost every subject, and never thought of asking for anything which I felt would not meet with her approval."

Marie Souvestre would have been horrified, had she lived to see her beloved Eleanor regressing in this way. Eleanor was rapidly losing any sense of herself. So much of her day was spent with Mama that she scarcely had time for friends her own age. Her one confidante was Isabella Ferguson, who was also pregnant, expecting her baby a few months after Eleanor. After five months Eleanor was already "the size of the Great Pyramid." To each other, the young women admitted they were afraid of childbirth.

At Christmas Mama handed her children a sketch of a house. Underneath she had written: "A Christmas present to Franklin & Eleanor from Mama. Number & Street not yet quite decided—19 or 20 feet wide." They were becoming heavily dependent on Mama's largesse, and it was clear that Mama liked it that way. Franklin's trust fund brought them $5,000 a year; Eleanor's brought them $7,000. Their combined annual income (the equivalent of $290,000 today) was impressive, but not enough to afford the grand living that Franklin, in particular, took for granted. They needed Mama's generosity. She needed their dependence and gratitude.

As it transpired, this gift had a bigger catch to it than usual. In the New Year, Mama bought a plot of land on East Sixty-fifth Street, between Madison Avenue and Park, and employed a prominent architect, Charles A. Platt, to design a handsome neo-Georgian double town house, with a single façade, common front entrance, and interconnecting doors. Franklin eagerly went over the plans with his mother and the architect. Eleanor took no part in the discussions. No one asked for her views.

When Anna Eleanor was born, on May 3, 1906, Eleanor felt more helpless than ever. The baby girl was the third generation of firstborns in Eleanor's family to be given this name. Unlike her mother, she was a beautiful baby. But Eleanor herself had never known maternal love; nor did she feel any real desire to be a mother herself. It was Mama who hired the nurse.

Eleanor had difficulty breast-feeding, and so Anna was bottle-fed. One evening, the nurse was off duty, and when Eleanor gave Anna her bottle and lowered her into her cradle, the baby started to scream. When the shrieks showed no sign of abating, Eleanor panicked and called the doctor. Might it be wind? he asked. Eleanor did not dare tell him that she had not thought to put the baby over her shoulder and pat her back.

That winter Eleanor had an operation for hemorrhoids, performed at home. Already weak, she nearly died on the operating table. For weeks she was in agony. "The pain was considerable, but as my own impulse was never to say how I felt I do not think I ever mentioned this until some time later on," she recalled. "I simply refused to speak to those who approached me."

Eleanor was consulting the best-known pediatrician in New York, Dr. L. Emmett Holt, and conscientiously followed the guidelines he gave in his manual, *The Care and Feeding of Children*. Holt decreed that crying was good ("it is the baby's exercise"); babies should never be kissed ("grave diseases may be communicated in this way"); whatever the weather, babies needed "an airing" for several hours a day; the cure for thumb-sucking was to tie the infant's arms to its sides at night. And so on.

Mama was appalled by these newfangled ideas. Behind Eleanor's back, she told the nurse that if the baby cried, she *must* turn her over and soothe her. But the worst was the airing business. When it was time for Anna's afternoon nap, Eleanor put her in a wooden basket and hung her out of a window at the back of the house. The backyard was cold and drafty, and Anna would scream for hours. This time, it was not Mama but the neighbor on the other side who intervened. The woman warned Eleanor that if she continued with this practice, she would report her to the Society for the Prevention of Cruelty to Children. "This was rather a shock to me," Eleanor recalled. "I thought I was being a most modern mother."

Mama was crazy about the baby, prided herself on always being there when needed, and believed that she was extremely generous with her money. She *was*, to a point. But she also used her money as a means of control. From her father and husband, she had inherited a vast fortune, and she retained absolute control of it until the day she died. Although she supposedly gave Franklin and Eleanor their half of the house at East Sixty-fifth Street as a gift, she kept the legal title. And the "gift" was very much in her own interest. She wanted to live with the family.

There were times when Eleanor, irritated by her mother-in-law's constant interference and disapproval, wanted to explode. And then she chastised herself for being ungrateful. In *This I Remember*, the second volume of her autobiography, published in 1949, when both her mother-in-law and husband were dead, Eleanor wrote that Sara Delano Roosevelt was "bent on being the head of the family":

> She disliked having any of the younger members of the family financially independent of their elders; keeping them financially dependent, she thought, was one way of keeping them at home and controlling them. She was most generous with her gifts when she wanted to make any. She gave her son and me and any of the grandchildren anything she felt was essential, but she did not like any of us to have regular incomes of our own. Nor did she like extravagance of any kind, though she permitted extravagances, for some unknown reason, more readily in the younger generation. I think she always regretted that my husband had money of his own from his father and that I had a small income of my own; and when I began to earn money it was a real grief to her.

During the summer of 1907, for the first time since their honeymoon, Franklin and Eleanor enjoyed a three-month break from Mama. She was in Europe, seeing family and friends. From Mama's house in Campobello, Franklin and Eleanor wrote her a running diary-letter. That summer, Eleanor seemed happier than usual.

Eleanor was pregnant again, but felt well—"far better than last time." Friends came and went. There were the usual walks and picnics, and canoeing, sailing, and fishing expeditions. When the sea was calm, they sometimes took Anna and her nurse out in the *Half Moon*. They were all getting tanned.

Franklin's "night episodes" continued. These had become family knowledge, which they chose to laugh about. One night that summer

Eleanor was woken by a strange sound, and found Franklin out of bed, still asleep, leaping up at the window shutters, convinced they were a bookcase. "I must get it, it is very rare." He was angry, as usual, when she tried to pull him back by his pajama tails.

In late July, Eleanor's brother, Hall, arrived. A tall, handsome lad of sixteen, he was doing well at Groton. That summer, the girls on the island vied for his attention. Eleanor and Franklin were reading aloud in the evenings. They had finished the gruesome book Mama had recommended to them, *Indiscreet Letters from Peking* (an eyewitness account of the 1900 siege), and were about to start *A Staff Officer's Scrap-book During the Russo-Japanese War*. "Two fat volumes but easy reading and most interesting to us (F. and me). Hall prefers lighter literature but is forced to listen!"

The island had been shrouded in thick fog for several days. Franklin had taken up his stamp collection again. They played bridge with friends, and Franklin nearly always won. He and Hall were going off in the *Half Moon*, with four friends, up the Magaguadavic River, in New Brunswick. If the weather held up, they would be away for four days. Eleanor was so enormous that she was sure it was going to be twins. "I see Franklin has omitted to chronicle the exciting fact that Anna can walk from one person to another."

At the beginning of September, they were packing up to go home. Now that Franklin had passed the bar, he was to start work at Carter, Ledyard and Milburn, an old New York law firm. "Just think," he teased his mother, "when you get back in less than three weeks I shall be a full-fledged office boy."

It was with "relief and joy" that Eleanor gave birth to a son on December 23, 1907. Franklin telephoned his mother at 2:45 a.m. "A son all right, Mummy." Sara was thrilled. "I hope it will be *James*," she wrote in her diary.

James's health was delicate. No food seemed to agree with him, and he cried most nights, sometimes the entire night. Already undersize for his age, in the spring of 1908, he developed pneumonia. Franklin and Eleanor did not want to be far from medical help, and now that Franklin was a practicing lawyer, there was no question of his disappearing to Campobello for the three summer months. Eleanor took the children to

Hyde Park, and felt like a guest in her mother-in-law's house. Neverthe-less, she was happy for Franklin when he left on a short trip to Virginia, Kentucky, and Tennessee with a maternal uncle, Warren Delano, who wanted to look into mining prospects.

It was Franklin's first journey south of Washington, D.C., and his letters to Eleanor brimmed with enthusiasm. "My own dear Babs—the trip today has been so wonderful to me that I can't begin to tell you about it now." The train trip through Virginia was spectacular. "In some places we were over 2000 feet up, and the train ran thro' gorges that for sheer beauty beat anything that we saw in the Black Forest." He and his uncle rode on horseback over the mountains to Harlan, Kentucky:

> The path was just about the steepest kind that I would care to take a horse up, following generally a water course filled with boulders and ledges of rock. We formed a cavalcade of five . . . We got to the top of the Cumberland Mountain about 10 o'clock and had one of the most magnificent views I have ever seen . . . We continued along the ridge for a mile or so, got lost, came over the top and started down into the valley over what they thought was a trail. I thought otherwise—for half an hour we slipped, slid and fell down the slope, the horses slipping, sliding and almost falling on top of us, and ended up in a heap in the stream at the bottom. Uncle Warren said it was about the roughest ride he has ever had here.

Franklin was enchanted by this backwoods world. They were stay-ing at the Imperial Hotel in Harlan, run by the county judge, who also waited on the tables. Franklin and his uncle had spent much of the previous day "chewing the rag" with the men of the town, but now the sun was rising and it was time to saddle up. They were going for an all-day ride, exploring the local terrain. "My one regret is that you aren't with me," he wrote to Eleanor.

At the end of August, Franklin took two weeks of leave, this time to go hunting in Newfoundland with Hall. This was the kind of vacation Franklin most enjoyed—roughing it in the wilderness, with male com-panions, boats, and sturdy boots. Eleanor was happy to stay home.

•

In the fall of 1908, the Roosevelt family moved into 47–49 East Sixty-fifth Street. The stately six-story house comprised two mirror-image residences: Mama lived at 47; Franklin, Eleanor, and the two children lived at 49. Mama could not have been happier. Through sliding connecting doors, she could enter the other half of the house at any time, and did not hesitate to do so. Eleanor never knew when her mother-in-law would come bustling into the room.

Not long after they had settled in, Eleanor had a crisis, which she would render, unforgettably, in *This Is My Story*:

> That autumn I did not quite know what was the matter with me, but I remember that a few weeks after we moved into the house in East 65th Street I sat in front of my dressing table and wept, and when my bewildered young husband asked me what on earth was the matter with me, I said I did not like to live in a house which was not in any way mine, one that I had done nothing about and which did not represent the way I wanted to live. Being an eminently reasonable person, he thought I was quite mad and told me so gently, and said I would feel different in a little while and left me alone until I should become calmer.

Six months later, on March 18, 1909, Franklin Delano Roosevelt Jr. was born. He was a big baby, cherubic, and full of smiles. But he was not robust, and by the time of his christening, in October, Franklin Jr. was ailing. The doctor found a murmur in his heart and diagnosed endocarditis, an inflammation of the inner layer of the heart. On November 2, 1909, Mama wrote in her diary:

> At a little before 7 am Franklin telephoned to my room, "Better come, Mama, Baby is sinking." I went in. The little angel ceased breathing at 7:25 . . . Franklin and Eleanor are most wonderful, but poor Eleanor's mother heart is well nigh broken. She so hoped and cannot believe her baby is gone from her. He was 7 months and 9 days old, a beautiful flower he always seemed.

Franklin Jr. was buried at St. James Episcopal Church in Hyde Park. "Sometimes I think I cannot bear the heartache which one little life has left behind," Eleanor wrote to Isabella Ferguson. Sadly for Eleanor, Isabella had moved with Bob, who had been diagnosed with tuberculosis, to the drier climate of New Mexico.

Eleanor's grief lasted for months. She felt, as she so often did, that she was somehow to blame. Her traumatic past was haunting her. There was in this era no therapy to help her—just her embroidery, knitting, and reading. "I made myself and all those around me most unhappy during that winter," she wrote later. "I was even a little bitter against my poor young husband."

Her "young husband" was only three years older than she was. But Eleanor felt world-weary that winter. No doubt her bitterness had to do with the fact that one month after the death of baby Franklin, she found herself pregnant again. Still dressed in mourning for her dead baby, she was already carrying another. In four and a half years of marriage, this would be their fourth baby. For most of their married life, Eleanor had been pregnant. It was hard on her body and hard on her nerves.

Eleanor apparently once told her grown-up daughter Anna that sex was "an ordeal to be borne." The comment (which has made FDR biographers sympathize heavily with Franklin) needs to be seen in context. For Victorian women, sexual intercourse went together with possible pregnancy. And yet it took Margaret Sanger, whose term "birth control" came into the English language in 1914, to make the obvious point that fear of unwanted pregnancy blighted the pleasure women might take in the sexual act.

Back in the 1870s, with the new advances in rubber vulcanization, condoms and diaphragms had been readily available, but it had not taken long for the moral crusaders in Congress to outlaw their sale. At the beginning of the twentieth century, when Eleanor was a young wife, the only respectable means of preventing conception were abstinence or withdrawal. Neither method was appreciated by lusty young husbands.

While Eleanor was battling with depression, Franklin was not happy at his law firm. His heart was not in the legal profession. He wanted to be in politics. Indeed, he once told his colleagues at the law firm that he had aspirations to be president one day. They did not laugh at him. As one of them recalled in later years, he made it sound "entirely reasonable."

In the summer of 1910, opportunity knocked. Democrat friends in Hyde Park urged Franklin to stand for the district's state senate seat. This had been solid Republican territory for decades, and the upstate Democrats badly needed a new face to represent them. On the national scene, the Republicans were still in power, but Theodore Roosevelt was no longer president. His two terms had ended in November 1908. Now William Howard Taft was president, and not at all popular. This freed Franklin to stand as a Democrat.

He talked it over with Eleanor. It would put her in an awkward position within the Roosevelt clan. It also meant that while Franklin positioned himself for his campaign, Eleanor, heavily pregnant, would spend the summer in Campobello without him. But she encouraged his political ambitions. She knew how much they meant to him.

They now had their own "cottage" on Campobello—a sprawling, thirty-four-room house next to Mama's. The woman who had lived there previously, Mrs. Hartman Kuhn, had been fond of Eleanor ever since Franklin first brought her to visit, in their early courting days on the island. When she died in 1909, Mrs. Kuhn stipulated in her will that Sara should have first option on the house, for a nominal price, provided she bought it for Franklin and Eleanor.

Mama had bought the cottage, fully furnished, and Franklin and Eleanor had been effusively grateful, as usual. Eleanor had rearranged Mrs. Kuhn's furniture and tossed some out, and for the first time in her life she almost felt as if she had a house of her own. But not quite. Mama lived less than five minutes away, and came visiting at any time of the day or night. And the house was still in Mama's name.

Eleanor loved it, nonetheless. A handsome house, with red shingles and green shutters, it stood at the top of the hill, facing west across the bay to Eastport, Maine. The place was simple—their visitors often expressed surprise at its modesty—but for her and Franklin that was part of its charm. There was no electricity on the island. For lighting they used kerosene lamps and candles. (Franklin was constantly worried about fire breaking out.) For refrigeration they used wooden ice chests. The sole source of heat was fireplaces. Water for bathing was pumped from the well. Their drinking water came from a spring on the other side of the island and was brought to the house by horse and cart.

Campobello always seemed like another world—a nineteenth-century wilderness. Even in August the evenings were so cool that they often lit a fire in the living room. That summer, Eleanor begged Franklin to write to her, and keep her informed about his campaign. She found it hard enough to be there without him, she told him. If he did not make the fleeting visit he had promised, she would weep.

Back in New York, on September 23, 1910, Eleanor gave birth to another son. Anna was four, James was three, Franklin Jr. was dead, and now there was Elliott. The baby cried a lot, and Eleanor blamed herself, as usual. She thought it was probably because she had been so depressed during the pregnancy.

Franklin had other preoccupations. Two weeks after his son's birth, he was nominated as the Democratic candidate for the Twenty-sixth Senate District, in New York State. "In the coming campaign I need not tell you that I do not intend to sit still," he told the convention. "We are going to have a very strenuous month . . . We have real issues and an excellent platform to lay before the people, and with the aid of the independent thinking voters of these counties we have little to fear from the result on November 8th."

Franklin knew that the odds were overwhelmingly against him being elected. Even his most optimistic Hyde Park Democrat friends gave him one chance in five of victory. He was only twenty-eight, with no previous political experience. His district, comprising three counties in the Hudson valley—Dutchess, Putnam, and Columbia—had voted Republican for the past thirty-two years. Franklin needed the farmers' vote. How was he, a posh-speaking New York City lawyer who had attended Groton and Harvard, going to inspire their trust?

Franklin needed a local base to begin his political career. As he saw it, he had nothing to lose and everything to gain. He was going to give this campaign every last drop of his energy.

He hired a motorcar for his campaign. It was the tail end of the horse-and-buggy era, and Franklin was the first candidate in the district to campaign in an automobile. His advisers told him that he was crazy. Farmers hated the noisy machines; they frightened their horses. A motorcar was a luxury, and Franklin's team was trying to downplay his patrician image. But Franklin was adamant.

With Democratic colleagues and a chauffeur named Harry Hawkey, Franklin spent a month bumping over country roads in a two-cylinder red Maxwell roadster, without a roof or windshield. They called it the

"Red Peril." Their top speed was twenty-two miles an hour, and whenever they met a horse or team—which was every half mile or so—they had to pull over and turn off the engine. But they drove two thousand miles and covered every corner of the region.

Franklin gave between ten and twenty speeches each day, talking in village squares, at storefronts, crossroads, railroad stations, and post offices. He took off his pince-nez, which made him look like a scholar, rolled up his shirtsleeves, and addressed his listeners as "My Friends!" He mentioned his father, a Democrat, who had served as town supervisor, church vestryman, and trustee of the local schools. He mentioned Theodore Roosevelt. "I'm not Teddy," he told the crowds, but like his Republican cousin, he deplored the "rotten corruption" and "boss rule" of the New York State administration.

Franklin poured $2,500 into the campaign—far more than his opponent. It helped that he was related to the former president. It did not hurt that he was handsome. But it was his personality that won people over. He impressed people as serious and energetic, with a genuine interest in local farmers and their affairs. On November 8, 1910, he won his seat by a narrow margin. It was a dazzling victory by any measure.

Whereas most state senators regarded it as a part-time job, Franklin threw himself into politics full-time. This meant moving the family to Albany, in upstate New York. For the first time since their marriage, he and Eleanor would be living at a considerable distance from his mother. Mama was not looking forward to the separation. Eleanor was relieved. "I think I knew that it was good for me," she wrote later. "I wanted to be independent."

They rented a furnished three-story house near the capitol, at $400 a month. Franklin's salary was $1,500 per annum. They offset the expenses by renting out their New York home. As for the rest—their three servants, the English governess, German nanny, and wet nurse for baby Elliott—Mama helped out.

FDR was sworn in on New Year's Day, 1911. The day after, Eleanor organized a lunch reception for 250 people at their new home. Mama helped them settle in, then returned to Hyde Park. "It seems like a very strange dream to be here," she wrote, "and to think of you dear things all settled in that big Albany house and my boy sitting in the state Senate."

Almost immediately, the Roosevelt house was taken over by politics. Tammany Hall, the Democratic Party machine in New York City, was putting forward William F. Sheehan as U.S. senator. Everyone knew that "Blue-eyed Billy," an Irish Catholic millionaire lawyer, made generous contributions to Tammany's coffers. Franklin, outraged by the corruption, rallied his supporters. For ten weeks some thirty men, soon known as "the Insurgents," held out against Sheehan's election. In the late afternoons, they gathered in the Roosevelts' living room, talked, smoked, went out for supper, came back, smoked, and talked. When the nannies complained that the children were coughing because of the cigar smoke, Eleanor moved the children's bedrooms to the top floor of the house.

It was daring of Franklin Roosevelt, a political novice, to lead an insurrection against the entrenched forces of Tammany. On January 22, 1911, *The New York Times* carried a gushingly admiring column: "Roosevelt is tall and lithe. With his handsome face and his form of supple strength he could make a fortune on the stage and set the matinee girl's heart throbbing . . . No one would suspect behind that highly polished exterior the quiet force and determination that now are sending cold shivers down the spine of Tammany."

One freezing evening in late January, a small, pockmarked, disheveled-looking newsman came to the house to interview Franklin. Louis McHenry Howe lived in Albany during the legislative session to cover politics for the *New York Herald* and the evening paper, the *New York World-Telegram.* A progressive Democrat, Howe was hugely impressed that Franklin Roosevelt had pulled off a hopeless fight upstate and was now taking on the Tammany thugs. He already knew he was bound to like this fellow. But he never expected to come away feeling as he did. He went home and told his wife, Grace, that he had just interviewed a man who was going to be president of the United States one day.

At the end of March 1911, Franklin's group of rebels actually succeeded in blocking Sheehan's election. In Tammany circles, Franklin was now an archenemy. In Democratic circles throughout the rest of the nation, the name Franklin Delano Roosevelt had a heroic ring to it.

As a couple, Franklin and Eleanor were happier and closer in Albany. Mama was no longer a daily irritation in their marriage, Franklin reveled in the maneuverings of political life, and Eleanor was finding that she enjoyed being a political wife. It was not something she would ever admit. "I took an interest in politics, but I don't know whether I enjoyed it! It was a wife's duty to be interested in whatever interested her husband."

During the campaign against Blue-eyed Billy, she had joined the men most evenings, listening to their talk, and handing around beer, cheese, and crackers. On some mornings she sat in the gallery of the capitol, listening to the debates. She made a point of calling on the political wives and the wives of the newspaper men. Most days she was out of the house until midafternoon, then spent time with the children until they went to bed.

Despite her interest in politics, she was taken aback when Franklin came out for women's suffrage. Even her aunt Bye, who was so politically astute that her brother Theodore had frequently consulted her for advice during his presidency, believed that women would represent the "stupid vote." But as a good wife, Eleanor adopted her husband's views. "I realized that if my husband were a suffragist I probably must be, too."

In early April 1912, Franklin set off for Jamaica, Cuba, and Panama, where he wanted to see the nearly completed canal. "It is hard enough to be away from the chicks, but with you away from me I feel too very much alone and lost," he wrote to Eleanor from the Bahamas. "I hereby solemnly declare that I REFUSE to go away the next time without you . . . I can't tell you how I long to see you again."

At the end of the month, Eleanor joined him in New Orleans. From there, they took the train to the Southwest, to see Bob and Isabella Ferguson. In Deming, New Mexico, they discovered that the train to Silver City ran only three days a week, so they hired a motorcar and drove over the desert, past mesas, cattle skulls, solitary cowboys on horses. The sun went down, it was bitterly cold, they were averaging a puncture every half hour and anticipating a night in the open. Finally, another car came into view. It was Isabella, worried, coming to meet them.

Isabella took them to the camp at Cat Canyon, where she and the two children lived in tents. Bob was at the tuberculosis sanatorium, three miles away, in Silver City. The camp had outhouses, no running water, and wood for fuel. When he was with the family, Bob had his own tent, to avoid contagion. His dishes had to be sterilized. There could be no intimate physical contact between him and Isabella.

Bob spent his days in bed, depressed. Twenty-six-year-old Isabella, across the country from her friends, was holding up the family. She looked thin and tired, but impressed Eleanor with her extraordinary courage and pluck. For her part, Isabella thought Franklin and Eleanor "much stronger and keener in their interests since the Albany experience."

In mid-June 1912, there was another Roosevelt wedding. Hall was marrying a beautiful Boston girl, Margaret Richardson. He was about to graduate from Harvard with an engineering degree, but he was not yet twenty-one, liked to party, drank too much, and Eleanor thought him too immature for marriage. Nevertheless, after her experience of her mother-in-law, she was determined not to meddle. "At this wedding I felt as though my own son and not my brother was being married," she wrote in *This Is My Story*. "I did have sense enough even then, however, to know that from then on he and his wife must lead their own lives, and I hope I was never an interfering sister-in-law!"

That summer and fall, the Roosevelt family was divided as never before. It was a presidential election year, and although Theodore Roosevelt had always said that presidents should limit themselves to two terms and had supported William Taft as his successor, he had once again thrown his own hat into the ring. At the Republican convention, when Taft was elected as the Republican nominee, Theodore Roosevelt broke away and formed a third party, the National Progressive Party. Claiming to be "as fit as a bull moose," he posed a threat to both Republicans and Democrats. His own party was soon known as the Bull Moosers.

While the Republicans were fighting among themselves, Eleanor accompanied Franklin to the Democratic National Convention in Baltimore. It was Eleanor's first political convention, and she observed the wrangling with "keen interest." But there was record heat that summer, and in the sweltering hall the noise and smoke were overwhelming. Franklin was busy, lobbying vigorously for Woodrow Wilson, the progressive governor of New Jersey. In the end, Eleanor decided that she could be of no assistance to Franklin there, and it would be better to take the children to Campobello.

Soon a wire arrived from Franklin: "WILSON NOMINATED THIS AFTERNOON ALL MY PLANS VAGUE SPLENDID TRIUMPH."

Throughout the presidential campaign, Franklin was optimistic that Woodrow Wilson would win. Eleanor worried that Wilson had none of Uncle Ted's magnetism. To Bob and Isabella Ferguson, fervent Bull Moosers, she confessed: "I wish Franklin could be fighting now for Uncle Ted, for I feel he is in the Party of the Future."

Eleanor came back early from Campobello, to help Franklin with his campaign for reelection as state senator. They left the children with Mama at Hyde Park, and moved temporarily back into their New York house. Franklin had hired the red Maxwell and the services of his chauffeur, Harry Hawkey. But on their very first evening at home, Franklin came down with typhoid fever. For ten days Eleanor ran up and down stairs with trays and medicine, and then she succumbed herself.

Franklin was bedridden, incapable of talking to a single Hudson valley farmer, let alone barnstorming the district giving speeches. This time, with Theodore Roosevelt's third party, he was up against not one but two opponents. He was not going to get any support from the Tammany people, who hated him. His chances of reelection did not look good.

Rescue came from an unlikely quarter: Louis Howe, the wizened little newspaperman from Albany who had predicted Franklin's brilliant political future. They had become friends. At the end of June, Howe had bashed out a high-speed invitation to Horseneck Beach, Massachusetts, where the Howes always took their summer vacation:

> Beloved and Revered Future President:
>   This is a line to remind you that you have a date with me to go in swimming. Also that your young hopefuls . . . have a date to come down and dig in the sand . . . You will notice that I have not mentioned particularly that I hope your better half will come along. This is not an oversight, but I fear that in adding this to my invitation I may make the invitation to her so warm and cordial as to arouse the green eyed monster in your breast. I will therefore hide my real feelings behind the "safe and Sane" statement that Mrs Howe hopes to see Mrs Roosevelt . . .
>
>   Yours, Howe

In early September, after an urgent call from Eleanor, Louis Howe hurried down from Horseneck Beach. Franklin turned his campaign over to him, with a blank check to do as he thought fit. Howe established his headquarters in the old Morgan House in Poughkeepsie and set to work. For the next six weeks, he blitzed the district with posters and pamphlets. To local farmers, apple growers, and fishermen along the Hudson he sent "personal letters" from FDR. He took out full-page advertisements in the local newspapers. "Here is your first ad," he wrote to Franklin. "As I have pledged you in it I thought you might like to know casually what kind of a mess I was getting you into. Please wire o.k. if it is all right . . . I'm having more fun than a goat . . . Your slave and servant, Louis Howe."

Howe was indeed working like a slave. "Keep that temperature down, so that you can get on the job," he urged Franklin from upriver. But while Eleanor was back on her feet, Franklin was still too ill to get out of bed. When Howe came to East Sixty-fifth Street to discuss strategies, Eleanor could not help but feel a little irritated by him. He stank of stale tobacco, and his crumpled suits were covered in ash. She and Franklin were sick, they needed fresh air in the house, and here was this gnomelike fellow sitting beside Franklin's bed, smoking one cigarette after another, coughing and spluttering as if he were about to die. Mama called him "that dirty little man."

But it was entirely due to Louis Howe that Franklin, without making one appearance in his district, was reelected, and with a larger margin than before. On November 5, the Democrats won New York State, and the Democrats won nationally. Woodrow Wilson was president.

That winter, it was clear that Franklin was likely to be given a government post in Washington. Eleanor was excited by the prospect. She liked Washington. Before she married, she had enjoyed her visits to Aunt Bye's house, on N Street, always a cauldron of political activity. For the moment, however, Eleanor had other things on her mind. Hall and Margaret's baby had died. Hall was in the hospital with appendicitis. And their own little Anna, six years old, was starting school.

On March 4, 1913, Franklin and Eleanor attended the presidential inauguration in Washington. Eleanor still could not warm to the austere Wilsons, neither of whom she found "overburdened with charm." Nor was she stirred by the largest suffrage parade in American history. "Nice fat ladies," she wrote to Isabella Ferguson.

Franklin had booked them into the Willard Hotel, two blocks from the White House, where most of the incoming administration was staying. In the lobby, he bumped into Josephus Daniels and congratulated him on his new appointment as secretary of the navy. The two men had first met in Baltimore at the Democratic National Convention, where they were both lobbying for Woodrow Wilson. Franklin liked and respected Daniels, a warm Southerner in his early fifties, and one of the more progressive members of the Democrat Party. Daniels was *very* impressed by Franklin. He later described it as "love at first sight."

Daniels, a newspaper editor from North Carolina, knew almost nothing about his new portfolio, and was well aware that the navy was Franklin's great passion. He had already decided whom he wanted to work with. How would Franklin like to be assistant secretary of the navy? he asked. Franklin grinned. "I'd like it bully well."

It was Theodore Roosevelt, as everyone knew, who used the word "bully" to mean "darn good." Sixteen years earlier, Theodore Roosevelt had been appointed assistant secretary of the navy. From there it had been a golden path to what he called the "bully pulpit"—meaning the White House, the best possible pulpit from which to tell the people what they needed.

Franklin Delano Roosevelt would be the youngest man ever to hold the post of assistant secretary of the navy. When President Wilson approved the appointment a few days later, Daniels was almost as pleased as Franklin himself. "His distinguished cousin TR went from that place to the presidency," Daniels observed in his cabinet diary. "May history repeat itself."

THREE

Somewhat at Sea

March 1913–February 1920

It was March 17, 1913, their wedding anniversary, and for the first time in eight years Eleanor and Franklin were not together to celebrate. Franklin had forgotten about it until the evening. For the past two weeks he had been waiting anxiously for the president and the Senate to approve his appointment as assistant secretary of the navy. While their future was being decided, Eleanor had gone back to New York to be with the children.

That evening, Franklin was in his new office on the third floor of the old State, War, and Navy Building, on Pennsylvania Avenue. He stood a while at the French windows, peering out in the dark at the South Lawn of the White House, then sat at his mahogany desk and took out a sheet of paper with its imposing navy letterhead. "My own dear Babbie—I didn't know till I sat down at this desk that this is the 17th of happy memory. In fact with all the subdued excitement of getting confirmed & taking the oath of office, the delightful significance of it all is only beginning to dawn on me."

After that, he wrote to his mother. "I am baptized, confirmed, sworn in, vaccinated—and somewhat at sea!"

"My dearest Franklin," his mother wrote back. "You can't imagine the happiness you gave me by writing to me yesterday. I just *knew* it was a *very* big job . . . Try not to write your signature too small, as it gets a cramped look and is not distinct. So many public men have such awful signatures, and so unreadable."

•

Two days later, Franklin wrote to Louis Howe: "Dear Ludwig . . . Here is the dope. Secretary—$2000— Expect you April 1, with a new uniform." He regularly teased Howe about his rumpled newspaperman appearance—the rolled-up shirtsleeves, crooked tie, and ash-spattered jackets—and from now on Howe was going to have to pass muster with the admirals. "I am game," Howe wired back, "but it will break me!"

Even though Franklin knew a great deal about the American navy, nautical techniques, and naval etiquette (his naval books, prints, and model boats were fast becoming the largest private collection in the country), the job was daunting. The navy department was vast and unwieldy, with an antiquated administrative structure, and every minor requisition involved paralyzing quantities of red tape. In those first weeks, the two friends joked that Franklin did the signing, Louis Howe did the blotting, and luck kept them out of jail.

They made a first-rate team. Franklin was the front man; Louis Howe maneuvered behind the scenes. Franklin thrived on the pomp and ceremony, inspection trips, seventeen-gun salutes, honor guards, speechmaking, and impressed people wherever he went. Howe was most comfortable behind a desk, on a phone, at a typewriter. Franklin, at thirty-one, was youthful, impetuous, and arrogant; Howe, ten years older, saw it as part of his job to "provide the toe weights." At the same time, Howe never lost sight of the goings-on in upstate New York, Franklin's political power base. He established a vast network of contacts for Franklin, and kept up an enormous correspondence.

If Franklin was able to boast that there were no serious labor conflicts during his time in the navy, it was thanks to Howe, who went down to the navy yards, befriended the labor leaders, and regularly ushered them into Franklin's office to talk to "the boss." Looking back on those navy days, Eleanor could see clearly how much Franklin owed to the man he called his "secretary":

It would have been easy for [Franklin] to have become just a nice young society man who, after his work in the department was over for the day, sat around in the Metropolitan Club for a while and talked with his friends. But Louis Howe, who went to Washington with us as Franklin's secretary, decided that this was a period in Franklin's life when he had better learn something new. Louis, though gnomelike and frail always, was an indefatigable worker . . . He insisted that Franklin find out something about labor conditions in the navy yards, which were his special province in the department, and come in contact with the men. And he succeeded in getting him interested. This was Franklin's first close contact with labor; and there is no doubt . . . that it was one of the turning points in his development.

Franklin's boss, Secretary Josephus Daniels, thought Louis Howe the strangest person he had ever met, but quickly came to respect him. "Always keeping himself in the background, he knew all the tides and eddies in the Navy Department, in the administration, and in the political life of the country," Daniels recalled. "Howe had boldness in as large measure as his chief. And he could write . . . His chief interest in life was to advance Franklin in his public career . . . Even in 1913 he expected to see Franklin occupy the White House, and to further that ambition he devoted his every effort."

Eleanor, too, plunged into the fray. Her first step as a Washington political wife was to call on her auntie Bye for advice. Bye's husband, William Cowles, had been an admiral in the navy before he retired, and Bye knew the navy scene inside and out. After New York, Washington still felt like a sleepy Southern town, but it had its own distinct social hierarchies and rituals. Bye gave Eleanor elaborate instructions about "calling."

Bye and her husband now lived in the Cowles's ancestral home in the hills of Farmington, Connecticut. This was partly so that they could be closer to their only son, Sheffield, who was at Groton, and partly because Bye, in her late fifties, was increasingly crippled from rheumatoid arthritis and had had to withdraw from Washington's social whirl. Their famous four-story red-brick house at 1733 N Street, twenty minutes from the White House, was empty. Within a few months, Franklin, Eleanor, three children, four servants, a nurse, governess, and chauffeur moved in. Eleanor disliked Bye's heavy, dark furniture, but she loved the little garden at the back, with its rose arbor, where Bye and Theodore had often sat in the past, taking tea and talking politics.

Bye Cowles had given Eleanor a list of names, told her to have calling cards made up, and instructed her to pay a brief visit to everyone who might ever have anything to do with Franklin. Since Franklin walked to work, their motorcar, along with the chauffeur, was at Eleanor's disposal. That first year, Eleanor averaged sixty calls a week. In addition, she received calls ("one long afternoon next to Mrs. Daniels until my feet ached and my voice was gone"), attended naval luncheons ("course after course reduces you to a state of coma which makes it almost impossible to struggle to your feet & leave at 4 p.m."), and almost nightly dinners ("last night a big Navy League affair for Mr. Daniels where there was some really good speaking"). She reported to Bye:

> I'm trying to keep up with my calls but it is quite strenuous. I've done all the Cabinet, Pres. & V. Pres., justices, speaker, N.Y. Senators & some others, also some Congressmen. All embassies, counselors, naval attachés, & there are only a few less important ministers & the military attachés left. Besides I've paid dozens of calls on people who've called on me! When I come to you I'm going to bring my book & try to find out something about the people who haven't been at home & are just names to me!

Franklin often brought colleagues back to the house for lunch, which meant that he wanted the meal served without delay, and in an atmosphere where the men could talk freely. Eleanor decided to use a little bell to call the servants, so that instead of hovering and inhibiting the conversation, they withdrew to the pantry. In the evening, she and Franklin either entertained at home or were invited out. On Sundays they made a point of having an "informal dinner" with friends.

In later life, Eleanor would wonder about this frenetic socializing—her "compulsion," as she called it. She put it down to wifely duty, and a fear she had carried over from childhood—"the terror of displeasing the people I lived with." She meant Franklin. But she did not have to carry her wifely duties this far. The fact is, she enjoyed it. While Franklin consciously modeled himself on Theodore Roosevelt, Eleanor was consciously modeling herself on Theodore's elder sister.

Unlike Mlle. Souvestre, Bye Roosevelt was no radical; she was not even in favor of women's suffrage. Nor was she a beauty; far from it. And yet she had skillfully transcended the limitations of her gender. Everyone sought out Bye's company. Her brother turned to her for political advice. She exerted real influence. The house at N Street had been such a social cauldron in President Theodore Roosevelt's day that it was known as the "Little White House." "She was a wonderful hostess," Eleanor wrote. "The talk was always lively . . . the unexpected guest was always welcome . . . Young or old, you really felt Auntie Bye's interest in you."

Eleanor would acquire her own reputation as a warm and gracious hostess, who was interested in everyone and had an extraordinary talent for putting people at ease. During those navy years, she lost her painful shyness. "I learned a liberating thing," she wrote later. "If you will forget about yourself, whether or not you are making a good impression on people, what they think of you, and you will think about them instead, you won't be shy."

In the spring of 1914, Eleanor accompanied Franklin on an inspection trip of West Coast navy facilities. They crossed the country on the *Santa Fe*, spent a few days with Bob and Isabella Ferguson in New Mexico, then headed to the coast, where they visited naval yards from San Diego to Seattle. The protocol was daunting. When Franklin inspected flagships, Eleanor had to know the ropes—"whether I went ahead of my husband, or whether he went ahead of me. What did I do while he stood at salute, whom did I shake hands with, and what parts of the ship should I not visit." Eleanor was never able to relax on the water. She could not swim, which made her feel vulnerable, and in rough seas she was prone to "feeding the fishes," as Franklin cheerily termed it. Whenever she was invited to a naval event at sea, she worried about letting Franklin down by being seasick.

Back in Washington, she kept up her afternoon house calls. In addition to the visiting round itself, it took hours to plan her calling list, send out invitations, answer them, and keep a log. Five months pregnant and tiring more easily than usual, she decided to employ a social secretary to help her.

Lucy Mercer came three mornings a week, and she soon became a part of the family. It might have been Bye Cowles who recommended her. Bye knew Lucy's parents, Carroll and Minnie Mercer, who had once lived on N Street, a few doors away. Carroll Mercer had fought with Theodore in the Rough Riders. Back in those days, he was a member of the Metropolitan Club (which Franklin now frequented), and had helped establish the equally exclusive Chevy Chase Club (where Franklin often played golf). But soon after Lucy was born, the Mercers had lost their fortune. Carroll took to drinking. Minnie, who was already once divorced, left him. A bohemian, who shocked the social set by smoking in public, Minnie brought up their two daughters on her own.

Everyone liked "the lovely Lucy," as Franklin called her. Eleanor treated her more like a friend than a secretary. Franklin liked to tease her. The children enjoyed her warm, smiling presence in the house. When Mama came to Washington to look after the children while Franklin and Eleanor were in San Francisco at the 1915 World's Fair, she was charmed. "Miss Mercer is here, she is *so* sweet and attractive and adores you, Eleanor."

Lucy Mercer was grateful for a job that was both eminently respectable and paid $30 a week. In small-town Washington, her social standing was precarious. She was twenty-three, a tall, slim beauty, with the manners and poise of the blue-blooded aristocracy from which she hailed. But she was Catholic, penniless, and her parents had created more than a whiff of scandal. Where was she going to find a suitable husband?

In the summer of 1914, Franklin was needed at his desk in the naval department. There were crises in Mexico, Haiti, and San Domingo. War was imminent in Europe.

Eleanor, who was now seven months pregnant, moved the household to Campobello without him. It was, as always, an arduous business. The luggage—some fifty trunks, suitcases, and boxes—was sent ahead. Eleanor followed with her "small army" of children and servants. The journey took two days—overnight train to New York, day train to Boston (where they rested for a few hours at the old Hotel Touraine), then the 11 p.m. sleeper to Ayers Junction, Maine. The next morning, they boarded an old woodstove-heated train through Passamaquoddy Indian reservation territory. They got to Eastport around noon, and took a horse and carriage to the dock. If the tide was right (this might mean a wait of several hours), the island ferryman, Frank Calder, transported them in his "chug chug" to Welshpool, on the west coast of Campobello island. From there they rowed around to the Roosevelt family pier, then clambered up the hill to the cottage.

Franklin came up on a naval vessel for the Fourth of July weekend, then hastened back to Washington to work. After long tense days arguing war policy with his navy colleagues, he liked to play a few rounds of golf at Chevy Chase. "Up to yesterday afternoon I seemed to live at the office," he wrote Eleanor one Sunday. "Today I have played 45 holes and am nearly dead!"

By early August, Europe was at war. "A complete smash up is inevitable," Franklin wrote to Eleanor. "These are history-making days. It will be the greatest war in the world's history."

To Franklin's despair, nobody in the navy seemed to realize what this war was going to mean for the United States. President Wilson called for neutrality. Secretary Josephus Daniels was, like most Democrats, a committed pacifist. "They really believe that because we are neutral we can go about our business as usual," Franklin fumed to Eleanor. "Mr. Daniels feeling chiefly very sad that his faith in human nature and civilization and similar idealistic nonsense was receiving such a rude shock. So I started in alone to get things ready and prepare plans for what *ought* to be done by the Navy."

Theodore Roosevelt thundered that the world was at war and President Wilson and his yellow-livered Democrats were doing nothing. Franklin agreed with him, though he could not openly criticize the Democrats. He put himself out on a limb with his passionate entreaties for "military preparedness." It was imperative, Franklin urged, to build up the American navy *fast*. In government circles, people were saying that Franklin D. Roosevelt sounded more like a Republican than a Democrat.

Eleanor was expecting the baby on August 26. Franklin, in Washington, was completely preoccupied by the war. For three nights in a row he had been at the office until 3 a.m. "The heat has come again, and today is the third scorcher, but one doesn't have time to think about it." In the navy, they were frustrated by the vague reports from Europe, he told Eleanor. It was difficult to fathom what was going on. "The Belgians are putting up a glorious and unexpected resistance . . . The Germans may be doing more than we suspect." He was right.

Eleanor was a pacifist by nature, and with another baby coming she had plenty of other things to worry about, but she went along with Franklin. "All one's thoughts these days are on war," she wrote from the island. "Life must be exciting for you and I can see you managing everything while Josephus Daniels wrings his hands in horror!"

It was Saturday, August 15, when Franklin arrived in Campobello. He and Eleanor had arranged that the family doctor, Dr. Albert Ely, would fly up from New York on August 19, in good time to deliver the baby. It was not to be. On Sunday, August 16, Mama came around to their house for dinner. All was calm when she left. An hour later,

Franklin was sending the *Half Moon* across the straits to Lubec, to fetch the only doctor for miles around.

Dr. Eben Bennet arrived soon after midnight, and Eleanor's pains went away. At 1:30 a.m., the household settled down to sleep. Mama went back to her house, but slept on top of her bed, fully dressed. Monday, August 17, was "a more or less uncomfortable day," she reported to Isabella Ferguson (who had just spent a few days on the island with Eleanor), "and *real* work from 5:30 to 6:30 when the 'bouncing boy' arrived. Dear Eleanor has done splendidly, and is nursing him . . . Baby is fat & fair and perfectly sweet & the local doctor proves excellent."

Eleanor's babies were all big; this one weighed ten and three-quarters pounds. They gave him his father's name, the same as the baby who had died—Franklin Delano Roosevelt Jr. "Eleanor had a harder time than before," Franklin wrote to Isabella. "Never again will I trust her mathematics!"

Franklin stayed two weeks, then spent three strenuous weeks campaigning in upstate New York—this time as a candidate for the U.S. Senate. Eleanor was preoccupied with her milk supply and the baby's bowel movements, but she encouraged him from afar.

Franklin was beaten by the Tammany candidate. His opponents claimed that at thirty-two he was too young to be a U.S. senator. But the campaign at least kept him in the political arena. For the moment, he was not unhappy to return to his desk at the Navy Department. It was an exciting place to be, at this particular moment in world history.

The following summer, Eleanor was pregnant for the sixth time. Later in life she wrote regretfully that she had approached motherhood "with a keen sense of responsibility but very little sense of the joy which should come with having babies."

Franklin had finally managed to persuade his mother to extend the old family home at Hyde Park. He had been trying for years to get her to agree to this. That year Springwood underwent a radical transformation. Franklin designed the two new wings, built out of local stone, in the Hudson valley Dutch colonial style he loved. A stately porch with a sweeping balustrade was added to the front of the house. The crowning jewel was the library, a vast room, with fine wood paneling, Italian marble fireplaces at each end, books everywhere, and views across the Hudson to the Catskills. It was now a mansion worthy of a president.

On March 13, 1916, John Aspinwall Roosevelt was born at the house on N Street. It was eleven years, almost to the day, since Franklin and Eleanor had married, and in that time Eleanor had given birth to six babies—a girl and five boys. Enough was enough.

Since there were no more pregnancies after this, some Roosevelt commentators surmise that Franklin and Eleanor resorted, from this point on, to the only truly reliable method of contraception available at that time—abstinence. They point out that in the extended house at Hyde Park, Franklin and Eleanor had separate bedrooms, albeit adjoining. They add that Franklin had unusual vitality and was not going to be happy with "enforced celibacy." And so, they conclude, he turned to Lucy Mercer.

It's a demeaning hypothesis, for all concerned. It is highly unlikely that Eleanor imposed abstinence on Franklin. Throughout her marriage, she had done everything in her power to please him. She still found it difficult to assert herself. Why would she start with something as major as forced abstinence? Nor is it likely to have been a mutual agreement. For a couple to end their physical relations in their early thirties, after eleven years of marriage, would have been a very dramatic decision. It is likely that Franklin and Eleanor began to take precautions.

They were also busier than they had ever been. Europe was at war. In Washington, there were important decisions to be made. Franklin, in the navy, was at the center of it all. Eleanor, in addition to her work as a navy wife, was preoccupied by five young children.

In the summertime, while Eleanor was in Campobello with the children, Franklin was baking in the heat-struck capital. His friends were either bachelors or married men who might as well have been. After long days at the office, he was ready for some fun himself. While Eleanor was away, Lucy Mercer continued to come to the house once or twice a week, to deal with Eleanor's correspondence. In later years Lucy would tell a friend that from the first time they met, she and Franklin were "inexorably drawn to each other."

Everyone who met Franklin Roosevelt at this period of his life mentions his good looks. He exuded vigor and vitality. Except when he was ill, which was rather often (Josephus Daniels remarked that there was never a passing virus that Franklin did not catch), he always seemed to be in motion. He relaxed by doing athletic things—golf, sailing, tennis, swimming, riding horses. During the war, as part of "preparedness," the navy organized an early-morning exercise group in Potomac Park, where a well-known football coach, Walter Camp, had government ministers doing calisthenics. "Mr. Roosevelt is a beautifully built man," Camp observed, "with the long muscles of the athlete."

People talked about Franklin D. Roosevelt as if he were a movie star. A journalist at the *New York Tribune* wrote about him: "His face is long, firmly shaped and set with marks of confidence. Intensely blue eyes rest in light shadow. A firm, thin mouth breaks quickly to laugh, openly and freely . . . His voice is pitched well . . . He doesn't disdain shedding his coat on a hot afternoon; shows an active quality in the way he jumps from his chair to reach the cigarettes in his coat. He is a young man, a young man with energy and definite ideas."

It was no wonder that Lucy Mercer was attracted to Franklin from the first. The romance probably began in the summer of 1916. In early July—baby John was four months old, and the muggy heat in Washington was settling in—Franklin accompanied the family to Campobello. He stayed three days, then returned to Washington to work on the Naval Bill. It was an election year and despite Wilson's campaign slogan, "HE KEPT US OUT OF WAR," the new Naval Bill planned to make the U.S. Navy the greatest navy in the world. Franklin was in the thick of it. "Kiss the chicks and take very good care of yourself, dearest," he wrote to Eleanor. "I long so to be with you and this bachelor life isn't what it's cracked up to be."

Despite his protestations to the contrary, Franklin seemed to be having a good time. "The heat in Washington was so fierce all of last week that it just about got my goat," he told Eleanor. "The nights were the kind that meant baths at 2 a.m. During the day the office itself got so baked that the fans did little good and when I got off in the afternoons I spent the hours until midnight driving the car around the country. It was a real comfort to have the car and Warren, Lathrop (who was there two days), Fletcher, Harrison and others were also appreciative of it."

Who were these *others* whom Franklin preferred not to mention by name? Eleanor must have wondered. She was feeling "marooned" on Campobello. The baby suffered from indigestion and was crying a great deal. Eleanor also worried about his heart. She yearned to decamp to Hyde Park, where there were doctors nearby and Franklin could visit more easily. But infantile paralysis had broken out in New York City—there had been more than a hundred cases in June—and the epidemic was spreading up and down the eastern seaboard. "I am too sorry about Bab's digestion, but do try not to wean him," Franklin wrote. "It would be an awful trip to come here, also the infantile paralysis is gaining."

In Campobello, Franklin had made a sport of trapping flies in one of the windows of the house, where they gathered in the sun, and he now worried that they might be carriers. "*Please* kill all the flies I left. I think it really important."

The epidemic was alarming. By early September there were nine thousand reported cases in New York City. Most were children under five. The medical profession was completely stymied by the disease. Was it the long period of damp weather that had incubated the germs? Were they carried in the air? In water? Were they spread by domestic animals? (Police in Brooklyn had killed hundreds of cats, just in case.) Children under sixteen were not permitted to leave New York City without a health clearance, but New Yorkers were fleeing, with or without clearances. "Various villages are keeping motorists with children out and it would be difficult to get to Hyde Park by motor," Franklin told Eleanor. "*No one* is thinking of moving children by rail."

He hoped to be able to borrow Josephus Daniels's personal navy vessel, the *Dolphin*, to fetch the family back to Hyde Park. They would land at their private dock on the Hudson so that the children had no contact with others. But then Franklin heard that on his mother's own estate, the coachman's three-year-old daughter, Mildred, had been struck with the disease. They would have to wait until she was out of quarantine, and everything she might have touched would have to be sterilized. The children should stay where they were for the moment.

By mid-September, Campobello was chilly. Thick fog rolled in most afternoons. Franklin, as always, was worried about fire. (A few months earlier, the Delano estate, Algonac, had been destroyed by flames, and was being completely rebuilt.) "Be careful of the sparks on the roof or too much heating of any one chimney," he warned Eleanor.

It was early October by the time the family left the island on the *Dolphin*. Never had Eleanor been more relieved to step onto a boat.

The United States entered the war on April 6, 1917. President Wilson called it "a crusade to make the world safe for democracy." At navy headquarters, Franklin insisted on immediate action. They had to be ready to withstand military attack, he said. In Europe, the Allies needed destroyers, mines, and men. For a year now, Franklin had been trying to get the U.S. Navy to lay a barrage of mines in the North Sea and English Channel to destroy German submarines. After the war, Josephus Daniels would admit: "Not laying that barrage earlier . . . was, in my opinion, the greatest naval error of the war."

Theodore Roosevelt, almost sixty and blind in one eye, was eager to gather a volunteer regiment—the Rough Riders all over again—and go to fight in France. His four sons enlisted. Bye's nineteen-year-old son, Sheffield, enlisted. Theodore urged Franklin to resign his job and join the war, and Franklin wanted to, but President Wilson was adamant that they needed him where he was.

It was taken for granted in the family that a Roosevelt man was prepared to sacrifice his life for his country. The women had to "understand." For Bye, it was utterly traumatic seeing her precious only son shipped off to the war in Europe, but she kept her feelings to herself. Eleanor hated the idea of young men dying at the front, but she could see that the Americans had to help their European Allies, and everyone—men and women, rich and poor—had to do their bit. When her brother Hall enlisted as an aviator, their grandmother was aghast. She could not understand, Mary Hall told Eleanor, why he did not buy a substitute, as gentlemen used to do during the Civil War. Eleanor argued heatedly that "a gentleman was no different from any other kind of citizen in the United States," and "it would be a disgrace to pay anyone to risk his life for you." Looking back, Eleanor would remember this moment, when she was thirty-three, as her first outspoken disagreement with any of her elders. She was finally daring to assert herself.

After work, Franklin saw a lot of Nigel Law, a young British diplomat in his mid-twenties, who was serving a term in Washington at the British embassy. Nigel was often at the Roosevelt house on N Street. It seemed as if a romance might be springing up between him and Lucy Mercer. At least, this was what Franklin was hinting to Eleanor.

Eleanor was not convinced. Her sulky "Griselda moods" came over her more often these days. One evening, they went to a party at the Chevy Chase Club, along with Franklin's cousin Warren Delano Robbins and his wife, Irene, who were staying with them for a few days.

Franklin was having a good time; Eleanor was not. Around 1 a.m. she whispered to him, "I'm going home. Stay here and enjoy yourself." According to one version of the story, Lucy Mercer was at the Chevy that evening, and Franklin danced with her rather too often. Whether or not this was true, Franklin and the Robbinses came rollicking home in the predawn hours to find Eleanor sitting on the porch in her evening dress. They were dumbfounded. If she did not have the key, why hadn't she rung the bell? "I didn't want to wake the servants." Why hadn't she gone back to the club? "I didn't want to spoil the fun." Cousin Alice, who loved to tell this story, said that she would not have blamed Franklin if he had hit his wife—*hard*.

Franklin was always organizing yachting trips on the Potomac with friends. Eleanor rarely joined in. She did not like boats, she could not swim, she was bored by light banter, and whereas Franklin and his friends loved their cocktails—rather too much, she thought—she never did more than sip at an alcoholic drink.

One weekend in mid-June, Franklin went off on a small navy yacht, the *Sylph*, for one of his jaunts. Inevitably, the party of friends included Nigel Law and Lucy Mercer. After they set sail, Eleanor, on a whim, decided to join them. They were downriver by this time, and sent a boat to the Indian Head naval facility to fetch her. No doubt the atmosphere was a little strained that evening. On Sunday the group went ashore to sightsee, picnic, and swim. Franklin, in high spirits, goaded Nigel Law to climb a wild-cherry tree to pick the fruit. The Englishman, in his bathing trunks, was stung by poison ivy.

One week later, Lucy left Eleanor's employ. Women had just been accepted into the navy. Was it Franklin who encouraged Lucy to enlist as a female yeoman? Or was it Lucy who decided she must leave a household that made her feel more guilty every day she went there? Her older sister, Violetta, had left for France, as a nurse in the American Red Cross. Whatever the case, on June 24, 1917, Lucy Mercer reported for duty in the navy. She was assigned, of all places, to the office of the assistant secretary.

Eleanor did not want to go to Campobello that summer. Franklin had seemed strangely distant recently, easily irritated with her and the children. It seemed to her that he could not wait to be rid of them. She talked of staying, to do war work. Franklin said she must go, for the children's sake. He promised to come soon.

The older children had gone on ahead, with servants and tutors. Not until July 14 did Franklin finally persuade Eleanor to leave. Two days later, he was still trying to reassure her:

> Dearest Babs, I had a vile day after you left, stayed at home, coughed, dozed, tried to read and work . . . I really can't stand that house all alone without you, and you were a goosy girl to think or even pretend to think that I don't want you here *all* the summer, because you know I do! But honestly *you* ought to have six weeks straight at Campo, just as I ought to, only you can and I can't! I *know* what a whole summer here does to people's nerves and at the end of this summer I will be like a bear with a sore head until I get a change or some cold weather—in fact as you know I am unreasonable and touchy now—but I shall try to improve.

"Dearest Honey," came the reply from the island. "Such a dear letter from you & I hate to think of you all alone, however I know you will be very gay & though I don't think Washington would have hurt me in the least I think the children need a dose of mother!"

Eleanor was just settling in when an embarrassing article appeared in *The New York Times*. With the United States at war, the Food Administration was urging austerity. A group of society women, Eleanor among them, had pledged to save food in whatever way they could. For some reason, the Food Administration had picked out the Roosevelt household as a model for other large homes. Before Eleanor left, a journalist had come to the house and interviewed her. Eleanor had naïvely boasted about the household management.

In the article, the journalist mockingly opined that the Roosevelt household might serve as a model for "fashionable summer resorts."

> Mrs. Roosevelt on her pledge card said that there were seven in the family, and that ten servants were employed. Each servant has signed a pledge card, and there are daily conferences . . . Mrs. Roosevelt does the shopping, the cooks see that there is no food wasted, the laundress is sparing in her use of soap, each servant has a watchful eye for evidence of shortcomings on the part of others; and all are encouraged to make helpful suggestions in the use of "left overs." . . . Menu rules allow two courses

for luncheon and three for dinner . . . "Making the ten servants help me do my saving has not only been possible but highly profitable," said Mrs. Roosevelt today.

Franklin was stupefied by Eleanor's insensitivity. There was no "Dearest Babs" this time. He started straight in. "All I can say is that your latest newspaper campaign is a corker," he wrote, "and I am proud to be the husband of the Originator, Discoverer and Inventor of the New household Economy for Millionaires! . . . Honestly you have leaped into public fame, all Washington is talking of the Roosevelt plan."

Eleanor was mortified. "I feel dreadfully about it because so much is not true and yet some of it I did say. I never will be caught again, that's sure and I'd like to crawl away for shame."

By the next day, Franklin had calmed down, and was back to "Dearest Babs" and "Kiss the chicks." He was pleased that the boys had not been too unruly on the journey up. "By the way, I meant to tell you that if by any perfectly wild chance a German submarine should come into the bay and start to shell Eastport or the Pool, I want you to grab the children and beat it into the woods . . . I am not joking about this, for while it is 500 to 1 against the possibility, still there is just that one chance that the Bosch will do the fool and unexpected thing."

The next weekend he was back on the *Sylph*. He dashed off a note on Monday evening—"We had a bully trip"—but was too busy to say more. He wrote again on Wednesday evening: "Since I got back on Monday morning I have been so rushed and so gay that I haven't sat down to think quietly for one second . . . The trip on the Sylph was a joy . . . Such a funny party, but it worked out *wonderfully*. The Charlie Munns, the Cary Graysons, Lucy Mercer and Nigel Law, and they all got on splendidly. We swam about four times and Sunday afternoon went up . . . to Richmond, . . . getting drenched to the skin by several severe thunder storms."

"I'm glad you are so gay," Eleanor wrote, "but you know I predicted it!" She was feeling decidedly insecure. "I wish you could come here but I want no one else! . . . I don't think you read my letters for you never answer a question!"

On Thursday Franklin wrote with the inevitable postponement: "I do miss you so *very* much, but I am getting busier and busier and fear my hoped-for dash to Campo next week for two days will not materialize."

In early August, Franklin came down with an infection of the throat, so serious that he was hospitalized. Eleanor left the children with Mama and their governesses, and came all the way back to look after him. Mama wrote from Campobello: "Dearest son— You certainly were unlucky to get that horrid illness, but I think fortunate to have the most lovely person rush to you as she did."

Eleanor stayed two weeks, then returned to Campobello. "I hated to leave you yesterday," she wrote on August 15, on her way back up. "Please go to the Doctor twice a week, eat well and sleep well and remember I *count* on seeing you the 26th. My threat was no idle one!"

Whatever Eleanor had threatened, Franklin's letters were no more reassuring than before. He was *very* busy. It was *very* hot. "No news." On Sunday, August 19, he drove to a friend's farm at Harpers Ferry, West Virginia, about an hour from Washington. "Lucy Mercer went and the Graysons and we got there at 5:30, walked over the farm, . . . had supper with them and several neighbors, left at nine and got home at midnight!"

In Washington that summer, there was a "heavy blast of gossip" about Franklin Roosevelt and Lucy Mercer. Franklin made little effort to hide the romance—not even within the Roosevelt family. Bye Cowles's son, Sheffield, saw Franklin and Lucy out together ("Often. I used to think too often"). Cousin Alice teased Franklin: "I saw you twenty miles out in the country. You didn't see me. Your hands were on the wheel, but your eyes were on that perfectly lovely lady."

Alice, who had always been jealous of Eleanor, encouraged the affair. More than once, she invited Franklin and Lucy to dinner at her house. "He *deserved* a good time," she remarked later. "He was married to Eleanor." Alice's own husband, Nicholas Longworth, had been unfaithful for years, and Alice was having an affair with a married senator, known on the Hill as the "Stallion of Idaho." While Eleanor had five children, Alice, after thirteen years of marriage, had none. She was certainly not going to waste time feeling sorry for Eleanor.

When Eleanor got back from Campobello, Alice did her best to tell her what Franklin was up to, but Eleanor was no more open to this news than she had been to hearing about the facts of life in her teens. She wrote to Franklin:

This afternoon I went to the Capitol about 4 . . . On the way out I parted with Alice at the door not having allowed her to tell me any secrets. She inquired if you had told me and I said no and that I did not believe in knowing things which your husband did not wish you to know so I think I will be spared any further mysterious secrets!

She was warning him. Over the years, Eleanor had never wanted to spoil Franklin's fun. She knew he was a flirt; everyone knew that. But this time, she was worried. She had never felt Franklin so far away from her. That fall, she was busy, moving the family out of Bye's house into a larger place at 2131 R Street. She also threw herself into war work.

The Red Cross had set up canteens in the Washington railroad yards, where women volunteers made soup, coffee, and sandwiches for the trainloads of soldiers passing through. Eleanor worked long shifts, and she soon made herself indispensable. She never seemed to tire, did not complain, and always kept calm, even in emergencies. She proved exceedingly good at raising money. With Mrs. Daniels, she organized the Navy Department Red Cross Auxiliary, which mostly involved knitting and distributing wool. "It is going to mean part of every day now except Sundays taken up at one place or another but that doesn't seem much to do, considering what the soldiers must do," she told Mama.

She was so good at her work that the Red Cross asked whether she could go to England to organize canteens there. "It is quite a temptation," she told Franklin. "One can't help wanting to do the real thing instead of playing at it over here." She sounded just like him. But she stayed at home. Her first duty, she knew, was the children.

Franklin had been impatient for some time to get to the combat zone. At the beginning of July 1918, he was sent to Europe, to oversee naval facilities. He crossed the Atlantic on a destroyer. The weather was stormy, the seas so rough that most of the crockery smashed, and they almost collided with another convoy. "We must come over when the world is safe again," he wrote to Eleanor, "but I will not ask you to try a destroyer, though I have loved every minute of it."

Tragic news came: Quentin, Theodore Roosevelt's youngest and favorite son, had been killed in air combat. In public, Theodore Roosevelt was the proud old warhorse. "It was very dreadful to have Quentin die.

All I can say is that it would have been worse if he had stayed at home." But Eleanor could guess the atmosphere at Sagamore Hill. "Think if it were our John," she wrote to Franklin. "But I suppose we must all expect to bear what France and England have borne so long."

Franklin's visit to Buckingham Palace and his forty-minute meeting with the king was on the front page of the American newspapers. Eleanor sent Mama the clipping from *The Washington Post*: "He is surely making a hit!" At the front, Franklin seemed boyishly thrilled by the danger, and inspired by the heroics of the civilian population—"men, women and children, who are still here taking the nightly raids as we would take a thunder-storm."

With the children in Hyde Park, Eleanor was alone in Washington, "canteening." For hours on end she made soup and sandwiches in the stifling tin shack, sometimes not getting home until one or two in the morning. "I've come to the conclusion that you only feel heat when idle," she reported. One day she cut her finger to the bone on a bread-cutting machine. She staunched the flow of blood with handkerchiefs, and kept on working.

Inspired by the front line, Franklin was more determined than ever to resign his post and fight. "I do not need to tell you how hard it will be for me to end our work together," he wrote to Josephus Daniels, "but know you will understand." To Eleanor he wrote from Brittany: "Somehow I don't believe I shall be long in Washington. The more I think of it the more I feel that being only 36 my place is not at a Washington desk, even a Navy desk. I know you will understand . . . Kiss the chicks—I wish I could see them each day and tell them of the wonderful things our country is doing here."

Louis Howe assured Eleanor that Franklin was unlikely to get his wish. "It has practically been decided to accept no volunteers whatever under the new draft, and also that married men with children are not going to be called. I feel that he will have a somewhat strenuous time getting the President to waive the regulations, particularly as I feel the President has sufficient judgment to know that things would go badly here if he should leave."

"I hate not being with you and seeing it all!" Eleanor wrote Franklin. "Isn't that horrid of me?" By mid-August, she was worried by his silence. "I do long for letters and don't quite understand the long delay after getting your first letters but perhaps we'll get some soon."

In early September, news came from Paris that Franklin was ill. Eleanor supposed he had been doing too much, and hoped that a restful trip back would fix him. But on September 19, the morning the *Leviathan* was due to dock in Hoboken, New Jersey, she got a wire, asking her to meet Franklin with a doctor and ambulance. When she and Dr. George Draper boarded the ship, they were confronted with a floating hospital. The Spanish influenza epidemic was decimating the men faster than the war itself. There had been several funerals at sea.

Franklin did not have influenza; it was double pneumonia. He had a high temperature, patches on both lungs, and was so weak that four navy orderlies had to carry him on a stretcher from the ambulance into Mama's house, on East Sixty-fifth Street. Their own half of the house was rented out.

While Franklin tossed in bed with a high fever, Eleanor unpacked his things. That's when she came across a bundle of love letters from Lucy Mercer, and felt, she told a friend years later, as if the bottom had dropped out of her world.

Those love letters were destroyed. All traces of the affair have been thoroughly expunged from history. We will never know the depth of Franklin's feelings for Lucy. We will never even know whether it *was* an "affair." This, after all, was 1918. The Roaring Twenties had not yet arrived.

It would have been difficult for them to conduct a full-scale affair. Franklin was never alone in the house; there were servants. Lucy lived with her mother. It was out of the question for them to go to a hotel. Franklin was known in Washington, and they could not have pretended to be a married couple, nor would they have dreamed of doing so. Franklin knew plenty of fellows who went a little wild in the summertime while their wives were away, but they had affairs with married women, like his cousin Alice. Lucy was single, and in all likelihood a virgin. She was twenty-six in the summer of 1917, when the romance really took off. For a devout Catholic, sex with a married man was a cardinal sin. Even if Lucy were prepared to incur the wrath of God, she and Franklin would both have been terrified of her becoming pregnant. Franklin had his own reputation to worry about, as well as Lucy's.

So what *did* take place on those summer evenings in that open car, under the silvery moon, on the back roads of Virginia? There has been plenty of speculation over the years, but no evidence has ever turned up. In his book, *My Parents: A Differing View*, published by the scandal-loving Playboy Press in 1976, James Roosevelt obligingly claimed that a "rather well-kept secret" was the appearance of "a register from a motel in Virginia Beach showing that father and Lucy had checked in as man and wife and spent the night." But "motels" did not exist until the 1950s. And why has no one ever set eyes on that register?

Apparently Franklin had been sufficiently besotted with Lucy to talk, at least briefly, about marrying her. "She and Franklin were very much in love with each other," two of Lucy Mercer's female cousins would tell Jonathan Daniels (son of Josephus Daniels) in 1967. "A marriage would have taken place but as Lucy said to us, 'Eleanor was not willing to step aside.'"

Is that really what Franklin told Lucy—that Eleanor was not prepared to grant a divorce? It would have been expedient for him to blame Eleanor, and perhaps he did. What we *do* know (even if Lucy did not) is that after she discovered the letters, Eleanor offered Franklin his "freedom." Several sources—including Eleanor's cousins Alice and Corinne—told biographers years later that there had been talk of divorce.

We know from Sara's diary that Franklin was seriously ill for weeks and was being kept very quiet. Dr. Draper called in two or three times a day. Eleanor fed Franklin jelly and read to him. His room was filled with flowers from friends and relatives. On September 27, he "sat up for first time." The next day, Mama went back to Hyde Park, "as I can do nothing." In early October, Franklin and Eleanor joined her at Hyde Park. Franklin did not get up until midday, then he sat quietly in the library.

There is no mention of it in Mama's diary, but somewhere in this difficult time there were some emotional discussions. Mama told Franklin that if he divorced Eleanor, left his children, and shamed the Roosevelt name, she would disinherit him, not give him another cent. Had he forgotten his good father? Had he forgotten his marriage vows?

Louis Howe, it seems, played a more healing role, going back and forth, mediating between Franklin and Eleanor, soothing Eleanor's hurt pride, telling Franklin that he was an idiot, that a divorce would destroy his political career, and that no man in politics could ask for a better wife than Eleanor.

Franklin was a stubborn man. He did not like to be thwarted, and generally got what he wanted in life. But he was no impetuous adolescent. He did not need Howe or his mother to tell him what was good for him. Against the melodramatic backdrop of war, he had been swept away by passion; he had fallen in love with another woman. But he was not going to stray from his chosen path for long. Lucy Mercer did not represent freedom. Quite the contrary. Marriage to her would condemn him to a future of ignominy.

Franklin still loved Eleanor. He knew what he owed to her; he knew how much he needed her. He asked for her forgiveness. He had not seen Lucy since he returned from Europe. He had to see her once more to say goodbye, he said, and after that, it would be over.

They returned to Washington in mid-October. On October 31, Franklin saw President Wilson, asked to be allowed to fight, in the navy, and was told it was too late. On November 11, 1918, the Armistice was signed. "Washington, like every other city in the United States, went completely mad," Eleanor wrote. "Bells rang, whistles blew, and people went up and down the streets throwing confetti . . . The feeling of relief and thankfulness was beyond description."

For the past two months Eleanor had felt that she was losing her husband—either to Lucy Mercer or to the war. She wrote to the Fergusons that Franklin had had a "horrid time," but he was now "quite well again . . . We've lived in suspense from day to day never knowing what would happen next no one making any definite plans so I put off even writing till things settled down a bit." Her handwriting and punctuation were even worse than usual, reflecting her complete disarray.

In January 1919, the navy sent Franklin back to Europe, to oversee the dismantling of U.S. naval operations. This time, Franklin asked special permission for Eleanor to go with him. The three youngest children—Elliott, Franklin Jr., and John—were recovering from the Spanish flu. In the past, Eleanor would have insisted on staying behind. But she chose to go with Franklin. The symbolism was not lost on either of them. This was their first trip to Europe together since their honeymoon, fourteen years earlier.

They boarded the *George Washington* on January 2, 1919. On the voyage over they heard the shocking news that Theodore Roosevelt had died in his sleep, at Sagamore Hill, of a coronary embolism. He was only sixty, and had not been ill. Eleanor wondered how Edith would bear it.

In the north of France, they saw battlefields, trenches, and shell holes. They saw stumps where there had been forests, ruins where there had been cathedrals, rubble where there had been houses. It seemed that every other woman was wearing a crepe veil. Eleanor developed a searing pain in one side of her body. It was pleurisy. While Franklin worked, she convalesced at his cousin's place, in London. The house was freezing, and Eleanor now experienced the harsh reality of war rations, something she and Franklin had not glimpsed at the Ritz Hotel in London. "Decidedly we are growing effete at home from too much comfort," she wrote to Mama, "and I always thought myself something of a Spartan!"

By the time she had recovered, Franklin was in Brussels and the Rhineland. Eleanor, feeling "blue," went back to Paris. With Mama's sister, Dora Forbes, who lived in Paris, she visited the Val de Grâce military hospital, where Dr. Hippolyte Morestin was leading the world in reconstructive surgery. Eleanor forced herself to smile reassuringly at the men's shattered faces, and was grateful that Dora found something to say to each one.

The survivors were letting go and whooping it up. At the Ritz in Paris, Eleanor was taken aback by the scene downstairs in the bar. "All the women . . . look to me exaggerated, some pretty, all chic but you wonder if any are ladies," she wrote to Mama. She was glad that they were taking Bye's son, Sheffield, back to the States with them. "It is no place for the boys, especially the younger ones, and the scandals going on would make many a woman at home unhappy."

In mid-February they sailed home with President Wilson, who had gone to Paris for the peace talks. The ship docked in Boston, where the Roosevelts were invited to take part in the presidential procession. Cheering crowds lined the route.

They took the train to Washington with the president's party, and arrived the following morning. "Greeted by chicks and Mama. All very well and very happy to be together again."

Now that the war was over, Franklin was eager to move ahead with his political career and leave his navy post behind. Eleanor felt lost. The world had changed, and so had she. Years later, with the wisdom of hindsight, she wrote:

> During the war, I became a more tolerant person, far less sure of my own beliefs and methods of action, but I think more determined to try for certain ultimate objectives. I had gained a certain assurance as to my ability to run things, and the knowledge that there is joy in accomplishing a good job. I knew more about the human heart, which had been somewhat veiled in mystery up to now.

The family was still her prime concern. Anna was eleven; James was ten; Elliott, Franklin Jr., and John were seven, four, and two, respectively. Franklin was making more of an effort as a father, and played all sorts of boisterous games with the children when he was home. But when he stayed out late or came home later than he said he would, Eleanor found herself flaring up, then hating herself. "Franklin nervous and overwrought and I very stupid and trying," she noted in her diary. "A dreadful fracas."

She was finding it difficult to trust his word. In the summer of 1919, she refused to go to Campobello. Instead, she took the children to Hyde Park, where she found herself exploding with Mama, and then to Fairhaven, Massachusetts, where there were good bathing beaches for the children and she and Mama could enjoy some distance from each other. "I feel as though someone has taken a ton of bricks off me," she wrote to Franklin, "and I suppose she feels the same!"

Eleanor was impatient when Mama trotted out her old certainties as if the world had not changed since the horse-and-buggy days. Whenever the children acted up, Mama made out it was for lack of discipline. But Eleanor was no longer convinced that the standard Victorian upbringing was the ideal:

> My mother-in-law often used to say to me, "Why don't you tell the children not to do this or to do that?"
>
> "Because," I would reply, "I'm not sure that my way is best for them."
>
> "Of course you are sure, my dear," she would say firmly. "There is only one right and one wrong."

She saw everything in black and white; there were no grays. Certain things were wrong, others were right, without any shading. And she could not take in the fact that many of her rules were based on conventions, on social conditions, on a whole frame of reference that had ceased to exist by the time she had become a grandmother.

Eleanor was no longer able to listen calmly to Mama's endless wisdoms about the children. "Mama and I have had a bad time," she told Franklin. "I should be ashamed of myself but I'm not."

Three days later, she apologized to Mama:

I know, Mummy dear, I made you feel most unhappy the other day and I am so sorry I lost my temper and said such fool things for of course as you know I love Franklin and the children very dearly and I am deeply devoted to you. I have, however, allowed myself to be annoyed by little things which of course one should never do and I had no right to hurt you as I know I did and am truly sorry and hope you will forgive me.

It was a brief reversal to the role Eleanor had played for years. But the truth was that she could no longer fall in with Mama's views, and no longer wanted to. Her "absolute judgments on people and affairs going on in the world make me want to squirm and turn bolshevik," Eleanor confessed to Franklin.

The world *was* changing, and it was bewildering for everybody. The Russian Revolution had inspired a new political radicalism in the United States, which had provoked the inevitable counterreaction, a paranoia toward "Bolsheviks"—anarchists, socialists, foreigners, anyone who might be promoting "disloyalty" against the government.

Woodrow Wilson's attorney general, A. Mitchell Palmer, who lived across the street from the Roosevelts, was convinced that Communists were planning to overthrow the American government. It did not help matters when in early June 1919, an Italian anarchist dynamited Palmer's home. The Roosevelts' front windows were also shattered. The anarchist blew himself up in the process, and body parts were all over the street. "Now we are roped off and the police haven't yet allowed the gore to be wiped up on our steps," Eleanor told Mama. "James glories in every new bone found!"

Palmer brought in new legislation, making government espionage and wiretapping legal. On November 7, 1919 (the second anniversary of the Russian Revolution), thousands of suspects were arrested in dawn raids. Needless to say, the ignominious "Palmer raids," as they became known to history, did not uncover any evidence of a Communist plot.

There was racial tension throughout the country. Many thought that African American soldiers fighting in Europe had enjoyed far too much freedom, consorting with the local women, and needed to be put back in their place. At the end of the war there had been a wave of horrific lynchings in the South, with black war veterans strung up in their army uniforms. The nation's capital, which was 25 percent black, was still an intensely racist, segregated Southern city. The Roosevelts, coming from New York, had stood out among their Washington friends by employing white servants. When they got back from Europe, Eleanor decided to adopt the Washington custom and change over to black servants. Mama was horrified. She considered black servants unreliable.

For Eleanor, it was her first real contact with black people, and she would look back on this as the beginning of her race consciousness. At that time, however, she still harbored the standard prejudices of her class. When the butler developed pleurisy the evening before a buffet luncheon, she admitted to Mama: "With darkies one is always suspicious, even of a death in the family."

The race riots that broke out in Washington that summer were among the worst in the country. On July 19, a vicious white mob let loose randomly on blacks in the streets. Within hours, Washington's black community was fighting back. Eleanor, who was in Fairhaven, sent anxious notes to Franklin. "Still no letter or telegram from you and I am worried to death," she wrote. "Even if something is wrong why don't you let me know . . . I couldn't sleep at all well last night, thinking of all the things which might be the matter." That evening, not having heard, she sent a wire.

Her anxiety irritated Franklin. "Your telegram came last night at ten," he replied. "As I was in my pyjamas and couldn't get to Western Union I did not answer it till this a.m. as soon as I got to the office . . . Luckily the trouble hasn't spread to R Street."

On the beaches of Fairhaven, Eleanor had time to reflect on her past year. "It has been so full of all kinds of things that I still have a breathless, haunted feeling about it," she wrote to Isabella Ferguson. In her diary she was slightly less vague: "I do not think I have ever felt so strangely as in the past year. All my self-confidence is gone and I am on edge."

On October 11, 1919, Eleanor turned thirty-five. She had spent the first half of her life trying to please others, do the right thing, subjugate her own desires to other people's. She had conformed to the rules, played her role dutifully, and done whatever was demanded of her, to the point that she sometimes wondered who she really was.

At the end of October, she attended the International Congress of Working Women, in Washington. These were activist labor women who had the courage to speak out at the height of the Red Scare. They talked about the exploitation of women workers, particularly black women and immigrants. They questioned the traditional role of women in marriage. Some lived in lesbian relationships. Eleanor was interested in their ideas and impressed by their courage. Within a few years, some of them would be her best friends.

In February 1920, Eleanor's aunt Pussie and her two young daughters died in the fire that raged through their Greenwich Village house. "It was one of those horrors I can hardly bear to think of," Eleanor wrote later. She was glad that her grandmother had died six months before, and did not have to experience the tragic death of yet another daughter and more grandchildren.

As Pussie and her girls were lowered into the family vault at Tivoli, Eleanor was filled with a sense of what might have been. Pussie, who had recently divorced, had been bitterly unhappy for years. In her twenties she had been a talented pianist; she had introduced Eleanor to the theater and opera; she had taught Eleanor to love poetry. But Pussie was brought up in a world where a young woman's mission in life was to find a suitably wealthy man. Like her older sister, Anna (Eleanor's mother), Pussie had lost her way in an unhappy marriage. Eleanor found herself thinking the same kind of thoughts she had had at her grandmother's funeral: "If she had had some kind of life of her own, what would have been the result?"

Ten days after that tragic funeral, Franklin and Eleanor were startled— both in quite different ways—by a marriage announcement. They were acquainted with Winthrop Rutherfurd—"Wintie," as they called him—an immensely wealthy man in his late fifties, who had once ridden to hounds with Theodore and Elliott Roosevelt. In 1917, after fifteen years of marriage, his wife had died, leaving Winthrop with six young children—five boys and a girl. Before she died, they had both converted to Catholicism.

The marriage was announced in *The Washington Post* on Valentine's Day—February 14, 1920. The groom was fifty-eight; his bride was twenty-nine. Eleanor, who liked to adopt a casual tone when dropping a bombshell, added a postscript to the letter she was writing to Mama: "Did you know Lucy Mercer married Mr. Wintie Rutherfurd two days ago?"

FOUR

Tragedy at Campobello

June 1920–March 1922

In early July 1921, Franklin, at Campobello with Eleanor and the children, was finally looking forward to a long restful vacation without interruption from work. In the past few years he had spent little time on his favorite island. This summer he did not have to be at a desk in Washington. He had left his navy post a year ago. Mama was in Europe until the end of August, which meant that there would not be the usual tensions between her and Eleanor. The Howes were coming up in mid-July for a few weeks. He and Louis would sit on the back porch, watching the sun set over Friar's Bay, carving their wooden boats, enjoying the rivalry, and making plans for Franklin's run as governor of New York.

At last Franklin would have time for the chicks. He had hardly seen them grow up. Anna was fifteen now, tall, with long blond hair and a dazzling smile. Her grandmother was always complaining that she was a tomboy and should act more like a young lady. Jimmy was thirteen, lonely at Groton, and relieved to be back with the family for some weeks. Elliott was ten, a mischief-maker, but old enough now to join in the more vigorous activities with the older children. Six-year-old Franklin Jr. and five-year-old Johnnie were looked after by Mlle. Seline Thiel, the pretty Swiss governess. It had not escaped Franklin's notice that Jimmy had a bit of a crush on mademoiselle.

Franklin was eager to organize tennis matches and get out on the golf course. He had told the older children that he would take them on a three-day camping trip up the St. Croix river in Canada, on the *Vireo*, the twenty-four-foot yacht that had replaced the *Half Moon*.

The idyll crashed on July 13. Louis Howe, still at his summer cottage at Horseneck Beach, trudged a mile and a half along the sand dunes to send a wire from the little store in Westport Point. He had just heard that a Senate committee was cooking up disgusting allegations about Franklin's role in the "Newport affair"—an unfortunate episode that had occurred during Franklin's term as assistant secretary of the navy—and a scandal was about to break.

Leaving behind the tangy sea breezes of Campobello, Franklin hurried down to the stifling capital to clear his name.

The past twelve months had been a demanding time for Franklin. Nineteen twenty had been a presidential election year. Woodrow Wilson had served two terms as president; the Democrats had been in power for eight years. It had been hard enough for Wilson to convince Americans that they needed to join the war, but ironically, it was the *end* of the war—the peace treaty—that lost him his popularity. Wilson's dream was the League of Nations, an international peacemaking body that would prevent further pointless bloodshed. But the American people did not want it. They were tired of Europe and its problems. In the United States, the economy was in the doldrums. The nation was wracked by strikes and racial tension.

Franklin had been a key figure at the Democratic convention in June 1920, in San Francisco. He set up his headquarters in San Francisco Bay, on a naval battleship called *New York*. The Democratic Party picked James Cox—a progressive, who had the advantage of not being associated too closely with Wilson—as its presidential candidate. Frances Perkins was one of the many delegates at the convention that year who had been far more impressed by Roosevelt:

> Franklin Roosevelt was in the thick of it. Tall, strong, handsome, and popular, he was one of the stars of the show. I recall how he displayed his athletic ability by vaulting over a row of chairs to get to the platform in a hurry. James M. Cox of Ohio was nominated to be the party's standard-bearer, and word came out that Franklin Roosevelt, then only thirty-eight, had been selected by the steering committee as his running mate.

Franklin was a Wilsonian, but the party felt they could take this risk in a vice presidential candidate. "I was delighted," Franklin would tell a biographer, Emil Ludwig, years later. "I was only thirty-eight . . . Theodore Roosevelt had been forty-two." Franklin would spend a lifetime measuring himself against his famous cousin.

He tendered his resignation as assistant secretary of the navy on August 6, 1920, and three days later accepted the Democratic nomination as vice president from the front portico of his mother's house in Hyde Park. Sara put up with some five hundred people swarming into her house and five thousand more trampling on her lawns. When Franklin addressed the crowd, she sat beside him, bolt upright, fingering her pearls, smiling proudly. Eleanor sat off to the side, in a simple blue-and-white summer dress, her feet up on the balustrade.

Franklin spoke in favor of that unpopular cause, the League of Nations. It was crucial, he said, that Americans throw their moral force behind world peace and join the league. "America's opportunity is at hand. We can lead the world by a great example." That year, for the first time in history, women would have the right to vote. He had faith, Franklin told the crowd, that women would stand for progress, not nostalgia for a past that no longer existed. "We cannot anchor our ship of state in this world tempest, nor can we return to the placid harbor of long years ago. We must go forward or flounder."

The Republican candidate, Warren Harding, a self-made businessman from the Midwest, talked about small-town virtues, patriotism, and the "good old days." The Democrats, with their talk of a "new world order," were on a slippery slope. But for the next three months, Franklin conducted the most extensive campaign ever undertaken by a candidate for national office. It was an opportunity to make himself better known on the national stage. If all went well, the Democrats might turn to him as their leader in 1924—or 1928.

On his campaign train, the *Westboro*, Franklin made two trips across the country, traveling more than ten thousand miles, stopping in small towns and large cities. He had brought together a first-rate team of men, most of whom were former journalists. (Thirteen years later, this same core group would join him in the White House.) His chief adviser and confidant was Louis Howe. Their advance man was Stephen Early, a journalist from Virginia, barely thirty, who went ahead of the party, drummed up press interest in Roosevelt's visit, tested the local atmosphere, and wired instructions back to the train—in code. Franklin's speechwriter was Marvin McIntyre, a cadaverous-looking fellow from Kentucky. Tom Lynch, a Dutchess County friend who, back in 1911, had put champagne aside for the day Franklin would be president, handled campaign funds. Coordinating the campaign from their New York headquarters was Charles McCarthy, helped by a highly capable young secretary from Boston, Marguerite LeHand.

And then, of course, there was Eleanor. She did not join Franklin on his first campaign trip. She had to take their eldest son to Groton. Jimmie was twelve, and though he seemed ludicrously young to be abandoned in that austere New England institution, it was the family tradition. Two weeks later, he was in the infirmary, and Eleanor was sure it was some sort of nervous collapse due to homesickness, but she was about to leave with Franklin on his second campaign trip, and it was Mama who went up to Groton this time.

Franklin thought it important that Eleanor should accompany him on his second cross-country trip. Before they left, a reporter from the *Poughkeepsie Eagle News*, the local Republican newspaper, interviewed Eleanor in the library of the family home at Hyde Park, and found himself very impressed by this political wife, the niece of Theodore Roosevelt, who was brought up in a famous Republican family and had turned Democrat, and who in her mid-thirties, as the mother of five, claimed that she was interested in politics but was "first of all a domestic woman."

It was the first time that Eleanor joined Franklin on his campaign, and she felt awkward in her new role. For four weeks, she was the only woman on board the *Westboro*, sharing the bathroom with the men, and dealing with the all-male press corps who followed them around. Whereas the men on Franklin's team had a clearly defined job, her role was simply to be the ever-gracious wife. While Franklin was busy every minute of the day—addressing crowds, discussing tactics with his team, liaising with presidential nominee James Cox, answering letters, and so forth—Eleanor got to listen to him ("for the umpty-umpth time") and look on with a benevolent smile when the women crowded around him afterward, gushing about his looks and charm, and asking her if she ever felt jealous. In the evenings, after dinner, the men relaxed by playing cards, with much animated talk and laughter. Eleanor worried that their black porter, Romeo, who was studying for the ministry, would not be able to get to sleep. She worried because Franklin was losing his voice and needed to get to bed. She worried about the children. And she worried, as usual, about her own performance. Had she said the right thing? Had she done all she could to help Franklin? It was Louis Howe who made Eleanor realize that she had a real contribution to make to the campaign. Indeed, Eleanor, with her kind blue eyes, ready smile, and genuine interest in people, proved a tremendous asset to Franklin.

During those four weeks in the train, "Mr. Howe" became "Louis." Over the years, Eleanor had been jealous of Franklin's friendship with Louis and resented his influence on her husband. But as the campaign team traveled through the Carolinas, Kentucky, Indiana, Missouri, Kansas, Colorado, and headed back east, she came to see Louis Howe in a completely new light.

As the train rattled along, Louis would knock on her door and ask her opinion about a draft of a speech. He talked to her about politics, the life of the journalist, his interest in the theater. And he listened to *her*. He made her feel that her ideas mattered. He encouraged her to take a more active role in politics. They had reached a point in history where women must get involved, he told her. Near the end of the trip— they were in upstate New York, Howe's home territory—they played truant for a day, and went off together to see Niagara Falls. She discovered how much he loved nature. Like Franklin, Louis was a fund of information, but he also knew how to be silent. Only now did she discover that he had "rather extraordinary eyes."

On November 2, the Republicans beat the Democrats sixteen million to nine million. It was a crushing defeat, but Franklin told his team that they had enjoyed "a darned good sail." Franklin, personally, had reason to be pleased. He had made a very positive impact on the national stage. After four years of Republican government, there was a good chance that the Democrats might get back into power. Franklin and his men had high hopes. "I confidently expect you to HEAD the ticket," Steve Early told Franklin, "and pledge myself meanwhile to do all in my power to accomplish that end."

To thank the men on his team for their hard work and commitment, Franklin gave them gold cuff links from Tiffany, individually inscribed. "The Cuff Links Gang," they called themselves. They pledged to get together for dinner each year, at the end of January, around Franklin's birthday. If all went well, they told themselves, they would meet in two years at the New York governor's residence, in Albany. And soon after that, the White House!

In January 1921, the Roosevelts moved back to New York. Their house at 49 East Sixty-fifth Street was still rented out, and so they crammed themselves into Mama's half, and spent weekends at Hyde Park. Franklin returned to law practice part-time. In the other half of his time, he dived—briefly, he hoped—into the financial world. A friend of his, Van Lear Black, a high-spirited Democrat with whom Franklin sometimes sailed in Chesapeake Bay, asked him to be the New York manager of his surety bonding house, the Fidelity and Deposit Company of Maryland. Neither of them had any illusions that Franklin knew much about finances, but politics played an important role in bonding and surety, and Franklin had prestige and a wide network of connections. His salary was huge—$25,000 per annum. Franklin told everyone that he was delighted no longer to be on a government salary.

In reality, he was determined to get back into politics as soon as possible. From Hyde Park he wrote to Steve Early: "If you can get off for a Sunday come up here and spend it with us. Very quiet but plenty to eat and wash it down." He wanted to discuss plans for the future. "You were so perfectly fine in the way you helped in the campaign, and I value your judgment so much that I look to you for many things in the days to come. Thank the Lord we are both comparatively youthful!"

With his salary from Fidelity and Deposit, Franklin was able to continue to employ Louis Howe as his assistant. To help with the correspondence involved in two jobs—not to mention the numerous organizations of which he was a patron—Franklin engaged Marguerite LeHand, the lively young woman who had worked in the New York Democratic headquarters during the election campaign.

This limbo was most difficult for Eleanor. After nine years away from New York, they were back with Mama. Eleanor no longer had the least interest in ladies' teas and luncheons, and was anxious not to be inveigled into becoming Mama's social companion again. What saved her that winter was a visit from Mrs. Frank Vanderlip, head of the New York League of Women Voters, who asked her to join the board.

Eleanor had not been involved in the campaign for women's suffrage, and she was a little intimidated by the educated professional women in the league, but she had not forgotten Howe's encouraging words on the campaign train. She willingly agreed. Her job was to go through the Congressional Record and write monthly reports on any national legislation that concerned women. One morning a week she worked with Elizabeth

Read, the league's lawyer, who helped her understand the more convoluted legal phrasing. At board meetings, Eleanor was a calm presence and would not allow herself to be drawn into factional disputes. While the others tended to get lost in theorizing, she focused on getting the job done. It was not long before the group considered her one of their leaders. In April 1921, Eleanor attended the league's national convention in Cleveland. "I've had a very interesting day and heard some really good women speakers," she wrote to Franklin. She added: "Much, much love dear and I prefer doing my politics with you."

Elizabeth Read lived with Esther Lape, a journalist who taught at Barnard and was active in the Women's Trade Union League. Eleanor sometimes went to dinner in their small Greenwich Village apartment. The three women read poetry to one another; there was lively discussion of social issues. Eleanor was reminded of her school days, those stimulating evenings with Marie Souvestre.

In June 1921, Elizabeth Read and Esther Lape, who were quite open about their lesbian relationship, stayed for a few days at Hyde Park. "My mother-in-law was distressed," Eleanor wrote. "I had begun to realize that in my development I was drifting far afield from the old influences."

The Roosevelts were shortly to leave for Campobello. The two women were returning to Manhattan. "Franklin took us to the station, carrying our bags," Esther Lape remembered. "He was wearing one of those baggy brown suits. He looked so strong and healthy." It was the last time they would see him walking.

The family had arrived on Campobello island in joyful spirits. The children were thrilled at the prospect of a whole summer with their father. So was Eleanor. It was a severe blow to everyone when, because of some scandal to do with his former navy job, Franklin had to hurry off to Washington.

On the way down to the capital, Franklin stopped in Boston to confer with Louis Howe, who traveled up from Horseneck Beach. They agreed that this was a deliberate frame-up on the part of the Republicans, to knock Franklin out of the political arena. More than a year had passed since the navy had cracked down on the infamous homosexual activity at the Newport naval base. Now the Republican muckrakers in

Washington were making vile allegations about the crackdown itself. Undercover agents, acting as sexual decoys, had engaged in the "most deplorable, disgraceful and unnatural" practices, they said. Franklin, as assistant secretary of the navy, must have known about this, and if not, they alleged, he "was most derelict in the performance of his duty."

Franklin asked Stephen Early to go with him to Washington to help clear his image, and Miss LeHand, to type up their statement. "As I expected I found all the cards stacked," he wrote to Eleanor from Washington on July 21, "only even worse than I thought." The headlines in *The New York Times* screeched: "Lay Navy Scandal to F. D. Roosevelt . . . Details Are Unprintable."

Franklin left Washington feeling frazzled. Miss LeHand accompanied him back to New York, where he responded to the accusations at greater length and attended to other work. He would be back in Campobello at the end of the month, he told Eleanor.

Meanwhile, the Howes—Louis, Grace, and their ten-year-old son, Hartley—had joined Eleanor and the children on Campobello. Louis was valiantly hitting tennis balls to the boys and whittling his model boats. Franklin wrote: "Tell Louis I expect those boats to be all rigged and ready when I get up there and I am very greatly put out not to be there now."

On Thursday, July 28, Franklin, who was on the board of the New York Boy Scouts, sailed up the Hudson to Bear Mountain, where he inspected the scouts' summer camps. That might have been the day he picked up the virus that would change his life forever. The photographs that were taken of him that afternoon—smiling, in shirtsleeves, striding around among the scouts—are the last in which he is seen standing without support.

That evening, Franklin returned to New York. Eleanor had expected him at the end of July. Now he wired that he would be coming up with his boss, Van Lear Black, in Black's yacht, the *Sabalo*. They would leave New York on Friday, August 5, and arrive at Campobello on Sunday, in the evening.

Eleanor had grown to love Campobello, with its rolling fogs, rugged rocks, rapidly rising tides, and bloodred sunsets. She and Franklin appreciated the simplicity of life on this island between Canada and the

United States, its isolation from the modern world. But these days, Campobello had an increasingly lost-world feel to it. From the 1880s until World War I the island had taken off as a summer retreat for New York and Boston aristocracy, seeking escape from the heat. Now the grand houses stood empty. The luxury hotels had closed. The world was changing. There was less leisure time, even for the aristocracy.

Eleanor was pleased to have the Howes there, keeping her company. They were all waiting impatiently for Franklin to return. But though it meant another week without him, Eleanor was relieved that he was not coming up by train in the blistering heat. She knew how distressed he was by the Newport saga. The sea voyage would help calm him.

It was close to dusk on Sunday, August 7, when the *Sabalo* docked in Welshpool. The voyage had been arduous. They had encountered dense fog off the coast of Maine, and Franklin had taken the helm, navigating blindly, guided by the booming of foghorns. It was fortunate, Van Lear Black kept saying, that Franklin knew these treacherous waters, the rocks and tides, like the back of his hand.

The Newport scandal seemed to have died away, but Franklin was still visibly disturbed by it. He was somewhat manic. "When Father was mad, his way of working off steam was through an outpouring of physical vigor," James Roosevelt wrote. "Immediately on his arrival, we began having a wild, whooping, romping, running, sailing, picnicking time with him."

On Monday, August 8, Franklin took Black and his party fishing from the tender of the *Sabalo*. In the process of baiting everyone's fishing hooks, he walked across a varnished plank, slipped, and fell overboard. He was used to those freezing waters and was only briefly immersed, but he was shocked by the impact. "I'd never felt anything as cold as that water," he said later. "It seemed paralyzing."

On Tuesday, Van Lear Black and his friends set sail for home, earlier than planned. Grace Howe wrote to their twenty-one-year-old daughter, Mary, who was spending the summer in France, that she imagined Franklin had exhausted them.

On Wednesday, August 10, Franklin took the older children for a sail in the Bay of Fundy. They observed smoke on one of the small islands, and sailed over to find that a grove of spruce trees was on fire. For hours they beat at the flames. By the time they put out the fire, their eyes were bleary with smoke, their skin blackened by spark burns. But no sooner had they docked the boat than Franklin suggested a swim in Glen Severn Lake, a freshwater lagoon on the other side of the island. They dogtrotted through the woods to the lagoon. The water was tepid. After that, Franklin suggested a plunge in the ocean. He felt strangely weary and was hoping that the icy water would revitalize him. It did not.

They returned to the house at a slower pace. The children, shivering, went upstairs to change. Franklin was distracted by the mail and the previous day's newspapers, which Frank Calder, the local sea captain, had brought from Eastport in his motorboat. Franklin sat reading for a while, too tired to move. Finally, he struggled upstairs, telling Eleanor that he thought he might have an attack of lumbago and would skip dinner.

He went to bed trembling with cold, and the chill grew worse in the night. The next morning, when he forced himself out of bed, his left leg buckled under him. He limped to the bathroom, stood awkwardly in front of the mirror, and shaved. He thought that the trouble with his leg would disappear with use. But after a bit the leg could not hold any weight at all.

He went back to bed. By the afternoon, he ached all over, and his temperature was 102. Eleanor asked Frank Calder to cross the narrow straits to Lubec and fetch Dr. Eben Bennet (the man who seven years earlier had delivered Franklin Jr.). The doctor, observing the fever, headache, aching body, and shivering, thought it might be flu. It was not an uncommon misdiagnosis. The initial symptoms of poliomyelitis were similar.

By Friday, Franklin was unable to support himself on either of his legs. "I don't know what's the matter with me, Louis," he kept saying. "I just don't know." By Saturday he was completely paralyzed from the chest down. His skin was so sensitive that he could hardly stand the pressure of the bedclothes or the breeze coming in from the window.

Never had Eleanor felt more trapped on Campobello. This was 1921. There were no helicopters back then to airlift Franklin to a hospital. There was no bridge on which an ambulance could cross. The one telephone on the island, at the small general store in Welshpool, offered no privacy. It would have caused panic on the island if Eleanor had described Franklin's condition on the phone. She and Louis relied entirely on Frank Calder and his motorboat, Dr. Bennet and his home telephone, and the two men's complete discretion.

On Saturday, August 13, Eleanor reported to Franklin's half brother, Rosy: "Louis Howe (who, thank heavens, is here, for he has been the greatest help) went with Dr. Bennet to Lubec, and they canvassed the nearby resorts and decided that the best available diagnostician was the famous old Dr. W. W. Keen of Philadelphia and he agreed to motor up and spend the night."

The eighty-four-year-old doctor, who was vacationing at Bar Harbor, Maine, arrived at seven thirty in the evening. "He thinks a clot of blood from a sudden congestion has settled in the lower spinal cord temporarily removing the power to move though not to feel," Eleanor told Rosy. "I have wired to New York for a masseuse as he said that was vital and the nursing I could do, and in the meantime Louis & I are rubbing him as well as we can."

The doctor could not have given worse advice. Not only did massage weaken the muscles and risk causing further damage but it caused excruciating pain, akin to torture. (Some polio patients required morphine when touched.) But the three persevered, believing it was for the best. Four days later, Eleanor hinted to Rosy, in her understated way, that Franklin was grappling with the depths of despair: "Yesterday and today his temperature has been normal, and I think he's getting back his grip and better mental attitude though he has of course times of great discouragement."

Rosy wrote back boyish, hearty letters, trying to buck Franklin up: "I am telling everybody who asks that you have had a very severe rhumatic [sic] attack from 'excess bathing' which makes it very difficult for you to move!!! . . . But I feel sure it is going to pass off very quickly . . . If it had happened on the yacht I might have guessed the reason, too much good food, *etc, etc, etc!!!* I wired Eleanor that I would not cable Ma anything about it. She would have forty thousand fits all the way over, and could do no good . . . What a pity you are not running for something this Fall. Judging by the last time when you were in bed, what a majority you would run up without legs!!!"

Franklin's condition had degenerated. Since he no longer had muscle power below the waist, his bladder became paralyzed, and for a time he also lost control of his bowels. Dr. Bennet showed Eleanor how to insert a catheter—with great care, to avoid infection—and how to administer an enema. She was nursing Franklin day and night, helping him on and off the bedpan, rolling him over to prevent bedsores, gently moving his inert limbs, washing him, trying to reassure him. She slept on the window seat by his bed.

From Bar Harbor, Dr. Keen sent a bill for $600 (one quarter of Howe's annual income), and wrote that on further reflection he was inclined to discard the clot idea. He now thought that inflammation might have caused a lesion in the spinal cord. This was more serious and the recovery would take longer, but it was important that they persevere with the massaging.

Louis Howe did not trust doctors. When he was thirty-seven, a doctor in Albany had given him just three months to live. Thirteen years later, though his heart played up sometimes, Howe was still very much alive. He strongly suspected that Franklin's condition was infantile paralysis. After careful deliberation, he and Eleanor decided to confide in Franklin's uncle Fred—Mama's younger brother, Frederic Delano, the patriarch of the Delano family, who lived in New York. Howe wrote him a detailed description of Franklin's symptoms and asked him to consult a specialist in the city.

Uncle Fred was away, and the letter sat there for three days. When he read it, on August 19, he wasted no time. By the end of that afternoon he had found out that the nation's leading authority on infantile paralysis was Dr. Robert Lovett, author of *The Treatment of Infantile Paralysis*, who worked at the children's hospital in Boston. That evening, Fred took the overnight train to Boston. Unfortunately, Dr. Lovett was at his summer home in Newport. Instead Fred saw a young specialist, Samuel Levine, and read him Howe's letter. Levine told him it was "unquestionably Infantile Paralysis."

Uncle Fred reported that Keen was "a fine old chap," but he was a surgeon, not a specialist in this disease, and "it would be very unwise to trust to his diagnosis." Dr. Levine said they should stop the massaging at once. It was Fred's view that Eleanor must arrange a consultation, without delay, with "the great Dr. Lovett." "Pardon my being so insistent, but you and Mr. Howe ask for my best judgment and I give it to you."

Louis Howe returned to Dr. Bennet's house in Lubec. They phoned Dr. Keen, who said he was sure it was *not* infantile paralysis, but he agreed to contact Dr. Lovett, in Newport.

By the time Dr. Lovett arrived on the island, on August 25, Franklin had been in agony for fourteen days. Lovett examined him gently. Franklin was paralyzed from the waist down. He was unable to move his toes, his hips were weak, but there was a slight response in his leg muscles. His bladder was paralyzed and he was unable to urinate. His upper torso was extremely weak, he had some movement in his arms and hands, but there was no strength whatsoever in his thumbs. He could not hold a pen. There was no respiratory involvement. His face was partially paralyzed. The diagnosis was not in doubt, Lovett told them. It was infantile paralysis.

Franklin took this news without showing any emotion. For a while he said nothing. "His reaction to any great event was always to be calm," Eleanor wrote. "If it was something that was bad, he just became almost like an iceberg." In later years, Frances Perkins, Roosevelt's secretary of labor, would notice that at a time of crisis, such as Pearl Harbor, there was a "studied quality" about Roosevelt's calmness. She thought to herself: "It's one way of controlling hysteria."

As soon as they left the sickroom, Eleanor turned to Dr. Lovett in a panic. There were six children in the house—Hartley Howe and their own five. Dr. Lovett assured her that if the children were going to succumb to the disease, they would almost certainly have done so already. He thought that they should aim to get Franklin off the island in mid-September. The period of quarantine was three to four weeks. After that, Franklin would no longer be infectious. For the moment there was nothing to do but wait.

Before he left, Lovett told them that the muscles could go any of three ways—complete recovery, partial recovery, or complete paralysis. The disease had come on fast—"not in a sneaking way"—and there had already been improvement in the muscles. Dr. Lovett thought this meant that Franklin's was a mild case, with the possibility of complete recovery.

The days dragged past. Franklin lay still, unable to move, watching the curtains flutter in the breeze, trying not to give in to despair. When Dr. Bennet came to see him on Wednesday, August 31, he was alarmed to find Franklin "unnerved." Franklin was feeling worse. In the last few days there had been a further falling off of muscle power. Franklin was wondering whether they did the right thing to stop the massaging. The pain had been hideous, but at least they were taking some action.

As soon as he got back to Lubec, Dr. Bennet sent a night wire to Dr. Lovett:

ATROPHY INCREASING POWER LESSENING CAUSING PATIENT MUCH ANXIETY ATTRIBUTED BY HIM TO DISCONTINUANCE OF MASSAGE CAN YOU RECOMMEND ANYTHING TO KEEP UP HIS COURAGE AND MAKE HIM FEEL THE BEST IS BEING DONE OR TELL HIM THOSE CHANGES ARE UNAVOIDABLE HIS WIFE ANXIOUS TO AVOID WORRY ON HIS PART.

Dr. Lovett was surprised to hear that there had been a further loss of power in the legs, and wondered if Franklin had been overexerting himself in an attempt to see how the muscles were working. "There is nothing that can be added to the treatment, and this is one of the hardest things to make the family understand." He explained that there were no drugs for this, though bromides for sleeplessness might be useful. Massage would merely prolong hyperesthesia and tenderness. "The use of hot baths . . . is really helpful and will encourage the patient, as he can do so much more under water with his legs." As he had told Mrs. Roosevelt, there was likely to be "mental depression and sometimes irritability" while the patient adjusted to his condition.

At the end of August, a young nurse, Edna Rockey, arrived from New York. After three long weeks of round-the-clock nursing, Eleanor finally had some relief. It meant that Louis Howe was able to dash down to New York for a few days to get some business done.

Louis Howe was still reeling from the shock; he had no idea how this was going to turn out for Franklin. What he *did* know was that he had a major task in front of him. He had to boost Franklin's spirits, help Eleanor in every way possible, be Franklin's stand-in at work, and keep up Franklin's political prospects. It felt almost like a calling. He was determined to do everything in his power to make sure that his friend and hero, Franklin D. Roosevelt, still had a future.

It was now Louis Howe who was Franklin's advance man. Before Sara Roosevelt's ship docked, Louis saw Fred Delano and tried to make sure he would not unduly alarm his sister. "I took breakfast with 'Uncle Fred' before your mama arrived," he reported to Franklin, "and filled him full of cheery thoughts and fried eggs."

He talked to Franklin's boss, Van Lear Black, and told him that Franklin was likely to be in the hospital for some weeks, and was ready to resign from his job at Fidelity and Deposit Company if Black thought it necessary, but Franklin felt sure he could manage the work, with Howe's help. Black, who a few weeks earlier had watched with ardent admiration as Franklin stood at the helm of the *Sabalo* navigating the boat through the densest of fogs, assured Howe that he would not dream of letting Franklin go.

Howe spoke to Franklin's colleagues at his law firm. He went to the Fidelity and Deposit office in lower Manhattan and briefed Franklin's secretary, Miss LeHand. He arranged for an ambulance to meet Franklin on their arrival at Grand Central. He went to the Presbyterian Hospital and spoke to Dr. George Draper—an old friend of Franklin's, who had graduated from Harvard a year ahead of him, and was keen to take on Franklin's care. An orthopedic specialist rather than a polio man, Draper would be liaising closely with Dr. Lovett in Boston. While he was with Draper, Howe also broached the delicate matter of dealing with the press.

Louis Howe's arrangements were crucial; a great deal was at stake. To everyone he stressed the importance of secrecy. The public must not know the nature of Franklin's illness—not yet. If the news of infantile paralysis were leaked, the Canadian and U.S. customs authorities might not let Franklin off the island. Howe was thinking ahead, and he did not know which word would kill Franklin's career the fastest—"cripple" or "infantile" or "paralysis." What he *did* know was that Franklin needed to feel that a semblance of normal life was awaiting him. The last thing Franklin needed was for the press to make "sob stuff" out of Franklin Roosevelt, the golden boy, having his political dreams crushed by infantile paralysis. Franklin did not need pity. He dreaded it.

Howe was careful to communicate directly with Franklin, rather than simply arranging things with Eleanor, as if Franklin were helpless. When Eleanor sent a wire asking him to purchase a Tiffany watch for Frank Calder, who had done so much for them these past weeks, Howe (whom Franklin teased about his poor taste in ties and pajamas), wrote to Franklin for more guidance:

> Dear Boss . . . I loved the way Eleanor telegraphed to go into Tiffany's to buy a watch for Calder without mentioning whether it was to be a $1200 Jorgerson or a Waterbury Radiolite; also to

have it inscribed without mentioning what to inscribe on it! Lord knows I have acted as your alter-ego in many weird commissions, but I must positively refuse to risk my judgment on neckties, watches or pajamas.

The obliging Howe had gone to the exclusive Fifth Avenue jewelers, and made notes on five different models. "They all have Tiffany & Co. on the dial, so the captain can exhibit it to admiring neighbors."

Marguerite LeHand had been devastated by Howe's news. Like everyone else who had been on Franklin's campaign team, the twenty-four-year-old adored her boss. As his secretary, she had been one of the last people to see him before he set off to Campobello. On August 17, Eleanor had written to her that Mr. Roosevelt had had "a serious chill . . . which resulted in fever and much congestion & I fear his return will be delayed." Miss LeHand had replied: "Dear Mrs. Roosevelt, I thought he looked quite tired when he left, so perhaps he will at least have a good rest." Now Howe told her that Franklin had temporarily lost the use of his legs. At the same time, Howe entreated her to keep up Franklin's spirits.

That day, August 29, Miss LeHand sent the first of a series of cheerful notes to Campobello. "Dear Mr. Roosevelt, . . . Mr. Howe came today, and it really was awfully good to see him. I like him so much." September 1: "By the way, Mr. Howe took me up with him in a *taxi*. Isn't that scandalous? I love scandal! . . . I have moved my desk and typewriter into your office, right beside the telephone. Do you object?"

September 6: "I am sincerely glad that you are gaining . . . It is getting ready to pour broomsticks, and *you know* how dark this office gets when that happens, so if I skip an occasional letter please forgive it!" September 8: "It is hot! There is nothing much more interesting than that I think. I wasted a perfectly good evening seeing George White's *Scandals* last night—it is terrible! I never heard such perfectly awful voices from chorus girls."

"The mouse came out and has made me very unhappy, otherwise things are deadly dull," she assured him. "By the way, I wish I could say, 'Your majesty!'"

Mama's ship berthed in New York harbor on Tuesday, August 30. Franklin had always been on the dock to welcome her home from overseas trips. When her brother Fred and her sister Kassie stepped forward, Sara knew instantly that something was terribly wrong. They pussy-footed about, trying to soften the news. It did not help when Fred handed her a letter from Eleanor, written four days earlier:

Dearest Mama,

Franklin has been quite ill and so can't go down to meet you on Tuesday to his great regret, but Uncle Fred and Aunt Kassie both write they will be there so it will not be a lonely home coming. We are all so happy to have you home again dear, you don't know what it means to feel you near again.

The children are all very well and I wish you could have seen John's face shine where he heard us say you would be home soon . . .

We are having such lovely weather, the island is really at its loveliest. Franklin sends all his love and we are both so sorry he cannot meet you.

Ever devotedly,
Eleanor

Sara finally wrung the details out of Fred. She left for Campobello the next day. During the two-day train journey north, she had ample time to reflect on life's cruel vicissitudes. Franklin's was "such a splendid young life," she wrote to her sister Dora, in Paris. "The lightning usually strikes when we *least* expect it."

She and Dora were familiar with tragedy. Their eldest sister, Louise, had died at twenty-three; their brother Philippe at twenty-four; their youngest sister, Laura, at nineteen. Laura's death haunted Sara to this day. Sara had been visiting Algonac with Franklin, who was eighteen months at the time. It was a Sunday morning and the family was shortly to leave for church. Sara was on the front lawn, talking to her father. Suddenly, from the third floor of the house, came an explosion, then a bloodcurdling scream, and as their wretched father put it later, "Laura flashed down the stairway, a cloud of fiery flame." She had been heating her curling irons over an alcohol lamp, which she knocked over, and burning alcohol was spilled on her muslin dress. While Laura writhed on the grass, Sara and her father smothered the flames with a rug. The burns were horrendous. Laura had been so brave that night, reassuring the family that she would recover. The next morning she was dead.

At Eastport, Sara took Frank Calder's motorboat across the bay. Eleanor was at the Welshpool pier to meet her, with the dray. Once at the house, Sara braced herself, walked into the hallway, kissed the children, and went upstairs. She knew that Franklin wanted her to be courageous. She *had* to be courageous.

The next day she wrote to her brother Fred:

> I got here yesterday at 1:30 and at once . . . came up to a brave, smiling, and beautiful son, who said: "Well, I'm glad you are back Mummy and I got up this party for you!"
>
> He had shaved himself and seems very bright and very *keen*. Below his waist he cannot move at all. His legs (that I have always been proud of) have to be moved often as they ache when long in one position. He and Eleanor decided at once to be cheerful and the atmosphere of the house is all happiness, so I have fallen in and follow their glorious example.

Sara stayed only a few days. She was afraid of being more of a burden than a help. It was clear that it tired Franklin to talk to her, and that Eleanor was utterly exhausted. Dr. Bennet was visiting, she told Fred. He was at that moment in Franklin's room. "I hear them all laughing. Eleanor in the lead!" Sara did not feel at all like laughing. Dr. Bennet came out and assured her: "This boy is going to get all right." Sara had grave doubts.

From Fairhaven, on her way home, Sara wrote to Eleanor with shaky handwriting that in no way resembled her usual bold scrawl: "My thoughts are with you and our dear invalid all the time and I ever wake at night with a longing to know how Franklin is and if there is continued gain."

Louis Howe was the mastermind behind the family's carefully orchestrated departure from Campobello. He did not want Franklin to be exposed to public view while he lay prostrate on a stretcher. Originally Louis had hoped they could travel by boat—if the waters were smooth it would be less jarring—but Uncle Fred, who had held managerial positions in railroad companies, arranged for a special railcar that would take Franklin from Eastport to New York without any transfers.

On Tuesday, September 13, Franklin was wrapped in blankets and strapped onto a homemade stretcher. Six local men carried him down the stairs, across the back porch, down the hill, onto the Roosevelt family pier, and into Frank Calder's bobbing motorboat for the two-mile trip across Passamaquoddy Bay to Eastport. The frightened children watched from the porch. "Don't worry, chicks," Franklin called out. "I'll be all right."

At Eastport the men had to climb the slippery wooden steps onto the sardine dock. They put the stretcher on a luggage dray, but the jolting over the cobbles was excruciating for Franklin, and so they carried the stretcher to the railroad siding. The final stage of the arduous journey involved maneuvering the stretcher through a train window.

Once on the train, Eleanor wiped the sweat from Franklin's face; Howe arranged the theatrical props. Through the window, curious onlookers had a brief glimpse of Franklin Delano Roosevelt supported by pillows, with a fedora on his head, Duffy the Scotch terrier on his chest, and his cigarette holder at a jaunty angle. Howe told them that Roosevelt was feeling more comfortable and had a good appetite. And the train took off.

Franklin was laid back more comfortably. Eleanor and the nurse fussed over him. Howe breathed out. The hardest part of the journey was behind them. Now they had to face two days on the train. The engine driver had been given instructions to go slowly, especially around the curves.

They arrived at Grand Central Terminal on Thursday, September 15, at 2:30 p.m. The news had leaked, as they knew it would. A handful of reporters was waiting at the station. Howe, who had arranged for an ambulance to whisk Franklin to the Presbyterian Hospital, told reporters that Mr. Roosevelt had had a "comfortable trip" and was "feeling very well."

On Friday, September 16, the story made front-page news in *The New York Times*:

F. D. ROOSEVELT ILL OF POLIOMYELITIS
Franklin D. Roosevelt, former Assistant Secretary of the Navy and Democratic candidate for Vice-President in the last election, was brought to this city from Campobello Island, Bay of Fundy,

yesterday, suffering from poliomyelitis, or infantile paralysis, which for more than a month has caused the loss of the use of both legs below the knees. Mr. Roosevelt was taken to Presbyterian Hospital, Seventieth Street and Madison Avenue, where it was said that the attack was very mild . . . Dr. George Draper . . . said that Mr. Roosevelt's condition was much improved, and that he was regaining control of his legs. He is still unable to walk, however. "I cannot say how long Mr. Roosevelt will be kept in the hospital," said Dr. Draper, "but you can say definitely that he will not be crippled. No one need have any fear of permanent injury from this attack." . . . His general condition, it was said, was better than at any time in years.

Louis Howe was peerless when it came to manipulating the press. He had persuaded Dr. Draper to go along with this upbeat version of events. But Howe also knew that it must never be said that Franklin was deceiving the public. That afternoon, Howe sent off a letter—allegedly coming from Franklin—to Adolph S. Ochs, the publisher of *The New York Times.*

> While the doctors were unanimous in telling me that the attack was very mild and that I was not going to suffer any permanent effect from it, I had, of course, the usual dark suspicion that they were just saying nice things to make me feel good, but now that I have seen the same statement officially made in the New York *Times* I feel immensely relieved because I know of course it must be so. I am feeling in the very best of spirits and have already been allowed to take up part of my somewhat varied interests.

It was a clever move. While teasing Ochs about the veracity of the press, Roosevelt and Howe were themselves laying a paper trail of half-truths. Where better to start than with the publisher of *The New York Times,* the most influential voice in the nation?

Over the next weeks, in the letters he dictated to Miss LeHand, Franklin kept up this sanguine façade. He told friends and colleagues he'd been diagnosed with infantile paralysis ("cheerful thing for one with my gray hairs to get") and that his "somewhat rebellious legs" were "temporarily out of commission," but the doctors were "most encouraging." He assured everyone: "I can keep up with everything and I expect to do this through Mr. Howe, my former assistant in Washington who will act as my go-between from 65th Street to 52 Wall and the F & D Company."

The reality was a great deal more bleak. George Draper greatly feared that Dr. Lovett had been too optimistic. At the end of the first week, he wrote to Dr. Lovett.

> I am much concerned at the very slow recovery both as regards the disappearance of pain, which is very generally present, and as to the recovery of even slight power to twitch the muscles . . . There is marked falling away of the muscle masses on either side of the spine in the lower lumbar region, likewise the buttocks . . . The lower extremities present a most depressing picture.

Draper was not convinced that Franklin would be able to walk again. And he now worried that his condition might be even worse than that. The tenderhearted doctor continued:

> I have studiously refrained from examining his upper extremities because he believes them to be untouched by the disease. It is fortunate that one does not have much opportunity in the re-cumbent position in bed to call upon the deltoids or the triceps. The biceps are fortunately pretty good so that he is able to pull himself up by a strap over his head and so help himself to turn in bed. This of course gives him a great sense of satisfaction . . .
> What I fear more than anything else is that we shall find a much more extensive involvement of the great back muscles than we have suspected and that when we attempt to sit him up he will be faced with the frightfully depressing knowledge that he cannot hold himself erect . . . I feel so strongly after watching him now for over a week that the psychological factor in his management is paramount. He has such courage, such ambition, and yet at the same time such an extraordinarily sensitive emotional mechanism that it will take all the skill which we can muster to lead him successfully to a recognition of what he really faces without utterly crushing him.

In mid-October, Draper was hugely relieved to report that Franklin had more muscle power in his back than he had thought. The bad news was that the pelvic girdle, thighs, and leg muscles remained almost entirely useless.

Throughout these terrifying weeks, Franklin astounded everyone with his remarkable courage and good cheer. It made things much easier for those who tried to help him. But George Draper was worried about his friend. He knew that it generally took at least two years—often more—for patients to come to terms with their disability. The loss Franklin faced was indescribable. Anyone stricken in this way experienced overwhelming grief. He feared that it was only a question of time until Franklin's defenses came crashing down.

Franklin, at the age of thirty-nine, was having to come to terms with paraplegia. He had been a man who liked to be seen leaping over a row of chairs to get to the stage, and now he could not walk, stand, dress, or go to the bathroom by himself. He was completely dependent on others. In society's eyes, he had become a "cripple"—a cruel word for a figure who aroused pity, even revulsion, a figure who was expected to hide away at home and not embarrass others. It was the most crushing blow that could have befallen Franklin. How could he possibly be *cheerful*?

Years later Franklin would confess to days when he was convinced that God had forsaken him. But Franklin was a stoic, with immense self-discipline. The Roosevelts did not complain about physical suffering. Bye Roosevelt Cowles, at sixty-six, was in a wheelchair, bent over, gnarled with arthritis, and deaf, but she did not complain. She was still interested in other people's lives. She was still good company.

It helped that Franklin believed in God. He also believed in destiny. During those long, cruel, sleepless nights when he could not even toss or turn, he told himself that this catastrophe was sent to test his moral fiber. This was his "trial by fire."

His good cheer was also a matter of consideration for others. Franklin had always tried to look after the morale of the people around him. His loved ones were doing everything they could for him; he did not want to burden them with his misery. Eleanor had put her heart and soul into caring for him; Louis Howe was unstinting with his loyalty, goodwill, and hard work. There were also his supporters, who believed in his political career. As Franklin saw it, he could not let these people down.

His chart read "Not improving." He could sit up for short stretches and gingerly maneuver himself around in a wheelchair, but this soon hurt him. "He is exceedingly ambitious and anxious to get to the point where he can try crutches," Draper reported to Lovett, "but I am not encouraging this."

Franklin was discharged from the hospital at the end of October. At 47–49 East Sixty-fifth Street, the ambulance men carried him upstairs to a quiet, sunny bedroom on the third floor. The Roosevelts were no longer a family; they had become a community. Louis Howe lived with them during the week. In addition to the servants, there were Franklin's full-time nurse, Miss Edna Rockey, and a "colored boy," Leroy Jones, who attended to the intimate details of Franklin's daily existence—helping him to the bathroom, dressing him, lifting him, and carrying him around.

At the center of this household was a man in a single bed, who was struggling to adjust to his starkly diminished circumstances. He knew that others felt sorry for him, he knew that old friends would feel awkward with him, and he did his best to make them feel at ease. Franklin's old navy boss, Josephus Daniels, entered Franklin's room with anguished trepidation. When he approached the bed, Franklin landed him a friendly punch. "You thought you were coming to see an invalid," he grinned, "but I can knock you out in any bout!" Isabella Ferguson came east on a visit and wrote to Franklin afterward: "We cannot realize that your life has in any way become handicapped—you have so entirely created a normal attitude. Eleanor had prepared me for your great courage, but even so, I didn't realize to what extent you had mastered the discouragement of it all."

James, exiled at Groton, had not seen the family since Campobello, and was tormented by the thought of his crippled father:

When I came home for the holidays that first Christmas, I dreaded the sight of him on his back with withering legs, but I went to his room determined to maintain my composure no matter what. He was propped up on pillows, exercising his upper body on trapezes and rings that hung over his head. Seeing me, he stopped, smiled broadly, thrust out his chin in that characteristic way of his, stretched out his arms to me and told me, "Come here, old man." I rushed to receive his embrace and was grateful to learn as he hugged me to him that whatever weakness had struck his legs, his arms were as strong as ever. I started to cry, but he just laughed and slapped me on the back and told me how "grand" I looked. Soon he . . . was roughhousing with me.

Franklin was immensely relieved when he was allowed to begin physical therapy in December. Mrs. Kathleen Lake, a physiotherapist who specialized in polio care, came to the house six mornings a week. The exercises were painful and progress was agonizingly slow, but she reported to Lovett: "He is a wonderful patient, very cheerful, and works awfully hard, and tries every suggestion one makes to help him."

On January 30, 1922, Franklin turned forty. The 1920 vice-presidential campaign team, the Cuff Links Gang, met as planned. They joked, clinked glasses, recalled the high and low moments of the campaign, and inwardly admired Franklin more than ever. But this was *not* what they had envisaged, a spirit-boosting exercise around the bedside of a man who had been paralyzed from the waist down. They hid their anguish, but each of them—with the possible exception of Louis Howe—privately doubted that there would ever be any more victories to celebrate. And Franklin knew it.

Soon afterward, Franklin suffered a setback. His hamstrings started to contract, and his knees curled toward his chest. To straighten them out, Dr. Draper was obliged to encase the legs in plaster, with wedges behind the knees that were hammered in deeper every day. It was yet another painful ordeal, which Franklin endured without complaint. But the whole family suffered, knowing what he was going through.

In March, Franklin was fitted with a heavy steel corset and braces that went from his hips to the outside heel of his shoes. He hated the medieval-looking contraption, a potent symbol of his invalidism. He felt confined, locked up. When he sat down, the thing almost cut him in two. The braces did not allow him to strengthen his muscles, and he worried that they were merely an obstacle to progress. But he knew that until he had some power back in his legs, it was only with braces and crutches that he was going to be able to "walk" at all.

Underneath the surface calm, the family was in turmoil. Sara and Eleanor were tense and unhappy. It broke their hearts to see Franklin in pain, to watch him struggling, to see him bravely smiling through it all. It was traumatic for the children, particularly Anna and James, now fifteen and fourteen, to see their father hauling himself across the floor on his behind, grimacing, with sweat pouring down his face. Everyone in the house was struggling to adjust to these new circumstances.

The shortage of space did not help. Anna had given her large third-floor bedroom and bathroom to Louis Howe and moved to a small dark room on the fourth floor, next to Elliott. The two youngest boys shared a room in Mama's half of the house. Eleanor did not have a room of her own. She slept in one of the boys' rooms, and dressed in Franklin's bathroom.

Mama resented Louis Howe's presence in the household. Behind the scenes, she worked up fifteen-year-old Anna about having to cede her room to that "dirty little man." The adolescent girl went and complained to her mother, who told her coldly that she was selfish. The hostility between mother and daughter lasted for weeks.

For the first time in her life, Anna was seeing her mother give affection—"much more openly than she ever gave it to her own children"—to Louis Howe, of all people. "I remember going into Mother's room and I would find Louis sitting in Mother's deep, comfy chair and Mother at his feet and he stroking her hair," she recalled. "I would be violently jealous."

In later years, Frances Perkins would comment: "I know that Mrs. Roosevelt loved Louis Howe. She loved him the way you love a person who has stood by you in the midst of the valley of the shadow and not been afraid of anything." When Corinne Robinson, Eleanor's cousin, came to the house, she was struck by Howe's presence in their midst. She had never met him before. "I was intrigued immediately. He seemed to be the dominant person in the group. He justly disciplined the rather recalcitrant children and spoke with authority to Eleanor."

From Monday to Friday, Louis Howe began and ended his day beside Franklin's bed, talking about politics, discussing work problems, encouraging him, joking with him. He spent the day downtown, either at Franklin's legal firm on Wall Street or the Fidelity and Deposit Company nearby. He was rapidly acquiring the skills involved in soliciting bonds and canvassing business, making good use of the vast network of contacts he and Franklin had made in labor, business, and politics during their Washington years. On Friday evenings, with a stack of newspapers under his arm, he took the New York Central to Poughkeepsie to join Grace and the children. Since their daughter, Mary, was attending Vassar

College, Louis and Grace had decided to send Hartley to the local public school. Poughkeepsie, a dignified old town on the Hudson, was a great deal cheaper than Manhattan and had the additional advantage of being close to Hyde Park, where Franklin was likely to convalesce.

Grace, who felt as if she had lost her husband to the Roosevelt family, even accused him of having an affair with Eleanor. From his messy smoke-filled room at 49 East Sixty-fifth Street, Louis wrote to her:

Dearest wife of mine . . .

I have given all my life to try and make you happy but I only make you more unhappy. When you told me 4 years ago that you hated me I tried to make myself believe you didn't mean it— when you told me 3 years ago that you loathed the touch of my body that it made you crawl and feel sick to have my arms around you I knew that I had lost out . . . It was all there was in my life that mattered to me except Kiddens and Bub and there has been no real fun in my life ever since . . .

I have said nothing of Eleanor for I know that in your heart you know there is not, nor ever *could* be anything to which you really could object— She has been dear and kind to Mary and Bub and you and she has done much to make what was a very hard place for me to be in endurable— Can you blame me if in my utter loneliness I have found her friendship a very pleasant thing— Do you want me to give *that* up too? . . . So many things you don't want—what is there that you do?

I still
love you love you love you
Your husband

Eleanor would remember that winter as "the most trying winter of my entire life." One afternoon, when she was reading to the youngest boys, she started to weep and could not stop. "Elliott came in from school, dashed in to look at me and fled. Mr. Howe came in and tried to find out what was the matter with me, but he gave it up as a bad job." Finally she wiped her face and resolved never again to let herself go in that way. She had to be strong for the children's sake and for Franklin's.

From the onset of this terrible crisis Eleanor had understood that Franklin did not want pity; he wanted hope. He did not want to be treated as an invalid, and she made sure that the family never treated him like one. That winter she worked tirelessly to keep him stimulated—cutting out interesting items from the newspapers, bringing friends and political associates to his bedroom, and insisting that he keep up his vast correspondence. He enjoyed it when Miss LeHand came, for an hour or so each day, to take dictation.

Mama had a different way of expressing her love. She had spent ten years treating her husband, James, as an invalid, and now she wanted to do the same with Franklin. He was a sick man, she insisted, and he did not need Eleanor and Louis Howe eternally discussing politics, legal questions, and financial matters with him. Mama did not understand why Franklin seemed so desperate to keep his Fidelity and Deposit salary. She would support the family while he convalesced. It seemed to Mama that the person who most wanted this salary was Louis Howe.

In *This Is My Story* (published while Mama was still alive), Eleanor wrote with unusual candor about the conflict that raged that winter at 47–49 East Sixty-fifth Street:

> My mother-in-law thought we were tiring my husband and that he should be kept completely quiet, which made the discussions as to his care somewhat acrimonious on occasion. She always thought that she understood what was best, particularly where her child was concerned, regardless of what any doctor might say . . . She had . . . made up her mind that Franklin was going to be an invalid for the rest of his life and that he would retire to Hyde Park and live there.

George Draper quickly understood "the intense and devastating influence of the interplay of these high voltage personalities one upon another." He and Dr. Lovett could see how domineering Franklin's mother was. In later years, both doctors would express the view that Franklin's mental rehabilitation owed an enormous amount to Eleanor.

Jealousy was rife among the women who cared for Franklin. His physiotherapist, Mrs. Lake, wrote to Dr. Lovett: "If only his wife could be persuaded that he does not need urging on all day & entertaining all evening, I think he would not be so tired and would do better physically." Mrs. Lake then discovered that Franklin's attractive young nurse, Edna Rockey, was giving Franklin late-night massages—needlessly tiring his muscles, she told Lovett. Nor could Mrs. Lake help noticing that Franklin was more animated when Edna Rockey was at his bedside. The whole household would hear bursts of laughter coming from his bedroom.

In March 1922, George Draper, who had the observational powers of a novelist, reported to Lovett:

> Mrs. R is pretty much at the end of her tether with the long hard strain she has been through . . . Another interesting thing in the complex tapestry is the fact that Mrs. Lake does not seem to fit perfectly smoothly into the picture. She is admirable as far as her technical work is concerned . . . As far as I can make out, the difficulty, if it amounts to a difficulty, is merely that she lacks the bubbling sense of humor which Miss Rockey possesses and which has been the mainstay of the whole outfit ever since the beginning. On the other hand, I think Miss Rockey occasionally gets on the nerves of Mrs. R.

Eleanor's friend, Caroline Drayton Phillips, wrote to Eleanor: "I am sorrier for you than Franklin, and I know what an ideal wife you are." Isabella Ferguson, who understood better than most what Eleanor faced, was full of admiration for Eleanor's "superb courage & determination." Isabella had looked after Bob, her invalid husband, for thirteen years now and hinted to Eleanor that she was beginning to find the self-sacrifice hard to bear. "Ours are the years when clear perception has come & with it the intense desire to live while we may."

For the moment, Franklin and Eleanor were struggling to make the best of their harrowingly difficult circumstances. But the tragedy that had occurred on Campobello was transforming their marriage. Little could they have imagined what the future would bring.

FIVE

The Wilderness Years

March 1922–November 1928

Who had ever heard of a man in a wheelchair winning high office?
The vocabulary of politics was one of mobility. You "ran" for office (in
England you "stood" for office), you were "in the running," you were a
"front runner," or if you didn't have a chance "you didn't have a leg to
stand on." If you were nominated, the other fellow on the ticket was
your "running mate." The campaign was a "race," after it kicked off
you were "in the lead" or you "trailed" or you were "neck and neck" and
in the last days of the campaign you were "in the home stretch." Until
the winner took office, the defeated incumbent was a "lame duck."

—Ted Morgan, *FDR: A Biography*

"Franklin's first drive," Sara noted in her diary on March 25, 1922. It
took place under cover of night, so that the neighbors would not see him
being carried in and out of the car. After seven months cooped up in his
bedroom, Franklin was ready to flee the claustrophobic atmosphere of
East Sixty-fifth Street. In the spring, accompanied by his nurse and
valet, he went to convalesce at Hyde Park.

It was better at Mama's house, in the Hudson landscape that Franklin loved so much. He did not have neighbors peering out of their
windows at him, and could spend more time outside. He immediately
felt more independent. To go up and down the stairs, he used the old
trunk elevator with its hand pulley, located in the servants' quarters.
Mama had ramps installed—she called them "inclined planes"—so
that he could wheel himself around. Franklin disliked bulky wheel-

chairs that reminded him of hospitals, and had wheels put on a simple wooden chair with no armrests. That way, he could maneuver himself through narrow spaces and be moved more easily into an armchair or bed.

His nurse, Edna Rockey, kept him company while he sat on the porch with his stamps and model boats. Eleanor, who came up from the city on weekends with the children, went out of her way to invite political friends whose company Franklin found stimulating. Louis was often at Hyde Park, discussing Fidelity and Deposit issues with Franklin. Marguerite LeHand, Franklin's secretary, stayed for days at a time. Mama disapproved of all this bustling activity.

Mrs. Lake came by train three mornings a week to supervise Franklin's physical therapy. She tried to rein him in a bit, fearing he would do more harm than good. "He has all sorts of new ideas about developing his muscles, and I have to discourage him periodically, as tactfully as possible," she reported to Dr. Lovett. Franklin worked hard at the parallel bars on the lawn, supporting his weight with his arms and dragging his legs along. But he dreaded the daily walk down the driveway.

An hour or so before lunch, Leroy Jones would help Franklin into his steel-and-leather corset and braces, wheel him out to the front of the house, and hand him his crutches. Each time, Franklin took a look at the Albany Post Road at the top of the drive, half a mile in the distance, and resolved to get a few steps closer to it than the day before. Over the years the family would hear him mutter to himself, "I must get down the driveway today." He never once made it to the end. It was far too grueling. He would take a few steps, then lean into his crutches and rest, sweat pouring off his face.

He called it "walking," but he was not walking at all. He could not hop, as most people do on crutches. His legs and hips were useless. Each leg brace weighed ten pounds, and maneuvering them would have been tiring even for someone with normal leg muscles. Franklin had to rely on his upper-body muscles to propel himself forward. Using his trunk muscles, he hitched one hip forward and then the other. He would fall sometimes, clattering to the ground in a humiliating tangle of crutches and helpless limbs. Leroy, who loitered nearby, had to lift him up and back into his wheelchair.

In the summer Eleanor and the children came to stay at Hyde Park. The women's daily battle over Franklin's destiny was resumed. Dr. Lovett, having gotten wind of this from Mrs. Lake, urged Franklin to come to Boston for a few weeks, to work at rehabilitation with Lovett's assistant.

Franklin traveled to Boston at the end of June. He stayed at Phillips House, close to the hospital, sharing his suite with his nurse, Edna Rockey. Leroy Jones stayed nearby, in a hotel for "coloreds." With the aid of Lovett's assistant, Franklin practiced various movements, including getting in and out of a chair (a complicated maneuver, which looked so awkward that he would never do it in public) and going up stairs. (The only safe method was to sit on his behind and haul himself up with his arms, dragging his legs after him.) Lovett stressed that Franklin must not overuse his muscles, or he risked doing himself more damage.

The Boston visit did Franklin good. He saw friends, took drives, and spent hours on the roof of Phillips House, relaxing in the sun and chatting with Miss Rockey. "I am so thankful that you have curtailed some of his work," Mama wrote to Dr. Lovett, "and that he is out of doors daily."

Back at Hyde Park, Franklin avoided his braces. He detested the ordeal of crutch-walking. His favorite exercise was swimming, especially in warm water, since the warmth relaxed his muscles. Three or four times a week he had himself driven to his friend Vincent Astor's heated pool at Rhinecliff, twenty minutes up the river, near Rhinebeck. Eleanor worried that Franklin was avoiding the one thing he most needed to do—learning to walk. Dr. Lovett agreed with her: "I think it is very important for you to do all the walking that you can within your limit of fatigue," he urged Franklin in mid-August. "Walking on crutches is not a gift, but an art, acquired by constant practice just as any other game, and you will have to put in quite a little time before you get about satisfactorily." And so "the strenuous life," as Franklin called it, began again.

His braces were cutting into him, and at the end of September 1922, Franklin went back to Boston to have them refitted. He and Edna Rockey checked in again at Phillips House. But Dr. Lovett now feared that Franklin was becoming too dependent on his nurse. What exactly Lovett meant by this—and whether the complaint had come to him from the other women in the house—is unclear. But it resulted in Miss Rockey taking up another job.

Miss Rockey's departure left a void, which was filled that winter by Franklin's other young attendant—his secretary, Marguerite LeHand. The youngest Roosevelt boys called her "Missy," and the name stuck. It was around this time that Missy started to call her boss "Effdee." The bursts of laughter from Franklin's room now came mostly when Missy was there.

Eleanor did not seem to mind. She liked Missy. Everyone did. Franklin had always hated to be alone, and these days, more than ever, he needed someone close at hand. Missy was twenty-four that year, just seven years older than Anna, their eldest child.

Like Louis Howe, Missy occupied an ambiguous place in the scheme of things. Like him, she was a sensitive and thoughtful character, who negotiated potentially treacherous waters with exemplary grace. Like Louis, she was Franklin's employee, and she was not Franklin's social equal. Missy came from an Irish Catholic family in Somerville, a working-class suburb of Boston. Her father was a gardener, who drank too much and deserted the family when the children were young. Like Louis, Missy had enormous respect for Eleanor, and never joined in when Franklin's other attendants complained about her. Unlike Louis, Missy was a pleasure to look at, with her jet-black hair, dark blue eyes, and slightly impish smile.

In February 1923, Franklin left Eleanor and Louis in charge of his affairs and headed to Florida with Missy. They were going to spend six weeks on a rented houseboat, the *Weona II*, cruising off the Florida Keys. Franklin was convinced that his muscles and circulation improved in warm water and sunlight. He had noticed that whenever he managed to have a "sunbath" in the morning, his legs did not get cold in the evenings; otherwise they froze up by about 5 p.m.

Eleanor understood that Franklin needed to get away from family tensions, his mother's solicitude, and her own pushing. She also understood that however grueling the physical struggle, Franklin's main battle was psychological. This restless, sociable, ambitious man faced the supreme challenge of remaking his life. If the adoring Missy could help him feel like a man again, Eleanor was not going to complain.

Franklin and Missy were not alone on the houseboat, of course. In addition to the four-man crew, there was Leroy, who lifted Franklin on and off the boat, carried him up on deck in the mornings, and transported him below when necessary. Friends came and went. "I am sunburned and in fine shape," Franklin wrote to his mother. "Cass and Ruth and Henry and Frances have been dear and look after me all the time. They are great fun to have on board in this somewhat negligée existence. All wander round in pyjamas, nighties and bathing suits!" He did not mention Missy.

Eleanor went down for a week, accompanied by her friend Esther Lape. Because she felt seasick in the cabin, Eleanor preferred to sleep on deck, braving the flies and mosquitoes. "When we anchored at night and the wind blew, it all seemed eerie and menacing to me," she recalled. "The beauty of the moon and the stars only added to the strangeness of the dark waters and the tropic vegetation, and on occasion it could be colder and more uncomfortable than tales of the sunny South led me to believe was possible."

Louis Howe arrived with a pile of Fidelity and Deposit paperwork for Franklin to sign. The doggerel he added to the ship's log suggests that he was no more enamored of shipboard life than Eleanor:

Colder, colder grew the night, we really suffered pain
We'd sat and sat with rod and reel and fished and fished in vain
And that, we thought, was reason fair to take to rum again.

Missy was willing to put up with cold nights, seasickness, sunburn, mosquitoes, and hours of vain rod-holding in order to be with Franklin. The following winter, they returned to the waters off Florida. This time, Franklin and a Harvard acquaintance had bought an old houseboat, which they renamed the *Larooco*. They were joined by an assortment of Franklin's friends, including a Hyde Park neighbor, Maunsell Crosby, a fellow bird-watcher, and Livingston Davis, a boyish show-off from Harvard, who had formerly been Franklin's favorite golfing companion. The party fished, swam, sunbathed in sheltered bays, played cards and board games. Crosby identified hundreds of different birds; Livy Davis pranced around in the nude. In the evenings, as they drifted under the moon, they mixed potent brews with bootleg rum and whiskey.

On February 10, Crosby went ashore in Daytona, Florida, for the mail and newspapers. He came back with a wire announcing that Missy's father had died. Missy departed for Boston the next morning. Two weeks later, she was back on the *Larooco*. Eleanor wrote to Franklin: "I haven't told Mama that Missy is back, because I think she has more peace of mind when she doesn't know things!"

Franklin's *Larooco* logbook never hinted at the dark side, but it had been two and a half years since he came down with polio, and in the last few months his doctors had broken the news to him that he might have reached the limits of the progress he was going to make. Years later, Missy would recall with tears in her eyes how Franklin struggled with his spirits that winter. "There were days on the *Larooco* when it was noon before he could pull himself out of depression and greet his guests wearing his lighthearted facade."

Eleanor and Louis sometimes wondered whether Franklin was going to spend the rest of his life in this pointless way—wisecracking with friends on a yacht, playing poker and bridge, mixing cocktails. He never used his braces on the boat, and prided himself on getting around—and pulling in enormous fish—with the strength of his upper body and arms. But there was one thing they all knew with certainty. If he was going to get back into political life he would have to be able to walk.

Louis insisted that Franklin's magnetic personality would "carry" him, and they would turn Franklin's lame legs to his advantage. He reminded them that Franklin's aristocratic heritage did not endear him to Democratic voters, and if they were clever, they could make one handicap cancel out the other. They knew, of course, that there would be strict limits to this public perception. Louis was adamant that Franklin must never be photographed in his wheelchair. Above all, the public must *never* see him being carried.

Thanks to Louis, the summer of 1924 marked the first "step" in Franklin's political comeback. If all had gone according to their original plan, Franklin would have been governor of New York by this time, about to run for the Democratic presidential nomination. Fate had intervened. But the gods were not entirely against Franklin. As it turned out, 1924 was not a good time to run for the presidency as a Democrat. The United States was entering a period of economic boom. Despite the scandals surrounding the Warren Harding presidency, the Republicans were identified with the new prosperity. The American people did not want change.

Instead of Franklin, it was Alfred E. Smith who was governor of New York and now aspired to be the Democratic nominee for president. Realistically, he never had a chance. Smith was a popular governor, but New York State was one thing and the rest of the country was another. Smith's nasal Bronx accent did not go down well outside New York. Nor did his progressive politics. Worst of all, he was Catholic, from an Irish immigrant family. There had never been a Catholic president, and Smith was unlikely to be the first.

Louis Howe managed to convince Al Smith that Franklin Roosevelt would be the ideal man to give Smith's nomination address at the Democratic convention in Madison Square Garden. Roosevelt's name carried weight; he came from a patrician Protestant family; and he was identified with rural upstate New York. Smith hesitated. It could backfire on him badly, the symbolism of having a cripple bat for him. But Roosevelt was popular and highly respected. Smith decided to take the risk.

Franklin disliked the speech that was handed to him, which ended with some sentimental Wordsworth lines about a "Happy Warrior." Convinced it was going to be a flop, he dictated a completely different version to Missy. But Smith's team insisted. They wanted the happy warrior speech.

The public knew that Franklin Roosevelt had polio, but it was generally believed that he had recovered his ability to walk. This was to be Franklin's first public appearance since polio. He and Louis agreed: he must not use his wheelchair; he had to be seen upright, on crutches. If he stumbled in public, it would be worse than humiliating; it would mean the end of his political career. This was going to be a nerve-racking test.

Franklin asked his son James to be his aide. For hours on end, they practiced together. James was only sixteen, still at Groton, but he was tall and strong and idolized his father. He went to the convention hall, measured the distance from the rear of the platform to the podium, and counted the number of steps Franklin would have to take. He made sure that the podium would be sufficiently solid and well anchored to support Franklin's weight.

The morning of June 26, 1924, was sticky and humid. The crowd at Madison Square Garden was restless; the speeches had been dull. At the back of the speakers' platform, out of sight of the audience, Franklin was helped to his feet and his braces locked into place. He leaned heavily on James's arm and one crutch; then James handed him the second crutch. Slowly, slowly, Franklin made his way across the stage. His eyes were riveted to the floor; his face was pale and concentrated. The audience was dead quiet. In her seat in the gallery, Eleanor knitted at high speed.

When Franklin reached the speaker's rostrum, James took away one crutch at a time. Franklin, holding fast to the podium, threw back his head and beamed. The crowd broke into loud cheering. Franklin spoke for a full half hour, tossing his head back and forth for emphasis. If there were any defects in the speech, his magnetic delivery more than made up for them. "He stood there in a gray and white suit, and the light poured down on him," Emma Bugbee, a prominent woman reporter, recalled. "The impact of this glorious white figure was terrific." When Franklin finished, by saluting Al Smith as "the happy warrior of the political battlefield," the crowd went berserk.

The speech was the high point of the convention. It did not win Smith the nomination; the party delegates decided that he was too risky a candidate. But it put Franklin D. Roosevelt back in the national political arena. In the press he was described in almost mythical terms as a "hero," who had been strengthened and purified by adversity. Ironically, it was FDR who was seen as the happy warrior.

At dusk on Friday, October 3, 1924, the Southern Railroad train pulled into a small station at Bullochville, Georgia, eighty miles southwest of Atlanta. Eleanor and Missy stepped out; Franklin was lifted out. The manager of the Warm Springs resort had come to meet them in his motorcar. The little party rattled along the unpaved roads, up the hill, through thick pine forests, to the resort, half a mile from the town.

The season was over. Everything was closed. The place was falling to pieces. The Meriwether Inn, a rambling wooden construction with turrets, gables, and wide verandas, gave off a whiff of grander days. Franklin took one look at the "firetrap," as he called it, and said he was glad they were staying in one of the cottages. Their cottage turned out to be as run-down as everything else on the property. Eleanor was shocked to see daylight through the walls. There was neither running water nor electricity, and the kitchen was primitive. Franklin said it was "delightful and very comfortable," and didn't they love the smell of pine? That night, they were woken by squirrels running across the roof and the mournful hooting of a passing train.

They had come to the mountainous backwoods of Georgia because a Harvard friend, George Foster Peabody, who had a financial interest in the resort, had written to Franklin about the startling improvement a local man with polio had made in these thermal springs. The young man's legs had been paralyzed, and after three summers exercising in the pool he was able to walk with a cane. Franklin often joked about the quack remedies people urged him to try. "It may be monkey glands or . . . the dried eyes of the extinct three-toed rhinoceros," he wrote to Dr. Draper. "Have any of your people thought of distilling the remains of King Tut-Ankh-Amen?" But he was as susceptible as any other invalid to the lure of a miraculous cure.

The next morning, Tom Loyless, the manager of the resort, drove them down the hill to the large open-air pool, set among pine and dogwood trees. The spring water flowed into the pool from the hillside, at a temperature of eighty-eight degrees Fahrenheit. The mineral salts made the water as buoyant as the ocean. Franklin declared that he had never found water more pleasant.

In the afternoon they drove to nearby Manchester to buy provisions. They passed fields of cotton and tobacco, tumbledown shacks, and bedraggled sharecroppers. The boll weevil was wreaking havoc on the crops. "Dollar and a half a day for a mule, dollar and a half a day for a nigger," a white farmer told Franklin. To Eleanor's horror, they returned with live chickens in the back of the car, tied by their legs. The wretched creatures wandered around in the backyard until the cook went out to wring their necks amid a pandemonium of squawking.

After a few days, Eleanor returned to New York, leaving Franklin and Missy to their rural idyll. "It is too bad that Eleanor has to leave so soon," Franklin wrote to Mama, "but she and I both feel it is important for her not to be away at the end of the campaign as long as I have to be myself."

A few weeks later, Eleanor and two friends, Nancy Cook and Marion Dickerman, turned into the driveway of Oldgate, Bye Cowles's house in Farmington, Connecticut. On the hood of their motorcar was a large papier-mâché teapot, from which burst forth steam. This was an allusion to the Teapot Dome scandal, which was causing the Republicans great embarrassment. In Teapot Dome, Wyoming, the Harding government had secretly leased public land with oil reserves to private companies.

The three women were campaigning for Al Smith, who (since he had not been nominated as a presidential candidate) was running again as governor of New York. Smith's Republican opponent was Theodore Roosevelt Jr., the eldest son of the former president—Eleanor's first cousin. As if this were not provocation enough for Bye Cowles, Eleanor and her friends tumbled gaily out of the car in brown tweeds and knickerbockers, looking like dapper young men.

Bye Cowles was aghast. No sooner had the merry trio departed when she sat down to write to her niece, Corinne Alsop: "I just hate to have Eleanor let herself look as she does. Though never handsome, she always had to me a charming effect, but Alas and lackaday! Since politics have become her choicest interest all her charm has disappeared, and the fact is emphasized by the companions she chooses to bring with her."

Politics had, indeed, become Eleanor's "choicest interest." It had begun in the spring of 1922, when Nancy Cook, executive secretary of the Women's Division of the New York State Democratic Committee, had phoned to ask her, as a "well-known name," to speak at a fund-raising luncheon. Since then, Eleanor had never looked back. Louis Howe vigorously encouraged her. Not only was it important that women play an active role in the Democratic Party, he told her, but it was the best way to keep politics alive in the Roosevelt household and the family name in front of the public.

As Louis had predicted, Eleanor was finding the political domain quite thrilling. She had the organizational skills, commitment, and charisma to make her remarkably good at it. Within a short time she had become a leading figure in the League of Women Voters, the Women's Trade Union League, and the Women's Division of the New York State Democratic Committee. At first Louis, who had performed in amateur theatrics as a young man, sat at the back of the hall when she gave talks. She must lower that wavering falsetto voice of hers, he told her. And why the nervous giggle? It was important not to ramble; she must make her point, then sit down.

Isabella Ferguson, recently widowed, had come east and found Eleanor "deep in politics, speechmaking all over the state." She understood that Eleanor was doing this primarily for Franklin. "The weight of the tragedy of this household almost suffocates me at times," she told a friend. "But Eleanor carries her head high and is a great woman and will go the whole distance of life triumphantly."

Eleanor's political activities had brought her in contact with a new type of woman—the "New Woman," as she was known in the press. At the turn of the century, Marie Souvestre had been a daring precursor. This was now the 1920s, the Jazz Age, the age of "flappers"—as these defiant young women were called who had their hair cut in a bob, wore knickerbockers, flaunted the inevitable cigarette holder, and exuded something called "sex appeal." Women were getting degrees at women's colleges, having their say in the political area, demanding the right to birth control, and brazenly having affairs.

Among her new circle of feminist friends, Eleanor was closest to Nancy Cook, an androgynous-looking figure with short wiry hair, blazing eyes, and a hearty laugh, who was a powerhouse in the New York State Democratic Committee. Nancy lived with Marion Dickerman, a tall, reserved, more ladylike character, who taught at Todhunter, an exclusive private girls' school in Manhattan. In 1917, during the First World War, the two women had gone to London as volunteers for the Red Cross. Faced with wards full of shockingly wounded men, Marion had fast acquired nursing skills, while Nancy (who could not stomach the gruesome sights and shrieks) turned out artificial limbs. When they returned to the States in September 1919, at the height of the Red Scare, Marion ran as a progressive candidate—the first woman ever—in the New York legislature. The couple shared an apartment in Greenwich Village, in a co-operative building with other activist women, mostly lesbians, all of whom Eleanor came to know.

Nancy and Marion had become part of Franklin and Eleanor's inner circle. "Our gang," Franklin called it. He was "Uncle Franklin"; they were "the girls." He and Louis jokingly referred to them as "she-males," but they liked and respected the two women. Nancy and Marion were fond of Louis. And never before had they met "so utterly charming a man" as Franklin.

The extended Roosevelt tribe was horrified by Eleanor's new friends. Behind Eleanor's back, cousin Alice called them "female impersonators." Franklin's half brother, Rosy, referred to them as "Eleanor's parlor pinks." Mama particularly disliked Nancy, with her masculine attire, loud laugh, and boisterous manners. Eleanor knew it. They all did.

One evening that summer, the "gang" had been picnicking in a favorite spot at Hyde Park—two miles down the road from Mama's house, on the banks of the Val-Kill stream. They were having a good time, and Eleanor was feeling wistful. She was about to turn forty and was finally finding her feet. The family was no longer all-consuming. Franklin was away a great deal, with Missy; Anna was eighteen, engaged to be married; their youngest son, Johnny, would soon be boarding at Groton. And yet, even now, Eleanor had nowhere she could call "home." At East

Sixty-fifth Street, Mama was always bursting in through the connecting doors. At Hyde Park, Eleanor still felt obliged to ask Mama's permission to invite friends to the house.

Voicing some of these thoughts aloud, Eleanor remarked that it was a pity winter was coming and this would be their last picnic for the season, for they could never feel entirely free like this in Mama's houses. Nancy and Marion agreed with her. Franklin looked around, and had a flash of inspiration. "But aren't you girls silly?" he said. "This isn't Mother's land. I bought this acreage myself . . . Why shouldn't you three have a cottage here of your own, so you could come and go as you please?"

The idea provoked great excitement. Franklin said he would lease the land to them, and the three could share the cost of the cottage. Did they see any reason why construction shouldn't start in the spring?

Franklin and Missy had Warm Springs to themselves that fall. Apart from the resort manager, Tom Loyless, who lived with his wife in the cottage next door, there were no other residents. Every morning, Franklin swam for an hour or more. For the first time in three years, he felt life in his toes again. "I walk around in water 4' deep without brace or crutches almost as well as if I had nothing the matter with my legs," he jubilated to friends. He spent another hour sunbathing on the concrete surroundings of the pool, then dressed for lunch.

In the afternoons, he and Missy sat on the cottage porch, and Franklin dictated correspondence, paid bills, worked at his stamp collection, or they played rummy. Sometimes they went motoring with Tom Loyless and his wife, who were keen to show them the surrounding countryside. "I like him ever so much and she is nice but not broad in her interests, but she chatters away to Missy on the back seat and I hear an occasional yes or no from Missy to prove she is not sleeping," he wrote to Eleanor.

There were numerous invitations from organizations in the area—suppers, talks, receptions. Missy accepted some and politely declined others. Franklin made a point of meeting Georgia's politicians and public personages. And he presided over the ceremony at which the town was renamed Warm Springs.

A reporter from *The Atlanta Journal,* Cleburne Gregory, asked permission to do a feature story. Franklin suggested that Gregory spend a few days in Warm Springs and get a real feel for the place. For the first time since his polio attack, Franklin allowed himself to be photographed in his bathing costume, both in the water and on the deck by the pool. The photos, which looked to all the world like casual snaps, were carefully staged. In the deck photo Franklin was sitting on a towel, beaming. By now, his upper body had the size and musculature of a prize boxer. His legs had been arranged so that he appeared to be quite agile. The left leg was curled along the ground, the right leg was bent, and Franklin draped his powerfully muscled arm over them to hide the emaciated calves.

The article, syndicated nationally, proclaimed: "Franklin D. Roosevelt . . . is literally swimming himself back to health and strength at Warm Springs." It was good both for Georgia's tourist industry and for Franklin's political aspirations to establish him as an adopted "Son of the South."

> Mr. Roosevelt plans to return to Warm Springs in March or April and remain for two or three months. At that time he will build a cottage on a hilltop.
> "Say! Let's get one of the hot dogs this man makes just outside the swimming pool. They're great," Mr. Roosevelt challenged. With him everything in Warm Springs is "Great" or "Fine" or "Wonderful." That is the spirit that has carried him to remarkable heights for a man just past his fortieth year, and it is the spirit that is going to restore him to his pristine health and vigor, for political and financial battles and successes in the years to come.

Franklin was still at Warm Springs at election time, in early November 1924. Riding high on the economic boom, the Republican presidential candidate, Calvin Coolidge, romped in. In New York State—thanks in large part to Eleanor and her energetic women friends in the Democratic Party—Al Smith was elected governor for an unprecedented third term.

"You need not be proud of me dear," Eleanor wrote to Franklin. "I'm only being active till you can be again . . . Hurry up for as you know my ever present sense of the uselessness of all things will overwhelm me sooner or later! My love to Missy, and to you."

Franklin and Eleanor celebrated their twentieth wedding anniversary—March 17, 1925—on board the *Larooco*. Louis Howe, with his flair for theatricality, organized the entertainment. There were formal place cards, speeches, skits, and much laughter.

Although those on board might not have thought so at the time, there was good reason for celebration. After twenty years of married life, the Roosevelts had achieved something rare. Their marriage was as strong as ever, and yet they had broken free from its traditional confines. By now it was clear to all their friends that Franklin and Eleanor were no longer a traditional couple. They had independent lives, which involved other close companions.

It was a daring direction to go in, particularly for Franklin, who as a paraplegic was already facing an uphill battle with his image. But polio had convinced him more than ever of the virtues and joys of communal life. He needed people close at hand. Since he could not get around like he used to, he needed the world to come to him. He could not stand being a burden, and while he had no choice in the matter of his dependence, he was careful not to depend too much on any one person. He liked reciprocity. If he depended on others, they also depended on him. One of the things that gave Franklin the most satisfaction was to provide the opportunity for people to do what they did best. He could see that Eleanor was happiest in New York, working in the political domain with her women friends; Louis was brilliantly suited to masterminding things behind the scenes; Missy enjoyed being Franklin's daily companion. While everyone in the group relied on everyone else, they also opened up each other's horizons. Franklin approved of this kind of bold social arrangement.

Eleanor, too, had grown bolder since Franklin's polio. It had been a long, painful struggle for her to come out of her shell, and she did not intend to crawl back inside it. She was no longer remotely interested in being a "gentlewoman," like Mama. Indeed, Eleanor had finished with trying to please Mama. Nor was she interested anymore in the path her aunt Bye had chosen: ladylike politics, moderate and well-groomed. Eleanor had embarked on a more radical path. "Courage is more exhilarating than fear," she told friends, "and in the long run it is easier."

She needed her courage. It had become clear that Franklin's "cure," whatever form it was going to take, involved a great deal of time away from the family. She tried not to burden him with her worries. Whenever he had momentary qualms about her and the children, she reassured him: "Don't worry about being selfish. It is more important that you have all you need and wish than anything else and you always give the chicks more than they need and you know I always do just what I want!"

But Eleanor did worry about the children. They rarely saw their father. She herself was spending more and more time away from home with her political activities. It was hard on the two younger boys, who still lived at home. Eleven-year-old Franklin Jr. complained to Anna that he and Johnny were becoming "more and more lonesome . . . The house seems just like an emty waistbasket [sic]. Now that Father has left, Mother seems always to be on the go."

The tension between Eleanor and Mama was worse than ever. Eleanor understood that Mama was bitterly unhappy. Mama found it agonizingly difficult to come to terms with her precious Franklin being in a wheelchair. She worried that he was fooling himself that he could somehow get back into politics; she worried about his friendship with that raggedy fellow Louis Howe; she worried about his frequent disappearances with young Missy. She thoroughly disliked the transformation she was seeing in Eleanor. But she had lost the battle of wills. Franklin had gone his own way; and Eleanor was now doing the same.

The children were another story. Because she had lost her influence with Franklin and Eleanor, Mama was more imperious than ever when it came to her grandchildren. There was not much Eleanor could do. Mama held the purse strings, and Mama laid down the law. Elliott did not want to go to Groton, but Mama had insisted: all Roosevelt boys went to Groton. Anna did not want to come out as a debutante, but Mama had insisted: all Roosevelt women came out in society. Franklin kept out of the conflicts. On the rare occasions when the children turned to him for support, he told them, "That's up to Granny and Mother. You settle all this with them."

Eleanor's letters to Franklin were full of her frustrations with her mother-in-law. "Mama has done nothing but get in little side slaps today," she reported. And on another occasion: "Mama was awful last Sunday and made us feel each in turn that we'd like to chew her up."

Franklin sympathized from afar.

•

On April 1, 1925, after spending six weeks on the *Larooco*, Franklin and Missy took the train to Warm Springs. The "Swimming Back to Health" article had attracted considerable notice, and now the news was out that Franklin was back at the resort. One day, Franklin and Missy were sitting on the shady porch chatting to Tom Loyless when a messenger arrived. "Two people have been carried off the train down at the station. What shall we do with them? Neither of them can walk." Polio patients were not allowed to travel with other passengers. One of the new arrivals, an emaciated young man called Fred Botts, had come all the way from Pittsburgh in the baggage car, strapped inside a wooden cage.

The "polios" kept coming. Franklin felt responsible, and took on a new role as "Doc Roosevelt." Passing on everything he had learned from Dr. Lovett, he drew up muscle charts and demonstrated water exercises. He even taught Fred Botts to swim.

When the season officially opened in June, there was consternation at the Meriwether Inn. The regular guests, frightened of infection, objected to polio patients using their pool and sharing their dining room. The polios were embarrassed by the lack of privacy. Franklin moved his "gang" to the basement of the Meriwether Inn for meals, and made arrangements for a second pool to be built.

He had come up with an ambitious plan. He wanted to buy Warm Springs: the pools, old hotel, cottages, twelve hundred acres of land—the whole caboodle. His idea was to turn this shabby resort in the hills and pine forests of Georgia into a modern hydrotherapeutic center for polio patients. He envisaged a friendly, positive place, where polio patients would have the best possible physical therapy and could encourage each other in a community atmosphere. Since polio patients were generally short of money, Franklin would find financial backing from public-spirited men and women. This resort in the mountains of Georgia would help handicapped people find their way back to a fulfilling life.

When Franklin returned to New York in mid-May 1925, the talk was of Val-Kill Cottage—the house by the stream for Eleanor and her friends. Franklin wanted a traditional Hudson River Dutch colonial farmhouse, made of stone. The women agreed. Nancy Cook drew up a model. Franklin drew up another. An architect friend, Henry Toombs, suggested putting a large window near the fireplace, looking out at the woods. The women loved the idea. Franklin insisted that such a feature did not belong in a Dutch cottage. "If you build it that way, I'll *never* come over."

Franklin was sure he could save money if he dealt with the contractors himself. "If you three girls will just go away and leave us alone, Henry and I will build the cottage," he told them. The women could see that there was no arguing with Franklin, and duly left on a long camping trip through the Adirondacks into Canada, with two Roosevelt boys and two of the boys' friends. Eleanor and Nancy took turns driving the Roosevelts' large Buick. Nancy was chief cook. With a tent for the women and two pup tents for the boys, they camped in national parks, woods, and farmers' fields. The last two weeks were spent in Campobello—a place Eleanor had avoided since Franklin's polio.

From Hyde Park, Franklin reported on progress: "Last Saturday and Sunday I shopped for lumber for the cottage . . . I mail you a small piece of the tulip poplar proposed for interior trim . . . The swimming pool is completed . . . Grass seed will go on in a few days." He was pleased with himself. "He works while you sleep."

Eleanor was indignant. Had Franklin forgotten what it was like to look after four young boys? Their sons were constantly quarreling. Franklin Jr. had gashed his foot with an ax. Franklin was duly chastened. "I knew you three older ones would find it awfully strenuous. Those kids are made of steel and rubber."

That fall, Franklin and Missy went to Marion, on the south shore of Massachusetts, to work with a neurologist, Dr. William McDonald, who claimed to have developed a special treatment for infantile paralysis. His theory was to discard braces, in order to develop the muscles. The exercises were agonizing, but Franklin managed to proceed for almost a hundred yards with a brace on his left leg and a cane in his right hand, and told everyone that within a year he hoped to throw his braces away forever. (Later he would realize that these exercises merely risked further deforming his legs.) He and Missy had intended to stay a month, but Franklin was so pleased with his progress that they ended up staying till December. Eleanor and her friends got to oversee the completion of the cottage.

Val-Kill Cottage was officially opened on New Year's Day, 1926. Friends and family, including Mama, were invited to a celebratory lunch. "The honeymoon cottage," Franklin called it. He had come across a children's book, *Little Marion's Pilgrimage*, which he gave Marion as a present. "For my little pilgrim . . . from her affectionate Uncle Franklin," he wrote inside, "on the occasion of the opening of the love nest on the Val-Kill." Franklin was taking a subversive delight in Eleanor's new life.

Mama hated it. With this house of her own, Eleanor had issued an unambiguous declaration of independence. It made Mama more difficult than ever. "Sometimes I think constant irritation is worse for one than real tragedy now and then," Eleanor wrote to Franklin, who was back in Warm Springs. "I've reached a state of such constant self-control that sometimes I'm afraid of what will happen if ever it breaks!" The explosion was not long in coming. "I had a run in with Mama about getting a little more coal, and then a real bust over the apartment."

Mama could be ludicrously tight about such things as the household supply of coal, but then she bought the children ridiculously extravagant presents. Nineteen-year-old Anna was shortly to be married to Curtis Dall, a thirty-year-old stockbroker at Lehman Brothers. Eleanor had just heard that Mama had offered to give them a luxury apartment as a wedding gift, and had instructed Anna not to tell Eleanor, since Mama was sure Eleanor would object. This time, Eleanor's self-control broke.

Mama put on her hurt voice and said that if Eleanor felt like that, she would cancel the gift. Anna and Dall were dismayed. Eleanor was made to feel like the villain of the family. A couple of days later, Mama apologized:

> Eleanor dear, I am very very sorry that I hurt you—*twice*, first by not letting Anna tell you before it was decided & then by saying I would not give it to them. I certainly am old enough not to make mistakes & I can only say how much I regret it—I did not think I *could* be nasty *or* mean, & I fear I had too good an opinion of myself— Also I love you dear too much to ever want to hurt you. *I was hasty*, & of course I shall give them the apartment. I only wanted them to decide for *themselves* & surprise you & Franklin— No doubt he will also be angry with me— Well, I must just bear it—
>
> Devotedly, Mama

With Franklin, Mama acted as if nothing had happened. She sweetly reported that Anna and her fiancé were staying in the Big House (Mama's house) that weekend and Eleanor and the two younger boys were at Val-Kill-Cottage. "They came over here for some hours today and tomorrow they will have lunch here. We three are invited for supper tomorrow at the cottage and they all lunch here on Sunday. Eleanor is so happy over there that she looks well and plump, don't tell her so, it is very becoming."

Franklin was about to sign the papers for the purchase of Warm Springs. "Don't let yourself in for too much money," Eleanor admonished him, "and don't make Mama put in much for if she lost it she'd never get over it! I think you ought to ask her down to stay for a week. She's dying to go and hurt at not being asked. I'll bring her if you want and Missy could move out while she stayed. I'm trying to be decent but I'm so conscious of having been nasty that I'm uncomfortable every minute!"

Eleanor went down to Warm Springs without Mama at the end of April 1926, and did her best to dissuade Franklin from buying the place. The resort looked as shabby as ever. The venture was risky. Franklin already had so many vital interests; did he really need another? It was surely not remotely practical for him to be involved in a project so far away from home. The price Peabody was asking, $200,000, seemed outrageous. Franklin was proposing to invest two-thirds of his entire capital in this; had he forgotten that they had five children to support?

When Franklin exploded in response, something he almost never did, Eleanor realized how close this project was to his heart. "He feels . . . that he's trying to do a big thing which may be a financial success & a medical and philanthropic opportunity for infantile [sic] & that all of us have raised our eyebrows and thrown cold water on it," she explained to Marion and Nancy. She added: "Missy is keen about everything here, of course!"

Eleanor's Val-Kill Cottage was altogether more modest in its aspirations than Franklin's plans for Warm Springs, but in each case these were to be community ventures that offered an alternative to traditional social institutions, whether that meant the dreary corridors of rehabilitation hospitals or the confining roles of conventional marriage.

Val-Kill, a simple stone dwelling, was cozy in a way that East Sixty-fifth Street could never be. The mess, such as it was, belonged not to unruly boys but to the women. The living room was full of books, political brochures, and newspapers. On a desk in the corner was a type-writer, with papers piled high. Upstairs were two bedrooms: the women shared one, leaving the other for guests. From her workroom behind the kitchen, Nancy turned out handsome Early American furniture—beds, tables, chairs, and chests. Eleanor embroidered the towels and linen with their initials, E.M.N.

Mama did not dare to drop in without an invitation, and the rickety old wooden bridge over the stream let them know whenever a motorcar was approaching. But the women were never alone for long. Since they were there on weekends, Eleanor was constantly inviting family and friends over. In the winter, there were dinners around the blazing fire. When spring came, there were picnics at the back, where they had built a large stone fireplace for grilling hamburgers and hot dogs. In the summer there were swimming parties in the pond that had been di-verted from the creek.

The women's lives soon became even more closely intertwined. One day that spring—Franklin had just been talking about the need to create local industries in rural areas, to discourage the exodus to cities—Nancy came up with the idea of a "cottage industry" at Val-Kill: a small furniture-making factory, where she would reproduce seventeenth-century Ameri-can furniture, employing local craftsmen to help. It was the beginning of Val-Kill Industries. All three women invested in it, and Eleanor, with her own trust money, paid for the construction of a sprawling two-story workshop at the back of the house. She loved to walk down the path and watch Nancy working among the sweet smell of wood shavings.

Louis Howe encouraged Eleanor to start a monthly magazine, *Women's Democratic News.* Eleanor gathered up her New York State Demo-cratic Committee friends, and made Caroline O'Day president, Elinor Morgenthau vice president, Nancy Cook business manager, and Mar-ion Dickerman secretary. But it was Eleanor, as editor, who did most of the work. She solicited articles and organized advertising to pay for the costs. Louis helped her with the editing and layout. "Your Missus is gaining in political wisdom every day," he told Franklin.

Marion Dickerman, the last survivor of the group, would admit to biographer Joseph Lash that there was "a definite attraction" between Nancy and Eleanor. "Eleanor loved Nan much more than she did me. She was very very devoted to Nan." Dickerman insisted that there was none of the "belittling emotion of jealousy."

It is significant, however, that when Eleanor was away, she wrote to Marion, not Nancy. She was careful with Marion, who had a tendency to take offense at things and overreact. "I hate to think that you've been unhappy dear," Eleanor apologized to her, that first spring at Val-Kill. "It is new for me to have anyone know when I have 'moods' much less have it make any real difference & if you'll try not to take them too seriously I'll try not to let myself have them!"

Not even Franklin was immune from Marion's prickliness. Since he was keen to use the swimming hole, he had promised to pay for its up-keep and maintenance. At some point that summer, Marion believed he had changed his mind, and proposed that she and Nancy should pull out of the entire Val-Kill arrangement. Franklin wrote back: "Do you know that I am dumbfounded by your letter? . . . Why the injured tone . . . Don't you poor idiots realize how much I care for you both and love having you at Val-Kill! . . . Think it over, my dears, stop talking about 'cheapening our relations,' stop listening to fairy stories . . . If I had you here I would spank you both and then kiss you."

But these tensions were rare. Val-Kill Cottage gave a new balance to the Roosevelt marriage. Franklin had Warm Springs; Eleanor had Val-Kill. Franklin had Missy; Eleanor had Nancy and Marion. Both had Louis Howe.

On Friday evenings, Eleanor and Louis generally left 49 East Sixty-fifth Street together—he to join his family in Poughkeepsie, she to go to Hyde Park. When Franklin was with her, Eleanor slept in the Big House, as they now called Mama's house. When Franklin was away with Missy, Eleanor rejoiced in her new independence at Val-Kill.

Franklin was away from home for 116 weeks between 1925 and 1928. His mother was with him for two of these; Eleanor for four; Missy for 110. There is never a hint of complaint in Eleanor's letters to Franklin. "I miss you very much and want your advice so often," she wrote, "but I imagine it is as well you are far away from all entanglements."

Over the years Eleanor had learned that she could not fulfill Franklin's every need. This was especially true since his polio. Later in life, in her book *You Learn by Living*, she would advise readers in a similar position: "You must learn to allow someone else to meet the need, without bitterness or envy, and accept it."

There is no doubt that Franklin's relationship with Missy was romantic. Whether it was sexual has been a matter of speculation. Hugh Gregory Gallagher, himself a polio victim, takes the view that it was unlikely:

By illness or accident a vigorous, virile, and narcissistic man finds himself a paraplegic. Perhaps, like Roosevelt, he had been successful and popular; admired by men, adored by women. And perhaps, like Roosevelt, he had always been uncomfortable with naked emotion and feeling. The loss of muscle power is a blow to a man's self-esteem. The strength of the blow is, indeed fearful. The feelings generated are hard to repress or deny . . . He can still make love, but not as before. In the sexual act he will be vulnerable to hurt and humiliation. More important and more frightening, is that he will be naked to himself—forced to acknowledge and confront the full extent of his loss and to cope with the fury engendered by that loss.

It is Gallagher's view that Missy would have repressed her sexual desires in order to be with Franklin:

The man then finds a woman who, by intuition, understands the loss, the pain, the fear. She responds with love, with caring and service. They develop a loving relationship. She learns all the little tricks to help him make his way in social situations—ways to make others feel at ease; ways to make him feel less disabled and dependent by anticipating his requests, knowing his habits. For her it is a career of service, a vocation of love—almost like a nun. And, too often, she is like a nun in another way. There is no physical expression of their love. This becomes the unspoken, unyielding act of their relationship.

We will never know. According to his medical reports, Franklin's paralysis did not affect his ability to have an erection. He was only thirty-nine when he was struck down by polio. Surely a man who was bold in every other aspect of his life, who was uninhibited about exposing his crippled legs to friends, who encouraged his wife's flirtations, and whose struggle to build up his body was of paramount importance to him, was unlikely to accept the end of any sexual vitality.

Whatever form it took, the relationship was hard on Missy. Eleanor felt quite sorry for her. Missy was in love with a married man, who was paralyzed from the waist down and almost twice her age. She could never be open about her feelings for Franklin—not even among their friends. She could not make emotional demands on him; she was officially his secretary, his employee. Her future with Franklin was completely uncertain. These pressures made her irritable at times, which in turn made her feel guilty. The previous summer, on a rare vacation without Franklin, she sent him a flower she had found embedded in the ice of a Norwegian glacier. "I'm going to be so good when I get back and never get cross or anything," she vowed. "Isn't that wonderful?"

Missy knew how much FDR hated tears and conflict, and she was grateful for the many things he did for her. He had opened up her world in a way she could never have imagined possible. She did her best to be the sunny, loving companion he wanted her to be. But in the spring of 1927, it suddenly became too much for her.

Franklin and Missy had arrived in Warm Springs in February, intending to stay for three months. Everything seemed to be going well. Franklin now owned a simple cottage a few hundred yards from the rest of the "colony." The furnishings, which included a replica of Thomas Jefferson's worktable and chair from Monticello, were from Val-Kill Industries. Naval paintings were everywhere. Missy slept in the second bedroom, and they shared a bathroom.

Franklin got about in an old Ford Model T with an ingenious system of hand pulleys and levers he had designed, which a local mechanic had rigged up. He was exhilarated to be behind the wheel again, and loved to drive down those red-clay roads at high speed, with Missy beside him, her hair blowing in the wind.

Some afternoons they visited the farm Franklin had bought on the side of Pine Mountain. Franklin had always been interested in farming, and his mother had never been willing to turn over to him any of the farming land at Hyde Park. Georgia was no longer doing at all well with its staple crops of cotton and peaches. The Great Depression, as it would prove to be, came early to Georgia. Franklin hoped to demonstrate to the locals the long-term investment potential of mixed farming—local cattle, goats, timber, vines, fruit, and vegetables. He was especially keen on cattle.

The Warm Springs Foundation, funded by benefactors, was to be officially opened in July. Franklin's wealthy friend, Edsel Ford, had donated the money for a magnificent new swimming pool, enclosed in a glass pavilion, which would allow the patients to swim year-round. Franklin had engaged Dr. LeRoy Hubbard, an orthopedic surgeon with nine years of experience in the aftercare of poliomyelitis, and Miss Helena Mahoney, a physiotherapist, both from New York. There were eighty patients by now, and the numbers were growing fast. Board, lodging, and medical treatment cost them a very reasonable $42 a week. For those who could not afford that, Franklin had set up a Patients' Aid Fund.

The atmosphere at Warm Springs was remarkably happy and cheerful; every visitor commented on it. In the mornings, Helena Mahoney and her team of female "physios" worked with the "polios" in and around the pool. At midday, the "pushboys"—strong local black lads—would help the patients out of the water and wheel them over to lunch. From three to four there were walking exercises on ramps. In between rigorous exercises, the polios sat on their shady porches and chatted. Franklin organized games of water polo, mixing polios with "a-b's" (able-bodieds). There were picnics at Franklin's favorite spot, Dowdell's Knob, a rocky outcrop on Pine Mountain with a breathtaking view of Shiloh valley. Evening meals were served in a charming dining room, with sparkling chandeliers, white linen tablecloths, and "Negro" waiters bearing linen napkins. Warm Springs was nothing like the standard austere institution for handicapped patients.

Franklin was practicing a new technique of walking with Helena Mahoney, the physiotherapist. It was all about balance, and required intense concentration. As always, his legs were firmly encased in braces, and he used his trunk muscles to hitch up his legs, one after the other, but now he was not using crutches. With his left arm he gripped Mahoney's forearm, which she held stiffly, at a ninety degree angle. In his right arm, which he stretched down, straight as a ramrod, he held a cane. Mahoney was opposed to this method of ambulation; she thought it terribly dangerous. If he fell, he would crash like a tree. Franklin, however, was determined. For two years he had been telling people that he was about to throw away his crutches. This method at least *looked* as if he were walking.

The peach trees were beginning to blossom when Missy started to act strangely. She was a much loved figure at the foundation. With the polios she was full of smiles and encouragement. She went everywhere with Franklin, and the two of them always seemed to be laughing. Helena Mahoney, a fellow Catholic, liked Missy enormously. But that spring, Mahoney was shocked by Missy's behavior. It began with her throwing temper tantrums in public. Missy raged against Franklin, raged about her life. This was followed by days of severe depression when she talked about suicide. Then Missy descended into delirium.

On April 23, Helena Mahoney wrote to Eleanor, who was about to come down to Warm Springs: "FDR is walking with two canes at exercise and also with my arm and a cane. Muscles improved and knees much stronger. Hope you'll persuade him to stay longer. Look forward to your visit . . . Missy improves daily but still needs care."

But Missy did not improve. She regressed into a childlike state, and clung to Franklin. She could not recognize people, could not remember anything, and her words no longer made sense. Franklin had to make a quick trip to New York, and left her in the care of Helena Mahoney and Dr. James Johnson, a doctor from nearby Manchester, the consulting physician to the Warm Springs Foundation. On Sunday, May 15, Mahoney wrote:

Dear Mr. Roosevelt, Missy is having a small wiggle for the wind is blowing a gale and with it the doors and windows. She is being such a good girl that I fear she will fly to New York on her own wings . . . She is so anxious to see you. She expresses it more picturesquely. Today Dr. Johnson said she could sit up in bed for fifteen minutes.

The letter was not finished till the following day. Mahoney explained to Franklin that it had been "written under much difficulty and many interruptions."

It is now Monday afternoon. Missy was too nervous to continue yesterday but did get settled down finally. Your telegram rather upset her for a while . . . She says she is dying . . . She is lonely for you. The improvement in health and increased strength makes her see things more reasonable than ever before she was sick. Missy would like a baby pillow and six covers for it . . . Missy is writing you a letter, which she hope [sic] you will appreciate as it is very hard and most fatiguing but will do it . . . Do not work to [sic] hard and come back soon.

Franklin returned on May 24 with a baby pillow, provided by Eleanor. Helena Mahoney wrote to thank Eleanor and confessed that it had been "a long weary time."

When Franklin left again, on June 11, Missy's condition had deteriorated to the point that she was hospitalized in Warm Springs' rehabilitation center. Sharp objects were forbidden her. Franklin was asked to stay away and not call her; his presence seemed to make her worse.

A month passed. On July 10, Missy's brother, Bernard LeHand, who had arrived from Boston, wrote to Franklin:

> Dear Mr. Roosevelt . . . I certainly had a most enjoyable afternoon with "Missy" on the lawn. She, of course, has not regained her strength—therefore moves and acts very deliberately and calmly, but such an improvement . . . Looks fine. Gained five pounds. Can read. Remembers everything—in detail except for the first eleven day period at the hospital . . . Since the 28th of June has been normal and it was her own suggestion that visitors be excluded until such time as she was convinced that she had "arrived." . . .
>
> She would like her fountain pen. A pencil does not appeal to her, although a pen is really considered a dangerous "weapon." . . . I am confident that you will decide to take her to Hyde Park for August.
>
> Sincerely, Bernard.

Franklin came back for a week at the beginning of August, and returned to Warm Springs at the end of September for two months. By November, after nine months of serious illness, Missy was finally better.

We can only speculate as to what might have provoked Missy's breakdown. What had changed? She had always accepted her role as Franklin's clandestine companion—his "second wife"—with the utmost good grace, even gratitude. She also felt beholden to Eleanor. Several years later, when they were all together in the White House, she would write in a Christmas card to Eleanor: "I hope you know how very much I appreciate being with you . . . I love you so much—I never can tell you how very much."

Missy did not count on sharing Franklin with yet another woman. There is no doubt that she knew about Franklin's past romance with

Lucy Mercer. He might even have told her himself. But Missy no doubt believed (just as Eleanor did) that this romance belonged to the past. It did not. A handful of surviving letters written between 1926 and 1928 reveal that Franklin and Lucy had kept in touch. Mrs. Lucy Mercer Rutherfurd was now living in Aiken, South Carolina, bringing up her husband's five children, along with her own daughter, Barbara. These letters tell each other of their comings and goings. In May 1926, Franklin had informed Lucy that he was buying Warm Springs. "Between now and the 16th I am in New York." He asked if she would be in Allamuchy, the Rutherfurds' New Jersey estate, that summer.

In April 1927, Lucy wrote to Franklin in Warm Springs, gave him her phone number, and asked him to call her. In early July 1927, she wrote from the SS *Belgenland* to say that she and her husband, their six children, and their nurses and tutors were on their way to Europe. "I hope you have a happy summer and that I shan't come home to find you President, or Secretary of State," she joked. "If there is anything I can do for you on the continent or in England let me know care Morgan and Co. Paris."

There were evidently other letters or phone calls that summer, since Franklin wrote on September 15, saying he hoped her children had recovered and that Lucy was "well—really well." He told her the dates for his next trip to Warm Springs.

Is it possible that for the second time in Franklin's life, Lucy had caused havoc in another woman's heart? Whether or not this was the case, Missy could sense, it seems, that her years of cozy intimacy with Franklin were coming to an end. She was realizing that she would always have to share him—not just with Eleanor but with the world in general. Franklin was determined to reenter public life.

In addition to their work in the New York State Democratic Committee, Eleanor, Marion, and Nancy already had Val-Kill Industries (Nancy's project) and *Women's Democratic News* (Eleanor's project). In September 1927, they embarked on another venture—Marion's project. For some years Marion had been teaching at the exclusive Todhunter School for Girls at 66 East Eightieth Street, off Park Avenue. Miss Winifred Todhunter, about to retire, suggested that Marion take over as principal and purchase the school from her. Marion discussed the proposition with Nancy and Eleanor. They decided to share the investment. Marion would be the principal, and Eleanor would teach American history and literature.

Eleanor, acutely aware that she did not have a college degree, would accept no pay for the first year, but she was thrilled by the prospect of teaching. "It is going to be such fun to work with you & Nan," she wrote to Marion from the South, "and you are dears to let me join in it all for I'd never have had the initiative or the ability in any one line to have done anything interesting alone!"

The Democratic National Convention was to be held in Houston, Texas, at the end of June 1928. For a second time, Al Smith was hoping to be nominated as the Democratic Party presidential candidate. For a second time, Franklin had agreed to give Smith's nominating address. Four years after his last major speech in front of the Democratic Party, Franklin wanted to be seen as "back on his feet." He was going to appear without crutches.

Since James was going to be in Europe that summer with Mama, Franklin asked Elliott, his second son, to be his aide. In early April, eighteen-year-old Elliott, proud that his father had entrusted him with this role, took the train to Warm Springs, and for a month the two of them practiced. While Franklin jerked himself forward, beads of sweat dripping off his brow, and Elliott suffered bruises from his father's steel grip on his arm, they worked up a routine of bantering and laughter to distract onlookers. "I'm telling everyone you are going to Houston without crutches," Eleanor wrote from Hyde Park, "so mind you stick at it!"

The speech was an unmitigated success, and this time the party chose Al Smith as their candidate for president. Once again, the press turned Franklin into a redemptive hero. He is "a figure tall and proud even in suffering," the *New York World* declared, "a man softened and cleansed and illumined with pain."

The election did not look at all promising for the Democrats. This was 1928 (a year before the onset of the Great Depression): the American economy was booming, the stock market was surging, and the nation's mood was optimistic. Herbert Hoover, the Republican candidate, boasted: "Unemployment in the sense of distress is widely disappearing . . . We in America today are nearer to the final triumph over poverty than ever before in the history of this land."

The Democratic candidate, Al Smith, was a progressive. In New York, he had created state parks, reformed the civil service, brought in workers' compensation, and improved labor conditions for women and children. He was a "Wet"—vehemently against Prohibition, and the bootleggers, moonshiners, gangsters, and speakeasy operators who made immense profits from the illegal trade in alcohol. But the American people did not want a progressive, a Catholic, or a Wet. They wanted continued prosperity.

By September, the Democratic Party calculated that Smith could win only if the Democrats carried New York State. They needed a compelling candidate to replace Smith as governor, someone New Yorkers knew and respected, someone who in his gubernatorial campaign would speak out passionately for Al Smith. There was only one man who fit the bill.

Down in Warm Springs, Franklin received endless phone calls, letters, and wires, trying to persuade him to stand. He could not be swayed. The answer was no. He was eager to get back into public service, he said, but this was not the moment. "My doctors are very definite in stating that the continued improvement in my condition is dependent on my avoidance of cold climate and on taking exercises here at Warm Springs during the cold winter months," he stated in a telegram. "As I am only 46 years of age, I feel that I owe it to my family and myself to give the present constant improvement a chance to continue."

His doctors said no such thing, of course. But Franklin could not tell the truth, which was that he and Howe were firmly convinced the time was not right. Louis Howe had worked out a schedule for Franklin. According to his reckoning, Hoover would win the presidential election, and would probably be reelected in 1932. Franklin should run for governor of New York in 1932 and get reelected in 1934, which would put him in a good position to win the White House in 1936. For the time being, Louis Howe was clear: Franklin must not stand!

For once, Eleanor did not agree with Louis. She believed that Franklin was ready to stand, his legs were as good as they ever would be, it would do him good to get back into politics, and furthermore, the party needed him.

On October 1, the New York Democrats were convening in Rochester, New York, to choose Al Smith's successor as governor. Franklin was going to be put under considerable pressure. Louis wrote to him, in Warm

Springs: "I hope your spine is still sufficiently strong to assure them that you are still nigh to death's door for the next two years."

Eleanor was a delegate to the convention. "I have to go to Rochester," she told Franklin, "but I wish I didn't have to, for everyone makes me so uncomfortable. They feel so strongly about your running and even good explanations can be made to sound foolish." She knew better than to push Franklin, but she felt strongly that he should accept the nomination.

Anna sent her father a telegram: "Go ahead and take it." Franklin wired back: "You ought to be spanked."

In Rochester, on October 1, the members of the nomination committee tried all day to get FDR on the phone. They were unable to reach him. In the evening, Al Smith begged Eleanor to call her husband, person to person. Surely he would talk to *her*. Eleanor said it was hopeless trying to persuade Franklin to do something once he had made up his mind. But finally she consented to call him.

Franklin came on the line and told her, laughing, that he and Missy had spent the entire day out of the house, to avoid the phone. Eleanor wasted no time with preliminaries. Al Smith had asked her to do this, she told him, and she was passing the phone over. Smith came on the line. "We need you Frank," he began.

In Warm Springs, Missy was by Franklin's side. As she saw it, Smith was using Franklin as a sacrificial goat. "Don't you dare!" she warned Franklin.

Other members of the committee came on the phone. They would make a contribution to Warm Springs to the tune of $100,000, they said. FDR did not need to undertake a vigorous campaign; he could give radio talks and limit himself to major addresses. Smith came back on the line. If they nominated him the next day by acclamation, would Franklin accept the nomination? Franklin was silent. Al Smith took that as a yes, and hung up.

The next day, Franklin D. Roosevelt was nominated by acclamation, and he accepted. Louis Howe was dismayed. "Mess is no name for it," he wired Franklin. "For once, I have no advice to give. Luhowe."

Franklin returned to New York without Missy. She was not sleeping, she was smoking too much—up to three packs of Lucky Strikes a day—and she could not stop crying. It seemed that she was falling into another black depression.

A difficult few days ensued, with the Republican newspapers playing up FDR's physical handicap. "There is something both pathetic and pitiless in the 'drafting' of Franklin D. Roosevelt by Alfred E. Smith," opined the *New York Post*. "Stung by the presidential bee, driven by the necessity of getting New York's electoral vote, the governor made this most loyal of friends agree to serve his ambition at a price that is beyond all reason."

"A Governor does not have to be an acrobat," Al Smith retorted. "We do not elect him for his ability to do a double back-flip or a handspring. The work of the Governorship is brainwork. Ninety-nine percent of it is accomplished at a desk."

Louis Howe, making the best of this "mess," swung into action. He set up his team of workers in the Democratic Party state headquarters at the Biltmore Hotel, across the street from Grand Central, and for the next five weeks he worked day and night, gathering information, issuing daily news releases, sending out thousands of "Roosevelt letters," and posting Franklin on the political landscape. His secretaries dubbed him "the Little Boss."

Al Smith and his colleagues did not think Franklin capable of doing much campaigning, but they had underestimated their man. Franklin barnstormed New York State. He traveled by automobile, with a steel bar installed on the back of the front seat so that he could pull himself up to give speeches. His campaign team had strict orders from Howe not to allow anyone to photograph him being lifted in and out of the car. "No movies of me getting out of this machine, boys," Franklin would tell the pack of pressmen.

Sam Rosenman, a thirty-two-year-old Jewish attorney who had joined the team as FDR's speechwriter, had been warned that FDR was aristocratic, aloof, and somewhat shallow. Rosenman could not have been more surprised:

> I had quite a detached, indifferent feeling toward this man at first. After all, I was going along just to do a chore . . . As the weeks went on, however, Roosevelt's warm, genial personality, his friendliness and cordial informality, drew me close to him. Nearly everyone who worked intimately with him had the same

experience. Roosevelt loved people, and they learned quickly to return that affection . . . He knew how to laugh, and he loved to laugh. He knew how to stop work, even when hardest pressed, for a joke or an anecdote or a minute of light conversation or gossip . . . He was not concerned with distinctions of wealth or social position or religious beliefs. This was a new kind of man in politics for me: one who did not seem to care—or even know—whether you were a Catholic, Protestant or Jew.

Rosenman marveled at FDR's courage and stamina. He could see that for FDR the simple act of standing up and sitting down required immense effort. It was tiring to stand in town halls, railway stations, and hotel lobbies anchored by a cane and his eldest son's arm. It was harrowing to be carried up the back stairs of halls like a sack of potatoes. But throughout it all, FDR never seemed ruffled. What everyone around him remembered was not his struggle but his smile.

For four hectic weeks, Franklin did his best to persuade people that Smith would make a good president. But what most impressed people was Franklin D. Roosevelt himself. Louis Howe was feeling more cheerful: "I am horribly afraid you are going to be elected."

While Franklin was traveling around, Eleanor was also working at fever pitch. In the mornings she taught at Todhunter School. As soon as her classes ended, she rushed over to her office at the Biltmore Hotel to do national campaign committee work. She had two secretaries working with her—Malvina Thompson and Grace Tully. Both women were learning to deal with voluminous piles of mail, high-speed dictation, late evenings, and weekend work at Hyde Park. In Manhattan, during the week, Howe would sometimes join them for dinner. "The conversation revolved constantly around politics," Grace Tully recalled.

The Republicans ran a disgraceful electoral campaign, stirring up prejudice, religious bigotry, and racism. According to the rumors they spread, Smith was a "Wet" because he was a drunkard; Smith was against lynching because he was a "Nigger lover"; and Southerners were warned that if a Catholic became president, their Methodist and Baptist marriages would be declared void and their children illegitimate.

On the evening of November 6, 1928, Franklin, Eleanor, and Louis were at New York Democratic Party headquarters, at the Biltmore Hotel, listening to the returns. The atmosphere was gloomy. The Democrats were suffering their worst defeat since the Civil War. Before midnight it was clear that Al Smith had failed to win even his own state of New York.

When Franklin and Eleanor left the Biltmore shortly after midnight, the returns from the Republican strongholds in upstate New York were pointing to a clear victory for Franklin's Republican opponent. Franklin was fervently wishing he had listened to Louis Howe. Eleanor felt terrible. Unable to bear Louis's black despair any longer, they went back to East Sixty-fifth Street to hear the bad news on the radio.

Around 2 a.m., the pendulum started to swing the other way. At 4 a.m. it was announced on the radio that Franklin Delano Roosevelt, by the narrowest of margins, had been elected governor of New York.

SIX

In the Governor's Mansion

November 1928–March 1933

The headlines in *The New York Times* read: "Mrs. Roosevelt to Keep on Filling Many Jobs Besides Being the First Lady." She would be mistress of the executive mansion in Albany for only half the week; in the other half she would live in Manhattan and teach at Todhunter School for Girls. "In spare moments she also will help to run a furniture factory, serve on a few committees and boards of directors and keep up with current history in which she is keenly interested. And all the time, as the mother of four boys away at school, she will be on call."

It was an unusual arrangement, certainly, for a governor's wife to be mistress of the mansion part-time. But her teaching was important to Eleanor. It was the only realm where she was not in FDR's shadow, she told an interviewer. "It is one thing that belongs to me." She did not add that she had no intention of giving up her political activity either, even if FDR's shadow loomed large in this domain.

She was obliged to resign as editor of *Women's Democratic News*. "I know if I take any part in politics everyone will attribute anything I say or do to Franklin & that wouldn't be fair to him," she told friends. In private, Louis Howe assured her that she could do much the same job behind the scenes.

Eleanor was keenly aware of the dangers facing the political spouse. FDR's future was entirely uncertain. The governor's term was two years—and then what? If she dropped her own interests to become "the governor's wife" and FDR were not reelected, she would find herself floundering again. By now she had become extremely wary of being subsumed by her role as wife. She firmly believed that "to develop, one must have a certain freedom of thought and action."

But she found herself in something of a bind. Over the past years she had become a powerful figure within the New York State Democratic Party. No woman had greater influence. Unlike the other women she worked with, however, she was not in the political arena in her own right. Her greatest advantage was also her greatest handicap: she was first and foremost Franklin's wife. By the general public, politics was still regarded as men's territory, rough and vulgar. To the outside world, as the smiling spouse, Eleanor had to pretend that she was not particularly interested in the political fray.

As she was well aware, she would not have been in politics in the first place were it not for her husband, and being the governor's wife gave her considerable political clout. On the other hand, she could not be seen as interfering with Franklin's work—not even by Franklin. More than ever before, she was going to have to walk a tightrope. She would have to do a great deal of her political work behind the scenes.

Two days after his election Franklin returned to Warm Springs to find a crowd of more than a thousand people at the little station. He had invited several colleagues to come down later that month, to "bat ideas around," as he put it. "Besides, I'd like you to see Warm Springs," he told Sam Rosenman, his speechwriter. "It will be a nice vacation, and we'll all have a fine time over some Brunswick stew." The chicken-and-pork dish, a Georgia specialty, was a favorite of Franklin's.

For his first few days back in Georgia, Franklin spent most of his time reassuring Missy. She had been ill for the past month and had taken no part in the gubernatorial campaign. While Franklin stumped New York State for four weeks, she had stayed in their cottage at Warm Springs, fighting off severe depression.

Missy felt as if her world was caving in. For seven years, while Franklin had struggled with body and soul, she had been his closest, most intimate companion. They had been able to retreat from public life for months at a time, in the South. Now Franklin was moving to the governor's mansion in Albany, where he would be surrounded by bodyguards and advisers, and scrutinized by the press. What would happen to Missy? As governor of New York, Franklin could not be seen taking time out with a woman who was not his wife. The gossip would be demeaning for him, for Eleanor, and for Missy herself. It seemed to Missy, in her despair, that she would never again be alone with him.

She would live in the governor's mansion with them, Franklin assured her. By now she was part of the family. As his secretary, Missy would spend far more time with him than anyone else. When Eleanor was in Manhattan, he wanted Missy to act as mistress of the mansion. Some evenings they would be alone together. When he had official guests, he would need Missy to be his hostess. And *of course* they would still come to Warm Springs!

While Franklin was in Warm Springs discussing future political appointments, Eleanor and Louis were doing the same at East Sixty-fifth Street. Having worked in the New York State Democratic Committee, Eleanor knew many of the people Franklin was dealing with better than he did. She and Louis were not surprised that Al Smith was finding it difficult to give up being governor. Smith was clearly hoping that Franklin would prove little more than a puppet governor, spending most of his time down in Warm Springs. When Smith tried to push his closest adviser, Belle Moskowitz, on Franklin, Eleanor warned her husband with playful earnestness: "You have to decide, and you have to decide it now, whether you are going to be Governor of this state, or whether Mrs. Moskowitz is going to be Governor of this state. If Mrs. Moskowitz is your secretary, she will run you."

But Eleanor admired Frances Perkins, whom Al Smith had appointed to the Industrial Board in 1919. "I hope you will consider making Frances Perkins labor commissioner," she wrote to Franklin. "She would do well and you could fill her place as chair of the Industrial Commission by one of the men . . . and put Nell Schwartz (now Bureau of Women in Industry) on the Commission so there would be one woman on it. These are suggestions which I am passing on not my opinions for I don't want to butt in!"

It would be a bold move to put a woman in charge of the Department of Labor. "You see, Al's a good progressive fellow but I am willing to take more chances," Franklin boasted to Perkins. "I've got more nerve about women and their status in the world than Al has."

They laughed. Perkins believed she knew who was behind this idea. And Franklin knew that she knew.

It was a cheerful bunch of "advisers" who joined Franklin at Warm Springs near the end of the month. They were mostly men, of course, but Eleanor had seen to it that Molly Dewson, a highly competent political leader from the Women's Division, was invited. The colleagues were lodged in the cottages. In between the discussions about policy decisions, there were swims, receptions, and picnics. At a barbecue in Franklin's honor, featuring Brunswick stew, one speaker remarked that after the 1932 election, Warm Springs was likely to become the "Summer White House." There was hearty applause. The national newspapers were already touting FDR as the possible next president.

In addition to policy planning and appointing his future staff, Franklin had a mountain of mail to deal with. Howe was doing his best in New York. ("Six hundred letters came in this morning," he wired, "of which 400 . . . refer to national affairs.") But though Howe and his secretaries were skilled at forging Franklin's signature, there was still plenty of correspondence that Franklin had to answer himself.

Eleanor had recommended one of her former campaign secretaries, Grace Tully, to Franklin. Grace Tully was twenty-eight, two years younger than Missy, and from a similar Irish Catholic background. Like Missy, she was a committed Democrat. She could act as Missy's assistant.

Grace Tully was thrilled to be invited down to Warm Springs, but she was understandably wary about stepping into Missy's territory. She wrote later, very discreetly, in her memoir:

I had never met Missy LeHand before this 1928 trip to Warm Springs and several mutual acquaintances had cautioned me that I must be extremely tactful in recognizing her authority as F.D.R.'s secretary and her long relationship with him. It was sound enough advice in such a circumstance but was completely unneeded. From the moment we met, Missy and I liked each other tremendously and our relationship from then until her death in 1944 was like that of two sisters who never quarreled . . . She did not display the possessive jealousy that is found so often between a confidential secretary and her boss. Missy was capable, confident and unselfish in her working relationship and welcomed rather than resisted the assistance of a "Number Two girl."

In the afternoons, Franklin worked with his two secretaries on the porch of his cottage. They made a good team. While Missy answered the more straightforward correspondence (Franklin would scribble a brief instruction in the margin: "Missy, to ack" or "Missy, tell him sorry"), Tully took dictation. Franklin would occasionally ask the women to remind him, once they were in Albany, to do this or that. Tully finally asked him whom he meant. "Why, I mean us, all of us. Of course you are going to Albany, child."

That was the way it was with FDR, as most people now called him. He had a flair for selecting colleagues, and knew instinctively who would make loyal, hardworking, good-humored members of his team. From now on he simply assumed that the chosen few would willingly give up their former duties to become part of the larger Roosevelt community.

While they were in Warm Springs, FDR took Sam Rosenman aside: "Sam, I shall want you to act as the Counsel to the Governor—we will have a fine, stimulating time together." They talked over the duties involved, and Sam promised to make up his mind within the week. A couple of days later, the newspapers announced Rosenman's appointment. Surprised and shocked, Rosenman put through a phone call to FDR. Was it true that FDR had announced Rosenman's appointment? FDR laughed and admitted it. "I made up your mind for you."

Rosenman forgave Roosevelt his imperiousness. Like most of FDR's close colleagues, he would find working with FDR a deeply rewarding, joyful experience. But it was a total commitment, which took a toll on partners and families. Alfred B. Rollins, Howe's biographer, who spoke to several of FDR's associates, could see the price they paid:

For many the most difficult part of the job was the absolute subordination of all personal concerns to the boss's needs and ambitions. No one in the Roosevelt staff made plans which conflicted with his. Louis often broke his promises of outings with Hartley or weekends with Grace when politics or the Governor's itinerary interfered . . . Marguerite LeHand, Grace Tully, and others would literally give up everything in the outside world to devote themselves to their 24-hour, seven-day jobs . . . For those who could not bend to the inexorable demands of a Roosevelt-centered world, there could never be a full measure of the rewards which he meted out.

Among the many rewards for the chosen few were the strong bonds that formed within the inner circle. "Missy" and "Tully," who in five years would become known throughout government circles as the loyal gatekeepers of the White House's inner sanctum, were as close as sisters. Indeed, FDR often referred to himself as "Father." He liked to think of the community around him as a big, happy family.

On the first weekend of December 1928, Eleanor motored to Albany with Nancy Cook to look over the Roosevelts' new home. The governor's mansion, a palatial red-brick Victorian building with a medley of cupolas, turrets, and towers, was at the top of a hill, guarded by state troopers. The Smiths had the coal fires blazing, but the place still seemed cold and austere. The furnishings, Eleanor and Nancy agreed, reflected "the official taste of the State of New York."

Eleanor wrote to Franklin, who was still down in Warm Springs, that she was shocked by the number of servants. She thought they could cut back, and she wanted to expand the servants' eating quarters, which were currently in the pantry and "not really decent." It seemed to her that the heated pool Franklin would need for exercise could be installed at the rear of the house, in place of Smith's three greenhouses. The flowers were magnificent, but the greenhouses cost $6,000 a year, and they could use commercial florists for far less. The library on the ground floor would make an excellent office for Franklin, and she thought they could transform Al Smith's office, upstairs, into a cozy family sitting room. Franklin would have the "grandest sunny room," a corner suite on the second floor, as his bedroom. There was a large, pleasant room down the hall, which Missy might like. "We will talk that over."

FDR's inauguration day as governor of New York was January 1, 1929. The streets of Albany were covered in snow. In the assembly chamber of Albany's capitol—the same room in which Theodore Roosevelt had been sworn in as governor of New York thirty years before—Franklin

Delano Roosevelt took the oath of office on his family's massive seventeenth-century Dutch Bible. TR was forty when he became governor; FDR was forty-six.

After the ceremony, Sara Delano proudly told friends that her son had finally "grown up." The reality was more complicated. Now that FDR was governor, he was once again financially dependent on his mother. In the fall, during the gubernatorial campaign, Mama had written to him: "Now what follows is *really private*. In case of your election, I know your salary is smaller than the one you get now. I am prepared to make the difference up to you."

As governor, FDR's salary would be $10,000 per annum. He had had to give up his job at Fidelity and Deposit, which meant forfeiting an annual salary of $25,000. As well as supporting five children and his personal aides, he also had to provide a salary for Louis Howe. They had decided that Howe was going to stay on in New York, at East Sixty-fifth Street, working behind the scenes, handling publicity, and positioning FDR for the presidency.

Sara had been forty-six when she inherited her husband's estate and took control of Hyde Park—the same age as FDR when he became governor. For the rest of her life—she lived to the age of eighty-six—Sara would give money to Franklin and his family. She had the satisfaction of knowing that her generosity made her son's political career possible. But she was never willing to do the one thing that would give Franklin his independence. She never increased the trust fund Franklin's father had left him, and she never turned over to him any of her capital. Even when he was president of the United States, arguably the most powerful man in the world, FDR would still have to go to his mother with his cap in hand. As Eleanor saw it, Franklin had generously made his mother part of his life. In response, Mama took away much of his authority as a husband and father, humiliating Franklin in front of his family. Eleanor could never forgive her for this abuse of power.

Now that Eleanor was the governor's wife she had to give some attention to her appearance. Even Lorena Hickok, a bulky, rough-edged, chain-smoking political journalist from South Dakota, was taken aback when she saw Eleanor during the election campaign, waiting for an elevator, about to go off and speak at a fashionable women's luncheon:

Mrs. Roosevelt that day, had she searched the world over, could hardly have found a more unbecoming costume. Waistlines, in 1928, were low, down around the hips. Her black skirt was longer than those worn by most women. She had on a knitted silk kind of jumper, very long, of a shade of green that made her skin look gray. Her hat, set squarely on top of her tightly netted hair, looked like a black straw pancake. "You poor thing," I thought. "It will be murder for you at that luncheon."

In four years, Lorena Hickok would become Eleanor's closest friend. In the intervening period she was often in the journalists' car that followed the governor and his wife around on their official duties, and was pleased to observe that Mrs. Roosevelt was choosing more elegant outfits. "I can see her now riding beside her husband in the open car ahead—very erect, wearing a light printed silk summer dress and a hat considerably more becoming than some of those she had worn when I first met her . . . But she still wore those hair nets!"

When they first moved into the governor's mansion, Franklin wanted Eleanor to use the governor's limousine. Eleanor had refused. She would do so for official trips, she said; otherwise she liked to drive her own car. In that case, Franklin insisted, she needed a bodyguard. He assigned state trooper Earl Miller to the job.

Earl Miller was a handsome thirty-one-year-old who had been a circus acrobat, amateur boxing champion, navy officer, and Al Smith's personal bodyguard. At the New York State Police barracks, Miller's colleagues saw the press photographs of the new governor's wife and smirked, "We don't envy you having to live with that old crab." But Miller, who had something of the gallant knight about him, loved his new job protecting "the Lady," as he would always call Eleanor. He had never met anyone like this woman, who hailed from the aristocracy and yet was so modest in her tastes and requirements. In no time at all, a warm friendship grew up between them.

For the next four years, Eleanor traveled all over the state with Earl Miller. When the governor and his wife made inspection tours together, Miller sat in front with the chauffeur. While FDR stayed in the car, touring the grounds with the superintendent and talking to the press, Eleanor went into the buildings. More often, FDR entrusted Eleanor to act as his "eyes and legs," and she went in his place, with Earl Miller. FDR's probing questions, after their visits to state prisons, hospitals, and asylums, taught both Eleanor and Earl Miller to look beyond the official façade. Rather than simply examining the menus, they learned to look into the cooking pots. Instead of relying on what the superintendent said, they noted the attitude of the patients toward the staff. By the end of FDR's two terms as governor, they would both pride themselves on their reporting skills.

But Eleanor hated having her photograph taken. She was self-conscious about her height, and tended to stoop. Her prominent jawbone made her look sulky when her mouth was closed. Over the years friends had often remarked that she was not "photogenic"; photographs did not capture her lively personality and warmth. Eleanor would retort, "My dear, if you haven't any chin and your front teeth stick out it's going to show on a camera plate." She was convinced that she looked worse if she showed her teeth.

It was Earl Miller who taught her to smile. He could see how stiff and awkward she became in front of reporters' cameras. Eleanor used to beg him, "Please don't let them take my picture." He cajoled her: "Now listen, try to smile for just one picture." He assured her that she had a beautiful smile. He joked with her; he stood behind the photographers making funny faces. When she saw how she looked in photos where she smiled and laughed, Eleanor was astounded. From this time on, she never forgot to smile for the camera.

Eleanor enjoyed being squired around by this dashing, chivalrous man, who was so fiercely loyal to her. Earl Miller gave her a new confidence in herself. Unlike Eleanor's sons, Earl did not mock her driving skills or laugh at her swimming stroke. They played tennis together. He encouraged her to take up riding horses again, and gave her a present of a docile chestnut mare, called Dot. In Warm Springs, Earl even got FDR back on a horse. It was not at all safe, since FDR could not grip with his knees, but they made the most of those few minutes when FDR was in the saddle to take photos for the press.

For Earl Miller, who had left home at the age of twelve, the warm, effusive Roosevelts provided the family life he had always hankered for. He adored the "Lady" and the "Boss," and felt honored to be included in the inner circle.

Mama disapproved of him, complaining to Marion Dickerman that he used to be "Corporal Miller," who ate with the servants in the kitchen, and now he was "Earl," and ate with the family. FDR liked Earl; Louis was a little jealous of Earl's place in Eleanor's life. Marion and Nan agreed with Mama: Earl was rough and uncultured. They disliked the liberties he took with Eleanor, particularly the way he touched her so freely. "He used to annoy me the way he talked to her," Marion recalled. "I didn't like his tone of voice sometimes when he told her what to do, or when he did not like what was being served at table." But Marion could see that it was "a very deep attachment."

Eleanor threw herself headlong into this romantic friendship. Earl often stayed in the guest room at Val-Kill. They went on horse rides together and on walks through the woods. On winter nights, the women sang around the piano while Earl played. Photographs from Nancy and Marion's personal album show Eleanor in her riding jodhpurs, with a hand on Earl's knee, looking radiant and relaxed, like a woman in love.

James Roosevelt, who was twenty-two when he first saw his mother with the state trooper, wrote later:

> I believe there may have been one real romance in mother's life outside of marriage. Mother may have had an affair with Earl Miller . . . He encouraged her to take pride in herself, to be herself, to be unafraid of facing the world . . . She seemed to draw strength from him when he was by her side, and she came to rely on him. When she had problems, she sought his help . . . He became part of the family, too, and gave her a great deal of what her husband and we, her sons, failed to give her. Above all he made her feel that she was a woman.

In Eleanor's relationship with Earl Miller, there were echoes of Franklin's relationship with Missy. Missy was sixteen years younger than Franklin; Earl was thirteen years younger than Eleanor. Missy and Miller were both "attendants"—a mixture of employee, close companion, facilitator, and protector. Missy was an attractive, smiling woman, whose flirtatiousness and devotion made FDR feel more like a man. Earl Miller was a good-looking fellow who liked to flaunt his muscled body, and whose tender affection and fierce protectiveness made Eleanor feel more like a woman. Missy and Earl both came from humble backgrounds, but this never bothered Franklin or Eleanor. Indeed, they loved to open up their friends' worlds, giving them opportunities they would otherwise never have had.

Earl had been married once. Although he had a reputation as a lady's man, he was unhappy in love. His romances did not last. Eleanor understood his loneliness. They trusted each other and exchanged confidences. Earl shared Eleanor's commitment to progressive politics, and to helping the "underdog."

There is no doubt that Eleanor was in love with Earl for a time. Her friends teased her about marrying him. But they are most unlikely to have had an "affair." Earl Miller believed in old-fashioned loyalty, straight down the line. Eleanor was the governor's wife. He called her "Lady." He was thirty-one; she was forty-four. He loved her, admired her, and took pleasure in helping her. He was flattered by the effusive affection that she lavished upon him. But Earl Miller's girlfriends—including the three women he would marry and divorce—were younger women, pretty women.

Eleanor once alluded to the hundreds of letters she and Earl wrote each other over the years. There was almost certainly a romantic edge to them, especially during the Albany period. At some point, significantly, they were destroyed. All that remain are a handful of notes in Earl's neat handwriting, addressed to "Dearest Lady," and signed "Much love always, Earl."

On October 29, 1929—just eight months after Hoover had taken office on a tidal wave of optimism—the New York Stock Exchange crashed. The speculation orgy of the past few years was over. The bubble had burst.

The collapse of the stock market rapidly turned into the most severe economic crisis the United States had ever known. By March 1930, unemployment had risen from 1.5 million to 3.2 million Americans out of work. President Hoover kept saying that the market would regulate itself, that renewed prosperity was "just around the corner." At the time there was no unemployment relief, no federal welfare, and no bank deposit insurance. Hoover insisted that such "socialist" measures would destroy American individualism and self-reliance.

Hoover believed in laissez-faire market capitalism, without government intervention. FDR believed that strict government regulation was needed to prohibit reckless banking and business practices. It was FDR's view that government had an obligation to help people who tried to help themselves but could not. According to him, the American people needed a minimum wage, an eight-hour day, a five-day week, old-age pensions, farm relief, cheaper electricity in rural areas, and unemployment relief through public works.

The new medium of radio was the ideal way for FDR to get his ideas out to the people. He needed to make an impact in upstate New York, where the newspapers were almost entirely Republican. From his study at the governor's mansion FDR told the people of New York what he was trying to achieve, and how the legislature in Albany was systematically trying to block his reforms. He had a calm sonorous voice, an informal chatty manner, and a talent for conveying complicated ideas in simple terms. Despite his aristocratic heritage and bearing, FDR was showing himself to be a confirmed liberal, with the courage to take on the entrenched conservatives in upstate New York. His fights with the Albany legislature were bringing him national prominence.

As governor, FDR had developed a daily schedule that would scarcely change when he became president. He had breakfast in bed around eight, during which time he read the newspapers. Still in bed, he received Eleanor, Missy, and his close advisers to discuss the day's schedule. His new valet, Irwin McDuffie—a black man from Warm Springs, previously a barber—helped him wash and dress. Around ten thirty, FDR's bodyguard, August Adolph Gennerich, wheeled him to the governor's limousine. "Gus" Gennerich—a gruff, good-humored, gum-chewing New York City policeman, originally from Yorkville, Manhattan's German district—had been assigned to FDR during the gubernatorial campaign. FDR liked him immensely.

At the capitol, FDR's official working day began at eleven and generally went through till five or six. Back at the governor's mansion, he had a swim in the pool, joined by Eleanor, Missy, or that evening's visitor. Then he and his colleagues would gather in his study for a predinner drink. "Children's hour," FDR called it. Prohibition was still in force, but FDR deplored this woeful manifestation of American puritanism. He loved to mix cocktails, using the shaker with mischievous glee. His own favorite was a "horse's neck"—ginger ale and whiskey.

Dinner was served at eight. Most nights they were at least six around the table, often more. Missy and Earl Miller ate with the family. Grace Tully, Missy's assistant, lived nearby, but often stayed for dinner, particularly when there was more work to do afterward. Other colleagues lived in New York City, and came up to Albany two or three days a week. These included Sam Rosenman, FDR's speechwriter; Malvina ("Tommy") Thompson, Eleanor's secretary; and Louis Howe, who had his own room in the executive mansion.

It was understood in the governor's mansion that dinner was a time for relaxation. The conversation was often about politics, but there was an unspoken rule not to talk "business." After dinner, FDR went back to work—talking to advisers, reading reports, editing speeches, or catching up on correspondence with Missy.

There was a constant stream of visitors—dignitaries and political leaders from all over the country. The mansion's nine guest rooms were frequently full. When FDR had a visitor he wanted to talk to, they retired to his study after dinner. Once the coffee cups were cleared away, FDR would turn serious. Sam Rosenman would observe him plying the visitor with questions, taking in vast quantities of information, remembering the important details. The talk generally went on until around midnight. Finally, FDR would ring for McDuffie. "I'm sorry," he would tell his guests. "I have to run now!"

FDR knew the importance of relaxation. Some evenings they would rig up a screen and watch a film. (Talking pictures, or "talkies," had just come into being.) On weekends, the Roosevelts usually decamped to Hyde Park, where their life continued much the same, in the middle of family, colleagues, guests, and dogs. Wherever they were, Franklin and his team worked for part of each day. "Albany was the hardest work I ever did," Missy said later, from the White House.

On Sunday evenings, Eleanor took the train to Grand Central, preparing her classes as she went. She arrived at East Sixty-fifth Street around midnight, soon after Louis Howe, who had spent the weekend with his family in Poughkeepsie. Eleanor's first class was on Monday at 9 a.m.

She often thought of Marie Souvestre, her old headmistress, who had managed to get her aristocratic protégées to question their most entrenched values. Todhunter School, like Allenswood, catered to girls from privileged families, girls just like Eleanor had once been, girls whose parents were invariably Republican voters. As Eleanor saw it, her challenge was to pry off her students' blinkers, widen their horizons, and encourage them to think for themselves. She had them analyzing newspaper articles and discussing social issues; she organized excursions to museums, the courthouse, and tenement buildings; she even invited the older girls to stay in the governor's mansion. The girls worshipped her.

At lunchtime, when her classes were over, Eleanor hurried to her small office at Democratic state headquarters. Her name had been taken off the masthead of *Women's Democratic News*—the official editor was now Caroline O'Day—but Eleanor continued to do most of the work. Behind the scenes, she was doing more than anyone else to build up the women's vote in upstate New York. In June 1930, Louis Howe sent FDR a clipping from the Hearst paper, the *New York Evening Journal*, with the heading: "Women to Begin Roosevelt Fight for Re-Election." The article stated: "Mrs. Caroline O'Day of Westchester, head of the women's division of Democratic State Committee, will rouse her group to concentrate on a campaign this Fall with the object of bringing about the most decisive defeat the Republicans have suffered."

On Wednesday at noon, as soon as her classes ended, Eleanor returned to Albany, arriving in time to host afternoon tea at four thirty, in the family sitting room. Anyone connected with the mansion was welcome to drift in—secretaries, bodyguards, friends, and guests.

From Wednesday afternoon till Sunday evening, Eleanor managed the governor's mansion, supervised seventeen servants, planned menus, attended functions and political gatherings, presided over dinners and receptions, wrote magazine articles, gave talks, and maintained a vast correspondence. A *New Yorker* journalist wrote admiringly: "No woman has a better grasp of the intricacies of state business."

In November 1930, FDR was reelected governor of New York with the largest majority in history. It made him a leading contender for the presidency in 1932. FDR firmly denied having any such aspirations. ("I have my hands full with the job of being Governor of the State of New York with its twelve million people and its many problems.") But Louis Howe went into top gear. He set up his headquarters at 331 Madison Avenue, across the street from the Democratic headquarters at the Biltmore Hotel. For the time being he could not be open about what he was doing. He called his organization Friends of Roosevelt.

Howe put out pamphlets boasting about FDR's achievements, and signed up a friend, Ernest Lindley, chancellor of the University of Kansas, to write FDR's biography. *Franklin D. Roosevelt: A Career in Progressive Democracy* was pure propaganda, but though Lindley stretched the truth, he took care not to actually lie. He made much of FDR's vigor:

> Roosevelt is recognized in Albany as . . . one of the hardest workers who has ever been Governor . . . The explanation of Roosevelt's vigor, of course, must lie in the extraordinary vitality and physique with which he was endowed, his athletic youth, and the good condition in which he keeps himself . . . At times, one is inclined to think that his handicap is really a great asset. Undoubtedly it conserves his energy for effective work.

Howe was FDR's chief campaign strategist, the only colleague who called him Franklin, and the only one able to get through to the Boss at any time of the day. When Howe called Albany, Missy put him straight through. Howe's staff could not believe the sort of things he sometimes yelled down the phone to the Boss. "Franklin, you damned fool! You can't do that. You simply can't do it, I tell you!" On one memorable occasion, there was silence—or rather, congested breathing—from Howe while FDR, at the other end of the phone, argued his case. "All right, all right, pighead," Howe shouted. "Go ahead and be a damned fool, if you insist. But don't say I didn't warn you. What's that? what's that? You're going for a swim? Well, go ahead, dammit, and I hope to God you drown!"

In Albany there was plenty of talk about the goings-on in the governor's mansion. No one quite knew what to think. At the beginning of FDR's second term, Sam Rosenman and his wife moved into the mansion; FDR wanted Sam close at hand. "Dorothy and I knew the gossip about Missy and FDR and tried to figure out what that relationship was," Rosenman told a biographer years later. The Rosenmans remained as mystified as everyone else.

Agnes Leach, the head of the League of Women Voters and a friend of Eleanor's, visited the mansion one Sunday and was puzzled by Missy's status in the family circle. Franklin proposed that they all motor down to Hyde Park for lunch. Eleanor told Agnes that Franklin would not be driving with them. "He has this new car and he wants to show it off to Missy." Afterward, Agnes asked Elinor Morgenthau, one of Eleanor's closest friends, whether Missy was Franklin's mistress. "Oh no," Elinor insisted. "He loves Missy. She's quite essential to him . . . But as to an affair—no."

By accepting Missy into the household as if it went without saying, Eleanor provided a cover. Her friends, just like Franklin's, knew not to add fuel to the endless gossip. Meanwhile, Eleanor's relationship with her bodyguard was also causing tongues to wag. Their frequent trips alone and the air of warm familiarity between them did not go unnoticed.

The rumors were slightly deflected when Missy and Earl got together in FDR's second term. This romance was almost inevitable. Earl and Missy were almost the same age (Earl was a year older), and they saw a great deal of each other. Both were part of the family group at dinners, picnics, and on special occasions. They shared the same fierce commitment to the Roosevelts—to the point that their love affair had a slightly incestuous edge to it.

The romance came to an end in May 1932, when thirty-five-year-old Miller became engaged to seventeen-year-old Ruth Bellinger. It is significant that Franklin and Eleanor heard the news before Missy did. They worried that she would fall into a heap. "Glad Earl told Missy," Eleanor wrote to Franklin a few days later. "I was sure she would rather know from him." Missy apparently spent several days in bed, weeping.

At the age of seventy, Earl Miller made out to biographer Joseph Lash that he squired Missy in order to stem the gossip about him and Eleanor. According to Miller, he was not successful, and so he went a step further. "That's why I got married in 1932 with plenty of publicity. I got married with someone I wasn't in love with."

Earl's marriage to Ruth Bellinger took place at Val-Kill Cottage in early September 1932. Elliott was the best man; Anna was the bridesmaid. Eleanor hosted the occasion; Franklin took time out from his busy schedule to attend. As a wedding present, Franklin and Eleanor gave Earl Miller a piece of land at Hyde Park.

•

President Hoover was now vastly unpopular. The Great Depression was worsening by the day. The newspapers were full of stories of bank failures, runs on banks, foreclosures. Farmers were hard hit. Severe drought combined with decades of bad farming practices had turned the panhandles of Texas and Oklahoma into a dust bowl. There was serious malnourishment in the mining areas of West Virginia and Kentucky. In the cities, the destitute gathered in cardboard and tin shanty towns, known derisively as "Hoovervilles."

For FDR, with his presidential aspirations, the biggest fight was going to be inside the Democratic Party. Each state seemed to have its own "favorite son." Al Smith was standing for a third time, with surprisingly strong support from the party machine.

In March 1932, FDR organized the Brains Trust, comprised of university professors, lawyers, and financiers—men on the left and right—who regularly came to the governor's mansion in Albany for discussions. The chief brain, Raymond Moley, professor of political science at Barnard, wrote the famous "forgotten man" speech that FDR delivered over the airwaves in April.

It was Eleanor who suggested that they bring James Farley on board Franklin's campaign team. As chairman of the New York State Democratic Committee, Farley had proved himself a master organizer, with a talent for getting on with people from all walks of life. FDR made him his campaign manager. Howe was the "inside man"; "Big Jim" was the "drummer," who dashed around the country drumming up support for the Roosevelt candidacy. Both were working eighteen or nineteen hours a day.

The Democratic National Convention was held in Chicago, at the end of June 1932. Louis Howe and Jim Farley went there well ahead of time, set up their headquarters in the Congress Hotel, where the convention was to take place, and jostled day and night to win delegates for FDR.

Chicago was blisteringly hot that summer. The convention hall was stifling; the infighting was bitter. Farley had handed out fans with FDR's picture on them, which even the Stop Roosevelt delegates were waving, in a desperate attempt to cool themselves. While Farley tried to rally votes in the hall below, Howe lay in room 1702 in front of two electric fans, struggling for air, coughing, strategizing, maneuvering, and rasping into the phone.

On nomination night, the nominating and seconding speeches went on until 3 a.m. FDR was well ahead, but no candidate got the required two-thirds vote. FDR was one hundred votes short of the number necessary for nomination.

Sam Rosenman recalled the scene at 3 a.m. in the governor's mansion:

> The Governor, his wife, his mother and I sat listening to the radio. He was in his shirt sleeves, silent, puffing on one cigarette after another. The phone was at his side, and he used it frequently . . . I have a keen recollection of Elliott, his son, leaning back in a chair with his ear next to the radio—sound asleep. My wife was sitting on the floor, dozing against my chair. Missy and Grace [Tully] were both asleep on couches. Out in the garage in the back yard the press associations had set up their wires and typewriters . . . Every once in a while the kitchen of the Executive Mansion would send them pots of steaming coffee to keep them awake, and Mrs. Eleanor Roosevelt made some scrambled eggs to go with their coffee.

Throughout the next day, the convention remained deadlocked. Howe and Farley were frantically working on the Texas delegation, whose forty-six members had voted for John Garner. If Garner would only give up a hopeless fight and release his votes to FDR, they were "in."

Louis Howe's raspy breathing filled room 1702. His secretaries were sure that he was dying. Jim Farley snapped at them: "Of course he'll last . . . You know he's not going to die until he sees Roosevelt nominated. He's one of the gamest little guys that ever lived."

In Albany, FDR and Rosenman were working on FDR's acceptance speech. "I hope we get a chance to use it," Rosenman said. "We will," said FDR.

That evening, the Roosevelt clan had just finished dinner when the phone rang. It was Louis Howe, wheezing down the line. FDR listened, smiled, and put down the phone. He refused to say what was happening. "Effdee, you look just like the cat that swallowed the canary," Missy said. An hour later, the news came through officially. The Texas and California delegates—ninety of them altogether—had switched their votes from John Garner to Roosevelt. FDR had won the nomination.

Tradition had it that the presidential candidate waited for as long as six weeks to give his acceptance speech. FDR had a different plan. He knew the importance of symbolism. The American people desperately wanted a bold, decisive leader. FDR had decided to arrive at the convention the next day, by plane, to accept his nomination.

Never before had a political candidate made a campaign trip by airplane. It was only five years since Charles Lindbergh had made the first flight across the Atlantic—from New York to Paris, in thirty-three hours. Airplanes were still considered risky and dangerous, only for the intrepid.

The next morning at dawn, a convoy of limousines left the governor's mansion for the little airport in Albany. A small three-engine Ford plane was waiting on the runway. Earl Miller and Gus Gennerich carried the governor inside the machine. Eleanor, Elliott, John, Missy, Grace Tully, and Sam Rosenman clambered in after them.

They flew into strong headwinds. Grace Tully worried that she had not made out a will. While his co-passengers turned green and reached for their airsickness bags, FDR quietly polished his acceptance speech. The flight took nine hours, with stops in Buffalo and Cleveland to refuel. They arrived in Chicago two hours behind schedule. On the tarmac in Chicago, a small figure in a straw boater stepped forward to greet the Roosevelts as they came nonchalantly down the ramp. It was Louis Howe, miraculously recovered.

"I regret that I am late," FDR told the crowd at Convention Hall, "but I have no control over the winds of Heaven and could only be thankful for my Navy training . . . You have nominated me for President and I know it, and I am here to thank you for the honor. Let it also be symbolic that in so doing I broke traditions." In former times Theodore Roosevelt had promised a "square deal" for every American. FDR finished his speech with the words: "I pledge you, I pledge myself, to a new deal for the American people." There was thunderous applause. The band struck up "Happy Days Are Here Again."

The following day, a newspaper cartoon showed a ragged farmer leaning on his hoe, looking up at an airplane with astonishment. On its wings were written, in big bold letters, NEW DEAL.

FDR's presidential campaign was now official. Louis Howe managed a vast staff of campaign workers, set up on the first and fourth floor of the Biltmore Hotel. He preferred to work from his small office across the street, on Madison Avenue, away from the hubbub.

Eleanor was busy in the Women's Division, which had been expanded into a major unit of the Democratic campaign. She and her colleagues—particularly Caroline O'Day and Molly Dewson—had organized a coast-to-coast program in which volunteers—the "grass trampers"—went from house to house, canvassing the female vote.

In October, Eleanor joined the *Roosevelt Special*, the six-car campaign train, in Arizona. As the train traveled through Colorado, Kansas, Nebraska, and Iowa, the signs of the Great Depression were everywhere. From the back of his train, on the arm of his son James, FDR gave speech after speech, promising bold action.

Among the reporters in the front cars of the train, Lorena Hickok, from the Associated Press, was profiling the presidential candidate's wife. Eleanor sometimes invited her onto the train for breakfast or a cup of tea. Louis Howe held "Hick" in high esteem: her articles were well written and firmly pro-Roosevelt. Eleanor liked this short, plump woman from South Dakota, who strode around like a hard-boiled newspaper man and smoked like a chimney, and whose deep sympathy for working people was quite evident when she talked.

Near the end of the campaign, Missy LeHand's mother died in Potsdam, New York, a small town near the Canadian border. Eleanor took time out to accompany Missy to the funeral. She sent a message to Miss Hickok. Would she care to come along, too?

Hickok recalled:

> I did not go to the funeral, but spent the time walking about the town . . . Later Mrs. Roosevelt looked me up at the restaurant where I was having lunch. She had borrowed an automobile and asked if I'd like to go for a drive . . .
>
> We drove along the St. Lawrence River, and she showed me where her husband hoped that some day a power project and a canal, connecting the Atlantic Ocean and the Great Lakes, would be built.
>
> "I don't see so many Democratic posters around," she observed as we drove back through the town. She looked thoughtful and a little sad.
>
> "Franklin is going to be dreadfully disappointed if he loses this election," she said. "For a while he won't know what to do with himself."

We dined with some of her friends that night. And when we boarded our train, the only space available was one drawing room . . . To my embarrassment, Mrs. Roosevelt insisted on giving me the lower birth and taking for herself the long, narrow couch on the other side of the drawing room.

"I'm longer than you are," she said when I protested. "And," she added with a smile, "not quite so broad!"

It was early, neither of us was sleepy, and so we started talking . . .

"May I write some of that?" I asked her fearfully before we finally said goodnight.

"If you like," she said softly. "I trust you."

It was on that trip to Potsdam that the two women became close friends.

Election Day was November 8, 1932. FDR and Eleanor gave a buffet supper at East Sixty-fifth Street for family, close friends, and a handful of reporters. When Lorena Hickok arrived, Eleanor opened the door herself and kissed her friend. "It's good to have you around tonight, Hick." Eleanor, who always looked at her best in evening dress, was wearing a white chiffon gown with a short train. Hickok thought she looked like a queen.

After dinner, the party moved to the Democratic National Committee headquarters at the Biltmore. In a large room on the first floor, FDR and Jim Farley took their seats at a long table rigged up with telephones, score sheets, and a dozen female telephone operators, who were answering calls from Democratic leaders throughout the country. Howe insisted on remaining holed up in his office across the street. Eleanor circulated between the state committee, the national committee, and the ballroom downstairs, where she greeted hundreds of campaign workers, who were growing more noisy as victory appeared certain.

The voter turnout was the biggest in American history. FDR carried 42 of the 48 states, with 472 electoral votes to Hoover's 59. Shortly before midnight, Herbert Hoover conceded defeat. Twelve years of Republican rule in Washington had come to an end.

A beaming FDR came down to the Biltmore's ballroom. Louis Howe had finally appeared. "I want to say just a word," FDR told his supporters. "There are two people in the United States more than anybody else who are responsible for this great victory. One is my old friend and associate, Colonel Louis McHenry Howe, and the other is that splendid American, Jim Farley."

The reporters crowded around the future first lady. Was she pleased? "Of course I'm pleased," Eleanor said. "You're always pleased to have someone you're very devoted to have what he wants." She paused. "It's an extremely serious thing to undertake, you know, the guidance of a nation at a time like this."

There were four months between the election and the inauguration. The Twentieth Amendment, which reduced the hiatus to two months, would not take effect until 1937. It was a busy, exhilarating, anxious time for the Roosevelts. The governor's mansion and the house at East Sixty-fifth Street looked like Grand Central, with the suitcases and packing boxes, friends and relatives calling in, and FDR's advisers coming and going.

Throughout the lame-duck period, President Hoover, convinced that Roosevelt's socialist experiments were going to destroy the country, tried to bully the president-elect into supporting his plans for rescuing the economy. FDR stood firm. Hoover repeatedly warned that FDR was about to turn the United States into a Bolshevik outpost.

The press, likewise, did its best to seed doubts about the country's new president. How was this wealthy aristocrat going to get the country out of its mess? It did not help FDR's reputation when he left on a Caribbean cruise, with Harvard companions, on Vincent Astor's luxury yacht.

On January 30, 1933, FDR celebrated his fifty-first birthday in Warm Springs with Eleanor and friends, then went down to Florida for a two-week fishing trip in the Bahamas. "When we land on the 15th I shall be full of health and vigor—the last holiday for many months," he wrote his mother from Vincent Astor's yacht. The press snidely remarked that FDR seemed to have no trouble putting "the forgotten man" out of his mind.

On February 15, FDR and his party docked in Miami, and FDR hurried to Bayfront Park, where he was to make an appearance at an evening rally. Among the notables present was the mayor of Chicago,

Secretly engaged, Campobello, summer 1904 (Franklin D. Roosevelt Presidential Library)

Eleanor in wedding dress. Studio portrait taken January 20, 1905 (Franklin D. Roosevelt Presidential Library)

ABOVE: The young married couple at Hyde Park:
Eleanor with his glass, Franklin with her knitting
(Franklin D. Roosevelt Presidential Library)

LEFT: Honeymoon, Scotland, summer 1905: one
of the rare shots in which Eleanor is seen smoking
(Franklin D. Roosevelt Presidential Library)

Campobello picnic, 1910 (From Laura Delano's scrapbook; Franklin D. Roosevelt Presidential Library)

Family group, Campobello, summer 1920, soon after Eleanor's discovery of Franklin's romance with Lucy Mercer. Back row (left to right): Franklin, Sara, Eleanor. Front row: Elliott, Franklin Jr., John, Anna, James; with Chief, Anna's dog (Franklin D. Roosevelt Presidential Library)

The swimming pool at Val-Kill: Franklin, Missy LeHand, and Eleanor (Franklin D. Roosevelt Presidential Library)

Peggy Levenson (Marion's sister), Nancy Cook, Eleanor, and Marion Dickerman, July 1926 (Dickerman collection; Franklin D. Roosevelt Presidential Library)

Franklin beside the pool at Warm Springs, October 1924. Cleburne
Gregory's article proclaimed: "Franklin D. Roosevelt . . . is literally
swimming himself back to health and strength at Warm Springs,
Georgia." (Franklin D. Roosevelt Presidential Library)

Missy LeHand at Dowdell's Knob, Franklin's
favorite picnic area at Warm Springs, circa
1928 (Roosevelt Warm Springs Institute for Rehabilitation Archive)

Whistle-stop on the 1932 presidential
campaign. Earl Miller, bodyguard, in
background (Franklin D. Roosevelt Presidential Library)

Louis Howe, June 29, 1932, at work on the presidential campaign (Associated Press; Franklin D. Roosevelt Presidential Library)

Aboard the *Amberjack II*, off Maine, before Franklin sailed to Campobello, June 1933. Back row (left to right): Frances Kellor, Mary Dreier, Marion Dickerman, Antonia Hatvary. Middle row: Nancy Cook, Franklin Jr., John Roosevelt. Front row: Eleanor, Franklin, James Roosevelt (Franklin D. Roosevelt Presidential Library)

Lorena Hickok and Earl Miller, in a photograph taken by Eleanor. Handwritten on back of photo: "Trip to New York–Canada with ER, July 1933."

(From Lorena Hickok album; Franklin D. Roosevelt Presidential Library)

The first couple: Eleanor and Franklin on south lawn at Hyde Park, August 4, 1933 (Wide World; Franklin D. Roosevelt Presidential Library)

On the front porch of Hyde Park, election night, 1940. Franklin on the arm of Franklin Jr., with John, Mama, Eleanor, and the sons' wives, Ethel Dupont and Anne Lindsay Clark (Franklin D. Roosevelt Presidential Library)

Eleanor with Earl Miller, Miami Beach, Florida, 1940 (Franklin D. Roosevelt Presidential Library)

Margaret Suckley in front of the FDR Library, Hyde Park, June 25, 1945 (Wilderstein Preservation)

Lucy Mercer Rutherfurd by Nicholas Robbins, Elizabeth Shoumatoff's photographer, Warm Springs, April 11, 1945 (Franklin D. Roosevelt Presidential Library)

Anton Cermak, a Democrat, who was eager to talk to the president-elect. Roosevelt, tanned and cheerful, had just finished giving a short impromptu talk from the back of his car ("I have had a very wonderful twelve days fishing in these Florida and Bahama waters") and Cermak had come forward to shake his hand, when shots rang out. A bullet hit FDR's car. Cermak crumpled to the ground. Gus Gennerich, FDR's stocky bodyguard, pushed FDR down on the seat and sat on him.

The chauffeur started the car, anxious to clear the crowd fast. FDR ordered that Cermak be lifted into the backseat with him. All the way to the hospital, he held the bleeding man, talking to him. FDR and his party waited in a back room while Cermak was on the operating table.

In New York, when the news came down the wire, Lorena Hickok rushed to East Sixty-fifth Street. She found Eleanor in Franklin's bedroom, looking pale. Louis was standing at Franklin's desk, trying in vain to get through to Miami. He kept jiggling the receiver and yelling, "Operator!" No sooner had he banged down the receiver, in frustration, than the phone rang. It was Franklin. Tony Cermak was in critical condition, he said. Three others had been injured. Franklin had not even been grazed by the bullets. His ribs felt a little sore, he said. Gus Gennerich was no lightweight.

Eleanor replaced the receiver. "That drive to the hospital must have been awfully hard on Franklin," she said. "He hates the sight of blood."

By midnight it was confirmed that the gunman, Giuseppe Zangara, a deranged Italian anarchist, had been aiming at the president-elect. In Florida, while FDR's companions were a bundle of nerves, FDR remained calm. Ray Moley reported later: "There was nothing—not so much as the twitching of a muscle, the mopping of a brow, or even the hint of a false gaiety. I have never in my life seen anything more magnificent." In the American press, the assassination attempt restored FDR's reputation as a hero.

The next day, reporters crowded around Eleanor to ask about her reaction. "That's apt to happen to any man in public life. He must always face the possibility, and so must his family," she said quietly. "One cannot live in fear."

Eleanor, as she prepared for her new role as first lady, was determined to be equally fearless about the way she lived her own life. She admired strong, independent professional women who made their mark in a man's world. Her closest friend was now Lorena Hickok, who, at the age of thirty-nine, was the nation's foremost female political journalist. Hick was a stimulating companion, committed to radical politics. It was her view that Americans were in trouble, and they needed a first lady who made use of her position to speak out.

Since the election, their friendship had blossomed into passion. The two women had seen each other almost every day. They traveled up to Albany together. When Eleanor went to look over the White House, they traveled down to Washington together. They went to concerts, operas, and plays. After the theater, they sometimes ate in Hick's one-bedroom midtown apartment. Hick was invariably at East Sixty-fifth Street for the casual family suppers on Sunday nights, when the Roosevelts ate scrambled eggs and sausages. Hick was present the day Eleanor had Mama and Mama's elder sister, Aunt Kassie, to lunch. When FDR was cruising in the Caribbean, Hick spent most nights at East Sixty-fifth Street. In early March, Hick traveled down to Washington with the future first family.

The evening before the inauguration, FDR and Eleanor were in their adjacent suites on the seventh floor of the Mayflower Hotel, in Washington. FDR's suite was a hive of activity. While FDR was polishing his inaugural address, President Hoover phoned twice (the last time was at 1 a.m.), still trying, even at this final hour, to get FDR to sign a presidential order controlling gold shipments.

That night, Hickok and Eleanor dined alone. Shortly after midnight, FDR sent Eleanor his speech to look over. She read it aloud to Hick. They approved of his fighting words. Around 2 a.m., James came in, sank into an armchair, and said, "They've all left. Pa's going to bed." Eleanor went to say good night to Franklin.

In her memoir, *Reluctant First Lady*, Hickok would muse that she could have slipped out at any point that evening and phoned the Associated Press. "There I was, a newspaper reporter, right in the middle of what, that night, was the biggest story in the world. And I did nothing about it." Hickok was already realizing that her closeness to the future first lady seriously jeopardized her professional career. Later she would discuss the problem with Louis Howe. "A reporter," Howe commented dryly, "should never get too close to the news source."

That night at the Mayflower Hotel, Hickok was, indeed, in the middle of "the biggest story in the world." Everyone in the political press corps knew that Lorena Hickok was a lesbian. By now most of the reporters had figured out that she was passionately in love with Eleanor, and that her feelings appeared to be reciprocated.

"And so you think they gossip about us," Eleanor would write to Hick a few months later. "I am always so much more optimistic than you are. I suppose because I care so little about what 'they' say!"

SEVEN

Grand Hotel

March 1933–November 1936

Inauguration Day—Saturday, March 4, 1933—was cold and gray, with a raw wind blasting through the streets of Washington. The crowds in front of the Capitol stomped their feet, turned up their collars, wrapped their scarves tighter. In the four months since the election of Franklin Delano Roosevelt as their new Democratic president, Americans had seen darker days than anyone could have imagined. The Great Depression had reached its lowest point. Unemployment stood officially at one-fourth of the workforce; the real figure was more like a third. Thousands of banks had failed, with people losing their entire savings. In the last few weeks, "bank runs"—panic-stricken depositors demanding their money—had reached epidemic proportions. No Western industrialized nation was worse affected than the United States. The country was a sinking ship.

Just after 10 a.m., FDR and Eleanor left the Mayflower Hotel with their eldest son, James, and his wife, Betsey, and drove the few blocks to St. John's Episcopal Church, just across Lafayette Square from the White House. Reverend Endicott Peabody, rector of Groton School, who twenty-eight years earlier had officiated at Franklin and Eleanor's wedding, prayed: "O Lord . . . most humbly we beseech Thee . . . to behold and bless Thy servant, Franklin, chosen to be President of the United States." Peabody, as the Roosevelts were well aware, had voted for Hoover. They were used to that. Most people in their own social class were frantically worried that FDR was about to turn the country socialist.

At 11 a.m., amid a roar of Secret Service motorcycles, two open cars made their way from the White House, up Pennsylvania Avenue, to the Capitol. In the first car, FDR waved his top hat at the crowds, smiled, and tried vainly to make conversation with Hoover, who sat in gloomy silence, refusing to say a word. In the second car, Eleanor had a somewhat easier time of it with Mrs. Hoover.

Just before noon, the Roosevelts appeared at the East Portico of the Capitol. FDR, on James's arm, advanced slowly, stiffly, down the carpeted ramp, to the inaugural platform. The throng on the Mall watched in silence.

Eleanor stood beside FDR while he was sworn in. "Her pale face and austere demeanor bore testimony to the solemnity with which she views Mr. Roosevelt's new position," Emma Bugbee reported in the *New York Herald Tribune*. "Many friends watched for an opportunity to wave to her, and strangers trained cameras upon her, but not once did she lift her eyes to the crowd or wave her hand or smile."

The new president moved to the rostrum. Above the battery of microphones, which would broadcast his speech to the nation, he looked out at the anxious throng. He did not smile, but he tossed back his head, and his clear voice rang out confidently: "This great nation will endure as it has endured, will revive and will prosper. So, first of all, let me assert my firm belief that the only thing we have to fear is fear itself." FDR knew better than most people the paralyzing effect of terror.

"The money changers have fled from their high seats in the temple of our civilization," FDR declared. "We may now restore that temple to the ancient truths." The biblical allusion was clear. It was Jesus who, in his sole recorded act of violence, had gone to Jerusalem, entered the temple of God, and overturned the tables of the money changers, accusing them of making a house of prayer into a den of robbers.

FDR announced that he would bring in "strict supervision of all banking and credits and investments," and end "speculation with other people's money." His government would generate public projects and put people to work. He would need the people's help: "We now realize as we never realized before our interdependence on each other; we cannot merely take but must give as well." At home, as well as in international relations, FDR proposed "the policy of the good neighbor—the neighbor who resolutely respects himself and . . . respects the rights of others."

He promised bold and immediate action. But he would need the co-operation of Congress. If this were not forthcoming, FDR would not evade "the clear course of duty." "I shall ask the Congress for the one remaining instrument to meet the crisis—broad Executive power to wage a war against the emergency, as great as the power that would be given me if we were in fact invaded by a foreign foe." The people cheered.

When FDR finished speaking, his face, solemn till then, burst into a radiant smile. The people went wild. "He's taken the ship of state and turned it right around," FDR's Brains Trust colleague, Raymond Moley, remarked.

"It was . . . a little terrifying," Eleanor said afterward. "The crowds were so tremendous, and you felt that they would do *anything*—if only someone would tell them *what* to do."

A buffet lunch in the Roosevelts' new home, 1600 Pennsylvania Avenue, was followed by hours in the reviewing stand watching the inaugural parade, then tea for three thousand guests in the East Room, the largest room in the White House. FDR briefly joined Eleanor in the receiving line, then went upstairs to the Oval Room, and swore in his cabinet. It was the first time a president had done this on inauguration day, and the first time a woman—Frances Perkins, secretary of labor—was included in the cabinet. After this "little family party," as he called it, FDR made his way to the Red Room, where he chatted with some thirty friends from Warm Springs, who sat around the fire in wheelchairs. At eight there was dinner in the State Dining Room for seventy-five members of the Roosevelt clan—nearly all of whom were ardent Republicans.

After dinner, FDR went back upstairs and spent an hour in the Lincoln Room, Louis Howe's new headquarters, having a quiet talk with his friend. Eleanor, who was wearing a silver-blue gown under her fur evening coat, slipped out into the cold Washington night. She would be the only first lady in American history to attend the inaugural ball without her husband.

In *This I Remember*, the second volume of her autobiography, Eleanor Roosevelt described herself as being "deeply troubled" by the prospect of becoming first lady. "As I saw it," she writes, "this meant the end of any personal life of my own." Lorena Hickok's biographical memoir, *Eleanor Roosevelt: Reluctant First Lady*, strongly reinforced this story. Hickok's book opens with her and Eleanor Roosevelt on a train, traveling from New York back to Albany in November 1932:

> "If I wanted to be selfish, I could wish Franklin had not been elected."
> Mrs. Franklin D. Roosevelt, wife of the newly elected President of the United States, gazed out the train window at the Hudson River, gray and misty under slanting sheets of rain. Her expression was wistful—and a little guilty . . .
> "I never wanted it," she said, "even though some people have said that my ambition for myself drove him on. They've even said that I had some such idea in the back of my mind when I married him. I never wanted to be a President's wife, and I don't want it now."
> She glanced at me with a slight smile.
> "You don't quite believe me, do you?" she asked . . .
> She was mistaken. I did believe her.

Hickok should have known better. Most of Eleanor's family and close friends knew not to take her outbursts too seriously. "*If* I wanted to be selfish," Eleanor had said. But Eleanor had never wanted to be selfish. She had always done—and would always do—everything in her power to help Franklin fulfill his political dreams. During the 1936 presidential campaign she would tell Hick, "I am doing all I can do without being accused of trying to run F.D.R."

It's absurd, this myth—perpetrated by Eleanor and credulously swallowed ever since—that Eleanor Roosevelt was a "reluctant first lady." Nothing could be further from the truth. Eleanor was immensely proud of the Roosevelt tradition of "public service." She believed in personal sacrifice for the public good. Moreover, she had never enjoyed a "personal life," as most of us know it. It was rare that she went anywhere on her own. She was sixteen when her uncle Ted became president of the United States. As a twenty-year-old bride given away by the president, she made national headlines. Ever since 1911, when FDR became a state senator, Eleanor had been in the public eye as a political wife. And the governor's mansion was scarcely a life of obscurity.

Eleanor's autobiography was in every way a political document. There was no way that she could have told the truth about certain things. FDR went through the first volume—the aptly named *This Is My Story*—with a blue pencil. Her narrative might have come across as beguilingly honest, but it is full of omissions and factual errors. So is the second volume, *This I Remember*, which she wrote after FDR's death.

Eleanor's writing was partly a response to the criticism that came her way. No sooner was FDR nominated than the press came out with cruel caricatures: Eleanor was hell-bent on the White House since the day she married; Eleanor had a "ruthless craving for personal publicity"; Eleanor "wore the pants"; FDR was a victim of "petticoat rule."

Eleanor trained herself to be impervious to it all. She had more important things to worry about. But like all independent-minded first ladies, she felt obliged to deny any personal ambition, deny ever influencing her husband, and deny having any real interest in politics herself. In her three-volume autobiography, she portrayed herself as the ultimate dutiful wife. She *was*. But not in either of the first two volumes did she admit that she actually enjoyed public life. In the third volume, *On My Own* (1958), she no longer had to hide the central fact of her life. Nothing gave her a greater sense of personal fulfillment than the political arena.

It was Lorena Hickok, not Eleanor, who was "reluctant" to see Eleanor become first lady. Hick was smitten and wanted time alone with Eleanor. From now on they would be living in different cities. Eleanor would be constantly busy, surrounded by people, followed by Secret Service and reporters, always in the limelight. Never again would they be able to do things together in relative anonymity. Hick was dreading it.

Between the inauguration ceremony and the public luncheon, Hick had scooped the first official interview with the first lady. Eleanor had been so besieged by people asking her things that the two women had retreated to Eleanor's bathroom for privacy. Eleanor had nothing new to say. Hick was finding it increasingly awkward to write about a first lady who was also her closest friend.

Early on Sunday evening, the day after the inauguration, Hick left the White House to return to New York. Around midnight, Eleanor sat at her desk: "Hick my dearest, I cannot go to bed tonight without a word to you. I felt a little as though a part of me was leaving tonight, you have grown so much to be a part of my life that it is empty without you even though I'm busy every minute."

On Monday night, Hick phoned from New York. A few hours later, Eleanor sat in bed writing: "Hick darling, Oh! how good it was to hear your voice . . . Jimmy was near & I couldn't say 'je t'aime et je t'adore' as I longed to do but always remember I am saying it & that I go to sleep thinking of you."

That had been their good-night ritual to each other over the last four months, when Hick had stayed at East Sixty-fifth Street. Now they had to be content with daily phone calls or letters. After Eleanor became first lady, Hick recorded their time together on a pocket calendar, circling the days they spent together and putting a cross through the days they spent apart. Eleanor had filled the wall in front of her sitting-room desk with photos of family and friends. "I can't kiss you," she wrote Hick, "so I kiss your *picture* good night and good morning!"

Hick had said she would like to write Eleanor's biography one day. Eleanor thought it a good idea; it might make Hick some money. With this in mind they agreed that Eleanor should include in her letters a daily "diary." Eleanor took pleasure in this.

By Monday, March 7, two days after the inauguration, the new first lady had launched cheerfully into her new life:

Well here goes for the diary (let me know when you get bored!) Breakfast downstairs Nan [Cook] and I, joined very late by James. Then E.R. interviews Mrs. Nesbitt [housekeeper] & begins at the top of the house, meets all the domestics & talks over work, then with Tommy [secretary] to meet secretarial force & 11:30 received [delegation of] Sioux Indians, at 11:45 the executive secretary of the "Girl Scouts" . . . Then lunch & tour the White House, then take Mama to the train & had tea & took a party to the concert. There I thought only of you & wanted you even more than I do as a rule. Home at seven & Tommy & I worked till 11:15 . . . Louis moved in & Mary Howe [Louis's daughter] came to stay today— Missy moves in tomorrow.

Hick was lonely and miserable. The jealous scenes began early on. "Oh, I'm bad, my dear, but I love you so," she apologized, after yet another tantrum. "At times life becomes just one long, dreary ache for you." In later life she would destroy their early letters, the most passionate. But the surviving correspondence gives glimpses of a sensuous physical relationship. "I've been trying today to bring back your face," she wrote to Eleanor. "Most clearly I remember your eyes, with a kind of teasing smile in them, and the feeling of that soft spot just northeast of the corner of your mouth against my lips."

For a long time Eleanor had been on the edge of the lesbian world, looking in. The woman who had been her teacher and mentor, Marie Souvestre, had been a lesbian. For the past ten years, Eleanor's closest friends—Nancy Cook and Marion Dickerman; Elizabeth Read and Esther Lape—were lesbian couples. Her activist friends, Molly Dewson and Mary Dreier, also had female partners. Even the secretary of labor, Frances Perkins (who was married to an invalid husband), had an intimate relationship with a female companion, which she kept extremely private. The women who had done most to encourage Eleanor to become more independent and politically active were lesbians.

Now Eleanor herself had fallen in love with a woman. For her, this was liberating, exhilarating, and decidedly rebellious. She could scarcely have taken a more radical step in the weeks surrounding Franklin's election as president. Furthermore, Lorena Hickok was no Marie Souvestre, who had shone in aristocratic circles with her beauty, elegant grace, and charm. Lorena Hickok liked to boast that she was a hick from the sticks, who made no compromises whatsoever.

From the beginning, their relationship was doomed. For Hick, lesbianism was her sole sexual identity, and she was besotted by Eleanor. For her part, Eleanor already had a husband whom she loved; she was about to lead a highly public life as first lady; and even now, when she was in love with Hick, she still saw herself primarily as a man's woman. Eleanor was prepared to commit herself to Hick, but Hick would have to share her with others. Hick would have to understand that.

For FDR, Sunday, March 5, the day after the inauguration, was a working day. That afternoon, he convened his cabinet to discuss emergency banking measures. In the evening he declared a four-day national bank holiday. It was close to midnight when his colleagues dispersed, "dog tired."

Monday and Tuesday were long days, when FDR and his associates discussed the details of the banking rescue package. On Wednesday, at

10 a.m., FDR gave his first press conference. The former president, Hoover, had met with reporters in the formal East Room, and made them write down their questions beforehand. FDR invited them into his private quarters—the Oval Office, in the West Wing—shook each reporter's hand, called them by their first names, fielded questions, talked off the record, and bantered with them. He was proud to have been editor of *The Harvard Crimson*, he told them, and knew the pressure of meeting printers' deadlines. He respected their job, and considered that the people deserved to be told what their president was doing. He would hold press conferences twice a week—on Wednesday mornings and Friday afternoons. When the session ended, forty-five minutes later, the newsmen broke into applause.

On Thursday, March 9, the House of Representatives convened in special session and passed the banking bill. This was the beginning of the period that would be known ever after as FDR's "first hundred days." In the next three months FDR would enjoy a honeymoon period with Congress. No American president in history would ever manage to get so much major legislation through Congress in one legislative session.

FDR's energy, accessibility, and unflappable good nature impressed everyone around him. "It seems queer to telephone at any hour to a president, to go into his bedroom at one in the morning," the budget director, Lewis Douglas, wrote to his father. "How strange for an insignificant man from Arizona to be in such a position."

One of FDR's first acts was to legalize the sale of beer. The reopening of the breweries gave work to half a million men and raised substantial money in taxes. FDR would soon end thirteen years of Prohibition. The signs went up outside bars: GOOD OLD DAYS ARE BACK AGAIN!

While Franklin was dealing with the nation's financial crisis, Eleanor set about putting their new house in order. Nancy Cook stayed on for a week to help arrange the second-floor living quarters. They made the beautiful oval library at the top of the stairs into FDR's study. This was the Oval Room, often confused with the Oval Office in the West Wing, where FDR spent his days. FDR's bedroom was the adjoining room, to the east of the Oval Room.

Eleanor had the suite next door, to the west. She made the larger room into her sitting room and study and the small space in the southwest corner (normally a dressing room) into her bedroom. Her rooms, like FDR's, looked out on the South Lawn, the magnolia trees planted by Andrew Jackson, and the Washington Monument, that handsome obelisk built in honor of the first president, which she found strangely reassuring.

On Monday, March 6, Eleanor held her first press conference, in the Red Room. It had been Hick's suggestion that she hold a weekly press meeting with women reporters, and Louis Howe thought it an excellent idea. There were no women in the official White House press corps at that time. Nor were female journalists permitted to attend the Gridiron dinner, the most important event of the year for the press, at which the president spoke.

Eleanor wanted to help the "press girls," as she called them. As she knew from Hick, it was a tough profession for women. Their jobs were tenuous, and they were confined to a limited range of "women's stories." She hoped to help them broaden their range of stories. Their discussions should not be directly political, but she saw no reason why they should not cover substantial topics and generate all sorts of interesting news. She was excluding men from these press conferences. She wanted the women to have a source of news not available to their male competitors. Until women were finally admitted to this bastion of male power, she would host a "Gridiron Widows" party at the White House—for women reporters, wives of newsmen, and cabinet wives. She was sure they would have a "grand time."

Eleanor shocked the groundskeepers by arranging for swings to be installed on the lawns for the grandchildren, and disconcerted the chief usher by insisting that she could run the elevator without his help. She had asked for a phone to be installed at her desk; on Wednesday she was told that the man had not wanted to enter the room while she was there. "Oh, spinach! Tell him to come on in and get started!"

At the end of his first week in the White House, on Sunday, March 12, at 10:30 p.m., FDR gave his first presidential "fireside chat." There was no broadcasting room in the White House at the time. FDR sat in a room draped with sound equipment and wires, at a desk loaded with microphones, in front of an audience of thirty or so White House associates.

Secretary of Labor Frances Perkins would attend nearly all of the thirty-one fireside chats FDR gave during the twelve years of his presidency, and she never failed to be moved. "His mind was focused on the people listening at the other end. As he talked his head would nod and his hands would move in simple, natural, comfortable gestures. His face would smile and light up as though he were actually sitting on the front porch or in the parlor with them. People felt this, and it bound them to him in affection."

With his first fireside chat, Roosevelt achieved what seemed almost impossible. He persuaded people to take their money back to the banks. He explained, simply but without condescension, why he and his advisers had decided to close the nation's banks and reopen them gradually, and he appealed to the people to play their part. "I can assure you, my friends, that it is safer to keep your money in a reopened bank than it is to keep it under the mattress . . . We have provided the machinery to restore our financial system; it is up to you to support it and make it work. It is your problem no less than it is mine. Together we cannot fail."

Better than any politician in his time, Roosevelt understood that the new art of radio was about informality. He managed to convey the impression that he was chatting with a neighbor by the fire, while beside him his mother sipped tea and Eleanor knitted. His publicists took photographs in which the three of them did exactly that.

FDR was a master at striking a pose for the camera. Stephen Early, FDR's press secretary, played a crucial role in this. He had strict rules for the press. Early decided when photos would be allowed, and these occasions were rare. There were to be no pictures depicting the president's handicap. It was not permitted to photograph FDR in his wheelchair. If his braces could be seen at the bottom of his trousers, the photos were to be retouched. Photography was banned when the president was at Hyde Park, Warm Springs, in the presidential railcar, or on the presidential yacht. There was no television in those days, of course, and all newsreel coverage of FDR was carefully orchestrated. FDR was shown standing; he was shown sitting; Early did not permit cameras to show FDR "walking."

From today's perspective, it is astounding that the press stuck to the rules. Even journalists who disliked Roosevelt respected the dignity of a handicapped man. On the rare occasion that a cameraman tried to photograph FDR as he was carried from his car, other reporters would step in and block his view.

The limitations on press coverage of FDR were so effective that for twelve long years, most Americans had no idea that their president could not walk. FDR's visitors were shocked to discover that he was a paraplegic. "What was impressed on everyone's senses," the famous transatlantic reporter Alistair Cooke wrote, "was the powerful upper body, the bull neck, the strong hands clasping the lectern, the handsome head tossing the spoken emphases, the happy squire waving to everybody from an open car."

FDR did not want to ask Congress for emergency executive power to deal with the economic crisis. It would not have looked good. The whole world was warily eyeing Germany, where Adolf Hitler had assumed dictatorial power at the end of January 1933, just six weeks before FDR became president of the United States.

It did not prove necessary. FDR had a majority in both houses of Congress, and Congress took the view that the house was on fire and FDR should be given whatever power he needed to put it out. One after another, the bills FDR sent over to Congress came back rubber-stamped.

In the first hundred days, FDR created a profusion of programs, which made up what had come to be called the "New Deal." The National Recovery Administration (NRA) set minimum wages and maximum weekly hours, outlawed child labor, and granted workers the legal right to form unions. The Federal Emergency Relief Administration (FERA), directed by Harry Hopkins, gave aid to the poor through local relief bureaus and departments of welfare. The Public Works Administration (PWA), headed by Harold Ickes, was a vast construction project that would oversee the building of bridges, buildings, roads, and schools. The Tennessee Valley Authority (TVA) aimed to build dams to control flooding and generate cheap power in one of the most poverty-stricken areas of the country. There were dozens more of these programs.

FDR's personal favorite was the Civilian Conservation Corps (CCC). The aim was to hire a quarter of a million young men to do conservation work—planting trees, cutting firebreaks, digging reservoirs, strengthening the national parks movement. They would live in camps run by the army, and their pay would be $30 a month, most of which they were obliged to send home to their families. There were murmurs of "fascism." The American Federation of Labor protested that such a scheme undercut wages. FDR left it to Louis Howe and Frances Perkins to iron out the wrinkles. The CCC would prove to be one of the New Deal's most successful programs.

Within the first hundred days, FDR turned the country's mood from despair to hope. "It's more than a New Deal," said Harold Ickes. "It's a new world."

Congress adjourned on June 16, 1933. FDR and his party—which included three of his sons, James, Franklin Jr., and John—boarded the schooner *Amberjack II* to sail up the coast of Maine to Campobello. It was FDR's first visit to the island since he was carried off on a stretcher twelve years before.

Eleanor drove up with Nan and Marion. She was fervently hoping that they would have sunshine on the island. "Especially do I want good weather when Franklin and his fleet are there," she wrote to Hick. From Lubec the women took the new car ferry across to the island. "Lunch & a trip to Eastport to buy essentials, with the engine breaking down as usual, & the rain in our faces for a time. We came in to tea before the fire. No telephone. Absolute peace. It is a joy!"

The next day, June 27, they were buying provisions for the big picnic to come. "The sun is out, and the fog is rolling out to sea, and I'm sitting in the bottom of the boat, sniffing salt air and every now and then looking over the water to my green islands and grey rocky shores."

The peace did not last. Louis Howe arrived with Grace and Hartley. Missy turned up with her brother, Bernard. The two houses—theirs and Mama's—swarmed with twenty-two guests. By midday on June 29, 1933, an excited crowd was waiting on the dock at Welshpool for the arrival of the president. Campobello was covered in thick fog. Not for the first time, Eleanor worried that Franklin would be late.

At 4 p.m., exactly on schedule, the *Amberjack II* appeared out of the fog, and there was Franklin, waving his old sea hat. Small naval boats circled the ship. A Scottish bagpipe band struck up. Brightly clad Indians from the nearby reservation greeted the president with war whoops. The beach picnic that evening was for naval officers, local dignitaries, friends, and reporters. Frankfurters were roasted on driftwood fires. Eleanor poured tea. The press cameras clicked and whirred. FDR said how pleased he was to be back. "After speeches he came home & I think he is happy," Eleanor wrote to Hick. She had taken some friends to the evening train. "Marion & I . . . drove home watching the sunset, & I recaptured a little serenity!"

That first summer, the first lady planned a three-week motor trip with Lorena Hickok, just the two of them, through Vermont and New Hampshire to Quebec and the rugged Gaspé Peninsula in French Canada. The Secret Service insisted that this was quite impossible. FDR, seeing Eleanor's face, agreed to let them go alone.

It was an idyllic trip, which the two women would always remember with nostalgia. In that remote part of French Canada, they sometimes went whole days without Eleanor being recognized. At one point they stopped to look at a little church, and the pastor came up to them. They exchanged names. "Are you any relation to President Theodore Roosevelt?" the pastor asked Eleanor. "I was a great admirer of his." Eleanor told the truth: "Yes, I am his niece." The pastor did not pursue the subject. "I was delighted to find that no recent history seemed to have penetrated this part of the world," Eleanor wrote later. "He apparently had no idea that my husband was at that time in the White House."

What attracted the most attention was their car. Whenever they parked in a village square, the women would return to find it surrounded by admirers. No one had seen anything like it. A chauffeured black Cadillac might have given the game away. But Eleanor Roosevelt drove a sporty ink-blue Buick roadster with a white convertible top.

With the Roosevelts in residence, the White House was full of laughter and vitality. "You know how it was when Uncle Ted was there—how gay and homelike," FDR had told his relatives at the inauguration dinner. "Well, that's how we mean to have it!"

Franklin and Eleanor enjoyed communal living. Neither of them liked to be alone, and they rarely were. They felt happiest when surrounded by talk, laughter, work, activity. They liked to have friends sleeping across the hallway, who wandered into their bedrooms in pajamas to discuss urgent matters. Life in the White House suited the Roosevelts to a tee.

Every morning at 9 a.m., after FDR had finished his breakfast, Missy and Louis Howe would find him sitting up in his narrow bed, wearing an old sweater, surrounded by newspapers, inserting another cigarette into his cigarette holder. His other two secretaries—Steve Early and Marvin McIntyre—would turn up for their daily bedside briefing. FDR was perfectly capable of talking to passing visitors while he was in the bathroom shaving. "Take a seat on the can," he would tell them cheerily. He would happily continue their discussion while McDuffie helped him dress. FDR was not inhibited.

Missy LeHand lived in a sunny little suite on the third floor, the walls of which were covered with photographs of FDR, Eleanor, and the Roosevelt children. Louis Howe lived on the second floor, in the Lincoln Room, across the West Hall from Eleanor. Like Eleanor, he had made the large room into his study, and slept in the small dressing room just off it. Tragically, just as he had realized his dream for Franklin, Louis's own health declined dramatically. Since moving into the White House, Louis was no longer strong enough for weekend commuting. Now his family came to him. Grace had moved to Fall River, Massachusetts, where she was active in the Democratic State Committee. Their daughter, Mary, lived in Urbana with her husband and little boy, Bobby, who was a favorite with the White House staff. Hartley, who had just graduated from Harvard, was a journalist, like his father.

That first year, Anna, who had separated from her husband, Curtis Dall, moved into the White House with her two children. "The grandchildren were the only ones allowed in Franklin's room while he ate his breakfast," Eleanor wrote later, "and occasionally I had to rescue him from the little darlings. Once I heard much noise and calls for help . . . Franklin sat trying with one hand to protect his breakfast tray from being swept off the bed, and holding the telephone in the other. 'Wait a minute, Hacky,' he was saying desperately to the operator. 'I can't talk to Paris just yet.'"

Eleanor was up by 8 a.m., and by 8:30 she was eating breakfast in the West Hall, usually with Louis Howe, then sometimes went for a horseback ride in Rock Creek Park with her friend Elinor Morgenthau. (The Morgenthaus, Hyde Park neighbors, had moved to Washington; Henry Morgenthau Jr. would soon be secretary of the treasury in FDR's cabinet.) After Eleanor had her daily consultation with the chief usher, housekeeper, and social secretary, she started on her own work—an endless round of engagements and talks, as well as the writing she did with her secretary, Tommy Thompson. In addition to answering the vast correspondence she received as first lady, Eleanor was writing books, articles, and a monthly column.

Around 10:30 a.m., Gus Gennerich wheeled FDR over to the Oval Office in the West Wing. FDR stayed there till about six, then returned to the residence for a swim in the White House pool that had been installed in the basement. Eleanor sometimes joined him; Missy had decided she did not much like exercise. After his swim, FDR was given a rubdown by the resident physical therapist, George Fox. Then came a brief consultation with Vice Admiral Ross McIntire, the White House physician, an ear, nose, and throat specialist, who administered FDR's daily sinus treatment. Around seven, FDR would hit the buzzers on his desk and call his colleagues for cocktails in the Oval Room.

They often had dinner guests, and more formal dinners were carefully stage-managed. Eleanor came late to cocktails, then distracted the guests, chatting about the portraits on the walls, until Franklin had been wheeled into the dining room and transferred from his wheelchair to his seat at the end of the table. As the group walked in, he would welcome them with his big grin. "It's strange to say now," one visitor commented after Franklin's death, "but you did not really notice he could not walk. He was a sort of Mount Rushmore being wheeled around, and all you noticed after a while was the Mount Rushmore part."

The cozy family dinners were a thing of the past. FDR was far too busy. If they did not have guests, he mostly ate with Missy and whichever colleagues he was working with that evening. Eleanor ate with friends, and frequently entertained White House guests by herself. If she wanted to talk to her husband alone, she had to wait her turn. "I learned to save anything I wanted to tell him till he was in bed," she wrote, "for that was likely to be the only quiet time in the whole day."

Hick was feeling, with some justification, that she had given up her career for Eleanor. In the summer of 1933, she resigned from her job at the Associated Press. By now she was known throughout the nation as a personal friend of Eleanor's. For a political journalist, this was disastrous.

Eleanor organized a job for Hick in the Federal Emergency Relief Administration (FERA), run by Eleanor's close friend, Harry Hopkins. It involved traveling around the country, reporting back to Hopkins on socioeconomic conditions in different regions. Hick's letters from bleak towns ravaged by the Depression made Eleanor poignantly aware of the plight of rural America. But Hick would have far preferred to be writing in a public capacity. She had left the profession she loved, and her new job took her away from Eleanor for weeks at a time.

In between her travels, Hick spent whole weeks at the White House. She ate with Eleanor's official guests; she slept a few feet from Eleanor, in Eleanor's sitting room. The White House publicity staff carefully snipped Hick's bulky figure out of the official photos. With the first lady always busy, rushing from one appointment to another, Hick felt like a ghost, pacing the long corridors alone, chain-smoking, wondering what she was doing there.

Missy LeHand turned thirty-five in September 1933, and her life still revolved completely around FDR. When he went away on cruises, she missed him badly. "Gosh, it will be good to get my eyes on you again," she wrote to him from the White House. "This place is horrible when you are away."

As the president's "Super-Secretary," Marguerite LeHand was now quite famous herself. There was an admiring profile of her in *Newsweek*, in August 1933: "She knows when he is bored before he realizes it himself . . . She can tell when he is really listening to an interlocutor and when he is merely being polite—which no one else can—and she sometimes even senses when he is beginning to disapprove of something that he still thinks he likes." It made Missy sound like the perfect wife, but the *Newsweek* piece went on: "Her devotion to the Roosevelts seems likely to extend her spinsterhood. Many a male visitor is struck by her charm, but even the most ardent swain is chilled at the thought that, to invite her to a movie, he must call up the White House, which is her home."

In the case of William C. Bullitt, the opposite was true: Missy's closeness to FDR greatly added to her appeal. In September 1933, forty-two-year-old Bill Bullitt, who hailed from a wealthy Philadelphia family, starting courting Missy. Bullitt had been psychoanalyzed by Sigmund Freud in Vienna. Twice married and divorced, Bullitt's second wife was Louise Bryant Reed, widow of the famous American Communist John Reed. FDR liked Bullitt a great deal. Bullitt's feelings for FDR were more a case of hero worship.

In November 1933—for the first time since the Russian Revolution in 1917—FDR extended diplomatic recognition to the Soviet Union, and made Bullitt the first U.S. ambassador. "Well, Russia is recognized, Bullitt goes as ambassador," Eleanor wrote to Hick. "I wonder if that is why F.D.R. has been so content to let Missy play with him! She'll have another embassy to visit next summer anyway!"

Eleanor distrusted Bullitt. It was her view—shared by others—that Bullitt used Missy to get close to FDR. "Missy was young and pretty and loved a good time," Eleanor wrote later, "and occasionally her social contacts got mixed with her work and made it hard for her and others."

The affair with Bullitt lasted a couple of years. There was gossip about a possible marriage. But Missy remained single. No one could replace Effdee.

Hick had sent Eleanor graphic reports of poverty in the coal towns of Pennsylvania and West Virginia. In mid-August 1933, Eleanor drove to Morgantown, West Virginia, to see for herself. The mines had closed. The former miners and their families were close to starvation, living in hovels, washing in a stream that ran with sewage. Eleanor toured the area, appalled.

She discussed it with Franklin, who said that this was the kind of thing he had in mind when he set up the Subsistence Homestead Program, which was run by Harold Ickes. The government purchased property near the town of Reedsville, West Virginia, started building houses, and selected suitable residents. Eleanor was dismayed that these did not include African Americans, but Ickes, despite his sympathy with blacks, did not want to risk the ire of local hillbillies.

The new town of Arthurdale became Eleanor's personal project. For the next three years she put most of her earnings from her talks and writing into the settlement. She employed a schoolmistress; she hired Nancy Cook to set up a small handicraft industry there. She sat with the families on their porches, talked to them about their lives, and square-danced at the high-school commencement hop.

But there were problems, which the Republican newspapers reported with glee. Louis Howe ordered fifty Cape Cod prefab houses that proved too flimsy for Appalachian winters. The porous rock under the settlement created complications for the water supply. The settlers were unable to attract industry to the area. Harold Ickes was embarrassed by this highly publicized failure. "We have been spending money down there like drunken sailors," he wrote in his diary. He blamed Eleanor.

Arthurdale became a favorite target for those who claimed that the New Deal was badly managed and "communistic." FDR took the view that even if Arthurdale had not been a successful investment, it had been a worthwhile social experiment. Eleanor could see that the government had brought hope, dignity, and work to a community. She would keep in touch with Arthurdale residents for the rest of her life, and was thrilled to see the ex-miners' children go to college.

Years later, one of the homesteaders recalled: "I never pass that little white meeting hall without remembering Mrs. Roosevelt—the First Lady—coming in there in a gingham dress and mud on her shoes one night to square dance with the settlers. That was real democracy."

The White House, with its four floors and sixty rooms, large porches, magnolia trees, and segregated restrooms, was like a grand, shabby, rather uncomfortable Southern hotel. The plumbing was rusty, the heating clanked and hissed, the roof leaked when it rained, and in summer the place was swelteringly hot. The beds in the guest rooms were lumpy, the kitchen was archaic, and there was only one elevator in the entire building. It did not take FDR long to start drawing up plans for renovations.

He hired an architect friend, Eric Gugler, and the work began in August 1934. For the next eighteen months, the White House would undergo a major transformation. FDR commissioned Frederick Law Olmsted Jr. (whose father had designed Central Park) to landscape the eighteen-acre grounds. The guest rooms were refurbished. The servants were given a cheery new dining room. The "New Deal Kitchen" was state of the art, equipped to provide a full-course meal for a thousand people. By the spring of 1936, the White House had become a truly grand hotel.

There was only one problem—the food. It was dreadful. FDR was always complaining to Eleanor about the cooking. White House guests traded stories about it. Eleanor had brought in the chief housekeeper, Henrietta Nesbitt, whose main job was to prepare menus and supervise the cooking. Mrs. Nesbitt was a Hyde Park neighbor, whom Eleanor had met at League of Women Voters meetings. She ran a little tea shop. Eleanor liked her baked goods and regularly sent down pastry orders for the governor's mansion. When FDR was elected president, Mrs. Nesbitt, a Republican turned Democrat, stood to lose her main source of income.

One wintry day in November 1932, the future first lady strode up Mrs. Nesbitt's front path, sat down in her kitchen, and dandled Mrs. Nesbitt's grandson in her lap. "I don't want a professional housekeeper," she explained. "I want someone I know." And so, at the age of fifty-nine, Mrs. Nesbitt had come to Washington to take on the White House cooking. She told her dubious husband, "You'll see how simple it will be. I've been keeping house for six. Now I'll multiply by ten, and keep house for sixty!"

In no time at all, Mrs. Nesbitt's culinary disasters were legendary in Washington. Eleanor sent her to New York, to learn from a restaurant chef how to cook vegetables. Eleanor passed on FDR's complaints, but ended up soothing Mrs. Nesbitt's ruffled feathers. Part of the problem was that Eleanor did not care about food, and hated to be extravagant while millions of their people were still going hungry. She liked to make out that FDR had little interest in food, too. This was quite untrue. FDR, who for security reasons almost never ate out, would have rejoiced in some culinary diversity at home.

Mrs. Nesbitt's little memoir, *White House Diary*, makes clear that she saw "plain cooking" as a form of patriotism:

Except for special occasions, the White House family was eating like any other American family. Some of the dishes I served regularly were corned-beef hash, poached eggs, and creamed chipped beef . . . Sometimes if the food was too simple, the President made wisecracks, and I'd have to stir myself and think up something fancy . . . He had simple American tastes, as a rule, but just the same he was a cosmopolitan and a connoisseur in foods, and if there were special things on the menu, he wanted them just so.

When international guests put in special requests for food, Mrs. Nesbitt chafed about their "presumptuousness." When FDR said he was bored with broiled calf's liver and green beans, Mrs. Nesbitt decided that the problem was his: "Whenever he became tense, he would get peevish about his meals. I figured out later that trapped as he was by his lameness in a great, strong body, yearning for action he had no other means of releasing his strain. He took it out on the food. But it took me some time and a lot of heartache to figure that out."

Eleanor Roosevelt's biographer, Blanche Wiesen Cook, speculates that Mrs. Nesbitt was Eleanor's revenge on FDR. "The housekeeper was one expression of her passive-aggressive behavior in a marriage of remarkable and labyrinthine complexity." Whatever the reason, Henrietta Nesbitt stayed on. For twelve long years, the Roosevelt White House would be famous for its stunningly mediocre cuisine.

"The Lord only knows when this will catch up with my Will o' the Wisp wife," FDR wrote to Eleanor in the summer of 1934. "Everywhere they spoke of your visit." FDR and his party were aboard the USS *Houston* on a four-week voyage to Panama and Hawaii, and had just spent two days in Puerto Rico. FDR was referring to Eleanor's triumphant visit there in March. The whole world had seen the photos of Eleanor walking through the squalid slums in her crisp white dress and white hat, surrounded by reporters, clamoring crowds, dogs, and pigs. "As long as my husband is in office, you have a friend in Washington," she told them.

The visit had been less successful on the personal front. Hick had accompanied Eleanor and was to report back to Harry Hopkins at FERA on conditions in Puerto Rico. She was enraged by the press reports that presented her merely as Eleanor's sidekick. *Time* magazine had written her off as "a rotund lady with a husky voice, a peremptory manner, baggy clothes," who was "in her day one of the country's best female news hawks" and was now "fast friends with Mrs. Roosevelt."

Eleanor was conscious that their friendship made things hard for Hick. "I'm glad you haven't had any more publicity," she wrote in April 1934. "It would hurt terribly & make work very hard, we must be careful this summer & keep it out of the papers when we are off together."

But they were never able to pull off this feat again. In July 1934, while FDR was cruising in the Caribbean, the two women spent three weeks in

California together. The trip was a disaster. Hick had dreamed of a quiet, lazy time alone together. Instead Eleanor had them camping, climbing, and riding horses in Yosemite Park (Hick, who was a chain-smoker and too fat, hated every minute of it), and the whole time they were followed by rangers, vacationers, and reporters—"in *droves*." Hick sulked, threw tantrums, and embarrassed Eleanor by swearing at people. "If only you weren't the President's wife—with all the fuss and pushing and hauling that goes with it," she brooded. "How I should love to travel with you!"

The trip was a turning point in their relationship. The two women would always be friends, but the passion was over. In August, Eleanor wrote to Hick from Chazy Lake, in the Adirondack Mountains, where she was enjoying the more restful company of Nan, Marion, and Earl Miller: "I'm afraid you & I are always going to have times when we ache for each other & yet we are not always going to be happy when we are together. Somehow we must find the things we can do & do them so that what time we have together is as happy as it can be in an imperfect world!"

"I blow off to you but never to F!" Eleanor would write to Hick. In truth, she occasionally lost her temper with Franklin. A sore point was Franklin's famous cocktails—potent mixtures of rum, gin, vermouth, and fruit juice, which their friends did not always hold well. Whenever anyone's glass was empty, it would be "How about another little sippy?" and Franklin would press a second or even a third drink on them.

Eleanor, who did not touch alcohol herself, was well aware that some of Franklin's associates, such as Sam Rosenman, surreptitiously tipped the second drink into the nearest White House plant. She was not amused by seeing people in an inebriated state. She had seen alcoholism at close quarters. Her brother Hall was yet another alcoholic in the Roosevelt family.

In November 1934, Eleanor accompanied Franklin to Warm Springs for Thanksgiving. Franklin was surrounded by the usual large party of associates. Eleanor was there with Tommy and Nan. In the evenings, FDR poured cocktails with his habitual enthusiasm. Eleanor wrote to Anna:

> I will probably fly home in a day or two. I'd like to leave at once but I injudiciously told Father I always felt like a spoil sport &

policeman here & at times elsewhere, because I lost my temper last night. He's been giving Nan a cocktail every night & for two nights it went only a little to her head but it was so strong last night that she not only talked incessantly much to their amusement but couldn't talk straight & I felt that he did it on purpose tho' he swears he didn't . . . I felt revolt physically from anyone in that condition & that made her unhappy & yet I hate to be the one to keep her from taking anything so I'd give the world & all to be out of the way . . . Father says however if I leave before I have to he will feel hurt so! I'm an idiotic puritan & I wish I had the right kind of sense of humor & could enjoy certain things. At least, thank God, none of you children have inherited that streak in me, it is as well to have some of Father's ease & balance in these things!

FDR understood why Eleanor reacted as she did, but for him, his cocktails were a precious moment of release. The fun was largely vicarious. He liked to test his friends' capacity to hold their liquor, but he lingered over his own drinks, sipping slowly. He had work to do the next day. He was also painfully conscious that he weighed 180 pounds, and that his life was far too sedentary. He had a horror of getting fat. It only made it even harder for the poor fellows who lifted him.

From the day he moved into the White House, Louis Howe's health grew worse. He nevertheless played a powerful role in the first eighteen months. Until illness made it impossible, Louis McHenry Howe was very much the "Assistant President," even if he worked in the background. He became a "telephone voice," as James Farley put it—"a sort of 'mystery man,' whom everybody respected and many feared."

It was Louis who organized the January 1934 Cuff Links Gang birthday frolic to which Franklin came clad in a purple roman toga and laurel crown, Louis clanked along as a Praetorian guard, and Eleanor, dressed as the Delphic oracle, made dire prophesies about the New Deal.

But in the fall of 1934, Louis's health took a turn for the worse. Eleanor knew how miserable he felt that his body was betraying him right now. She canceled other engagements to be with him. She took him for afternoon drives in the Virginia countryside, in the flashy Lincoln convertible he had proudly bought when he came to the White House and had never been strong enough to drive himself. They sometimes tried to walk a little, but Louis could not take more than a few steps without gasping for breath. Whenever she left Washington for a few days, Eleanor reminded Franklin: "Be nice to Louis."

At the end of January 1935, Louis was so ill that FDR called off the annual Cuff Links Gang party. In early March, Louis was placed in an oxygen tent. Franklin put off his cruise in the Bahamas; Eleanor canceled her engagements; Grace and the children hurried to Louis's bedside. On the morning of March 19, Mary wired her husband: "No hope beyond 24 hours." A special train was brought into a siding at Union Station, in preparation for Howe's last journey, to Fall River.

Later that afternoon, Louis opened his eyes and said irritably, "Why in hell doesn't somebody give me a cigarette?" A few days later, he reached out from under his oxygen tent for the telephone and talked to Harry Hopkins for fifteen minutes about the new work relief bill. Two weeks later, Howe's improvement was such that Franklin went off on his cruise. "If he is not too 'fuzzy' give him my love," he wrote Eleanor, "and tell him I expect him to be sitting up in bed when I get back."

The White House doctor, Ross McIntire, could not believe the iron will of this wizened little man. "Louis Howe is a New Deal in patients," the Washington *Evening Star* reported, "and he has confounded them all."

Louis lived on for a whole year, most of it under an oxygen tent. "He is no better & no worse," Eleanor reported to Anna in August. "It is like a living death." Louis slipped in and out of a coma. When he felt strong enough, he would shuffle across the hall in his pajamas and slippers to Eleanor's sitting room. He still came up with brilliant ideas, he still fretted about Franklin's speeches, but he was not always lucid.

The summer of 1935 was one of the hottest Washington summers on record. The White House renovations were still not finished, and the air-conditioning was not working. FDR was stuck in Washington, fighting with Congress over the details of his groundbreaking Social Security Bill. In July, Eleanor went to Campobello with Marion and Nan. Louis was too ill to go anywhere.

Louis was demanding that summer. His wife, Grace, read to him—from history books, whodunits, the newspapers. One evening, when she closed the book, hoarse from reading, he asked plaintively, "What's the matter, my dear? Don't you *like* to read to me?" He kept telephoning Mrs. Nesbitt and ordering special food. "I want some plain rat cheese," he told her. "The kind they set traps with." Another day he was furious with her. "You don't know how to cook a steak," he said. "Get one two inches thick. Cover it with coarse salt and broil it under a hot fire . . . Then scrape the salt off the steak, slap on some hot butter, and bring it to me." It took a courageous man to take on Mrs. Nesbitt.

The dust and fresh paint were playing havoc with FDR's sinuses and Louis Howe's lungs. These were no conditions for a dying man. At the end of August, Louis was moved to the Bethesda Naval Hospital. Eleanor went with him, to help him settle in. His room was pleasant, with two exposures and a porch, but Louis was dismayed to find that he did not have a phone by his bedside. He insisted that he needed to be able to call the White House at any hour of the day or night. On Franklin's orders, Louis was given a phone connection from 10 a.m. to 4:30 p.m.

FDR told his staff that whenever Louis Howe called, however bizarre his requests, he was to be treated with the greatest courtesy. Eleanor visited Louis most days; Franklin was wheeled in at least once a week. But Louis chafed to be away from the action. FDR's press secretary, Steve Early, sent a memo to his colleague, Marvin McIntyre: "Louis is feeling 'hurt' because he says the President promised yesterday and again today to talk to him—he feels like he is on the outside, cut off. He wants the President to call him."

Eleanor Roosevelt's first "My Day" column appeared on December 30, 1935:

I wonder if anyone else glories in cold and snow without and an open fire within and the luxury of a tray of food all by one's self in one's room. I realize that it sounds extremely selfish and a little odd to look upon such an occasion as festive. Nevertheless, Saturday night was a festive occasion for I spent it that way.

The house was full of young people, my husband had a cold and was in bed with milk toast for his supper, so I said a polite good night to everyone at 7:30, closed my door, lit my fire and settled down to a nice long evening by myself. I read things which I had had in my briefcase for weeks—a report on educational work in the CCC camps, a copy of "Progressive Education" dealing with the problems of youth . . . and I went to sleep at 10:30. Because I haven't been to bed for weeks before 1 a.m. and often later, this was so unusual that I woke this morning with a feeling that I must have slept for several years . . .

Louis Howe had encouraged Eleanor to take on the daily newspaper column. Franklin thought it would be a burdensome chore, in addition to Eleanor's other work. But from the beginning she loved it. It was an opportunity to air her own views, while also promoting FDR. Every day, six days a week, she dictated her five hundred words to Tommy, and prided herself on never missing a deadline.

She was no writer; her prose style was pedestrian and awkward. She was no intellectual; the "My Day" column would contain plenty of platitudes. But in the long run these things did not matter. She was a great communicator, with a beguiling fireside quality that she shared with her husband. Her goodness and moral integrity shone out. Her vitality was inspiring. Her calm good sense lowered the political temperature when FDR was criticized.

At first "My Day" appeared in twenty newspapers. Within a year it was appearing in seventy-five, many of them anti-Roosevelt papers. As author of one of the most popular columns in the American press, Eleanor could not have done her husband a greater service.

Margaret Suckley—"Daisy," as she was known—was a distant cousin of FDR's, from one of the Hudson River families that had lost their fortune. She lived with her mother and brother in a rambling Queen Anne house with gingerbread trim and a Rapunzel tower, near Rhinebeck, farther up the Hudson. As the paid companion of an invalid aunt, she lived a sequestered life. To most of the world, Daisy Suckley appeared to be a mousy spinster.

She and Franklin had become friends in the spring of 1922, when FDR went to Hyde Park after he came down with polio, and his mother, worried about her restless invalid son, used to invite Daisy to tea. Over the years they saw each other when Franklin came back to "the River."

When FDR was elected president, he invited Daisy to the inauguration. That first summer in the White House, since Missy was being serenaded by William Bullitt, Franklin was feeling lonely.

"A Red Letter Day," Daisy wrote in her diary on August 1, 1933. "The President of the United States of America called me up on the telephone!" He invited her to Hyde Park. Things had changed since her first visits there. There was now a guardhouse at the entrance to the driveway, with a Secret Service man who telephoned the house to announce Daisy's arrival. The president's valet told her that the president was delayed and led her to the library, where she spent an hour looking at the president's old books. Finally he arrived, and two men lifted him into his car.

> The Pres. & I drive in his roadster through his woods—followed by 4 detectives in a state trooper car. On the swamp lot we think we see an egret which turns out to be a quart bottle on a stump! . . .
>
> On our return Pres. shows me more books; also illustrations of birds, etc.
>
> Mrs. R. somewhat surprised to see me!
>
> 6 p.m., Miss LeHand & I drive with the President to the "cottage," where the Rs have a picnic for the press. Mrs. Franklin, Mrs. James, . . . Anna Roosevelt Dall all there. I choose a hot dog, potato salad, beer . . . About 8 pm I leave . . .
>
> The President is a MAN—*mentally, physically, & spiritually*— What more can I say?

Daisy was dazzled. FDR felt genuine tenderness toward this prim-looking little woman, with her quirky imagination and astute observations. They shared a love of Dutchess County, historic homes, old books, and local gossip. "I miss the River," he told her.

In March 1935 he wrote to her, "There is a hill—in the back country—perhaps this spring we can go to it. Why is it that *our* River & *our* countryside seem so to be a part of us? Perhaps it is the 'common' Beekman ancestry!" He wrote in longhand, on White House notepaper, and addressed the envelopes himself. These were not letters he could dictate to Missy.

The fall foliage was out when FDR finally drove Daisy to his favorite hill, the highest point on his property, with a magnificent view of the river and the Catskill Mountains on the other side. One week later, FDR wrote from the *Presidential Special* in Colorado, where he and Eleanor had just dedicated the new Boulder Dam: "I love the desert and rocks, but not to live among—still true to Dutchess!" he told Daisy. "There is no reason why I should not tell you that I miss you *very* much. It was a week ago yesterday."

Daisy was following the president's western trip in the newspapers and listening to his speeches on the radio. "Early this morning I had a *very* serious talk with a Certain Person," she wrote back. "I told her she must come to earth, attend to her job, and stop looking at the moon (there is a particularly silvery new one)— She took it *very* nicely— agreed with me *perfectly*—said I was *entirely* right."

Their letters were tender, playful, full of teasing ambiguity. Daisy had a head full of fantasies; Franklin enjoyed making some of these come true. On October 3, 1935, Mussolini's troops marched into Ethiopia. Two days later, Franklin wrote to Daisy, who had sent him a sketch of a house for "Our Hill":

> First of all—why have I only just discovered that you paint and draw adorably? Why hide such a delightful light under a bushel? . . . You said once "log cabin"— But I don't think so— . . . I think a one-story fieldstone two room house— . . . one with very thick walls to protect us against the Indians and a little porch on the West side. Do you mind—then—if I tell you fairy stories till it gets very late?

Daisy was about to spend the winter looking after her aged aunt in New York. Franklin told her: "I truly want you to see lots of people and do lots of nice things in town—and perhaps some day find just the right kind of 'Gentle Man' who will take very good care of you—and even then will you remember that your old Country Cousin from H.P. is to be counted on and leaned on very much."

In April 1935, FDR replaced FERA with the Works Progress Administration (WPA), still headed by Harry Hopkins. The WPA gave an unprecedented level of work to people on relief. The next few years would see the construction of public buildings, roads, bridges, parks, schools, and housing. The WPA also fostered artistic creativity. The Federal Arts Project employed artists to decorate buildings with murals and sculpture that celebrated the dignity of the American people; the Federal Writers' Project paid writers to research and write about every aspect of American life; the Federal Theatre Project had playwrights, actors, and directors bringing theater to the people.

FDR was particularly proud of the Social Security Act, on which he had worked closely with Frances Perkins. For the first time in American history, there would be social security benefits, old-age pensions, disability benefits, aid for dependent mothers and children. By the time Congress had finished with it, the bill was not nearly as inclusive as FDR had hoped, but he could still boast that this was watershed legislation—"historic for all time."

In four years, the New Deal had transformed the lives of Americans. Six million jobs had been created; industrial production had doubled; unemployment had dropped by a third. But predictably, the New Deal was meeting with plenty of opposition. Conservatives called it socialism, and complained that it was killing the enterprising spirit of American individualism. They liked to refer to the WPA as the "We Piddle Around" or the "Whistle, Piss and Argue" gang. Socialists complained that FDR was propping up capitalism. Southerners deplored the power of the central government. But the New Deal's worst enemy was the Supreme Court, which claimed that it was "unconstitutional" for the federal government to undermine states' rights. For a year now, the Supreme Court had been blocking New Deal initiatives.

As usual, the fight was "bringing out the Dutch" in FDR. As Grace Tully observed: "With each adverse decision, his jaw set a little harder and his cigarette holder tipped a bit more belligerently."

Louis Howe was still at the Bethesda Naval Hospital, clinging to life. He had just turned sixty-five. On April 12, 1936, Franklin called at the hospital after the Easter Sunday service. He stayed half an hour, joking and laughing. Fannie Hurst, a novelist friend of Howe's, met the president as he was coming out. "Louis is not doing too well," he told her. "Try to cheer him up, and stay with him as long as you can."

Fannie Hurst saw how happy Franklin's visit had made the patient. Louis had once said to her, "At heart I am a minstrel singing outside the window of beauty." That spring day, Louis was struggling to breathe, as usual. But he seemed to want to talk to her, in his whispery, wheezy voice, about Franklin and Eleanor—their goodness to him, their devotion. "I have been as close to Franklin Roosevelt as a valet," he told her, "and he is still a hero to me."

One week later, on Sunday, April 19, Eleanor wrote to Hick:

> I got in from speaking last night & Dr. McIntire called me to tell me Louis had died in his sleep. They just noticed his breathing was changing, called the doctor who did what he could but he never responded & was never conscious. A merciful way for him. We got Franklin as soon as the Gridiron dinner was over & I spent hours getting Mrs. Howe & Hartley on the telephone, but finally succeeded & they took it calmly, thank Heavens! . . .
>
> For a long time the real person has been gone . . . He was like a pitiful, querulous child but even when I complained I loved him & no one will ever be more loyal & devoted than he was.

On April 21, Howe was given a state funeral in the East Room, attended by numerous dignitaries. There was singing by the choir of St. Thomas's Parish, in which Howe had sung, back in his navy days. Later that evening, Franklin and Eleanor boarded the funeral train for the overnight journey to Fall River.

The streets of the old mill town were lined with onlookers as the funeral cortege made its way to the Oak Grove Cemetery. The trees had sprouted new leaves, though there were still patches of snow on the burial ground. During the short service, the press cameras whirred. A few paces back from the grave, Franklin and Eleanor stood with their sons, their heads bowed. *The New York Times* noted that the president "appeared oblivious to everything around him, both during the service and when he returned to his car for the ride back to the station."

"This little man," Eleanor would write of Howe, "was really the biggest man I have ever known."

At the Democratic National Convention in Philadelphia, FDR and John Garner, his vice president, were renominated by acclamation. On Saturday, June 27, one hundred thousand people waited in the University of Pennsylvania's outdoor stadium to hear FDR's acceptance speech. At 10 p.m., the Roosevelts' limousine arrived.

It had been raining and the ground was muddy. FDR and James began their laborious walk to the stage. FDR stopped to greet an old friend. The crowd surged forward, he was jostled, his right leg brace came unlocked, and he lurched forward. Mike Reilly, the chief Secret Service man, dived to the ground and caught the president before he hit the ground. FDR's aides clustered around and hid him from view. Gus Gennerich snapped the brace back into place. "It was the most frightful five minutes of my life," FDR said later. Nobody in the audience saw what happened, but Eleanor was told immediately.

The sheets of FDR's talk had scattered in the mud. Not until he stood at the podium did he discover that they were out of order. Eleanor had to watch him rearranging them while he held himself up. Somehow he performed at his brilliant best. "We have won against the most dangerous of our foes," he told the crowd. "We have conquered fear!" He went on to say that in America they were waging a war for the survival of democracy. "This generation of Americans has a rendezvous with destiny." There was wild cheering.

The president and first lady did two victory laps around the running track in their open car. The cheering went on and on and on. "I think F *felt* every word of his speech," Eleanor wrote in her "My Day" column. "It was a wonderful sight."

The Republican presidential candidate was Alf Landon, a businessman from Kansas. The Hearst newspapers made him out to be a man of the people, who believed in protecting the Constitution against the ravages of the New Deal. Landon's wife assured people that *she* would not be taking part in politics. She would devote all her time to caring for her family.

Eleanor Roosevelt was regularly lambasted and caricatured in the white Southern press. Stephen Early, FDR's press secretary, was a Southerner, and he did not share the late Louis Howe's opinion that Eleanor was one of FDR's best assets. Early did not approve of Eleanor's daily column, or her talks, or her weekly press conferences. He wished the first lady would shut up.

One day, Eleanor asked Early's permission to include a colored reporter at her women's press conferences. Early was incredulous. The president's press corps was white only, he told her; this would create "a terrible precedent." When Eleanor held a White House garden party for the inmates of a local Negro reformatory school, it provoked an avalanche of criticism in the press. Early was outraged. Had the first lady lost her mind?

In the months before the election, Eleanor cut back on her talks and was careful not to make her columns too political ("I might get myself into trouble!"), but behind the scenes she was as active as before. In October 1936, she joined the campaign train in the west. As FDR's "legs," she inspected the New Deal's national parks, roads, bridges, tunnels, dams, waterways, and hydroelectric power schemes. When she did not appear on the train platform, the crowds shouted for her.

"Hick dearest," she wrote from the train, "we are surfeited with candy & flowers & crowds! I never have seen on any trip such crowds or such enthusiasm." She allowed herself an immodest P.S.: "How I hate being a show but I'm doing it *so* nicely!"

November 3, 1936: As usual, Franklin and Eleanor were at Hyde Park on election night. At 6 p.m., Franklin settled in the dining room with Missy, his sons, and telephone operators to listen to the returns. In the library, Eleanor and Mama were hosting a buffet supper for friends.

Some pundits had predicted a close outcome. They were wrong. It was a record-breaking landslide for FDR. There had never been anything like it in American history. Every state except Maine and Vermont voted Democrat. FDR won 523 electoral votes to Landon's 8. The popular vote—61 percent—was the second highest since 1820. "You could be a king or a dictator and they'd fight for you," Eleanor told him. "Lucky you have no aspirations!"

EIGHT

Embattled

November 1936–November 1940

Following his reelection, FDR had planned a three-week trip to South America. He considered it important for diplomatic relations, but he hesitated to go away right now. He was deeply pessimistic about the international situation. The fascist Italian leader, Benito Mussolini, had invaded Ethiopia. Hitler had begun to remilitarize the Rhineland, the territory along the Rhine in the west of Germany that had been demilitarized by the Treaty of Versailles. In Spain, General Franco's coup d'état against the elected Popular Front government had turned into bloody civil war, with Germany and Italy sending armaments and weapons to aid Franco. "As President I have to be ready, just like a Fire Department!" FDR said. After the frenetic pace of the campaign, however, he badly needed some sleep, fresh air, and sunshine. On November 18, he and his party set sail from Charleston.

Eleanor was in the Midwest with Tommy, on a lecture tour. They would be back in good time for the busy Christmas season. From the *Indianapolis* FDR wrote that the seas had been smooth, they had enjoyed the "crossing the line" ceremonies, and he was happy to have James with him. At dawn they would be docking in Rio, where they had a hectic schedule. They would be leaving in the late evening, with a special illumination of the harbor as they went out. "Loads and loads of love—and try to get lots of sleep preparatory to that—Social Season. Another year let's cut it out and take a trip to Samoa and Hawaii instead!"

"I do wish you could see Rio," he wrote his "dearest Babs" four days later. He had been delighted to see that his "Good Neighbor Policy" was having some impact. There had been vast crowds of cheering people, who threw orchids at him. "Three years ago Latin-American public opinion was almost violently against us."

On December 1, Eleanor was back in Washington and about to go to breakfast when Louise Hackmeister, the White House switchboard operator, announced a phone call from Buenos Aires. "My heart sank," Eleanor wrote in her "My Day" column, "for I knew that only something serious would make my rather careful husband telephone from that distance." She was right. Gus Gennerich, FDR's fifty-year-old bodyguard, had died of a heart attack.

Franklin had spoken at an official dinner, and Gus helped him to bed, at the U.S. embassy. After midnight, Gus and two naval-officer friends had gone to the famous Tabaret cabaret. At 1:30 a.m., just back from the dance floor, Gus had toppled over dead.

For Franklin, it was a painful loss. Gus Gennerich had been at his side since 1928. Gus had helped him bathe and dress; Gus carried him in and out of cars, up and down stairs; Gus pushed his wheelchair; Gus had ducked him under water in water polo games. The entire Roosevelt family loved the man. FDR had even helped him buy land at Hyde Park. "That part of it accentuates the tragedy," he told Eleanor, "for Gus was really living for that farm—he thought about it day and night and was buying things for it in Rio and B.A."

By mid-December, the *Indianapolis* was approaching Trinidad, on the way home. In Britain, King Edward VIII, who had not yet been on the throne a full year, wanted to marry the twice-divorced American, Mrs. Wallis Simpson. FDR and his party placed bets on how the scandal would end. FDR was convinced that the king would make the lady Duchess of Cornwall, marry her, and keep the throne.

"Tomorrow we go ashore for 4 hours and lunch with the Governor," Franklin wrote to Eleanor. "Word having just come of King Edward's abdication, do I or do I not propose the 'health of the King'? Awful dilemma . . . Ever so much love. I've missed you a lot and it will be good to be back."

When he got back from South America, FDR was tense, preoccupied by the fight he saw coming with the Supreme Court. "Pa has no time to be talked to except on matters of business," Eleanor wrote to Anna, who had remarried and was living in Seattle. Eleanor missed Anna and the grandchildren.

The rain came down in torrents at FDR's second inauguration. FDR insisted that he and Eleanor drive back to the White House with the top of their car down. They were, Eleanor wrote in her column, "soaked through."

Ten days later, on January 30, 1937, they celebrated FDR's fifty-fifth birthday. He had aged in the last year, and looked more like sixty. With Louis and Gus gone, there were no birthday frolics. After dinner, the men played poker and Eleanor set out to do her rounds of the Washington "birthday balls"—a national fund-raising effort for polio.

FDR, who was feeling lonely these days, had asked their twenty-nine-year-old son, James, to take a four-year leave from his Boston insurance business to become a presidential secretary—at the same rank as Stephen Early and Marvin McIntyre. Eleanor was "appalled" to hear this, and tried to talk them out of it. James resented her attitude.

Eleanor's fears proved well founded. In the conservative Hearst press, which liked to refer to the New Deal as the "Raw Deal," James was dubbed the "Crown Prince," or even the "Clown Prince." James would last eighteen months before he resigned with severe gastric ulcers and a broken marriage.

James's appointment reinforced the hostility toward Eleanor that had been simmering in FDR's circle ever since Louis Howe died. James had boundless admiration for his father but was ambivalent toward a mother who all too often seemed cold and disapproving. His colleagues, Steve Early and Marvin McIntyre—both Southerners with traditional Southern attitudes—could not understand why the president did not keep his wife on a tighter rein.

The tensions were intensified by James's wife, Betsey Cushing. A socialite from a prominent Boston family, Betsey fawned over her famous father-in-law. She made sure she was present at cocktail hour, and sometimes took over hostess duties when Eleanor was away. Betsey was careful to cultivate Missy. But she disliked Eleanor, and the antipathy was reciprocal. On New Year's Eve, Eleanor briefly left the dancing downstairs and went up to her room, where she added two sentences to her letter to Hick: "I think our young people look very nice in a crowd! But Betsey has a dress I hate, it is so undressed!"

Betsey stirred up the ongoing feud about the housekeeper, Mrs. Nesbitt. Betsey was contemptuous of "La Nesbitt," as she called her. She objected to Mrs. Nesbitt's bossy manner. Betsey had noticed dust on the banisters. Above all, Betsey could not for the life of her understand why they put up with Mrs. Nesbitt's terrible cooking.

One evening at dinner, FDR pushed aside his watery spinach with disgust and launched into a tirade about the bland cooking in the White House. Eleanor wrote about it in her column. There were mocking headlines in the papers: FDR DEMANDS NEW DEAL—REFUSES SPINACH—CRISIS STRIKES. Mrs. Nesbitt was humiliated. ("I was sensitive and overworked, and this was ridicule that curled up my very soul.") The White House received dozens of indignant letters, pointing out that millions of Americans were still undernourished. Steve Early ranted and raged. Eleanor, mortified, poured her woes out to Anna:

> Pa is both nervous and tired . . . I thought stupidly his little outburst of boredom on meals was amusing & human & used it in my column & it was taken up by papers & radio & over the ticker & Steve & Jimmy got hate letters & were much upset & Pa was furious with me. James came and reproved me and said I must distinguish between things which were personal and should not be said or none of them would dare to talk to me and he thought I should apologize to Father. I did before McDuffie Monday night before leaving as I couldn't see him alone and Pa answered irritably that it had been very hard on him and he would certainly say nothing more to me on any subject! So it has become a very serious subject and I am grieved at my poor judgment . . . Will I be glad when we leave the WH and I can be on my own!

If FDR was unusually irritable in the spring of 1937, it was because he had just made what would turn out to be the biggest mistake of his entire presidency. For two years now, the Supreme Court had been blocking important New Deal legislation. Time after time, the court ruled FDR's bills "unconstitutional," claiming they gave too much authority to the executive. As FDR saw it, he had been reelected with one of the biggest popular majorities in American history, he owed it to the people who voted for him to bring about change, and he was being thwarted by "nine old men."

Seven of the nine Supreme Court justices had been appointed by Republican presidents, and six of them were over seventy. In early February 1937, FDR asked Congress for a constitutional amendment that would allow him to appoint a new Supreme Court judge for each judge over seventy who refused to retire—up to a possible maximum of six. This meant that instead of nine judges, the Supreme Court might find itself with fifteen.

The outcry was immediate. Former president Herbert Hoover accused FDR of trying to "pack the court." The press called him "power mad," a "dictator." Most hurtful for FDR was that even some of the progressives in his own party felt that he was placing American democracy in jeopardy. Eleanor's lawyer friend, Elizabeth Read, told Eleanor that when she read about FDR's proposed bill in the newspaper, she sat at her dining-room table and wept.

In one of his best fireside chats ever, FDR pointed out that the president did not run the country. Using one of his simple, homely analogies, he described the U.S. government as a "three-horse team":

> The three horses are, of course, the three branches of government— the Congress, the executive, and the courts. Two of the horses, the Congress and the executive, are pulling in unison today; the third is not. Those who have intimated that the president of the United States is trying to drive that team, overlook the simple fact that the president, as chief executive, is himself one of the three horses. It is the American people themselves who are in the driver's seat. It is the American people themselves who want the furrow plowed.

Eleanor, who was in the Deep South on another lecture tour, cabled Franklin that it was "a grand talk." She was defending his bill at every opportunity. As she pointed out in her "My Day" column: "Here are these people all so scared for the Supreme Court, because it 'protects our liberties.' *Whose* liberties has it protected?"

For a while it looked as if FDR's bill might pass, but there were maneuverings behind the scenes, not least by the Supreme Court. On July 22, 1937, Congress rejected what the press was now calling the "court-packing bill." The political satirists had a field day. One cartoon depicted FDR with a fishing line, cursing "the big one that got away." For FDR, it was the most bitter defeat of his twelve-year presidency.

Such were the vicissitudes of political life. FDR's second term had started out with a blazing triumph; he had looked forward to making real progress with New Deal legislation. Instead, throughout his second term, he was to be buffeted by one storm after another. In the fall of 1937, stock-market prices fell, production declined, and unemployment rose. Conservatives claimed the New Deal was strangling business; progressives believed that the problem was reduced government spending—but they all saw the fault as FDR's. Just as Hoover had been blamed for the Depression, FDR was blamed for the "Roosevelt recession."

In the congressional elections of 1938, the Republicans made major gains. Martin Dies, a Texas politician who hated the New Deal, was stirring up paranoia about "socialists" and "communist subversives." In the House of Representatives he had created the "House Un-American Activities Committee" (HUAC), which aimed to ferret out those Reds to whom the Roosevelt government had given jobs.

By the summer of 1938, FDR's popularity had plummeted to an all-time low. Overseas, the situation was more and more alarming. Japan had invaded China. Nazi troops had marched into Austria. Franco, aided by the fascist powers, was winning in Spain. FDR was privately convinced that there would be another world war. Just as he had done in his navy days, he was pushing hard for "preparedness," wanting to build up the navy, air force, and armed forces. The press called him "the warmonger in the White House."

Throughout these turbulent times, FDR retained his famous calm. "Once you've spent two years trying to wiggle one toe," he told friends, "everything is in proportion."

While FDR's star was waning, Eleanor's was rising. In an NBC radio poll, she was elected "the outstanding woman of 1937." In January 1939, a Gallup poll showed her beating her husband in popularity. *The New York Times* made the astounding claim: "After her hundreds and thousands of miles of industrious travel and sightseeing and myriads of questions and explanations, the probability exists that she is, except for the President, the best informed individual on the American scene." Tommy Thompson, Eleanor's secretary, joked to Anna Roosevelt: "There may be something in this rumor of running your mother in 1940!"

There *were* rumors about Eleanor Roosevelt following in her husband's footsteps at the end of FDR's second term. Louis Howe had sometimes joked to Eleanor that if only she said the word, he would make her the next president. She had laughed.

In January 1938, while her autobiography, *This Is My Story*, was on the best-seller lists, her short book, *This Troubled World*, was hailed in *The New York Times* as a "valued, tough-minded assessment of the world's gravest problems."

Eleanor did not play safe to win fans. In *This Troubled World* she supported FDR's most unpopular cause—"preparedness." She knew what she was up against. Isolationists were in the majority, both on the right and left. They called this the "European war." They pointed out that forty thousand Americans had been killed in the so-called Great War, just to save Britain, and they did not want to fight in another imperial war. The money spent on war preparation would be far better spent on housing, schools, old-age pensions. Eleanor thoroughly agreed with the last argument, but she had come around to FDR's point of view: the United States needed to be strong, in order to exert moral power.

With *This Is My Story*, Eleanor—the only first lady to write an autobiography while in the White House—had taken another major risk. So had FDR, who gave his permission. His mother thought the idea preposterous, and in many ways it was. How could Eleanor tell the truth? How could she preserve a dignified discretion? How could she write her story without looking like a vulgar propagandist for herself and her husband? Somehow, she managed to turn a minefield into a triumph.

Harper and Brothers bought the book on the basis of the early chapters. *Ladies' Home Journal*, thrilled by Eleanor's "startling honesty and courage," offered $50,000 for first serial rights. Eleanor's literary agent, George Bye, raised the bid to $75,000. This was a huge sum, equal to FDR's presidential salary. Eleanor gave most of it to good causes, such as Arthurdale. But she was proud of her earnings.

Nevertheless, Eleanor had a terrible struggle with the later chapters. Bruce Gould, the editor of *Ladies' Home Journal*, told her frankly that he did not want a list of places she and Franklin had gone to, and the people they had met. He wanted to know more about Eleanor's mother-in-law. He wanted to know FDR's first words when he discovered he had polio. He wanted the "inner story."

Not for the first time in her life, Eleanor felt trapped. There was so much about her marriage that she could not talk about. She could not betray the true extent of Franklin's paralysis, nor could she go into her own long and difficult conflict with Mama. She could not mention Lucy Mercer, and she could not tell the truth about Missy LeHand. With Bruce Gould pushing hard, she did make some chary comments about her dominating mother-in-law, which would certainly have hurt eighty-three-year-old Sara Delano Roosevelt.

As the installments appeared in *Ladies' Home Journal*, the magazine's sales exceeded the editors' wildest hopes. From housemaids to politicians, everyone in the country seemed to be reading Eleanor's life story. The prose was pedestrian; the narrative, even at its most emotional moments, was oddly flat. But readers could see that Eleanor was telling the story herself, without a ghostwriter. They understood that a first lady could never be entirely open, and they appreciated the candor that was there. *The New York Times* described the book as "arresting in its combination of frankness and charm."

The success of her autobiography gave a further boost to Eleanor's "My Day" column. With her daily message to millions of readers Eleanor had acquired her own bully pulpit. It was rare that she spoke directly about politics. Rather, she used it to promote people and causes she admired. Above all, it was an opportunity to make the first family appear more human and lovable—which, of course, reflected favorably on FDR.

The fact that Eleanor seemed to be everywhere at once helped conceal FDR's lack of mobility. She wrote from New York, where she was having coaching to lower her voice. ("I came to New York on the midnight train last night, and I have today taken my first lesson to improve my speaking voice.") She wrote from Boston, where her son John was having four wisdom teeth removed. ("There is no doubt about it, the hours spent sitting around in a hospital are conducive to doing a great deal of knitting.") She wrote from Hyde Park, where she read the newspapers and mused about the government balancing its budget. ("Like almost every other woman I know of moderate means, I am always terribly nervous until all my bills are paid . . . I do hope, however, that in this budget balancing business we make our economies without making people suffer who are in need of help.")

Ten years after his mother's death, Elliott Roosevelt would have this to say about his mother's writings:

In the hundreds of thousands of words, possibly even millions of them, which she ultimately set down on paper, reaching her zenith with her "My Day" column started in 1936, she managed to conceal her personality completely. She pictured herself as a calm, contented woman deeply concerned with the world and her family. We read her articles and marveled how she created the image of a total stranger, not the detached, harried, fault-finding wife and parent we knew. Only deep below the surface of her careful prose could be found an occasional clue to her conflicts. "I have always wanted to try to write fiction," she said, "but I never had the time."

Elliott Roosevelt's own memoirs would prove completely unreliable, but his comment is a salient reminder that Eleanor's writings, just like FDR's, always had a political purpose. Even the stories they told their friends were less concerned with truth than effect. Sam Rosenman, FDR's speechwriter, never ceased to be amazed by FDR's talent for dramatic invention: "He would tell anecdotes which some of us had heard time and again, but which always seemed to gather additional embellishments as well as additional charm in the telling." It was not a question of lying—Franklin and Eleanor were too upright and too clever for that. It was more a question of omission and embellishment. A good politician—the kind who could persuade the nation that a paraplegic could walk—had to know what to leave out. It was an integral part of the spellbinding Roosevelt charm.

The White House press had long ago understood that FDR was brilliant at *not* saying things. At one of the Gridiron dinners, the reporters were much amused by a massive papier-mâché model of Franklin as an Egyptian sphinx, with a long cigarette holder jauntily positioned in a grinning mouth.

She might have been the most influential woman in Washington, but Eleanor had to steer her path with great tact. She once wrote that for women to be effective in politics they needed "the wisdom of the serpent and the guileless appearance of the dove." She was first lady, not an elected official. She made suggestions to Franklin, brought people to see him, and was widely regarded as the "back door" to the president. But she had to be careful that Franklin did not feel she was telling him what to do. She had to show due deference to FDR's advisers, who easily resented her. And with the public, she had to use her position of power while making it appear that she was not trying to influence her husband. One of the refrains in her autobiography would be: "I never tried to exert any political influence on my husband or anyone else in the government."

The records tell another story. Eleanor was always firing off memos to Harry Hopkins, head of the Works Progress Administration, a fellow humanitarian to whom she was close:

Dear Harry,
    Is it true that wages for Negroes in regions #3 and #4 under the works relief act, are lower than those established for white people? Very cordially yours, ER

Dear Harry,
    This family seems to be very much in need of assistance . . . Would you be good enough to have the case looked into?

She wrote to Harold Ickes, secretary of the interior:

I hope you do not think that I was the person who suggested Mrs. Rohde for any position. I simply wrote you because the President asked me to do so. There is such a concerted effort being made to make it appear that I dictate to F.D.R. that I don't want the people who should know the truth to have any misunderstanding about it. I wouldn't dream of doing more than passing along requests or suggestions that come to me.

She wrote to Louis Fischer, an American journalist who urged her to speak to the president about sending arms to help the Loyalists in the Spanish Civil War:

Dear Mr. Fischer,
    I talked to the President— He agrees with you, but feels that it would be absolutely impossible to repeal the Neutrality Act, because the people of this country feel that it was designed to keep us out of the war.

When Louis Fischer asked permission to thank her in his book, she wrote back:

My dear Mr. Fischer,

I would rather you left out my letter and any reference to the President . . . I do not want it said that I interfered. Very sincerely yours, ER

With the "Negro question," as it was called, Eleanor was walking on eggs. White Southerners held strategic posts on the House and Senate committees. FDR needed their vote. This did not stop Eleanor speaking out, with FDR's consent.

Whenever Eleanor was seen with African Americans, there was an outraged reaction in the white Southern press. A photograph in the *Alabama Sun* carried the caption: "Eleanor and Some More Niggers." The white reporter was hopping mad:

> Every time Eleanor opens her big mouth, it's big news for the Negro newspapers, who boast of a circulation of over 2,000,000 in the South. The past week, Eleanor was journeying as usual but stopped at Newark, New Jersey, where a bunch of Negroes were having a jamboree, and naturally Eleanor had to stop there and have her picture taken with a nigger.

When it came to race consciousness, Eleanor herself was still learning. In *This Is My Story* she twice used the word "darky." She did not realize that it was derogatory. Her editors did not question her use of this word. Nor did Franklin, Anna, or Hickok, all of whom read the manuscript. An African American woman from Chicago wrote to the first lady and told her how shocked she had been to come across this expression, from someone who otherwise did so much for her people. Eleanor wrote back: "My dear Mrs. Carey: 'Darky' was used by my great aunt as a term of affection and I have always considered it in that light. I am sorry if it hurt you. What do you prefer?"

Eleanor regularly invited African American leaders to the White House for discussions, and sometimes arranged for them to meet FDR. She and Walter White, the executive secretary of the National Association for the Advancement of Colored People, tried hard to get FDR to promote the passage of federal anti-lynching legislation. FDR was strongly in favor of it, but could not risk antagonizing white Southern Democrats.

After a brutal lynching in Florida—attended by thousands of frenzied spectators and ignored by local officials—Eleanor wanted to speak at a protest meeting. "FDR, I would like to do it," her memo read, "but will do whatever you say." The answer came back through Missy. "President says this is dynamite." It was one of the occasions when Eleanor wished she did not live in the White House. "I feel a skunk not to do more on the lynching thing openly," she told Hick.

But when the Daughters of the American Revolution refused to allow Marian Anderson, the world-famous contralto, to perform in Washington's Constitution Hall because of the color of her skin, Eleanor resigned from the organization. Eleanor's action brought international attention to the "Negro question" in the United States. Walter White suggested a free open-air concert in front of the Lincoln Memorial. Eleanor threw her support behind it, and FDR gave his approval. On Easter Sunday—April 9, 1939—in an atmosphere electric with excitement, 75,000 people gathered to hear Marian Anderson sing. It was the first time in American history that black and white Americans came together in such numbers to pay tribute to a black American.

As Marian Anderson came down the marble steps of the Lincoln Memorial and stood at the feet of the Great Emancipator, the setting sun bathed the reflection pool in a pink glow. "In this great auditorium under the sky, all of us are free," Harold Ickes declared. Throughout the concert people were weeping for joy.

"The Marian Anderson concert on Sunday was one of the most thrilling experiences of our time," Walter White wrote to Eleanor. "Only one thing marred it—that you couldn't be there. But I understand thoroughly the reason you could not come."

Eleanor admitted in her autobiography that her actions would "sometimes serve as a trial balloon" for FDR. "If some idea I expressed strongly—and with which he might agree—caused a violent reaction, he could honestly say that he had no responsibility in the matter and that the thoughts were my own." She was bitterly disappointed when FDR refused to do what she saw as the right thing. But she understood. FDR was the politician and she was the "agitator." It was a delicate balance, but it worked.

FDR's second term would be over at the end of 1940. After that, FDR intended to live at Hyde Park, surrounded by his usual community of colleagues, friends, and family. His plan was to establish the FDR Library—the first presidential library in history—on his mother's property, and spend his retirement putting his papers in order and writing his memoirs.

Franklin and Eleanor were encouraging their friends to build houses in the vicinity. Harry Hopkins intended to. So did Earl Miller, to whom they had given land as a wedding present. Eleanor's brother Hall lived with his girlfriend in a small house on the edge of the Hyde Park estate. Gus Gennerich had bought a farm nearby. After Gus's death, FDR wrote to Daisy Suckley: "I hate to see that place just sold to anybody—don't you? Should I buy it—& you & I manage it? I long so to talk it all over with you."

FDR was putting pressure on Sam Rosenman, his speechwriter, to move into the area. Rosenman recalled:

> One weekend . . . [the President] had asked Mrs. Rosenman and me to come up to Hyde Park; we found, much to our surprise, that he had arranged with a real estate agent to pick us up directly after lunch to take us to see some Dutchess County property near his own place. At that time we had no thought of buying a country place. He said that he wanted us to have a country home up there as his neighbors. And he added significantly: "When I come back here . . . we can work on the papers together at Hyde Park."

In the fall of 1937, Franklin began drawing designs for Hilltop Cottage—or Top Cottage, as it came to be known. It was to be a simple Dutch fieldstone house, on the highest hill on his part of the property. His mother was upset. It was beginning to seem to her that everyone was fleeing the Big House. Franklin promised her he would never stay in the cottage overnight. He visualized it as an occasional daytime retreat—a place where he could escape from the world. The hill was surrounded by seventy acres of forest. There would be no telephone. He wanted to be able to sit on the porch, gaze out across the Hudson to the Catskills, listen to the rustle of the trees, and work on his memoirs.

Writing to Daisy Suckley, Franklin dubbed it "our house on our hill." He designed a modest cottage with two wings, a large living and dining room, opening onto a wide porch that faced west, toward the river. Daisy wrote back playfully: "You have made the wings much bigger than

I, & we've both planned for lots of book space! . . . Just one thing *really* worries me! And that is the angle of the attic floor!! The trunks will be continually coasting down to the eaves."

FDR was also enjoying a flirtatious friendship with Dorothy Schiff. An attractive thirty-three-year-old from a prominent New York Jewish financier family, Dorothy Schiff had been active in the Democratic campaign of 1936. She and her husband, George Backer, were among the friends at Hyde Park on election night. Their marriage (like all of Dorothy Schiff's four marriages) was somewhat casual. In the spring and summer of 1937, Dorothy received several invitations to Hyde Park. She would be "summoned," she recalled, by Missy LeHand. Dorothy did not want Eleanor to think she was flirting with FDR behind her back, and so she would call Eleanor's secretary to accept. To her initial surprise, she found herself staying overnight at Val-Kill with Eleanor and her friends. FDR would turn up in his car and honk his horn (Dorothy found this horribly embarrassing), then take her for a drive in his blue Ford V-8. "He loved driving recklessly along his miles of wood roads," Dorothy Schiff recalled, "particularly pleased at giving his secret service agent the slip."

Dorothy was flattered by the president's interest in her. "If he had said let's go to bed, I probably would have," she told Ted Morgan, FDR's biographer, years later. She thought of Franklin as a "sun god"—warm, beaming, cheerful. But she was never in love with him. She was bored by his "juvenile stories," which he told again and again. She wished he were a little more inhibited about being carried around in front of people, and was embarrassed when he asked her to push his wheelchair. At Warm Springs, she was repelled to see him in the pool "with all those other cripples."

In the summer of 1937, Franklin coerced her, as Dorothy saw it, into buying half shares, along with him, in a property near Hyde Park. (This was most likely Gus Gennerich's farm.) Dorothy found it hard to say no to FDR, and was relieved when he seemed to have forgotten about it. In December she got a letter saying he had closed the deal and would she please send a check for $9,000. Dorothy had a cottage built on the property—"the Red House," she called it—but it was mostly Sam Rosenman and his wife who stayed there. The year it was finished, 1939, Dorothy Schiff bought the *New York Post*, which under her direction would be strongly pro-Roosevelt, but the romance, such as it was, was over.

By now, Eleanor knew clearly that she no longer wanted to be caught up in the hurly-burly around Franklin. She needed her own space. When they left the White House, she intended to live at Val-Kill Cottage—close to Franklin but not with him.

She did not feel at home in Mama's house, and she realized now that she never would. The same was true of their half of the house at 47–49 East Sixty-fifth Street. She and Franklin wanted to sell it, but Mama did not want to, and the deed was hers. In the meantime, Eleanor had rented a small top-floor apartment at 20 East Eleventh Street, a walk-up in Greenwich Village owned by Eleanor's friends Elizabeth Read and Esther Lape, who lived downstairs. Eleanor gave keys to Hick and Earl, telling them that they should consider it their home as well.

Eleanor had fallen out with Nancy Cook and Marion Dickerman. In May 1936 they had closed the Val-Kill furniture factory, which had always run at a loss. Eleanor, who had paid for the building in the first place, asked Nancy and Marion if she might turn it into a house for herself, leaving them the stone cottage. She was thinking of life after the White House, and felt the need for a place of her own, where she could have guests without feeling that she was imposing. She knew that Nancy and Marion, who were quite snobbish, had never warmed to Earl, Hick, and other of her friends.

They agreed, though Nancy was clearly hurt by the arrangement. The sprawling two-story factory was converted into a residence, and Eleanor and her secretary, Tommy Thompson, moved in during the summer of 1937. The house had none of the charm of the stone cottage. The gray stucco exterior had an industrial look. The front door was the old tradesman's entrance—two stucco steps at the side, where Eleanor would receive world leaders. The interior was modest but cozy, with a maze of small pine-paneled guest rooms, which looked out at the woods. Few of Eleanor's visitors were enthusiastic about the skin of a tiger on the living-room floor, teeth bared in a threatening snarl. Eleanor loved it. Her father had shot the tiger in India.

"My house seems nicer than ever," Eleanor wrote to Anna in October, "& I could be happy in it alone! That's the last test of one's surroundings I think!" She slept most of the year on the wide screened-in porch off her bedroom, where she could enjoy the cold night air, the frog noises from the pond, the dawn chorus of birds. Tommy had her own apartment on the ground floor.

But tensions were brewing with the women who lived just down the path, in the stone cottage. Nan felt lost without the furniture business, and sensed that Eleanor was slipping away from her. Marion often complained to Eleanor that the Roosevelt connection made life difficult for her as headmistress of Todhunter (these days, the mere mention of the Roosevelts and the New Deal provoked rage in the girls' Republican parents), and yet whenever she needed something Marion turned to Eleanor, wanting her to pull strings.

It was due to Eleanor's influence that Marion was in Europe in the summer of 1938. She had been appointed to a committee, headed by Frances Perkins, whose task was to study labor relations in England and Sweden. (Perkins said later that Marion should never have been on the committee. This was not her area of expertise, and she did not take it seriously. To Perkins's embarrassment, Marion spent most evenings whooping it up in the bars of Stockholm with a woman friend.) Eleanor and Tommy were installed in their new house. Nan was alone in the stone cottage, feeling morose.

Late one night Nan made a comment to Eleanor that she would regret for the rest of her life. According to her, she and Marion felt that everything the three of them had ever done together—the Women's Democratic Committee, Todhunter School, Val-Kill Furniture Industries, Arthurdale—was always, ultimately, for the purpose of building up Eleanor.

Eleanor was hurt to the quick. She stormed off. The next day, she strode back up the path and told Nancy that the friendship was over. Since she and Marion lived next door, Eleanor would continue to invite them to social occasions; they would share the swimming pool; she hoped they would treat each other with courtesy. But that was it.

When Marion got back from Europe a week later, Nancy was alone on the dock, with red eyes. Marion tried to talk to Eleanor, in vain. Eleanor would not talk to her or Nancy. Finally, the two women went to Franklin. "As a peace negotiator you are Number One!" Nancy wrote him afterward. "Bless you dear and a world of thanks and love."

Franklin, with his lifelong experience of Mama, knew how to appease and coax, but in fact he, like all of Eleanor's friends, took the view that Marion and Nancy had abused Eleanor's goodwill over the years. Eleanor herself was now in full martyr mode. Since Marion was quibbling about the settlement, Eleanor employed Elizabeth Read, her lawyer friend, to sort out their financial affairs, but Eleanor insisted on a settlement that was ridiculously generous, and Read told her so.

"Elizabeth, what you say is true," Eleanor wrote back, "but I can never forget that these two girls are afraid of the future and I am not."

Eleanor's closest companion these days was her secretary, Malvina Thompson. Tommy was nine years younger than Eleanor, short and stocky, with a deep, husky voice from incessant smoking. Born in the Bronx of working-class parents, she was levelheaded, eminently sensible, and game for anything—Eleanor called her a "brick"—but Tommy lacked Eleanor's culture, and had little interest in art and literature. Their friendship was really about work. Tommy was an indefatigable worker, who had sacrificed her personal life to a boss she adored. Her husband resented it. In the fall of 1937 he asked for a divorce. Tommy was miserable for months. Nevertheless, she considered herself immensely privileged to be doing that job. "My boss is a very big person," she told Hick, "just about the biggest person in the world. Anything I can do for her—no matter what—justifies my existence."

Tommy now went almost everywhere with Eleanor. She came up with ideas for the column; she corrected Eleanor's spelling and grammar; and she was not afraid to say what she thought. "You didn't do that very well," she would sometimes chide Eleanor. "You didn't take enough time to prepare for it."

Her loyalty was reciprocated. Tommy was part of the Roosevelt family, and particularly close to Anna. The grandchildren loved her. When Tommy had an operation in the fall of 1938, Eleanor hovered by her hospital bedside. Back home, Eleanor took over the nursing. "Did she tell you that . . . once each week she gives me a jab in my posterior?" Tommy wrote to Anna. "She is really expert, it never hurts a bit."

Eleanor liked Tommy's new boyfriend, Henry Osthagen, the engineer who had supervised the conversion of the factory building. He would often stay at Val-Kill, in Tommy's apartment. In future years, he wanted to marry Tommy, but Tommy refused. She was not going to make that mistake again, she said. She loved Henry, but she was wedded to her work.

"Did you hear Hitler today?" FDR wrote to Daisy in September 1938. "His shrieks, his histrionics and the effect on the huge audience. They did not applaud—they made noises like animals." He scarcely dared to plan trips even to Hyde Park, he told her. The European situation needed "hourly watching."

Daisy saw what was coming. Rumors had been flying since the beginning of his second term that FDR would be "the first third-term president." The prospect of war made it likely. By the time Top Cottage was completed, in the spring of 1939, Daisy had understood that he was never going to retire with her to a little house in the woods.

Most Americans at the time took the view that the rest of the world was not their problem. The government officially espoused "neutrality." FDR, though, had no illusions about the danger Hitler posed to the world. He already knew that the United States was going to have to play its part in Hitler's defeat. For the time being, he wanted to build up American military power so that they could supply arms to Hitler's opponents. This meant repealing the neutrality law and yet another protracted fight with Congress.

Eleanor was well known as a peace advocate. She, like her husband, had seen the horror of war close up, she told audiences, and hated war. She was the mother of four boys of fighting age. But she was a "realistic pacifist." Hitler was threatening freedom and democracy throughout the world. It was no good disarming the United States while the evil leaders armed their countries to the hilt.

In November 1938 the world heard the shocking news of *Kristallnacht*, the "Night of Broken Glass." Nazi storm troopers set fire to Jewish homes, schools, synagogues, businesses, and cemeteries, murdering as they went. Thousands of Jews were taken from their homes and sent to concentration camps. Adolf Hitler, who had already stripped German Jews of their civil rights and assets, announced that he would happily send them to any country willing to take them. He now talked of "complete extermination." FDR was the only major world leader to condemn Hitler's actions publicly.

The American people were shocked by events in Europe, but continued to have what FDR called an "ostrich" attitude. They did not want any more immigrants, and particularly not penniless Jews. Anti-Semitism was as rife in the United States as everywhere else. The reactionary American newspapers—along with the Führer—liked to call the New Deal the "Jew Deal." (They made frequent mention of treasurer Henry Morgenthau Jr., speechwriter Samuel Rosenman, Supreme Court Justice Felix Frankfurter, and FDR's "confidant," Bernard Baruch.) They even called Roosevelt "Rosenfelt," making out he had Jewish ancestors. FDR retorted: "In the dim distant past, they may have been Jews or Catholics or Protestants. What I am interested in is whether they were good citizens and believers in God. I hope they were both."

A group of activists introduced the Wagner-Rogers Bill, which proposed allowing special entry to twenty thousand Jewish children from Germany. Eleanor worked behind the scenes with the committee. "My husband says that you had better go to work at once and get two people of opposite parties in the House and Senate," she advised, "and if possible, get all the Catholic support you can."

But two-thirds of Americans opposed the bill. Laura Houghteling, FDR's cousin and the wife of the immigration commissioner, went around saying that "twenty thousand charming children would all too soon grow into twenty thousand ugly adults." The Southern Democrats were against it, and FDR needed their support to repeal the neutrality law. As he kept reminding Eleanor, he was obliged to focus on the "big picture."

In February 1939, Eleanor telegraphed FDR, who was on a cruise in the Caribbean, to ask whether she could say they both supported the Wagner-Rogers Bill. "You may," he wrote back, "but it's better that I don't for the time being."

Eleanor, bitterly disappointed, wrote in her column: "Democracy requires not the action of one man, but the conviction and courage of many."

FDR had planned the visit of King George VI and Queen Elizabeth with exhaustive care, down to the last detail. The visit carried a symbolic charge. It was clear that war in Europe was imminent, and Americans were wary of Britain pulling them into the fray. For his part, FDR could see that the United States was going to need Britain, just as Britain would need the United States. It was his hope that if Americans opened their hearts to the British king and queen, the mood in the States might become less isolationist.

FDR had written to the British monarch in August 1938, broaching the subject of a possible visit. He had heard that the royal couple was planning to travel to Canada in the summer of 1939, and hoped they might come to the United States as well.

> My dear King George . . . It would give my wife and me the greatest pleasure to see you, and frankly, I think it would be an excellent thing for Anglo-American relations if you could visit the United States . . . If you should be here in June or July you might care to avoid the heat of Washington, and, in such a case, it would give us the greatest pleasure to have you and Her Majesty come to visit us at our country home at Hyde Park which is on the Hudson River, about eighty miles north of New York and, therefore, on the direct route between New York City and Canada. Also, it occurs to me that a Canadian trip would be crowded with formalities and that you both might like three or four days of very simple country life at Hyde Park—with no formal entertainments and an opportunity to get a bit of rest and relaxation.

In November, when the visit was becoming a definite possibility, FDR wrote another long letter, equally warm and charming, which made his aim quite clear. "Probably the official visit to the Capital should be made, and also a visit to New York, but if you could stay with us at Hyde Park for two or three days, the simplicity and naturalness of such a visit would produce a most excellent effect."

The entire country was vicariously involved in the royal visit. In her "My Day" column, Eleanor had divulged that she and the president were planning a picnic at Hyde Park, with simple American food, such as hot dogs. The idea provoked an outcry. Eleanor was enjoying herself:

MY DAY, MAY 26, 1939

Oh dear, oh dear, so many people are worried that "the dignity of our country will be imperiled" by inviting royalty to a picnic, particularly a hot dog picnic. My mother-in-law has sent me a letter she received, which begs that she control me in some way and, in order to spare my feelings, she has written a little message on the back: "Only one of many such."

But she did not know, poor darling, that I have received "many such" right here in Washington. Let me assure you, dear readers, that if it is hot there will be no hot dogs, and even if it is cool, there will be plenty of other food, and the elder members of the family and the more important guests will be served with due formality.

The arrival of Their Majesties at Union Station and the procession through the streets of Washington took place in sweltering heat. The crowds were immense. The king, attired in his formal regalia, admitted to FDR afterward that he had feared he might "pass out." But all went well. The royal couple, gracious and smiling, captivated the American people. In the world press photos, Franklin and Eleanor, who towered over the diminutive British royals, exuded American vigor and hospitality.

The weather was pleasant when the royal couple arrived at Hyde Park on Saturday, June 10, 1939. That evening, a proud Sara Delano presided over dinner. She was dismayed not to be able to use her own servants; the staff had been brought from the White House. Halfway through the meal, an overladen serving table collapsed and a stack of Limoges china plates clattered to the floor. After dinner, they repaired to the library, and the butler, who was bringing in a tray with decanters, glasses, and bowls of ice, caught his heel on the steps. The tray went crashing. Franklin made a joke of both incidents. Sara was mortified.

On Sunday, June 11, 1939, the little parish at Hyde Park, St. James Episcopal Church, received world attention. The royal couple was attending an 11 a.m. service with the Roosevelts. Daisy Suckley had arrived an hour early, and from her aisle seat in a front pew she observed the terror that lurked beneath the glamour. That evening she wrote in her diary:

Mrs. James Roosevelt & the Queen walked up together, followed by the King & Eleanor R. The Pres. followed on Jim's arm . . . The Pres. walked with great difficulty & told me later that only one side of his right brace was fastened & if it had broken, he would have collapsed in the aisle! . . . At the close . . . the King & Queen walked out together, smiling from side to side—followed by the R. ladies & F.D.R. "stumping" along, as he puts it, as fast as he could.

After the church service came the picnic, attended by 165 people. Top Cottage, FDR's new hilltop hideaway, did not yet have running water or furniture, but FDR had insisted that this was the perfect place for a royal picnic. Eleanor had been rushing around for days, seeing to last-minute details.

There was a delicious cold buffet. Outside, on the large porch, a single dish of hot dogs was served on a silver tray. Eleanor, her admiring niece observed, "was dashing about in a little brown gingham dress, seeing that the lunch was properly served and that everybody was comfortable, just as though it were only a family party."

Later that afternoon, the Roosevelts asked their royal guests over to Val-Kill Cottage for tea by the pool. Franklin went into the water, exposing his shriveled legs. The king joined him. The queen sat in the shade with her lady-in-waiting, and confided in Eleanor that she and her husband had known that Franklin used a cane, but they had not had the *slightest* idea that he could not walk.

It was close to 11 p.m. when the Roosevelts drove the royal couple to the Hyde Park railroad station. There had been a heavy thunderstorm during dinner, with dramatic flashes of lightning over the Catskills. The air was fresh after the rain, and the moonlight on the river had a magical quality. There were people everywhere, on the steep banks of the river and up the hill. The mood was somber. Recent events in Europe made it almost certain that Their Majesties were going home to face war. The king and queen, standing on the rear platform of the train, waved and smiled as it pulled slowly away. FDR called out: "Good luck to you! All the luck in the world!" Somebody began to sing "Auld Lang Syne," and soon everyone joined in. Many had tears in their eyes.

Eleanor could not resist talking about the crashing china in her column. She checked it with FDR. "Why mention that?" he asked. Eleanor said she liked these touches, which showed that they were just as human as everyone else. FDR laughed, and let it pass. "My mother-in-law was very indignant with me for telling the world about it," Eleanor wrote later, "and not keeping it a deep, dark family secret."

FDR, an avid reader of detective stories, liked to call it "the Hyde Park Cataclysm." The story of the royal visit to Hyde Park became a favorite in his repertoire.

•

Three months after that mellow picnic by the Hudson, war broke out in Europe. On September 1, 1939, just four days after the shocking news of the Nazi-Soviet Pact, Missy, asleep in her apartment, was woken by the jangling of the phone. It was William Bullitt, currently the American ambassador to France, calling from Paris. Germany had invaded Poland, he told her. Would she wake the president?

Two minutes later, FDR woke to a ringing phone, turned on his bedside lamp, glanced at the clock—it was 4:30 a.m.—and picked up. He knew this was not going to be good news. Bullitt told him that Nazi divisions had entered Poland, the fighting was heavy, and there were reports of bombers over Warsaw. "Well, Bill, it's come at last," FDR said. "God help us all."

Missy dressed and came downstairs. She spent the next few hours in the Oval Room, fielding phone calls for FDR. At 5 a.m., FDR phoned Eleanor, at Val-Kill. Hitler was about to address the Reichstag, he told her. Eleanor and Tommy turned on the radio and listened, until 6 a.m., to that strident voice.

That evening, Americans all over the country were glued to their radio sets to hear the far more gentle, fatherly tone of FDR. "My countrymen and my friends— Until four-thirty o'clock this morning I had hoped against hope that some miracle would prevent a devastating war in Europe," he said. "I hope the United States will keep out of this war . . . It is, of course, impossible to predict the future . . . When peace has been broken anywhere, the peace of all countries everywhere is in danger."

On September 3, 1939, Britain and France, declared war on Germany. FDR had a major challenge ahead of him. While reassuring the American people that he would not be sending their boys abroad to fight, he had to convince Congress to spend almost a billion dollars on defense. The prevailing mood in the United States was "peace at any price," but FDR knew that the defeat of fascism was going to mean all-out war.

In her column, Eleanor was now gently preparing her readers. "I hope that, in spite of the contagion of war, we can keep out of it, but I hope that we will decide on what we believe."

Eleanor scorned the Red Scare that was sweeping away civil liberties in her own country. "We must not reach a state of fear and hysteria that will make us all cowards!" Over the years, in her fight for progressive causes, Eleanor had often found herself mixing with Communists. (The American Communist Party had 65,000 members in the 1930s, and played a major role in the Labor Movement and campaign against lynching.) Eleanor had been a strong supporter of the Federal Theatre Project which, because of its radical politics, the House Un-American Activities Committee (HUAC) had managed to destroy. And she had friends in the American Youth Congress (AYC), some of whose members were known to be Communists.

HUAC, claiming that it was a Communist front, had issued a subpoena to the leaders of the Youth Congress. The hearings were to take place on November 30, 1939. Eleanor asked FDR's permission to turn up unannounced in the audience. Her arrival caused a flurry among the members of HUAC, who, full of Southern chivalry, invited her to sit with them. She shook her head and sat with the student leaders. The HUAC interrogations were noticeably less antagonistic that morning.

By noon the youth leaders had still not been summoned, and a three-hour adjournment was announced. Eleanor asked the young radicals back to lunch at the White House. The students had no money, and they were obliged to find accommodation in Washington while the HUAC men made sport of them. Eleanor invited the entire contingent—there were ten of them—to be guests of the White House until the hearings were over.

The militants arrived with their shabby bags and settled into the guest rooms. That evening, they found themselves at the dinner table with FDR. He had a lot on his mind—the Soviet Union had invaded Finland that day—but he nevertheless wanted to hear all about the day's proceedings. He declared HUAC "sordid." There was joking and laughter about its methods. Then the subject of Finland came up. FDR said the Soviet invasion was "a terrible thing." The Communists in the group were silent.

Eleanor found herself particularly drawn to an intense, dark-haired, troubled-looking young man who sat across the table from her. Joseph Lash, the son of Russian Jewish émigrés, admitted that he had been devastated by the Nazi-Soviet Pact and the invasion of Finland. As an active member of the American Socialist Party, he had viewed the Soviet Union as a bastion of progress and a bulwark against fascism. At the very moment when HUAC was trying to make him look like a Soviet spy, his own faith in the USSR had crashed.

After dinner, the president withdrew to his study, and Eleanor invited the group up to her sitting room. The animated talk continued. The young radicals, most of whom had voted for FDR in the 1936 election, expressed dismay that the president was so focused on war. An international war was necessarily against the interests of American workers. What about the "Second New Deal" that FDR had promised? What about Negro rights? Eleanor pointed out that they should not underrate the difficulties the president faced with Congress every time he tried to pass progressive legislation. This was why they needed a socialist movement, outside the Democratic Party, to put pressure on the government. This was why they needed the youth of America to speak out.

The next day, Joe Lash gave his testimony in front of the committee. Eleanor was slightly deaf these days, and she moved closer to the front to hear him. Joe's political confusion and personal turmoil were evident. Afterward she wrote him a note. If he would like to talk to her, alone or with a friend, she would be glad to see him.

Joe Lash turned up with a Youth Congress girlfriend to the first lady's small apartment on East Eleventh Street, and the three of them talked politics for almost an hour. Joe confessed that until recently he had been a fervent advocate of American neutrality, but now believed that the United States could not sit back while the rest of the world went to hell.

The first lady asked questions and listened intently. Lash could not believe how kind she was, how understanding. She invited him to use her cottage at Hyde Park to do some thinking and writing. It was a quiet place, she told him, where he could figure out his beliefs.

A couple of weeks later, the Youth Congress was meeting in Washington for a conference, and Eleanor invited the leaders back to the White House. The group went down to the pool and Joe Lash had his first view of the first lady diving. ("She dove in with an awful splash!") They were invited to the Oval Room for cocktails. The president mixed manhattans, which Missy ("soft, silver-haired, smiling") handed around. At dinner, some of the youth leaders argued that the government should be spending less on armaments and more on social services. The president said, "Let's accept the opinion of youth, but I want my protest vote recorded for history." There was a 50 percent chance of a Nazi-Soviet victory in Europe, he told them, and the United States had a stake in preventing it. The United States *had* to be armed.

The next day, Eleanor invited Joe to lunch to discuss his stay at Val-Kill. There was only one maid there, so apart from occasional visitors he would be by himself. She hoped he would invite a friend up on the weekends. There was a docile horse he could ride—hers. If it were cold enough, he could skate on the pond. She told him where to find wine, cross-country skis, and cigarettes. "Perhaps I'll drop in and lunch with you on the 3rd if you will have me?"

On January 23, 1940, Joe took the train to Poughkeepsie. Mrs. Roosevelt's groom met him at the station and drove him to the cottage. Alice, a shy "Negro girl" showed him to his room, which was full of books, with a lovely view of white birches, pines, and the frozen pond. There was a note from Mrs. Roosevelt on the desk: "I find the woods & the hill top conducive to thought & I hope you will find peace up there. Eat & sleep well, the rest will come."

When Joe came downstairs, he was greeted by Earl Miller ("a big, bluff man, exuding health"), who said he happened to be in the vicinity. They had lunch together—hearty chops cooked by Alice—and went for a walk ("the Lady's favorite," Earl said) through the woods to the top of the hill where the president had built Top Cottage.

Joe spent two weeks at the cottage. A Youth Congress friend came up for a few days. Joe went down to New York for a meeting. His socialist comrades disapproved of his new friendship. It would be seen as "sycophancy," they said, and destroy his political credibility. Was he looking for a mother? Could he not see that though Mrs. Roosevelt was a "good woman," their views were poles apart?

On Saturday, February 3, the president and first lady arrived at the Big House for the weekend. That afternoon Mrs. Roosevelt phoned Joe, and came around to the cottage. She lit a fire in the living room, and knitted while they talked. On Sunday morning, she invited Joe to the Big House. She showed him the library, and they walked back to the cottage, both of them slipping at times on the icy path through the woods. At 1 p.m., the president drove up with Missy in his Ford. His guards formed a seat with their hands and carried him in, and they sat down to eat.

After lunch, some political neighbors turned up to talk to the president. Mrs. Roosevelt, Missy, and Joe cleared the table and chatted in the sitting room. The president and Missy drove off, and Mrs. Roosevelt and Joe took the 4:07 train to New York. Joe asked Mrs. Roosevelt if she would be willing to serve as a reference for a Harvard fellowship. Mrs. Roosevelt said she would be glad to. Joe was thinking of writing a book on the president's political philosophy; Mrs. Roosevelt said she might be able to organize a foreword from FDR.

They arrived at Grand Central. Joe Lash gave the first lady a farewell hug. Then she rushed off to catch another train, which was to depart in ten minutes.

Although it was not written in the Constitution—not until 1951—it was an established tradition, from George Washington onward, that presidents would not run for a third term. But in 1940, the world was in disarray. FDR was perceived internationally as a bold leader who was willing to stand up to Hitler. Where was the suitable presidential candidate in the Democratic Party, if not Roosevelt? Some Democrats were begging FDR to stand again. Others were dismayed by the idea. The Republicans were outraged.

Eleanor had urged FDR to prepare a successor. FDR told her that he could not do more than provide opportunities. Leaders rose to the surface themselves.

In January 1940, FDR turned fifty-eight. The strain of the presidency was taking its toll. FDR was becoming acutely aware of his own mortality. One evening in February, while he was having dinner in the White House with Bill Bullitt and Missy, he suddenly lost consciousness. Dr. McIntire declared it a minor heart attack and the incident was hushed up, but it was ominous. Theodore Roosevelt, FDR's eternal yardstick, had died at sixty. FDR's own life was far too sedentary, not at all good for his circulation.

For months the war in Europe had been at a standstill. It was being called the "Phony War." Suddenly, in the spring of 1940, Hitler moved fast. In April and May, the Nazis invaded Denmark, Norway, and Holland. In early June, they swept through the Maginot Line and France fell. Winston Churchill, the new British prime minister, warned the world: "I expect that the Battle of Britain is about to begin . . . If we fail, then the whole world, including the United States . . . will sink into the abyss of a new Dark Age."

In early July, just before the Democratic National Convention, FDR put an end to months of intense speculation. If he were nominated, he would run again. But he wanted Henry Wallace, his secretary of agriculture, as vice president. Without Wallace, FDR said, he would not accept the nomination.

FDR wanted Wallace because he was well aware that he himself might not survive a third term, and Wallace was in his prime. Wallace had done an outstanding job at modernizing American agriculture; he would help carry the farm belt; he was a New Dealer; and he was loyal. But Wallace was not a popular choice. He had never run for elective office; many considered him too left wing; in his personal life he was seen as something of a crackpot mystic; and he had no support from the business sector.

The Democratic National Convention was held in Chicago in mid-July. The atmosphere was poisonous. The party delegates did not want Wallace, and were furious about FDR's imperious behavior. Two days into the proceedings, Frances Perkins phoned Eleanor, who was at Val-Kill with friends, and pleaded with her to come out and speak. Eleanor Roosevelt was a much admired figure in the party and people trusted her. The party needed to hear from her.

Eleanor was not keen. This would only bring on more accusations of "petticoat government." She phoned FDR, in the White House. He urged her to go. Eleanor made some notes, stayed up till 3 a.m. with her friends, packed an overnight bag, and flew eight hours to Chicago. By the time she got there, the party had unanimously nominated FDR. The sticking point was Wallace. FDR held to his position: no Wallace, no Roosevelt.

There was pandemonium in the convention hall as Eleanor walked onto the stage that evening. As she started to speak the audience grew quiet. "This is no ordinary time," she told the 50,000 delegates. She pointed out the burden her husband was being asked to bear. "I know and you know that any man who is in an office of great responsibility today faces a heavier responsibility, perhaps, than any man has ever faced before in this country." If FDR "felt that the strain of a third term might be too much . . . and that Mr. Wallace was the man who could carry on best," then surely FDR was entitled to have Wallace to help him.

Wallace was nominated. Eleanor sped to the airport. Her plane was moving down the tarmac when it was flagged back. Franklin was on the phone to say she had done a sterling job. While she was flying home, the president gave his acceptance speech, broadcast from the White House at 12:25 a.m.

Letters praising Eleanor flooded into the White House. "You turned a rout into victory," Senator George Norris, a relieved progressive, wrote to her. "You were the Sheridan of that convention . . . That victory was finally realized is due, in my opinion, more to you than to any other one thing. That one act makes you heroic."

The Roosevelts now faced yet another presidential election. FDR ruled out the campaign train. With the situation in Europe so volatile, he needed to stay close to the White House. At the end of September 1940, Germany, Italy, and Japan—the countries known as the Axis—signed the Tripartite Pact in Berlin, agreeing to come to one another's defense if attacked. This was a warning—primarily to the United States—not to interfere with their expansion program.

FDR's Republican opponent was Wendell Willkie, a handsome, charismatic forty-eight-year-old, who appealed to middle-of-the-road voters. A lifelong Democrat, he had turned Republican because he believed that FDR had swung too far toward big government, and the very idea of a third term was a threat to American democracy. But Willkie was not against the New Deal, and on foreign policy he supported aid to Britain. People called him a "me too" candidate.

By September, when the polls made it clear that Willkie was losing, the Republican campaign changed tactics. The New Deal suddenly became a Communist plot. Willkie was cast as the protector of democracy and FDR as a dictator. Willkie was the peace candidate and FDR the warmonger. Isolationists sported buttons: A VOTE FOR ROOSEVELT IS A VOTE FOR WAR. By mid-October, it was looking as if Willkie might win.

Two weeks before the election, with Eleanor and his colleagues prodding him, FDR was finally persuaded to do some campaigning himself. Too much was at stake. The Republicans were pushing Willkie more and more to the right.

FDR gave five speeches, among his finest ever. "I have said before, but I shall say it again and again and again," he told a huge rally in Boston. "Your boys are not going to be sent into any foreign wars." Sam Rosenman thought this a rash promise. FDR assured him: "If we're attacked it's no longer a foreign war."

Eleanor accompanied FDR to the rallies. Her chatty columns carried a gentle punch: "Some of the things which I have heard on the radio and read in the papers seem to me to appeal to prejudice and emotion rather than to clear thinking and seasoned judgment."

The election looked as if it was going to be a cliffhanger. The pundits agreed that if Willkie moved even more to the right, he would definitely win. At the time, Charles Lindbergh, an anti-Semitic Nazi sympathizer who preached that Nazi victory in Europe was certain and that Roosevelt and his Jewish friends were leading the United States into a pointless war, was a national hero.

On the evening of November 5, 1940, Eleanor organized a supper at Val-Kill for friends and neighbors, leaving FDR, his mother, and Missy to dine at the Big House in peace. Eleanor's party returned to the Big House at nine, and clustered around the radio sets. FDR sat in a small room off the dining room, listening to the returns with Missy. He asked the head Secret Service man, Mike Reilly, not to let anyone in—not even family. Reilly noticed that the president had broken into a heavy sweat.

FDR won, with a far better margin than he had dared hope for—54.8 percent of the popular vote, and thirty-eight out of forty-eight states. "It was a narrow escape," FDR told the gathering of friends and supporters. "There were altogether too many people in high places in the Republican campaign who thought in terms of appeasement of Hitler."

NINE

"I am a bit exhausted..."

December 1940–March 1945

It was on the *Tuscaloosa*, cruising in the Caribbean, that FDR came up with the Lend-Lease scheme. A bold plan, brilliantly conceived, it combined altruism with national self-interest and was to be a critical factor in the eventual success of the Allies. The idea was that, while officially remaining neutral, the United States would embark on massive war production—ships, planes, arms, tanks, bombs—and "sell, transfer, lend, lease" armaments, foodstuffs, and other material to countries whose defense was considered crucial to its own. The United States, which after years of isolationism was totally unprepared for war, would be helping the Allies as well as buying its own security. It would take six weeks of impassioned debate for FDR to convince Congress that the best way to keep the United States out of the war was for it to become "the great arsenal of democracy." On March 11, 1941, FDR signed the bill into law.

Eleanor was feeling sidelined. FDR had appointed Harry Hopkins to administer the Lend-Lease program, and Hopkins had become FDR's closest colleague. The former social worker and New Deal relief administrator had developed an astute grasp of foreign policy and was proving an excellent negotiator. FDR asked him to move into the White House as his round-the-clock adviser. Hopkins was hardworking and loyal. He was also a very sick man, who was living at death's door. But he was no Louis Howe. Hopkins was eight years younger than FDR, and had difficulty standing up to him. As Eleanor put it: "Because he knew Franklin did not like opposition too well . . . he frequently agreed with him regardless of his own opinion, or tried to persuade him in indirect ways . . . This was not as valuable a service as forcing Franklin in the way Louis did, to hear unpleasant arguments."

In the past Hopkins had been closer to Eleanor than Franklin. Both had been idealistic New Dealers, intent on relief and reform. Eleanor had helped Harry through hard times. When Harry's wife died, leaving behind their five-year-old daughter, Diana, Eleanor became Diana's legal guardian and promised Harry that if anything should happen to him she would see to it that Diana was well looked after. Now Hopkins was obsessed by war strategy, and his loyalty had shifted entirely to the president. Eleanor felt betrayed.

She was also put out by the attention FDR was paying to a Norwegian princess. In January 1940, FDR had written to Crown Prince Olav of Norway, saying that he was painfully conscious of the danger that faced the Scandinavian counties. "If by any unfortunate chance things should go from bad to worse and it should become advisable to send the children out of Norway, I hope you will really consider sending them over here for us to look after. My wife and I would be only too glad to take charge of them."

In the spring of 1940, when the Nazis invaded Norway, Crown Prince Olav set up an exile court in London and gratefully accepted FDR's offer of refuge for his wife and children in the United States. After a harrowing voyage through mined waters, Crown Princess Märthe and her three blond children disembarked from the USS *American Legion* at the end of August 1940. For several weeks the royal guests stayed at the White House. Throughout September, while Wendell Willkie was warning the electorate that Roosevelt was becoming a dictator, FDR took several afternoon drives with the princess, looking at houses to rent. Martha (as she called herself in the United States) finally settled on a grand estate at Pooks Hill, Bethesda.

FDR regularly drove over to Pooks Hill to visit "the Norwegians." Martha and her retinue—lady-in-waiting, chamberlain, children, nurse for the children, and their dog—were frequent guests at the White House and Hyde Park. Martha called FDR "Godfather." He called her "Godchild." Everyone noticed how animated FDR was in her company, and how Martha twinkled and blushed.

Missy, too, was feeling tense and neglected. At a dinner party in the State Dining Room on June 4, 1941, Missy told Grace Tully that she felt ill. Grace urged her to excuse herself and go upstairs. Missy said she did not want to draw attention to herself and would stay until the Boss left. FDR was wheeled out at nine thirty. A few minutes later, Missy slumped to the floor, unconscious. She was rushed to her apartment on the third floor, where Dr. McIntire observed that her speech was slurred. He thought it might be a slight heart attack.

Eleanor, who was traveling and getting only vague reports, assumed it was yet another of the strange collapses to which Missy was prone. "Missy is very ill again," she told Anna. "She's been taking opiates and had a heart attack and then her mind went as it does, so now we have three nurses and the prospect of some weeks of illness before we get her straightened out."

Two weeks later, Missy had a massive stroke. This time there was no ambiguity about it. Her right arm and leg were paralyzed, and she completely lost her power of speech. She was taken to the nearby Doctors Hospital.

By then Eleanor was in Campobello with Joe Lash, who was holding a five-week leadership training institute under the auspices of the International Student Service, a noncommunist movement, separate from the Youth Congress. Eleanor, who did not yet know the seriousness of Missy's stroke, was more anxious about Franklin, who had been unable to shake off a persistent fever. She no longer had faith in Dr. McIntire, an ear, nose, and throat specialist. "They don't know what it is," she wrote to Anna on June 22. "I telephoned every day since I've been here & today begged [Pa] to have an outside doctor & he said he would tomorrow. Missy was taken to the hospital today & has been worse for the last few days & that may be at the bottom of much of the trouble."

Missy's stroke was devastating for Franklin. For twenty years, Missy had been his closest companion. She had had other boyfriends, he flirted with other women, but their affection for each other had not diminished. With the exception of his cruises, he and Missy were rarely apart. Most evenings, Missy sat with him in the Oval Room, typing letters, making arrangements on the phone, reading—a calm, smiling presence. And now, at the age of forty-three, Missy had turned into a helpless invalid.

Franklin could be brave for himself, but he could not be brave for Missy. Just as he had done in the past with Louis Howe, he had himself wheeled into her hospital room and did his utmost to cheer her up. But what could he say? She could not walk; she could not speak. It was catastrophic.

He arranged for twenty-four-hour nursing care, and took charge of all Missy's medical expenses. She stayed in the hospital for three months, and then FDR suggested that she go to Warm Springs to try to learn to walk again. She did not like the idea, but agreed to go. Warm Springs was the place where her beloved Effdee had struggled to walk. Warm Springs was where they had been happiest together.

Franklin promised her that he would be down at Thanksgiving, in a few weeks, and a tearful Missy departed on the train with her nurse.

Eighty-six-year-old Sara Delano had looked quite sprightly at Franklin's third inauguration, but in the spring she fell ill. Eleanor took her to Campobello that summer, with a nurse to look after her while Eleanor was busy with the International Student Service. In early September, when Mama got back to Hyde Park, Eleanor found her so weak that she urged Franklin to come home without delay. Franklin arrived the next morning, on Saturday, September 6, and sat for several hours beside his mother's bed, quietly talking. On Sunday, around midday, Sara Delano slipped away in her sleep.

There was a simple funeral service at St. James Episcopal Church, Hyde Park. Sara was buried next to her husband, James Roosevelt—not far from the tiny grave of Franklin Jr. Throughout the internment, Franklin stood alone, a few feet from the grave, supporting himself on the door of his car.

"Father has begun to forget all that was ever disagreeable in his relationship to Granny," Eleanor wrote to Anna, "but he was not emotional . . . I kept being appalled at myself because I couldn't feel any real grief or sense of loss & that seemed terrible after 36 years of fairly close association."

A few weeks later, FDR and Grace Tully were sorting out memorabilia for the FDR Library at Hyde Park. They opened some boxes that had been labeled in Sara's hand, and found, carefully wrapped in tissue paper, a lock of Franklin's baby hair, his first shoes, his little boy's kilt, his childhood toys, and every note he had ever written her, from the age of five onward. The president's eyes filled with tears. He asked to be left alone. Tully withdrew. She felt quite shaken. She was not at all used to FDR showing his feelings.

A few hours after her mother-in-law's burial, Eleanor hurried to the bedside of her brother. Hall Roosevelt, who lived with his girlfriend in a small house on the Hyde Park estate, was in a state of delirium. Eleanor was up most of the night.

She took him by private car to the Walter Reed General Hospital in Washington, and for the next three weeks she hovered by his bed watching her fifty-year-old brother die of alcoholism. "It's such an unattractive death," she wrote to Anna. "He's mahogany color, all distended, out of his head most of the time . . . he moves insistently & involuntarily so you try to hold him quiet & it is really most distressing."

Hall Roosevelt drew his last breath on September 25, 1941. Back at the White House, Eleanor sat on the sofa in the Oval Room, telling Franklin and James about the last few days. Suddenly she could not speak. James never forgot that moment. FDR wheeled himself over to Eleanor. "He sank down beside her and hugged her and kissed her and held her head on his chest. I do not think she cried. I think mother had forgotten how to cry. But there were times when she needed to be held, and this certainly was one."

Missy was much on Franklin's mind. He had changed his will. It now seemed likely that Missy would be in a wheelchair for the rest of her life. Her medical expenses were costly and she had limited savings. How would she manage, if he were no longer there to support her? He told James: "I left half my estate to mother, and I left half my estate to Missy for her medical bills. Some may try to make something of that. They shouldn't, but they will. If it embarrasses mother, I'm sorry. It shouldn't, but it may."

It was not possible for FDR to be in Warm Springs at Thanksgiving. He was involved in urgent negotiations with Japan and could not leave the White House. But he did not want to let Missy down. He suggested to his friends at the foundation that they have a belated celebration, one week later.

On Saturday, November 29, 1941, FDR arrived in Warm Springs in the late afternoon. He and Grace Tully drove straight to Missy's cottage. They found Missy sitting up in her wheelchair, eagerly waiting for them. But the sounds she made, with considerable effort, were scarcely comprehensible.

That evening, FDR did the ritual turkey carving, and gave as cheerful a talk as he could muster. During the night there was an urgent phone call from the White House. The president should come back immediately. Negotiations with Japan had broken down, Japanese troops had been seen moving south, and aggressive action was expected in the next few days.

FDR had planned to stay in Warm Springs until Tuesday. After barely twenty-four hours there, he and Grace said goodbye to a weeping Missy, then boarded the presidential train. It now looked inevitable that the United States would enter the war.

On Sunday, December 7, 1941, Eleanor was entertaining guests at a luncheon in the Blue Room. She apologized that FDR was not able to join them.

FDR was expecting a Japanese attack at any moment—in the Philippines, Siam, the Dutch East Indies, or Malaya. He had been tense for weeks, wondering how to convince Congress and the American people that this would mean the United States joining the war.

FDR and Harry Hopkins had just finished lunch in the Oval Room when news came through that Japanese aircraft were bombing the American naval base in Hawaii. They were dumbfounded. Pearl Harbor, the home base of the U.S. Pacific Fleet, was a long way from Japan, and the only U.S. military installation in the Pacific that was known to be well equipped. Hopkins did not at first believe the report. FDR thought it likely to be true. The Japanese were bold.

FDR assumed that the U.S. Army and Navy commands were well prepared. The entire Pacific area had been on war alert for weeks. But the reports coming in were appalling. The Japanese had launched their attack at the break of dawn, and the American military had been caught off guard. An hour later, a second wave of attacks—hundreds of horizontal bombers, dive bombers, torpedo planes—was even more lethal than the first. By 10 a.m., when the last plane disappeared from the skies above Pearl Harbor, 2,403 American servicemen were dead, 188 military aircraft had been destroyed on the ground, and most of the battleships in the U.S. Pacific Fleet had been sunk.

The next day, FDR stood up in Congress, looking grim and defiant, and announced that since the "unprovoked and dastardly attack" the day before—"a date which will live in infamy"—the United States was at war with Japan. His speech was received by thunderous applause. The press reacted the same way. The entire country, formerly isolationist, was filled with patriotic emotion.

Three days later, Hitler addressed the Reichstag in Berlin. He ranted about "that man who, while our soldiers are fighting in snow and ice . . . likes to make his chats from the fire-side." Hitler hated Roosevelt. He hated Roosevelt's patrician good looks; he hated Roosevelt's Jewish advisers; above all, he hated Roosevelt's Lend-Lease program. Hitler finished by declaring war on the United States. Italy immediately followed suit.

"The clouds of uncertainty and anxiety have been hanging over us for a long time," Eleanor wrote in her "My Day" column. "Now we know where we are . . . No one in this country will doubt the ultimate outcome."

The White House had blackout curtains in every room. Gun crews paced around on the roof. There would be no more cruises on the presidential yacht—not even day trips down the Potomac. Nor was it considered safe for the president to eat in a hotel. For the duration of the war, the new Office of Censorship called upon a "patriotic press" not to report the president's movements outside the White House.

All four Roosevelt sons were already in uniform. James was in the Marine Corps reserve, Elliott the army air corps, Franklin Jr. the naval reserve, and John was an ensign in the navy. In mid-December 1941, Franklin and Eleanor said goodbye to James, who had been ordered to Hawaii, and to Elliott who had been attached to a bomber squadron on the European front. Eleanor, who hated not being in control of her emotions, found herself bursting into tears in front of Joe Lash. "She knew they had to go," Lash wrote in his diary, "but it was hard. Simply by the laws of chance not all four would return."

There were no Roosevelt children or grandchildren at the White House that Christmas—just Diana Hopkins, a lost little soul, who reminded Eleanor of herself as a young girl. The Norwegian royal children were there, excitedly opening their presents with Diana, while

Fala, the president's Scottie, ran around poking his nose in everything. But mostly there were closed doors and war meetings. "The house is full of official business & official people," Eleanor told Lash. "Franklin with his historic sense is enjoying it greatly."

Winston Churchill and his party were staying. The British prime minister had traveled in high secrecy, through waters infested by German U-boats. The return trip would be riskier still, since by then the Germans would be looking out for the British party. When FDR expressed concern about the danger to Churchill, Churchill had shrugged. "There is great danger in our not having a full discussion at the highest level."

The two leaders depended on each other. Churchill had far more military experience than FDR, and the British had superior forces. FDR was the Lend-Lease savior, who supplied vital munitions and supplies, and would now be supplying men. Sam Rosenman, who sat in on many of their meetings, was proud of his president—his knowledge of history, geography, and grasp of military tactics. This, Rosenman told himself, was probably "the most important partnership in the history of the world."

A genuine friendship was growing up between Franklin and Winston, as they called each other. They respected each other's broad culture, interest in history, and love of the navy. Franklin enjoyed Winston's puckish humor and British eccentricities. Winston admired Franklin's calm optimism and the courage with which he bore his physical affliction.

Eleanor tried to like Winston, since Franklin did, but she thought him a class-bound conservative, who did not yet understand that the British Empire was no more. With his podgy body, massive head, scowling face, and pink skin, Winston reminded her of a baby. He paced around the corridors in a bizarre-looking one-piece woolen outfit with a zip up the front. (His "siren suit" was a "joy," Eleanor told Lash, and she was having one made for FDR.) Instead of a pacifier, he had a fat cigar permanently jammed in his mouth. He drank like a fish. Worst of all, he did not emerge from his room till 11 a.m., and took a nap in the afternoons, then kept FDR up until 1 or 2 a.m. After three weeks of trying to keep "Winston hours," FDR was ready for a sleep marathon.

"You don't really approve of me, do you, Mrs. Roosevelt?" Winston Churchill ventured years later, after the war. "Looking back on it," she wrote in her autobiography, "I don't suppose I really did."

•

Lorena Hickok was now working with the Democratic National Committee in Washington, and Eleanor had suggested that she move into the White House during the week. "I'd like to very much, because it gives me at least a few glimpses of you," Hick told her, "but I'm *not* going to hang around the place the way I used to. That business of moping around the W.H.—never again."

It helped that Hick had a new girlfriend—a judge, who lived with her mother in the affluent Washington suburb of Chevy Chase. On weekends the two disappeared to Hick's little house in Moriches, Long Island, where Hick liked to dig in the garden, far away from the White House whirl. Eleanor was "like a pea on a hot shovel"; Hick needed calm.

Meanwhile, Eleanor was lavishing her affection on Joe Lash. She loved this dark-haired young man, with his socialist ideals and tormented soul. She was moved by his difficult childhood (his father had died when Joe was nine, and Joe's mother worked fifteen-hour days in their Harlem grocery store to feed her five children), and impressed that Joe did not just talk about things; he acted. At the City College of New York during the Depression, Joe became a Socialist student leader. When Franco staged his coup d'état, Joe went to Spain to support the Spanish Loyalist Army. Now, as General Secretary of the International Student Service, he was trying to arrange help for student refugees.

Just before Eleanor met him, Joe had fallen in love with a fellow political activist—a married woman with three children. Gertrude ("Trude") Pratt had come to the United States in her early twenties from Germany. Trude reciprocated Joe's feelings, but was terrified of losing the children in an ugly divorce settlement and regularly told Joe she would have to stay with her husband and give up Joe. Eleanor had spent the past two years listening to the agonies and elations of their love affair, and dispensing advice.

Joe and Trude had become part of Eleanor's entourage. The Secret Service was dubious about Joe Lash, the Jewish socialist radical, and even more dubious about Trude Pratt, the militant from Germany. But FDR liked Joe, and he liked the warm and spirited Trude even more. One afternoon, Harry Hopkins took Trude aside and warned her about loyalties in the White House. If Mrs. Roosevelt ever felt that Trude was becoming part of the president's circle, he told her, Trude would never be forgiven.

Joe was flattered by Mrs. Roosevelt's affection, and sometimes more than a little overwhelmed by it. "I've grown to love you so much," Eleanor told him. "I could have wept when you left! I realize you want to work & it is better for you, but you forgive me for being selfish & missing your presence, don't you?"

No sooner had Joe moved into a new one-bedroom apartment in Manhattan than a crate arrived from Wanamaker's with a luxurious armchair. For Joe's thirty-second birthday, the first lady bought him a Pontiac convertible. She wrote to him from Val-Kill: "Do come up whenever you are free. I'll be at the house soon after six & waiting to both kiss and spank you & I would love it, if you have nothing else that calls, to have you stay the night. It would be nice to tuck you in & say goodnight on your birthday!"

There were times when Lash backed away. "Why have you returned to 'Aunt Eleanor' in your letters? Did 'ER' seem too familiar?" Eleanor asked him. Lash went back to "Dearest ER." He noticed that with Earl Miller, similarly, Eleanor made strenuous efforts "to make him treat her as one of his ladies," and it did not work. "With Earl and me she would ask for an old-fashioned [a cocktail], try puffing on a cigarette, do household chores, but there was always a slight distance that separated her from those who loved her."

On April 29, 1942, Lash was inducted into the armed services. Eleanor paid for his going-away party at the old Lafayette Hotel in New York. She had written him a series of letters, in separately numbered envelopes, that he was to open during his first week in the service. "A little bit of my heart seems to be with you always Joe," she told him. "You'll carry it round wherever you go . . . This is just to say goodnight & I love you. Sometimes I think if we have *chosen* to love someone, we love them even more than we do the children of our bodies & so that is why I shall be looking forward to every chance of seeing you & longing for the day when you are home for good. God bless & keep you."

It was perhaps inevitable that Franklin and Eleanor were spending more time apart. Franklin had become the Allies' chief planner, strategic initiator, and main source of authority. It was an enormous responsibility. Eleanor had no interest in military strategy, and Franklin's discussions took place behind closed doors. When Franklin took time out, he needed to relax. This was not Eleanor's forte.

Missy had come back to the White House from Warm Springs, but she still could not walk, and despite spending hours each day with a speech therapist, she could barely speak. She sometimes wheeled herself down to the Oval Room to sit beside FDR for the evening. But she could no longer be any use, and she felt a burden. In June 1942, she went to her family in Boston, to live with her sister, Anna Rochon.

FDR was spending most of his time with Harry Hopkins. Eleanor felt excluded. She could sense Harry's impatience when she pushed Franklin on domestic reform. She also noticed—and so did the press— that Harry, the former New Dealer, had developed a marked taste for glamorous society. His new girlfriend, Louise Macy, was a pretty social-ite, who had worked as the fashion editor of *Harper's Bazaar*. Both of them loved to hobnob with the Roosevelts' royal friends.

On July 30, 1942, Harry Hopkins, fifty-two, married Louise Macy, thirty-six, in the flower-decked Oval Room. Without consulting Eleanor, FDR pressed Harry and his bride to stay on at the White House. The first Eleanor heard of it was from Harry, who asked her whether she minded. Eleanor marched in to see Franklin. Had he thought through what it meant to have another married couple, plus ten-year-old Diana, in the White House? Had he thought through what it would be like for Louise, not having a home of her own? It was wartime, Franklin said, and he needed Harry on hand. "That settled that," wrote Eleanor.

In her autobiography, Eleanor dropped hints about the antagonism. "I met Louise occasionally in the hall as we both went our busy ways, and we saw each other at dinner when we wanted to," she wrote. "By this time I had come to feel that there were sides to Harry Hopkins which were alien to me and that perhaps we could get along better if we did not build up too much intimacy."

"Gosh, I shouldn't think he'd be any bargain as a husband," Hick wrote to Eleanor. "He looks as though he might die any minute! And how awful to take his poor bride to live at the White House. They won't have any life of their own at all, will they? It may have been the presi-dent's idea, but I'll bet Harry didn't fight it much. Kitty-kitty! And what a Hell of a thing for *me* to be saying."

Franklin did not forget Missy. He wrote her little letters, with news of the Roosevelt family. Phone calls were difficult. At Christmas in 1942,

FDR sent a gift but failed to call her, and Missy's sister wrote him an aggrieved letter:

> Missy . . . started crying New Year's Eve about 11:30 and we couldn't stop her and then she had a heart spell and kept calling "F.D., come, please come, oh F.D."—it really was the saddest thing I ever hope to see, we were all crying, she was very depressed all through the Holidays and that was the Climax—she was expecting you to call all Xmas day and when we sat down to dinner, her eyes filled with tears and she said, "A Toast to the President's Health." . . . She watches for the postman every trip . . . She worries so about you all the time.

FDR had more than enough burdens in his life. In his rare moments of relaxation, he turned to other women for the calm and lighthearted gaiety that Missy had once brought him. None of these women ever became real companions, as Missy had been. They were merely figures in the backdrop of his life, who brought him some joy.

Shortly before Missy became ill, Lucy's eighty-year-old husband, Winthrop Rutherfurd, suffered a stroke. FDR had arranged the best possible care for him at the Walter Reed General Hospital in Washington. It meant that Lucy came to town, staying at her sister's house, in Georgetown. On June 5, 1941, Franklin, for the first time ever, invited Lucy to visit him in the White House. She was given a code name on the visitors' list in the White House press room—"Mrs. Johnson." Eleanor was away. But Missy knew, of course. Indeed, it was the night before Lucy's visit that Missy collapsed at the dinner table.

That summer, with both Winthrop Rutherfurd and Missy incapacitated by strokes, Franklin and Lucy resumed their clandestine romance. On several occasions, when Eleanor was out of town, "Mrs. Johnson" was whisked into the White House—for afternoon tea or a quiet dinner with the president.

Theirs was a romance that seemed to flourish under conditions of war. The landed gentry, which was the world in which Lucy Rutherfurd moved, had detested "that man Roosevelt" until December 1941. (Lucy described her world to Franklin as "a community of pleasure-seekers, who cannot see farther than the gloves in their hands.") But since Pearl Harbor, Roosevelt was widely seen as a hero, even by the upper classes. "One feels that the responsible heads of the Democracies must indeed be supermen," Lucy wrote to Franklin, "clothed with the power of life and death."

At fifty, she was still the "lovely Lucy." People always described her that way. "She is tall & good-looking, rather than beautiful or even pretty," Daisy Suckley would write in her diary, when she accompanied FDR on a clandestine visit to Lucy's English manor house in New Jersey. "It was a really lovely day, centering around Mrs. Rutherfurd, who becomes more lovely as one thinks about her."

Lucy leaned heavily on Franklin. Her youngest stepson was looking for a job in politics. Another stepson was hoping for a navy assignment. A friend wanted to secure a place on a plane to Europe. "This kind of letter is best unwritten and unmailed, and poor darling, to give you one more thing to read on or think about is practically criminal," Lucy wrote to Franklin. But the requests came often.

Lucy's visits were a carefully guarded secret, though the Secret Service knew, and so did FDR's inner circle. Privately, Franklin and Lucy were allowing themselves to be flirtatious again. Lucy wrote to say that she now had Franklin's cold—"Caught over the telephone?" Franklin dropped hints about the past: "I *do* remember the times—so well—à toujours et toujours." He spoke to her on the phone about sharing a cottage together one day, when the world was at peace. Lucy wrote back dreamily:

> A small house would be a joy—and one could grow vegetables as well as flowers—or instead of—oh dear—there is so much I should like to know—how much hope you have—and the thousand questions one does not like to ask—
>
> I know one should be proud—very very proud of your Greatness—instead of wishing for the soft life—of joy and . . . the world shut out.

This had once been Daisy Suckley's dream. These days Daisy no longer had illusions of romance, but considered herself extremely fortunate to be Franklin's friend. Her invalid aunt had died, leaving Daisy, at fifty, without an income. "Save any problems for the broad shoulders of F," the president wrote her. Within a month he made her one of the archivists in the newly opened FDR Library at Hyde Park. Daisy loved her new job, immersed in Franklin's world, and it gave them a perfect excuse to spend time together.

She teased Franklin about his "girlfriend." She meant the woman the press corps was gossiping about. Whenever the Norwegians were at Hyde Park—this was often—it was Princess Martha whom Franklin took for drives, tea at Top Cottage, and to picnics at Val-Kill. "I can see why FDR likes her so much," Daisy wrote bravely. "She is gentle & sympathetic, has a sense of humor & is very responsive. He teases her all the time & she is very teasable & reacts with laughing and blushing." Daisy's diary was not entirely candid. She intended it for posterity.

Eleanor took the princess in her stride—she was used to Franklin's torchlight charm and the adoration it provoked—but Trude Pratt was irritated on Eleanor's behalf. "It is not even catty to say [Princess Martha] behaved like an 18-year old flirt," Trude wrote to Joe Lash. "Mrs. Roosevelt seems to grow in situations like that."

One afternoon, Eleanor and Trude Pratt took a walk to Top Cottage, where they found Franklin and the princess on the porch, taking tea. Trude reported to Joe:

> Martha was there and as always I was puzzled why he seems to be so attracted. She says nothing, just giggles and looks adoringly at him. But he seems to like it tremendously—and there is a growing flirtatious intimacy which is of course not at all serious. Mrs. R. explained to me last night that there always was a Martha for relaxation and for the non-ending pleasure of having an admiring audience for every breath. She is just a bit annoyed.

For FDR, these flirtations were a distraction, a respite from his personal sorrows and the heavy responsibility of the war. He was happiest when he could think of himself as the center of a closeknit community in a bucolic setting—beautiful women laughing with him, dogs chasing one another, smiling servants bearing trays of food and drink, high-spirited children playing. He liked Martha's three children, and enjoyed teasing her five-year-old son, Harald, the heir apparent to the Norwegian throne, a handsome Little Lord Fauntleroy with long blond ringlets, who showed a lively boyish interest in the local flora and fauna. One day, Franklin was telling him about skunks. Harald mentioned that he had been bitten by mosquitoes. "But Harald," Franklin said, "there are no mosquitoes in Hyde Park—it must have been a skunk."

•

The real skunks, in Eleanor's view, were the House Un-American Activities Committee and FBI investigators, who spied perfidiously on perfectly law-abiding American citizens. When she discovered that the FBI was snooping around her social secretary, Edith Helm, she wrote a furious letter to the FBI director, J. Edgar Hoover, complaining about the bureau's "Gestapo methods." Since Joe Lash had already been called in front of HUAC, it came as no surprise that the military refused to give him a commission as a naval intelligence officer, but Eleanor (who had been one of Lash's recommenders) wrote to the attorney general, Francis Biddle: "I think to hound someone who has lived up to his convictions is really unwise procedure . . . It has a very bad effect upon youth in general when they think something unjust is being done."

In February 1943, Joe Lash was sent to the air force base at Chanute Field, in Illinois, for training as a weather observer. It did not take him long to notice that the things in his foot locker had been tampered with. He was not surprised. As an activist, he took it for granted, he told Eleanor, that army intelligence was keeping an eye on him. But he worried about being an embarrassment to her. And she worried that he would be made to suffer because of their friendship.

During his three-month training period in Illinois, Eleanor and Tommy met Joe in an Illinois hotel. An FBI informant was at the scene:

About nine o'clock on March 4, 1943, informant stated, a soldier came to the desk of the Urbana-Lincoln Hotel, and announced that he was JOSEPH LASH, and he understood that MRS. ROOSEVELT had a room reserved for him. He was directed to room 330.

Informant stated that MRS. ROOSEVELT had ordered dinner for three sent to room 332 about 8:30 pm. He also said that upon the arrival of Lash, MISS THOMPSON had her luggage moved into the room occupied by MRS. ROOSEVELT.

Neither MRS. ROOSEVELT nor LASH left their hotel rooms during the entire day of March 6, 1943 except to have lunch in the Hotel dining room. Other meals were served in their rooms, according to informant.

MRS. ROOSEVELT checked out of the Hotel at 7:35 am, March 7, 1943 and LASH left the hotel a few minutes before that time, according to informant. The hotel bill for all parties occupying room 330 and 332 was paid by MRS. ROOSEVELT.

Two weeks later, when Trude Pratt checked into the same hotel to spend a weekend with Joe, their room was bugged. The FBI informant reported: "Subject and MRS. PRATT appeared to be greatly endeared to each other and engaged in sexual intercourse a number of times during the course of their stay."

It seemed that the FBI deliberately conflated Lash's two women friends. J. Edgar Hoover and his underlings decided that the first lady was having "an affair" with Joe Lash. The sole "evidence" were their letters, which the FBI informants opened as often as possible. "I'm sorry I was such a drowsy soul after dinner, but it was nicer drowsing in the darkness with you stroking my forehead, than playing gin rummy," Lash wrote to Eleanor after their hotel meeting.

At the end of April 1943, Lash's regiment was shipped to New Caledonia. Eleanor, who had been visiting military hospitals on the West Coast, saw him off from San Francisco. "I watched you through the back of the car until I could see no more for the tears & I think I shall never forget how your back looked," she wrote. "I called Trude & she tried to be cheerful but I knew from her voice she felt as I did." Years later, Lash would find a photocopy of this letter in his FBI file.

Neither Eleanor nor Lash ever imagined that the FBI would apply their "Gestapo methods" to *her*, the wife of the nation's commander in chief. The FBI file on Eleanor Roosevelt was to be more than three thousand pages long, one of the thickest files in the entire FBI collection. Throughout the war, counterintelligence circles in Washington were obsessed with the first lady's "extreme familiarity" with the young Jewish radical who, like her, was "suspected of Communistic affiliations." It was clearly evidence of a "gigantic conspiracy."

Since the United States had joined the war, Eleanor's back-door diplomacy had become far more difficult. All too often the president's door was closed. Civil rights, women's rights, workers' rights—everything was put on hold. Protest was "unpatriotic." While FDR was proving a mastermind at war strategy, the war left Eleanor deeply torn.

For all its horror, the war had put an end to the Great Depression. The United States had reached new heights of productivity. There were plenty of jobs. The factories were going day and night. The paradox, which Eleanor felt keenly, was that this was war production. Every Christmas, she told friends: "I shall be praying that . . . another year will bring us a happier world in which all of us can feel that we are building up instead of destroying." She visited military hospitals, and saw the suffering up close. "I wake up in the night, & imagine every horror & can't go to sleep again."

And yet she was having to beat the war drum. When the United States first joined the war, it had taken a serious thrashing in the Pacific. Eleanor reminded her compatriots that they, the peace lovers, were paying the price for their "ostrich" behavior. At the same time she did her best to boost morale. "We should remember . . . that day by day the opposition . . . is wearing itself out far more rapidly than we are. Some day, when we have reached the full power of our production, the day of victory for those who love peace will come."

Soon after the fall of Singapore to the Japanese, in February 1942, FDR ordered that all citizens of Japanese descent were to be evacuated to internment camps. It was a controversial decision, even at the time. More than two-thirds of those herded behind barbed wire in the desert were American citizens. Eleanor pointed out that "the same Bill of Rights covers all our citizens, regardless of the country of origin." But when her friend Pearl Buck wrote to her protesting that this "inhuman and cruel treatment" of the Japanese was "so much more German than it is American," Eleanor replied: "I regret the need to evacuate, but I recognize it has to be done."

It became Eleanor Roosevelt's wartime refrain: "I regret, but I recognize . . ." She worked with the Emergency Rescue Committee; she was honorary president of the United States Committee for the Care of European Children, and a sustaining member of the International Rescue and Relief Committee. She assisted these organizations financially and did everything in her power to push the State Department, but all too often she found herself telling the committee members: "It is not possible to get children out of the countries which are occupied by Germany at the present time. The German authorities do not allow them to leave."

The bind she found herself in was greatest when it came to the black community. African Americans were angry that the armed forces under FDR were segregated. The United States supposedly deplored Hitler's racism against Jews, and yet the American military forces practiced blatant discrimination against Negroes. At home, whites resented the promotion of black workers in the auto and munitions plants. In the summer of 1943 there were race riots in Detroit, in which thirty-five people were killed. Eleanor sympathized, but preached moderation. "If I were a Negro . . . I would not do too much demanding," she wrote in the *Negro Digest*. "I would take every chance that came my way to prove my quality and my ability and if recognition was slow, I would continue to prove myself, knowing that in the end good performance has to be acknowledged." Black militants were dismayed by this patronizing talk coming from the woman they had seen as their ally. Meanwhile, white Southern newspapers managed to blame Eleanor Roosevelt even for the race riots.

Eleanor could say only what FDR was willing to let her say; FDR could say only what the Southern Democrats were willing to let him say. She needed the president's backing; he needed congressional backing for essential war bills. "It is one of the prices that we who live in democracies have to pay," FDR pointed out. "It is, however, worth paying if all of us can avoid the type of government under which the unfortunate population of Germany and Russia must exist."

During the war, Eleanor was at her splendid best when FDR sent her abroad as a goodwill ambassador. In October 1942, she went to war-torn Britain. Her official task was to visit the U.S. armed forces in Britain. Her real task was to tighten the bond between Britain and the United States.

She crossed the Atlantic by plane, accompanied by Tommy. It was an arduous twenty-hour journey, but Eleanor far preferred clouds to waves. "The blackout here is real, you never saw its like & when mixed with fog it is dreadful," she wrote to Joe Lash from London. She was horrified by the shell holes, the ruins, the "wanton destruction." Even Buckingham Palace had taken a direct hit. She and Tommy were guests of the king and queen for the first two nights, under the same restrictions as everyone else. Food was rationed, their rooms were freezing, and they were permitted only five inches of bath water.

For the next three weeks, Eleanor visited American troop units, British women's auxiliaries, clubs, shipyards, hospitals. There were receptions, official dinners, and visits from European leaders who wanted to send messages to FDR. Every day—huddled beside peat fires that gave out almost no heat—Eleanor dictated her "My Day" column to a coughing Tommy. After a seven-day tour of the Midlands, Ulster, and Scotland—

one reporter estimated that the first lady had walked "fifty miles through factories, clubs and hospitals"—Eleanor came down with a "vile cold." She did not cut back her hectic schedule.

The British newspapers were rapturous in their praise. She might be the first lady, but this was no spoiled American. Mrs. Roosevelt was a "working woman," "a staunch and sympathetic friend," "the wife of a great leader of the people," and the mother of fighting boys. Prime Minister Churchill was delighted by the impact of her visit. "You certainly have left golden footprints behind you," he told her.

The American papers gave the first lady front-page coverage. "More than anyone else in the world, *you* are holding the British and us together right now," Hick wrote to Eleanor. "And in your own straightforward, honest way. Oh, I'm *so* proud of you! Your press over here is wonderful."

The flight home was in a freezing army transport. On the tarmac in Washington, Eleanor and Tommy peered through the window and saw black limousines, with clusters of Secret Service men, and realized that FDR had taken time off to meet them. Eleanor climbed into the car beside him, and the press clicked their cameras as the president and first lady gave each other a kiss. "I really think Franklin was glad to see me back," Eleanor wrote in her private journal. "Later I think he even read this diary and to my surprise he had also read my columns."

On January 9, 1943, FDR handed his Scottish terrier, Fala, to Daisy Suckley ("he hates to be left behind—take him to the library with you every day, & walk him during lunch") and left on a secret trip to Casablanca, Morocco, where he was to meet Churchill. It was initially planned as a meeting of the Big Three, but Stalin refused to leave the Russian front at that time.

The president's departure was top secret. The American press did not know at first that he had left the White House. The presidential party flew to Trinidad (ten hours), Belém in Brazil (nine hours), across the Atlantic to the west coast of Africa (nineteen hours), then to Casablanca (eight hours). Soon the world headlines blazed: "President's Daring Air Trip."

It was the first time FDR had traveled by air since his flight from Albany to Chicago to accept the presidential nomination in 1932, the first time an American president had been to Africa, and the first time a president had left the country during wartime. FDR hated being cooped up for so long in a plane, and suffered from the altitude. With no strength in his legs to brace himself against the jolts, and no padding on his behind, the air pockets and bumps were agony for him.

In Casablanca, FDR and Churchill discussed the next steps in the war. The Anglo-American landings in North Africa had been successful, the Russians had encircled the Germans at Stalingrad, and the Japanese had lost the Battle of Guadalcanal, but the Allied leaders knew there was still a long and bloody road ahead.

"I'm a bit tired—too much plane," Franklin wrote to his "Babs" on the way home. "It affects my head just as ocean cruising affects yours!"

In mid-August 1943, Eleanor traveled to the South Pacific. It was to be the longest time she had been on her own, without a personal companion, in her entire life. She did not feel she could justify Tommy's presence; the press liked to complain about the cost of her "jaunts." And Tommy was not sure she could keep up with Eleanor's pace.

In five weeks, Eleanor traveled to seventeen Pacific Islands, Australia, and New Zealand. She went as a representative of the Red Cross, and for the duration of the trip she wore the Red Cross uniform. She found this a relief, and it also allowed her to take a typewriter and remain within the forty-four-pound baggage limitation. She flew in a four-engine Army Liberator, bumped over rough terrain in jeeps, and slept on army cots in rooms that crawled with tropical bugs. She visited army camps, lining up with her tin tray in the mess halls. She walked through hospital wards, leaning over to kiss young soldiers whose bodies had been shot into pieces. At night, after a long day, she pecked out her "My Day" column on her typewriter.

Admiral William F. Halsey, commander of the South Pacific forces, had been appalled to hear that Mrs. Roosevelt was to "junket" through the battle area, wasting good aviation fuel and a fighter escort. After a few days in her company he was completely won over:

> When I say that she inspected those hospitals, I don't mean that she shook hands with the chief medical officer, glanced into a sun parlor, and left. I mean that she went into every ward, stopped

at every bed, and spoke to every patient: What was his name? How did he feel? Was there anything he needed? Could she take a message home for him? I marveled at her hardihood, both physical and mental; she walked for miles, and she saw patients who were grievously and gruesomely wounded. But I marveled most at their expressions as she leaned over them. It was a sight I will never forget.

For Eleanor, the highlight of the trip was her visit to Guadalcanal, the largest of the Solomon Islands. After months of heavy fighting, the Battle of Guadalcanal had been the first significant victory by Allied forces over the Japanese in the Pacific. Halsey insisted that the island was still too dangerous for the first lady to visit. Eleanor fretted about the trouble she caused, but pushed hard to go there. She wanted to thank those men on behalf of the president.

There was another reason why Eleanor was intent on visiting Guadalcanal. Joe Lash was there, assigned to a weather station. Halsey finally agreed, and she flew in at 6 a.m., shortly after another bombing raid. Her presence caused a sensation. "Gosh, there's Eleanor!" one soldier shouted. She had a busy day of official duties. In between, she and Joe had a brief meeting, when she introduced him to Admiral Halsey. "So this is the young man," Halsey said. Finally, in the evening, Eleanor went back to her guest cabin, had a bath, and waited for Joe.

"We sat on a screen porch and talked until 11:30 but I have never seen her so weary," Joe Lash wrote to Trude. "And today she had to be up at 4:15 and fly and then another round of hospitals . . . You and Tommy must make her rest, really rest, when she returns . . . She must have been going at a terrific pace, because while she was going through hospitals here this afternoon, the officers who have been with her gratefully took time out to sleep."

Eleanor returned home physically exhausted and emotionally drained. Those hospitals would haunt her for the rest of her life. More than ever, she felt that she and FDR had to do everything in their power to work for lasting peace. They owed it to those young men. Once the war was over, the returning veterans must not be forgotten. FDR was already fighting the members of the House and Senate over the GI Bill of Rights—groundbreaking legislation that would provide war veterans with jobs, benefits, and free education. Eleanor was not going to let him give up. She was reluctant to push FDR too much these days. She knew how tired he was. But if she didn't, who would?

In late November 1943, on his way to Tehran, FDR spent a few days with Churchill in Cairo. While they were there, they celebrated Thanksgiving. The Americans had brought along two enormous turkeys, and FDR carved for more than twenty people with a dexterity acquired from years of practice at Warm Springs. Harry Hopkins had arranged for an army band, which belted out tunes like "Marching Through Georgia" and "Carry Me Back to Old Virginny." Several of their offspring had joined them, adding a family touch to the occasion. Harry Hopkins's eldest son, Robert, was there. He and Elliott Roosevelt danced with Churchill's daughter, Sarah. To everyone's amusement, Churchill did a jig with Pa Watson, FDR's military attaché.

From Cairo, the presidential party proceeded to Tehran to meet Stalin. This was the first meeting of the Big Three, and they had some delicate diplomacy ahead of them. The war had seen a shift in world power. Until recently Britain had been the dominant partner. By now, all three leaders were aware that at the end of the war there would be two superpowers: America and Russia. FDR had traveled a long way to meet Stalin in person. He was determined to forge a good relationship with him.

"No lover ever studied the whims of his mistress as I did those of President Roosevelt," Churchill admitted, after the war. In Tehran, Churchill experienced FDR's slippery side. Churchill wanted FDR to stay with him at the British legation; FDR stayed at the Soviet embassy with Stalin. Churchill asked FDR for another private meeting; FDR refused, and had a one-on-one with Stalin instead.

The three-way discussions were tense. Churchill and Stalin had a strained relationship, and by common consent FDR sat in the middle, as arbitrator, but FDR came down far more often on Stalin's side. During the official dinners, Stalin mercilessly needled Churchill, and FDR smiled.

On the third day of their conference, FDR, who was busy playing up to Stalin, started in on Churchill himself, making jokes about his Britishness, his eccentricities. Churchill scowled. Stalin guffawed.

"I realized at Teheran for the first time what a small nation we are," Churchill said later. "There I sat with the great Russian bear on one side of me, with paws outstretched, and on the other side sat the great American buffalo, and between the two sat the poor little English donkey."

Looking back later, the inner circle would see Tehran as a turning point in FDR's health. FDR was never the same again. He came home exhausted. Over Christmas, he developed what he called "grippe"—an influenza-like illness to which he had always been susceptible.

Harry Hopkins usually spent Christmas with the Roosevelts, but while the men were in Tehran, Louise Hopkins had moved the family to a rented house in Georgetown. She wanted to protect Harry, who was far too frail, she felt, to be always on hand for FDR. She felt FDR was driving him much too hard.

Anna came home for Christmas (her husband, John Boettiger, was overseas with the army), and she was shocked by the sight of her father. He looked ravaged. When Franklin asked her if she might consider resigning her job with the newspaper in Seattle and staying on as his assistant, she did not hesitate. She and the children moved back to the White House.

Anna did not have an official job title or salary. FDR was not going to risk that again, not after the fiasco with James. "Father and I never had any discussions as to what my job or jobs should be," Anna told biographer Bernard Asbell later. "Actually, they grew like Topsy, because I was there all the time and it was easy for Father to tell someone to 'Ask Anna to do that,' or to look at me and say, 'Sis, you handle that.'"

For the next thirteen months—until FDR's death—Anna looked after her father devotedly. "It was immaterial to me whether my job was helping to plan the 1944 campaign, pouring tea for General de Gaulle or filling Father's empty cigarette case," she told Asbell. "All that mattered was relieving a greatly overburdened man of a few details of work and trying to make his life as pleasant as possible when a few moments opened up for relaxation."

After Franklin's death, Eleanor wrote in her autobiography:

Anna's presence was the greatest possible help to my husband. Ever since Miss LeHand's illness, though Miss Tully did a remarkable job in taking her place, there had been gaps which could have been filled only by someone living in the house. Now Anna filled them. She saw and talked to people whom Franklin was too busy to see . . . She also took over the supervision of his food. The doctor thought he should have a dietitian to plan his menus . . . Anna also had her hands full keeping peace between the cook and Mrs. Nesbitt. In fact, she helped Franklin in innumerable ways . . . She brought to all her contacts a gaiety and buoyance that made everybody feel just a little happier because she was around.

This was the public account. In reality, there were some tensions. Eleanor, who had spent most of her married life contending with a dominating mother-in-law, now found herself displaced by her beautiful daughter. Anna was close to both parents, and her new duties placed her in a difficult position. Her father was visibly tired, and her mother's missionary zeal was stronger than ever. There were times when Anna— or "Sis," as she was known in the family—played the ungratifying role of protecting her father against her mother. Although it was an unwritten rule that Franklin did not like serious talk during cocktails or dinner, Eleanor found it difficult not to bring up burning political issues with her husband. Everyone else at the table could sense FDR's fatigue and impatience. Anna once piped up, "Mother, can't you see you are giving Father indigestion?"

Franklin let Anna mix the cocktails these days. Eleanor would arrive near the end of cocktail hour, just before they were called to dinner. Anna would never forget the occasion when Franklin came close to exploding:

[Mother] came in and sat down across the desk from Father. And she had a sheaf of papers this high and she said, "Now Franklin, I want to talk to you about this." . . . I thought, Oh, God, he's going to *blow*. And sure enough, he blew his top. He took every single speck of that whole pile of papers, threw them across the desk at me and said, "Sis, you handle these tomorrow morning." I almost went through the floor. She got up. She was the most controlled person in the world. And she just stood there a half second and said, "I'm sorry." Then she took her glass and walked toward somebody else and started talking. And he picked up his glass and started a story. And that was the end of it.

Eleanor could be insensitive when it came to the family, and she knew it. Scenes like these always provoked in her an agony of self-recrimination, and made her want to run away in a funk. After all this time—even now, as first lady—Eleanor still felt like the ugly duckling, the orphan, the girl who deserved love only if she were good.

"I think she is a very *great* person, and that her greatness springs in a large measure from the depth of her love for him," Daisy Suckley wrote in her diary when she heard about the grueling three-week schedule ahead of Eleanor. On March 4, 1944, Eleanor, this time accompanied by Tommy, set off on a thirteen-thousand-mile plane trip, visiting military posts and hospitals in the Caribbean and South America.

While Eleanor was island-hopping with her usual manic energy, FDR was feeling exhausted. He had not recovered from his "grippe," and the doctors worried that it was something else. He had a racking cough, felt breathless with any physical exertion, and was plagued by headaches. His hands shook more than ever when he lit his cigarettes. When he was dictating to Grace Tully, he sometimes nodded off.

In late March, FDR went to Hyde Park to rest for a few days. He took a nap before lunch, and spent the afternoons in a deck chair on the porch. He told Daisy that he felt like Robert Louis Stevenson in the last stages of consumption.

On March 26, Lucy Rutherfurd arrived. Her husband had died six days before. With Eleanor abroad, Franklin wanted to show Lucy his home while he had the chance. Lucy came for lunch, then Franklin showed her around the Big House, the FDR Library, and Top Cottage. She left at six thirty, and soon after, Franklin went to bed.

Daisy Suckley knew about the visit. So did Anna and FDR's aides. They all understood that they were not to breathe a word about it to Eleanor.

Ever since the United States joined the war, there had been talk of a *fourth term* for Roosevelt. No one in the Democratic Party inspired the same trust. Roosevelt was winning the war. He was on good terms with both Churchill and Stalin. Under his leadership, the United States had become the most powerful nation in the world. Having come this close to bringing about victory, it made sense that he see the war through to the end and negotiate the peace. In January 1944, the Democratic National Committee asked FDR to run for a fourth term.

FDR would not commit himself. Privately, he did not know whether he was up to another election. But he wanted to see the war out, he did not trust anyone else to deal with Stalin, and he was determined to set up the conditions for lasting peace.

On March 28, the day Eleanor returned from her Caribbean trip, FDR underwent a battery of tests at Bethesda Naval Hospital. The chief of cardiology, Dr. Howard Bruenn, was appalled by his findings. FDR was on the verge of heart failure. He had dangerously high blood pressure, an enlarged left ventricle, and acute bronchitis. The diagnosis could scarcely have been worse.

Three days later, Dr. Frank Lahey, from Boston, was brought in to give a second opinion. He examined the president and his findings supported Bruenn's. "Mr. President, you may not care for what I have to say," Lahey began. FDR said, "That will be all, Dr. Lahey."

FDR knew what Bruenn had found, and knew why he had been reexamined. He also knew, from long experience, the need for silence. The reason why FDR had employed Ross McIntire as his personal doctor when he first entered the White House was not because McIntire was an ear, nose, and throat specialist and FDR had a chronic sinus problem, but because McIntire was known for his complete loyalty and discretion. Over the years, McIntire had proved himself loyal to the point that he was prepared to put his own reputation on the line rather than disclose facts that the president did not want disclosed. There had been many cover-ups. This was going to be the biggest of them all.

From March 1944 to the day of FDR's death, Dr. Bruenn, a cardiologist, became FDR's full-time attending physician. He saw FDR every morning and evening, and accompanied FDR on all his trips. He took his orders from McIntire, and was led to understand that he must not discuss the president's condition—either with the president or anyone else.

FDR could not tell *anyone* the truth about his health. Not Eleanor. Not Anna. Not his sons. *No one*. This was a pact between him and his doctors. Posterity must never know that FDR had run for a fourth term when he knew he was dying. The cover-up began that same day. "The P. called up to report on the Doctor's examinations of the morning," Daisy noted in her diary on March 28. "He said they took x-rays & all sorts of tests, found nothing drastically wrong, but one sinus clogged up . . . They are going to put him on a strict diet, a good beginning."

On April 10, 1944, the newspapers reported that FDR had left for an undisclosed location in the South for two weeks, to "shake off a persistent attack of bronchitis." FDR went to his friend Bernard Baruch's estate, Hobcaw Barony, in South Carolina. He stayed away not two weeks but a month. Dr. Bruenn, Dr. McIntire, and their assistant, George Fox, kept a close eye on him. FDR slept ten-hour nights, woke around nine thirty, read the newspapers and dictated correspondence from bed, made his first appearance at lunch, napped, sat on the screened porch with his stamps, and later went for a drive around Baruch's vast property. The doctors reduced his diet to 1,800 calories, and got him to cut back to six cigarettes a day. Before dinner, he usually drank a couple of dry martinis. Dinner was at seven. "The conversation was animated," Bruenn wrote later, "with the President playing the dominant role."

The press, bound by wartime regulations, was under oath of silence, and could not reveal the president's location until his return. Barred from Baruch's estate, which was patrolled by marines, they took rooms in the nearby village of Georgetown. The presidential train was parked there, and there was a great deal of coming and going to the train (which had a direct telephone connection to the White House), but the reporters never set eyes on FDR. After a few days, they were convinced that the president was no longer at Hobcaw. Rumors flew. Someone had heard that he was in a hospital in Chicago. Another had heard that he had had a heart attack and was under Dr. Lahey's care, in Boston. Someone else had heard that he had a malignant melanoma, from a brown sunspot over his left eye, which had mysteriously disappeared. They plagued Mike Reilly, head of the Secret Service, for information. To put an end to the rumors, Reilly let the press see FDR passing in his car. FDR was furious. "Those newspapermen are a bunch of God-damned ghouls."

Eleanor and Anna flew in from Washington for lunch with the prime minister of Australia, John Curtin, and his wife. "He looked much better," Eleanor wrote to James, "but said he still had no 'pep.'" Lucy Rutherfurd drove down from Aiken, South Carolina, on an "off the record" visit. Daisy Suckley came for two days and returned to D.C. with FDR on the presidential train. "Under his tan, he looks thin & drawn & not a bit well," she wrote in her diary. "He says they don't know what is the matter with him—I wonder if perhaps they don't want to tell him." FDR also said that he did not believe the doctors were telling him everything.

Daisy never asked herself whether FDR was telling *her* everything. Did Eleanor? No doubt she wondered, but she knew better than to ask. She understood what was at stake. "I think all of us knew that Franklin was far from well, but none of us ever said anything about it," she wrote in her autobiography. "I suppose because we felt that if he believed it was his duty to continue in office, there was nothing for us to do but make it as easy as possible for him."

Eleanor fell in with the cover-up, telling friends and family that Franklin was allowing himself to be lazy. A stoic to the core of her being, that kind of thinking came easily to her. She felt strongly that FDR had chosen to sacrifice his private life to a higher cause, and he must do everything in his power to fulfill his promise to the people. At the end of May, she wrote to James: "The doctors are very pleased with Pa's comeback & say he is really fine again— They took some last digestive tests last week that I haven't heard from but I'm sure they turned out well or Anna would have told me . . . Pa is enjoying not doing things which bore him & he's getting so much pleasure out of having Anna around that I think he's going to shirk any but the office hour things for some time but it isn't necessity—just preference!"

FDR was sixty-two, and looked ten years older. If he stood for a fourth term, he would be up against Thomas Dewey, the governor of New York, who was at forty-two the youngest man ever to win the Republican presidential nomination. Dewey called FDR a "tired old man."

For the first time in the war, the United States had more combat troops than the British. The U.S. Navy was three times bigger than the British navy. "I cannot think of any moment when the burden of the war has laid more heavily upon me or when I have felt so unequal to its ever-more entangled problems," Churchill wrote to FDR. "I greatly admire the strength and courage with which you face your difficulties, especially in a year when you have, what I may venture to call, other preoccupations."

Shortly before the Democratic National Convention, at which the presidential candidate would be chosen, FDR underwent an official examination at the Naval Medical Center at Bethesda. Dr. McIntire made a public declaration that the president was in better physical condition than the average man of his age. "His health is excellent in all respects."

FDR's friends were not fooled. Some begged Eleanor to use her influence to stop him from running again, for his own sake. "I don't know what Franklin will decide," she said, "but if he thinks he is needed I'm sure he'll make the fight & if he loses, I shan't be as sorry as I would be if he didn't accept the responsibility when he felt he should."

In early July, one week before the Democratic National Convention in San Diego, FDR announced his position with respect to a fourth term. "Reluctantly, but as a good soldier, I will accept and serve in this office, if I am ordered to do so by the Commander in Chief of us all—the sovereign people of the United States." He and Eleanor traveled by train to San Diego. FDR was nominated easily, as he knew he would be. The only question was his running mate. He would have liked Henry Wallace again, but the delegates did not want Wallace, and FDR was not willing to take on another fight. When the party chose Senator Harry S. Truman of Missouri, FDR agreed.

Eleanor flew home. FDR was going on to Pearl Harbor to confer with General Douglas MacArthur on the future strategy of the war in the Pacific. Before boarding his ship, FDR wanted to see James, who was convalescing from malaria in nearby Camp Pendleton. After that, FDR was to officiate at a landing operation by the Fifth Marine Division.

James was shocked to see how frail his father looked. They talked in FDR's private railroad car. Suddenly FDR groaned, clutched his heart, and dropped to the floor, convulsing with pain. He would not let James fetch a doctor; he would not let James cancel his engagement. It would cause alarm, he said, and jeopardize his chances of reelection. Somehow he managed to rally himself, and attend the landing exercise. He was smiling in the press photos.

The next day FDR wrote home with a carefully rearranged account of the events: "Dearest Babs: Off in a few minutes—All well . . . Jimmy & I had a grand view of the landing operation at Camp Pendleton and then I got the collywobbles and stayed in the train in the p.m. Better today." He added: "It was grand having you come out with me—and the slow speed was a good thing for us both."

At the end of July, FDR was in Honolulu when a wire arrived to say that Missy had died. She was forty-five. FDR would learn later that Anna, Missy's sister, had taken Missy in her wheelchair to a movie theater in

Harvard Square. The newsreel, which had included a segment about Fala and the president, upset Missy. When she got home, she took out her old photos—photos of FDR in Warm Springs, on the *Larooco*, in the White House. She was still poring over them when Anna went to bed. At 2 a.m., Anna heard strange noises coming from Missy's room. She looked in. Missy had collapsed, with photos of FDR in her hand. She died at dawn, in the Boston Naval Hospital.

FDR could not attend the funeral. He was on his way to Alaska and the Aleutians for further war meetings. Later that day, he received a second telegram from Steve Early: "All concerned have been advised. Mrs. Roosevelt will attend the funeral. Your absence has been carefully explained to Missy's family . . . Have arranged for flowers. Everything we can think of has been done."

In his public statement that day, FDR said that "Miss LeHand was utterly selfless in her devotion to duty." The truth, of course, was that Missy was utterly selfless in her devotion to *him*. She had never seen it as duty. She acted out of love.

The Republican presidential candidate, Thomas E. Dewey, was a little man with a dark, pencil-thin mustache, who bore an unfortunate resemblance to the man the Allies were fighting in Germany. FDR and Eleanor despised him. While the world was in conflagration, Dewey conducted the dirtiest campaign they had ever experienced. FDR was accused of corruption, treachery, and lies. He was harboring a Communist wife, and was clearly protecting his four sons, none of whom had died at the front. FDR was incensed. "His Dutch is up," his colleagues observed. "Nothing will stop him now."

FDR had not wanted to give campaign speeches. He knew he looked bad, and his voice was weak. But there had been an alarming rise in Dewey's popularity. With Eleanor's vigorous encouragement, FDR began to get involved in the campaign. On September 23, he gave what came to be known as "the speech about Fala" to the Teamsters Union in Washington:

> These Republican leaders have not been content to make personal attacks upon me—or my wife—or my sons—they now include my little dog, Fala. Unlike the members of my family, Fala

resents this. When he learned that the Republican fiction writers had concocted a story that I had left him behind on an Aleutian Island and had sent a destroyer back to find him—at a cost to the taxpayer of two or three or twenty million dollars—his Scotch soul was furious. He has not been the same dog since.

The public loved Fala. The little dog was part of the presidential image. The short MGM newsreel movie *Fala, the President's Dog*, showed FDR giving Fala his supper; Fala chasing a squirrel up a tree on the White House lawn (the squirrel, in a cage, was released as the cameras were rolling); and Fala sniffing with intense interest at a scrapbook Diana Hopkins was reading (a piece of bacon was hidden under the book). The film was a hit. So was FDR's Fala speech. Most newspapers agreed that in the contest between Dewey and Fala, the dog was winning.

The Republicans kept on about FDR's frailty. A photograph of FDR speaking in San Diego had escaped Steve Early's clutches, and FDR did look like a ravaged old man. But FDR had always enjoyed campaigning, and his fighting spirit was back. In the weeks before the election he looked almost robust again.

On Saturday, October 21, FDR and Eleanor were to make a well-publicized tour through the five boroughs of New York. At dawn that day it began to pour and did not look like letting up. His doctors wanted FDR to travel with the roof up. FDR would not hear of it. He and Eleanor traveled for four hours through driving rain in an open car.

When they got to Ebbets Field, the major league baseball park in Brooklyn, FDR threw off his navy cape and hat, and gave a magnificent speech. Afterward, his aides rubbed him down in a Coast Guard truck, and helped him into dry clothes, then FDR and Eleanor traveled through Queens, the Bronx, Harlem, and down through Manhattan, past millions of cheering people, to Eleanor's apartment in Washington Square. Thoroughly drenched, FDR was dried off again and allowed to rest a few hours before his big speech that evening at the Waldorf-Astoria.

The weather had been on FDR's side once again. The whole country was impressed that after a four-hour ride in the rain and two major speeches in one day, FDR still had that radiant smile.

On November 7, 1944, FDR won the election for a fourth time. The popular vote was close, but he won easily in the electoral college—432 to 99. It took Dewey till 3 a.m. to concede. At 4 a.m.—Eleanor was still talking to friends—FDR had himself wheeled off to bed. "The little man made me pretty mad," he said.

On January 20, 1945, Franklin Delano Roosevelt was sworn in for a historic fourth term. He insisted that the grandchildren be there—all thirteen of them, ranging in age from three to sixteen. It meant considerable organization on Eleanor's part, but she could see that it was important to him. Later she wondered whether he had "a premonition that he would not be with us very long."

FDR wanted the simplest possible inauguration. The nation was at war. This was no time for pomp and circumstance, and he had to spare his strength. The ceremony was held on the South Portico of the White House. James flew back from the Philippines to be by his father's side for their fourth inauguration. FDR put on his braces for the occasion, a painful ordeal now that he was so thin. It was to be the last time he stood on his feet.

There was snow on the ground, and it was bitterly cold, but FDR refused, as always, to wear a coat or hat. His inaugural address lasted five minutes, the shortest in history, but he had worked on it carefully. Afterward, Eleanor received a vast throng of people, while FDR had a quiet lunch in the Red Room with a few friends—Princess Martha, Daisy Suckley, and others. Later in the afternoon, there was tea for yet another crowd, with Eleanor once again alone on the receiving line.

Two days later, FDR set off for Yalta, in the Crimea, where he was going to meet Churchill and Stalin. Stalin was not willing to move from his home turf. This was going to be an arduous trip for FDR, a sick man, but he had to go. He and Churchill were worried about Stalin. The Red Army controlled Poland and the Balkans and was advancing toward Berlin. It was imperative for the Big Three to remain united, to bring about the defeat of Germany and Japan. Eleanor had asked Franklin whether she might go with him. "Darling, there won't be any other wives present," he told her. He took Anna instead.

The presidential party boarded the *Quincy* for the ten-day voyage to Malta, where FDR was to have a preliminary meeting with Churchill. ("I said Yalta, not Malta," Stalin joked.) From Malta FDR and Anna departed at 3:30 a.m.—a bumpy ride in a noisy little plane through

German-occupied territories—to a small airstrip at Saki, in the Crimea. Then came a freezing five-hour drive over rough winding roads, across the mountains, past bombed-out buildings, to Yalta, on the Black Sea.

FDR was the youngest of the three leaders (he had celebrated his sixty-third birthday on the way there), but looked by far the oldest. For seven days he had a heavy schedule of meetings. He got the Russians to agree to enter the war against Japan within three months of victory in Europe. He pushed hard for the United Nations. He and Harry Hopkins left Yalta looking like dead men, but feeling triumphant.

"Dearest Babs," FDR wrote home, "We have wound up the conference—successfully I think . . . I am a bit exhausted but really all right."

"Your diplomatic abilities must have been colossal!" Eleanor wrote back. "I think having the first U.N. meeting in San Francisco is a stroke of genius . . . Much love dear, congratulations & I hope you enjoy the return trip & that it is placid & uneventful so you get a rest."

But the return trip was harrowing. Harry Hopkins, who had done so much to lay the groundwork for the conference, had been living on his nerves in Yalta, and fell seriously ill. FDR had to deliver a speech on Yalta to Congress on his return and was relying on Hopkins's help, but Hopkins left the *Quincy* in Algiers to fly back for treatment at the Mayo Clinic. The two friends said goodbye stiffly. They would never see each other again.

While the presidential party was at sea, headed homeward, FDR's cherished companion and military aide, General Edwin ("Pa") Watson, had a stroke, lay in a coma for two days, and died. FDR got back to Washington on February 28, thin and weary, and accompanying yet another coffin.

For the first time ever, FDR remained seated while giving an address to Congress. "I hope that you will pardon me," he told the members. "It makes it a lot easier for me not to have to carry about ten pounds of steel around on the bottom of my legs." Everyone was shocked by the president's appearance. His skin was waxen, his voice muffled, and his delivery halting. "It has been a long journey," he said. "I hope you will all agree that it was a fruitful one."

Eleanor was trying hard to carry on as usual. One evening, they had dinner with their old friend Harry Hooker, who advocated compulsory military service as a peacetime measure. Eleanor argued heatedly against it. Franklin was visibly tense. Afterward, Harry took Eleanor aside and told her she must not subject Franklin to these energetic dinner discussions again. Eleanor felt dreadful.

On March 17, Franklin and Eleanor celebrated their fortieth wedding anniversary. There were cocktails in the Red Room, then a small formal dinner in the State Dining Room. The table was covered with St. Patrick's Day decorations—pipes, green hats, shamrocks. FDR told one of his favorite stories. "Complete contrast . . . to the scene forty years ago when the bride was given away by her 'Uncle Ted,'" FDR's new secretary, Bill Hassett, wrote in his diary. "T.R., in the very heyday of his popularity, stole the whole picture—wedding, press, everything—so that the obscure young bridegroom and bride in their early twenties were almost unnoticed."

After dinner the group went downstairs and watched a new British thriller, *The Suspect*, starring Charles Laughton, whose character murders his nagging wife when she threatens to expose his "friendship" with a beautiful younger woman. At 10:30 p.m., FDR excused himself and went to bed, saying he intended to sleep until noon. "Thus another milestone is passed," Bill Hassett noted, "in the career of an extraordinary man and wife."

TEN

The Rose Garden

March 1945–November 1962

Spring had come early this year. The wisteria on the South Portico of the White House was in bloom when Franklin and Eleanor left Washington on Saturday evening, March 24, 1945. The next morning, on the train, they opened their shades to find the trees in the Hudson valley covered with green fuzz. They drove up to Wilderstein that afternoon— Daisy Suckley's house, just outside of Rhinebeck, where Daisy's Scottie, Button, had given birth to two presidential puppies.

"A Big Day!" Daisy Suckley wrote in her diary:

> The Pres. and Mrs. R came for tea at our house, to see the puppies . . . Mrs. R. drove her open car with the pres. by her side & Fala in the back seat. We had tea in the enclosed porch, the puppies fast asleep in their box, at the President's feet . . . I took them out to be seen by the SS [Secret Service] . . . Fala came up with great interest, to see his offspring, & Button flew at him & ran around with him for a while.
>
> Mrs. R. was very sweet & charming, as always. The President looks terribly badly—so tired that every word seems to be an effort. They stayed for about 3/4 of an hour, Mrs. R. doing her best to get him started home to see some people at six—more people for dinner.

For four tranquil days at Hyde Park, FDR looked into matters at the FDR Library and gave instructions for work to be done around the farm.

Eleanor warded people off, trying to let FDR rest. Bill Hassett, who came to the president's bedroom each morning with the mail, found FDR frighteningly weary but in good spirits.

The Roosevelts were back at the White House on the morning of Thursday, March 29, and FDR did a few hours' work before departing for Warm Springs at 4 p.m. He was accompanied by the usual barrage of Secret Service, aides, colleagues, secretaries, and reporters. Dr. Bruenn and his assistant, George Fox, were going; Dr. McIntire, for once, was staying behind in Washington. As his personal guests, FDR had invited Daisy Suckley and his more flamboyant Rhinebeck cousin, Laura ("Polly") Delano.

Eleanor had her regular round of engagements in Washington and New York. Anna had to stay in Washington to look after her youngest son, Johnny, who was at the Bethesda Naval Hospital with an abscess in his throat. The two women waved goodbye as the fleet of cars set off for the train. Franklin had never looked more exhausted. The doctors had recommended total rest. Franklin said he intended to "sleep and sleep and sleep."

The presidential train arrived at Warm Springs the next day, around 1 p.m. There was the standard crowd at the railway station to welcome the president. Mike Reilly wheeled him to his dark-blue Ford, with the deep-red license plate FDR 1, and lifted him in. Reilly found him dead weight, far heavier than usual. It worried him, he told Dr. Bruenn that night.

FDR no longer took the wheel, but sat in the front seat, beside the chauffeur. Daisy and Polly climbed in behind with Fala, and Polly's Irish setter, Sister. In contrast to Daisy, who looked as prim as a nun, the eccentric Polly jangled with jewelry and sported bright-blue hair. They drove along the familiar rough wood roads to the foundation, slowed to a standstill in front of Georgia Hall, where the patients had gathered, as they always did, to greet the president, and proceeded up the hill to the Little White House.

The president's closest colleagues stayed in the cottages. That evening, Bill Hassett, FDR's secretary, met Dr. Bruenn in the compound, and stopped to talk about the Boss. "He is slipping away from us and no earthly power can keep him here," Hassett ventured. Bruenn looked surprised, and asked what made him say that. Hassett said he had "maintained the bluff" for a year with the Boss's family and associates, but Hassett could see—everyone could see—that the president had no strength, no appetite, no zest. He was wasting away.

Bruenn finally admitted that there was some cause for alarm, but maintained that the situation was not beyond hope, if only they could spare the president from any additional strain. After twelve years in the White House, the Boss was tired. No president had ever faced greater burdens, and certainly not for four terms. But the war was coming to an end, and Bruenn hoped there would be no disasters in the coming weeks. In the meantime, he was glad that the president was having a break from his wife. Hassett nodded.

The two men parted in front of Georgia Hall. "We said good night with heavy hearts," Hassett wrote in his diary.

Efforts to rescue FDR from his wife had taken on the momentum of a conspiracy among his inner circle. Over the years FDR's friends had often resented Eleanor; Louis Howe was the notable exception. The current situation resembled the dramatic winter of 1921–1922, when Franklin's mother, nurse, and physiotherapist all complained that Eleanor was pushing him too hard. Back then, the doctors were on Eleanor's side. This time, they were trying to keep a dying man alive.

Eleanor took the view that Franklin had taken on this job, and so he must do it. She knew how ill he was, but so much was at stake—the war, the peace, the men who were dying on the battlefields. As she saw it, she and Franklin were on the battlefield themselves, fighting to the last for their country. As Dr. Bruenn saw it, the president desperately needed rest. Even while Franklin was in Warm Springs, Eleanor would continue to harass him with requests. One day she called him urging help for Yugoslavia. The phone call lasted forty-five minutes. Franklin did not agree to her request. When he hung up, the veins on his forehead were bulging and his blood pressure was up by fifty points. Bruenn was furious.

There was something obsessive about the love FDR inspired in others. The members of his inner circle almost vied with each other to prove how much they loved him. Dr. Bruenn told Daisy Suckley, "You realize that like all people who work for this man—I love him. If he told me to jump out of the window, I would do it, without hesitation." Daisy wrote in her diary: "To be in a position to see FDR every day . . . to wait on him, to be at hand when he wants anything, whether it's a cigarette or just some one to talk to, is the greatest privilege in the world." Lucy Rutherfurd had written to Daisy: "I have been hoping for word from F. You who live within the radius of the arc lights do not know how hard it can be when one is beyond their rays."

Under the surface, jealousies were rife. In the Little White House at Warm Springs, Franklin's women friends were on the lookout for signs of preferential treatment. Who would get the special guest room, next to the bathroom, where Missy used to sleep? Whom would FDR invite to go driving with him that day? Whom would he ask to act as hostess at dinner?

The women liked to tell themselves that the president *needed* them, that they were making up for Eleanor's lacks. When Lucy Rutherfurd left Warm Springs on their previous sojourn there, in November 1944, Daisy mused in her diary: "We understand each other perfectly, I think, and feel the same about F.D.R. She has worried & does worry, terribly, about him, & has felt for years that he has been terribly lonely." Three weeks later, when Lucy made another of her clandestine visits to Hyde Park, Daisy observed: "She & I have one very big thing in common: our unselfish devotion to F."

While FDR's acolytes were looking after him in Warm Springs, Eleanor conferred with ministers, fielded requests, prepared for the United Nations meeting, entertained official guests, helped Anna look after her sick son, transmitted pressing memoranda to FDR, gave talks, and wrote her daily column. On Friday evening, April 6, she and Tommy took the train to Hyde Park and spent the weekend sorting through Sara Delano's china cupboards. At sunset they walked back through the woods to Val-Kill. Over the radio came news of bloody battles in Germany and the Pacific. "We went out on the porch which opens out of my sitting room on the second floor and looked at the rolling fields and the trees, with their feathery red and green spring attire," Eleanor wrote in her column. "Somehow it was hard to believe that somewhere far away our ships and planes were shooting down the Japanese, and our soldiers and more planes were chasing the Germans."

•

FDR was coughing at night; Polly and Daisy could hear him through the thin walls. He ate breakfast in bed around nine. Bill Hassett turned up around ten with a batch of letters for him to sign. Grace Tully came at eleven, and FDR dictated urgent correspondence. (He and Churchill were now worried that Stalin was not fulfilling the promises he had made at Yalta.) He did not emerge from his room till around midday. After lunch, he napped for a couple of hours. In the late afternoon, he took the women for a drive.

FDR sat in front beside the chauffeur, and pushed his windshield aside so that he could enjoy the wind on his face. Polly and Daisy sat behind with the dogs, and an extra windshield to protect their hats and hair. The countryside was magnificent in its spring mantle. "Lots of azaleas in bloom and some dogwood trees," Daisy noted. "The peach trees are covered with fruit, the size of walnuts, already."

At dinner, FDR still dominated the conversation, entertaining the women with amusing anecdotes and memories. One evening, after dinner, the little group sat by the fire and told ghost stories. FDR grumbled like a schoolboy when Dr. Bruenn and George Fox came at nine thirty and insisted that he repair to bed. There were the usual wisecracks while the doctors examined him. The women could hear the laughter coming from his bedroom. Then FDR's Southern valet, Arthur Prettyman, got him ready for bed.

When Prettyman came out of FDR's room, Polly and Daisy went in to say good night. Daisy had asked Dr. Bruenn's permission to give Franklin a small cup of gruel. She was convinced it would help him sleep better; Bruenn said it would do no harm. In front of Polly, Daisy now performed a nightly ritual:

> I sit on the edge of the bed & he "puts on an act": he is too weak to raise his head, his hands are weak, he must be fed! So I proceed to feed him with a tea spoon & he loves it! Just to be able to turn from his world problems & behave like a complete nut for a few moments, with an appreciative audience laughing with him & at him, both!

Later, Daisy crossed out that passage in her diary with a thin pencil line. She hoped to publish her diary one day. Such details were not for the eyes of posterity.

The routine at Warm Springs was calm and pleasant, and FDR's colleagues privately resented the interruption ahead. Lucy Rutherfurd was about to arrive. She was bringing a friend, the Russian society painter, Madame Shoumatoff, an arrogant woman and a committed Republican. Two years ago, Lucy had arranged for Elizabeth Shoumatoff to paint a watercolor of FDR. It was hanging in the White House. Now Lucy had pushed for a second portrait. FDR had kindly agreed. This time, it was to be Lucy's.

It was not the first time that the president's party had been conspirators in the secrecy surrounding Lucy Rutherfurd. Everyone knew that Lucy's visits were "off the record." And everyone knew why. Lucy was an "old friend," Daisy wrote in her diary. She put "old friend" in quote marks.

It was generally understood that Lucy was at the top of the hierarchy of FDR's women friends. When Lucy came to Warm Springs the previous November with her twenty-two-year-old daughter, Barbara, the Rutherfurds had stayed in the cottage with FDR, and Daisy and Polly had moved to the small guesthouse at the back. "I felt badly to have been the cause of evicting you," Lucy wrote to Daisy afterward, "but you can imagine how very wonderful it was for me to feel myself under the same roof and within the sound of the voice we all love after so many, many years." This time, since Shoumatoff was a stranger in their midst, Daisy and Polly were remaining in the Little White House, and Lucy and "Shoumie" (as FDR called her behind her back) were to stay in the guesthouse.

On Monday, April 9, FDR asked Daisy to go with him to the town of Macon, where he had arranged to meet their visitors at 4 p.m. Lucy and Shoumie were driving down from Lucy's home in Aiken, South Carolina, in Shoumie's convertible Cadillac sedan.

FDR and Daisy got to Macon and waited, but nobody came. FDR asked his chauffeur to turn back. In Manchester, they stopped for a Coke in front of the drugstore and Lucy and Shoumie drove up. The women piled into the president's car. Lucy sat in the front seat beside FDR. Daisy moved to the back with Shoumie. A Secret Service man followed in Shoumie's car. It was late by the time they got home, and chilly. FDR looked exhausted. That evening his blood pressure was far too high.

On Tuesday, April 10, FDR emerged from his room around eleven thirty. Shoumatoff made sketches while FDR sat on the porch and worked. That afternoon, after his nap, he took Lucy for a drive to his favorite spot, Dowdell's Knob, on Pine Mountain. His chauffeur walked over to join Mike Reilly and the Secret Service men, who had parked behind some trees, keeping a respectful distance. For more than an hour Franklin and Lucy sat in the car and talked.

April 11 was another glorious spring day. The windows of the Little White House were thrown wide open. Dr. Bruenn told the president, "Keep lazy, sir!" Franklin came out of his room at noon, wearing a double-breasted gray-blue suit and crimson tie, and sat in the living room reading his mail, while Shoumatoff painted. They decided that she would paint FDR with his navy cloak around him, for more color. In his left hand he would hold a scroll, symbolizing the United Nations charter.

After lunch, while FDR napped, the women talked and knitted. "Lucy is such a lovely person," Daisy wrote, "but she seems so very immature—like a character out of a book. She has led such a protected life with her husband, who was much older than herself, always living on a high scale, that she knows little about life . . . F says she has *so many* problems & difficulties that she brings to him . . . I cannot blame her, but at the same time I can't help feeling that she should face her own life & not put too much of its difficulties on *his* shoulders."

By the time FDR emerged from his room, Daisy and Polly had made tactful plans to take Fala for a walk, so that Franklin could go for another drive with Lucy. But this time Franklin wanted either Daisy or Polly along, too. "I was delegated," Daisy wrote. She flung on her hat and raincoat. "Off we went for a two-hour drive in warm, wonderful air—little Fala on the little seat, so he could look over the side once in a while. Most of the time he just lies on the floor, with, usually, his head on his master's foot."

On Thursday, April 12, 1945, FDR woke with a slight headache and stiff neck, but he was full of smiles when he emerged from his room and looked "very fine," Daisy thought, in his gray suit and crimson tie. Madame Shoumatoff set up her easel and fussed around. FDR sat in his stout leather chair, his feet up on a wicker stool, and a card table in front of him.

Bill Hassett arrived with papers for FDR to sign, and found himself extremely annoyed by Shoumatoff's imperious manner. She kept interrupting, walking up to take measurements, asking the president to turn this way and that. Hassett resolved to speak to Bruenn about it and "put an end to this unnecessary hounding of a sick man." As Hassett prepared to leave, FDR said they would see him at the barbecue later that afternoon. The manager of the Warm Springs Hotel was cooking FDR's favorite dish, Brunswick stew.

At 1:15 p.m., the Filipino butler was setting the table for lunch when FDR passed his right hand over his forehead with a jerky gesture, then slumped forward. Daisy thought he had dropped his cigarette. She sprang up and went to him. FDR murmured, "I have a terrific pain in the back of my head." Then he lost consciousness. Daisy seized the phone and asked the operator to get hold of Dr. Bruenn. Arthur Prettyman and the Filipino butler heaved the president to his bed.

FDR was sweating profusely. His breathing was loud and labored. He had not regained consciousness. Lucy waved camphor in front of his nose. Dr. Bruenn came rushing in, and asked the women to leave the room so he could get the president undressed. Polly Delano telephoned Eleanor and told her that Franklin had had a fainting spell. Lucy and Madame Shoumatoff hastily packed their bags and departed. An internal-medicine specialist sped down the road from Atlanta. At 3:35 p.m., the breathing stopped.

That morning, Eleanor had held her press conference as usual. She told the press women that she was looking forward to traveling across the country with the president for the United Nations charter meeting in San Francisco.

At 3 p.m. she was having a meeting in her sitting room when Tommy called her to the phone. It was Polly Delano, phoning from Warm Springs, to say that the president had had a fainting spell. Moments later, Dr. McIntire called. He had just heard from Dr. Bruenn, and although Bruenn was not alarmed, McIntire wanted Mrs. Roosevelt to be ready to fly with him that evening to Warm Springs.

Eleanor asked whether she should cancel her 4 p.m. engagement. McIntire thought she should proceed with her plans. A cancellation followed by an unexpected trip might provoke comment.

At 3:40 p.m., Eleanor was at the Sulgrave Club, supporting a benefit tea for the thrift shop, when she was called to the phone. "Steve Early, very much upset, asked me to come home at once," she wrote later. "I did not even ask why. I knew down in my heart that something dreadful had happened."

Back at the White House, Steve Early and Dr. McIntire came to Eleanor's sitting room and broke the news that FDR had died of a cerebral hemorrhage. Eleanor phoned Anna, who was at the Bethesda Naval Hospital, then sent a wire to her four sons: "Darlings: Father slept away this afternoon. He did his job to the end as he would want you to do. Bless you. All our love. Mother."

At 5:30 p.m., Vice President Truman arrived at the White House. Eleanor placed her arm on his shoulder. "Harry, the President is dead." Truman could scarcely speak. Then he asked if there was anything he could do for her. Eleanor looked at him with her gentle eyes. "Is there anything we can do for *you*? You are the one in trouble now."

Eleanor attended the swearing in of the new president, then left for Warm Springs, accompanied by Early and McIntire. It was a five-hour journey by plane and car. They arrived at the Little White House at 11:25 p.m.

"The president is dead!" Newspaper vendors across the country were shouting the headlines. People were stunned by the news. "An air of complete demoralization pervaded every government office and business house," a Washington correspondent observed. "On the streets people gathered in small groups to discuss the incredibility of the reports. A mantle of silence seemed to creep over the scene. Pedestrians walked more slowly . . . Strong men wept openly."

It seemed such a tragic, untimely death. FDR had led the free world to the threshold of victory. Berlin was about to fall. Hitler was on the verge of surrender. Japan was on its last legs. In two weeks there was to be an international meeting in San Francisco that would establish the conditions for world peace. And FDR, the man who had done so much to bring about this victory, had not lived to see it.

In Britain, Churchill choked up when he told the House of Commons: "In Franklin Roosevelt there died the greatest friend we have ever known, and the greatest champion of freedom who has ever brought help and comfort from the New World to the Old."

Men and women in the street felt as if they had lost a friend or relative. The New York poet, Carl Lamson Carmer, put it well:

> . . . *I never saw him—*
> *But I* knew *him. Can you have forgotten*

How, with his voice, he came into our house,
The President of the United States,
Calling us friends . . .

People all over the world were already missing FDR's smile—the smile they had seen for the last twelve years on newspapers and in newsreels. "His face was the very image of happiness," Albert Camus wrote in the French Resistance newspaper, *Combat*. "History's powerful men are not generally men of such good humor . . . There is not a single free human being who does not regret his loss and who would not have wished his destiny to have continued a little longer. World peace, that boundless good, ought to be planned by men with happy faces rather than by sad-eyed politicians."

In Warm Springs, Eleanor hugged Daisy and Polly and patted Grace Tully on the shoulder. "Tully, dear, I am so very sorry for all of you." Before she went in to see Franklin, she sat down on the sofa in the living room and asked the group to tell her what had happened. It was Polly Delano who revealed that Lucy Rutherfurd had been in the room when FDR collapsed, that Lucy had been with them for the last three days. The others sat around like guilty schoolchildren. They knew what this would mean to Eleanor, but they could not be caught lying. FDR had put them in a very awkward position.

Eleanor listened quietly, then turned to Grace Tully. "Were you here, Grace?" She was trying to take it in—the fact that Franklin had been seeing Lucy Rutherfurd, that Lucy had been with him at the end, that all his friends and associates knew about Lucy, everyone, it seemed, except her.

Eleanor got up, went into Franklin's bedroom, and closed the door. She was there for about five minutes, then came back out. Her eyes were dry, Tully observed. Her face was "grave but composed." Then Eleanor sent the women to bed, while she made arrangements, with FDR's aides, for the funeral.

Hick was one of several close friends who phoned Eleanor in Warm Springs the next morning, around eight. "I guess I never realized what implicit faith I had in him until now—since he has gone," Hick told Eleanor. "No use burdening you with *my* bewilderment and terror. After all, I guess I only feel like millions of other people in the world . . . God, he used to be strong, so vital, so full of energy!"

The funeral procession left the Little White House in Warm Springs, Georgia, at 10 a.m. Marines lined the streets. Military bands led the procession, followed by soldiers in uniform. Then came the dark-green hearse bearing the president's body. Eleanor sat in the next car, with Grace Tully, Daisy Suckley, and Laura Delano. Behind them were a convoy of cars bearing secretaries, aides, and Secret Service. The most wrenching moment of all was when FDR's casket stopped in front of Georgia Hall, as FDR always did when he left Warm Springs, to say goodbye.

The train trip to Washington—through Georgia, South Carolina, North Carolina, and Virginia—was slow and solemn. All night long, people lined the tracks. Some sang hymns. Many were weeping. The back of the presidential car was lit up, displaying FDR's flag-draped casket surrounded by flowers, with four guards standing at attention. Eleanor could not sleep. "I lay in my berth all night with the window shade up, looking out at the countryside he had loved and watching the faces of the people at stations, and even at the crossroads, who came to pay their last tribute."

The train got into Washington on Saturday, April 14, at 10 a.m. It was raining as the funeral procession made its way from Union Station down Pennsylvania Avenue to the White House. A throng of 500,000 mourners filled the streets. As Roosevelt's casket passed on a black caisson pulled by six white horses, people gasped, held handkerchiefs to their faces, bowed their heads, knelt in the rain, sobbed aloud.

The funeral service was in the East Room at 4 p.m., officiated by the bishop of the Episcopal Diocese of Washington. In his will FDR stated that he wanted Reverend Endicott Peabody to administer his funeral rites, but Peabody had died, at the age of eighty-seven, three months before, on the day of FDR's fourth inauguration. Eleanor asked the bishop to recall FDR's first words as president: "The only thing we have to fear is fear itself."

Harry Hopkins had left his hospital bed in Minnesota to be in the East Room that day to say goodbye to his friend. He had not seen FDR since they parted in Algiers, on their way home from Yalta. Hopkins looked like a dead man himself (he would not survive the year), but that afternoon he told his colleagues, with feverish emotion, that now it was up to them:

> We've had it too easy all this time, because we knew he was there, and we had the privilege of being able to get to him. Whatever we thought was the matter with the world, whatever we felt ought to be done about it, we could take our ideas to him, and if he thought there was any merit in them, or if anything that we said to him started on a train of thought of his own, then we'd see him go ahead and do it, and no matter how tremendous it might be or how idealistic he wasn't scared of it. Well—he isn't there now, and we've got to find a way to do things by ourselves.

At 11 p.m., the funeral train—seventeen cars packed with dignitaries, diplomats, military, and security men—left Washington for Hyde Park.

As dawn broke, crowds were standing by the railroad tracks to catch a glimpse of the funeral train as it steamed through New York and up the Hudson valley. Trude Lash, who had married Joe when he came home on leave the previous year and was now expecting their baby, had spent the night at Hyde Park. She watched from the rose garden as the funeral cortege made its way up the hill, headed by the marines, the West Point cadet band, and the caisson, which was pulled by thirteen horses bridled in black and scarlet. Eleanor walked behind in a simple black dress and veil, wearing the small pearl fleur-de-lis brooch Franklin had given her on their wedding day forty years earlier. Anna and Elliott (the only son to get back in time) followed their mother. Trude reported to Joe:

> The funeral was very beautiful. The day was gloriously snappy, very sunny and blue, white lilacs were in bloom—and early in the morning there was a mist over the Hudson—the birds were singing . . . Soon the cannons were booming, then the music started, getting louder as the cortege wound up the hill (how on earth did they have enough breath to climb and blow the brass instruments!)—then the caisson came to a rolling stop outside of the hedge. You heard the coffin grate as it was lifted off the

caisson—a simple coffin draped with a flag—old Mr. Anthony [the local minister] quavered the Episcopal service—there were rifle shots . . . Fala barked once after each shot . . . and then it was all over.

Eleanor traveled back to Washington in the last car of the train. James joined the train at Penn Station, having flown in from the Philippines. Eleanor asked a secretary to notify the White House that there would be nine for dinner that night. "Mrs. Roosevelt was wonderful," Trude wrote. "We discussed whether Truman could . . . carry on the President's Program. We were both scared, and she looked thin and old and drawn."

Eleanor was sixty when Franklin died. He was sixty-three. They had been married for forty years. "There was a big vacuum which nothing, not even the passage of years, would fill," she wrote later. "My husband and I had come through the years with an acceptance of each other's faults and foibles, a deep understanding, warm affection and agreement on essential values. We depended on each other."

She missed his voice, the booming laughter, the boyish joy he took in simple things. They had been apart a great deal during their marriage, but Franklin had remained the center of her world. He had always been there, in the background, as her anchor. "I have never known a man who gave one a greater sense of security," she admitted. Now she was cast afloat.

The Trumans urged her to take her time, but Eleanor was determined to move out of the White House within a week. By the afternoon of Thursday, April 19, the packing was done. She and Tommy were going to spend the weekend in her New York apartment with Hick:

Hick dearest,

The Trumans have just been to lunch & nearly all that I can do is done. The upstairs looks desolate & I will be glad to leave tomorrow. It is empty & without purpose to be here now . . . Franklin's death ended a period in history & now in its wake those of us who laid in his shadow have to start again under our own momentum & wonder what we can achieve . . . I may be a bit weary when we get home tomorrow but I'm so glad you will be at the apartment.

The following week, Eleanor and Tommy supervised the unpacking at Hyde Park. Eleanor slept on her upstairs porch at Val-Kill, finding comfort in the croaking of frogs in the pond and the chorus of birds at dawn. She was glad to have Tommy with her.

We walked tonight up to the top of the hill back of my cottage and saw the sun go down . . . Then, as we came home, the rain began to fall very gently—that soft spring rain which gives you the feeling you can almost see things grow. My lilies-of-the-valley are just young green shoots coming up out of the ground . . . The lilacs are out, and as we walked through the woods two white dogwood trees gleamed, almost in full bloom. Yes, the world does live again. Perhaps nature is our best assurance of immortality.

At the end of April, Mussolini was captured and hanged by Italian partisans. Two days later, Hitler and his mistress, Eva Braun, took cyanide in their Berlin bunker, then Hitler shot himself. On May 8, Churchill and Truman declared V-E Day—victory in Europe. "Unconditional surrender has been accepted by the Germans," Eleanor wrote. "I can almost hear my husband's voice make that announcement." But she was in no mood for celebration. The war in the Pacific was still raging. Many young American men, including her own sons, were in danger. And the details that were emerging from the newly liberated concentration camps were horrendous.

In the evenings she and Tommy tried to make headway with three large clothes baskets that overflowed with condolence letters. Eleanor was acutely aware that she shared her grief with millions of other women who had lost husbands and sons in the war. The task ahead of them, she wrote in her "My Day" column, was to see that their loved ones had not died in vain. "There is only one way in which those of us who live can repay the dead who have given their utmost for the cause of liberty and justice. They died in the hope that, through their sacrifice, an enduring peace would be built and a more just world would emerge for humanity."

She hoped that Congress would pass FDR's Fair Employment Practices bill, which would commit the government to fighting discrimination in the workplace. Its opponents saw it as a concession to minority groups, she wrote, but this bill was vital to each and every citizen of the United States:

> Are we learning nothing from the horrible pictures of the concentration camps which have been appearing in our papers day after day? Are our memories so short that we do not recall how in Germany this unparalleled barbarism started by discrimination directed against the Jewish people? . . . The idea of superiority of one race over another must not continue within our own country, nor must it grow up in our dealings with the rest of the world.

In his will, FDR left Hyde Park to Eleanor and the children for the duration of their lives, but in a private letter to Eleanor that she opened after his death, he urged her to turn the Big House over to the government as soon as possible. He did not think that she and the children could afford the upkeep.

Eleanor understood that this was also about keeping history intact. She now realized that when his mother died, in September 1941, Franklin was already thinking of the Big House as a future museum. Eleanor had suggested changes at the time, to make the house more livable. Franklin had blankly refused. He wanted the house kept exactly as it had been left by his mother. For Eleanor, it was one of those moments of hurtful realization that sprang up from time to time in their marriage, which made her question her place in Franklin's life. She had had no desire to live in a monument to her mother-in-law.

Eleanor still did not want to live in the Big House, and she was relieved when the children agreed to hand the house to the government. She was proud of FDR's gesture. It was the first time in American history that a former president was opening his home to the people. For the next few weeks, Eleanor was busy seeing executors and appraisers. The Big House, the FDR Library, and surrounding grounds would be opened to the public on April 12, 1946, the first anniversary of FDR's death, in a ceremony attended by President Truman. The library and museum were to be the permanent repository for FDR's naval books, prints, and model boats (the most significant private collection in the country), his stuffed birds (the best collection in Dutchess County), and 150 albums, with stamps from all over the world. Over the years the manuscripts, correspondence, books, photographs, newsreels, sound recordings, and other mementos from FDR, Eleanor, and their circle would never cease to grow.

"Franklin had pictured the estate, under federal auspices, as a place to which the people of our own country and even of the world might come to find rest and peace and strength, as he had," Eleanor told the gathered crowd that April day. "His spirit will always live in this house, in the library, and in the rose garden where he wished his grave to be."

In *This I Remember*, Eleanor hinted that for reasons she could not say, she felt drained of emotion in the days and weeks following Franklin's death:

> I had an almost impersonal feeling about everything that was happening. The only explanation I have is that during the years of the war I had schooled myself to believe that some or all of my sons might be killed and I had long faced the fact that Franklin might be killed or die at any time . . . That does not entirely account for my feelings, however. Perhaps it was that much further back I had had to face certain difficulties until I decided to accept the fact that a man must be what he is, life must be lived as it is . . .

She was thinking, of course, about Lucy Mercer Rutherfurd. In Warm Springs, Eleanor had been confronted not just with Franklin's dead body but with his betrayal. On the long slow funeral trip through the South to Washington, she was sharing the train with his conspirators. Never had she felt more alone.

When she got back to the White House, she had gone straight to Anna. Did Anna know that Lucy Rutherfurd was in Warm Springs with Pa? Did Anna know that Pa was still seeing Lucy? Had Anna betrayed her, as well as Franklin?

It was the most painful confrontation mother and daughter would ever have—and it happened on the day of Franklin's funeral. Anna had known for years about her father's past romance with Lucy. Eleanor had told her when Anna was seventeen. (As it happened, Aunt Susie Parish, the gossip of the family, had already informed Anna a year before.) The adolescent girl had been shocked to realize that her father was capable of such betrayal.

Twenty years later, as Franklin's "secretary," Anna was taken aback when Franklin asked if she would object to his inviting an "old friend," Mrs. Lucy Rutherfurd, to dinner. Did she know who Mrs. Rutherfurd was? he had asked her. Anna said she did. Franklin said no more. Anna knew what she was being asked to do. Her mother would be devastated if she found out.

After that, there had been other occasions with Lucy. Naturally Anna had felt conflicted. She had not wanted to hide anything from Eleanor, but neither did she want to run to her mother with tales. It was clear to Anna that whatever it had been in the past, her father's friendship with Lucy was now perfectly innocent. There were always other people present when they met. Franklin was tired, ill, and burdened. He liked the comfort of old friends. Anna had not wanted to deny him this small pleasure.

She did *not* know that Lucy was in Warm Springs, Anna assured her mother. She had spoken to Pa every day on the phone—he was very worried about little Johnny—but he had never mentioned Lucy. As they both knew, Pa liked to keep his life private, she said weakly.

But a president's life was *not* private, as they well knew. Franklin had been playing with fire to invite Lucy to Warm Springs, and now the White House was trying to conceal a potential bombshell. If it came out that Lucy Rutherfurd had been on the scene when FDR died and the White House had covered this up, there would be an international press frenzy. FDR would topple from his pedestal and Eleanor would be publicly humiliated. The United States would lose its moral leadership in the peace negotiations.

The press was buzzing with stories about the president's last days in Warm Springs. The news was out that Elizabeth Shoumatoff was painting the president when he died. She was hounded by reporters, but declined to comment. A few days after FDR's death, Shoumatoff—after an intensive briefing by Stephen Early—managed to pull off an entire press conference without mentioning Lucy Rutherfurd.

While Eleanor was supervising the packing up of the White House, she learned that it was Lucy Rutherfurd who had commissioned Shoumatoff's previous portrait of Franklin. Eleanor had known only that Shoumatoff made three visits to the White House in the spring of 1943, and produced a small watercolor, somewhat idealized, which Franklin had liked.

Through Daisy Suckley, Eleanor sent Lucy a present. A few days later, a letter arrived from Lucy:

Dear Eleanor,

Margaret Suckley has written me that you gave her the little water color of Franklin by Mme. Shoumatoff to send me. Thank you so very much— You must know that it will be treasured always—

I have wanted to write you for a long time to tell you that I had seen Franklin and of his great kindness about my husband when he was desperately ill in Washington, and of how helpful he was to his boys—and that I hoped so very much that I might see you again—

I can't tell you how deeply I feel for you and how constantly I think of your sorrow— You—whom I have always felt to be the most blessed and privileged of women—must now feel immeasurable grief and pain and they must be almost unbearable—

The whole universe finds it difficult to readjust itself to a world without Franklin—and to you and to his family—the emptiness must be appalling—

I send you—as I find it impossible not to—my love and my deep deep sympathy

As always—
Affectionately
Lucy Rutherfurd

It was a dignified letter. There was no apology, no defensiveness. Lucy wrote as an equal. Indeed, as much as she dared—to a wife she had betrayed—Lucy was declaring her love for Franklin. Her wording was not tactful. If anyone had made Eleanor feel less than "blessed and privileged" to be married to Franklin, it was Lucy.

A few days later, Lucy wrote to Anna. They had met several times in the year before Franklin's death, and got on well. Lucy had always felt grateful to Anna for facilitating their meetings, and now—when she heard in a phone call from Anna what it had cost her—she felt it more than ever. This time, Lucy was writing a vicarious love letter to FDR:

Anna dear—

Your telephoning the other night meant much to me. I did not know that it was in me just now to be so glad to hear the sound of any voice—& to hear you laugh—was beyond words wonderful.

I had not written before for many many reasons—but you were constantly in my thoughts & with very loving and heart torn sympathy & I was following every step of the way. This blow must be crushing to you—to all of you—but I know that you meant more to your Father than any one and that makes it closer & harder to bear . . .

I have been reading over some very old letters of his & in one he says: "Anna is a dear fine person—I wish so much that you knew her—" Well, now we do know one another—and it is a real joy to me—& I think he was happy this past year that it was so.

. . . Through it all one hears his ringing laugh & one thinks of all the ridiculous things he used to say—& do—& enjoy. The picture of his sitting waiting for you that night with the Rabbi's cap on his extraordinarily beautiful head is still vivid.

The world has lost one of the greatest men that ever lived—to me—the greatest. He towers above them all—effortlessly . . .

Forgive me for writing of things which you know so much better than I—& which are sacred—& should not ever be touched on by a stranger—I somehow cannot feel myself to be that—& I feel strongly that you understand.

My love to your husband—and to you—Anna darling—because you are his Child and because you are Yourself,
I am very devotedly & with heartbroken sympathy—
Lucy Rutherfurd

On July 31, 1948, Lucy Mercer Rutherfurd died of leukemia, at the age of fifty-seven. By then she had destroyed all of Franklin's old letters. She had decided that the details of their romance should remain a sacred secret between her and Franklin. Posterity did not need to know.

There would continue to be awkward moments during Eleanor's lifetime when someone mentioned in print that Franklin had once loved another woman, and that there had been talk of divorce, but that the woman was a Catholic, who refused to marry a divorced man. It was humiliating for Eleanor but, fortunately, the gossip never came to much.

In her 1949 memoir, *F.D.R., My Boss*, Grace Tully broke the news that Madame Elizabeth Shoumatoff had not arrived in Warm Springs alone. "Mrs. Winthrop Rutherfurd, who had commissioned her to do the portrait, had accompanied her." The extreme right-wing gossipmonger, Westbrook Pegler, did his best to turn this into a full-scale scandal, but he was such a notorious Roosevelt hater that he had undermined his own credibility.

And so the gossip came and went. There were other whiffs of scandal, but they, too, died down. In 1950, Earl Miller's third wife, Simone Miller, sued for divorce on the grounds that Earl had consorted with "a woman of prominent reputation." Simone Miller was granted custody of the two children (named Eleanor and Earl) and a very generous settlement. There were more unpleasant columns by Westbrook Pegler, but though the innuendos were clear, he was not able to name names. "Miller got in a lather, but it didn't bother your mother," Tommy told Anna.

On the whole, FDR's circle—those in the know—respected Eleanor's privacy and honor. It was not until the mid-1960s, after Eleanor's death, that scandalous stories began to seep out about the Roosevelt marriage.

"The story is over," Eleanor Roosevelt told reporters when she moved out of the White House. She was wrong. The story—or rather, stories— about the Roosevelt marriage had scarcely begun. And in her own life she was merely beginning another chapter. For the next seventeen years, as FDR's widow, she would accomplish what many believed to be her best work ever.

In December 1945, President Harry Truman asked Eleanor if she would serve as a member of the United States delegation to the United Nations General Assembly. The first meeting was to be held in London in January 1946. Eleanor felt proud to be carrying on the work FDR had begun. Like him, she viewed the United Nations as the only hope for lasting world peace.

She was the only woman in the U.S. delegation, and her leadership was crucial to its success. "The Russians seem to have met their match in Mrs. Roosevelt," *The New York Times* reported. "Never have I seen naiveté and cunning so gracefully blended," said a State Department adviser. On December 10, 1948—in large part thanks to the steely determination of Eleanor Roosevelt—the United Nations General Assembly adopted the Universal Declaration of Human Rights. The assembly gave Eleanor a standing ovation. For the first time in history, the nations of the world had come together to proclaim the dignity and equality of all human beings.

For seven years, Eleanor regularly shuttled across the Atlantic for UN meetings. When her official appointment ended in late 1952, she continued to work for the UN in a voluntary capacity. At the same time, she wrote books, a daily column, gave an average of 150 lectures a year, spoke on the air, and led a roundtable discussion on politics and society, *Eleanor Roosevelt's Weekly Forum*, on the new medium, television.

The contract for her "My Day" column had been renewed when Eleanor left the White House, with the proviso that it would be dropped if the column did not turn out to be "profitable." Strangely, it would prove more successful than ever. Eleanor Roosevelt's columns carried the whiff of a more heroic age in American history—an age when the whole of the free world looked to the White House for reassurance and inspiration. Eleanor's daily diary would remain a reassuring fixture of the American press until September 27, 1962, a few weeks before her death. Her readers loved Eleanor both in her own right and because she had been married to FDR.

Throughout the 1950s, as a thick fog of conservatism settled over the United States, Eleanor continued to be a strong voice of liberalism. She supported civil rights, equal pay for women, national health insurance. And she deplored the new brand of anticommunist paranoia whipped up by Joe McCarthy and the House Un-American Activities Committee, which soon had the entire nation involved in a witch hunt.

She insisted that fear was the greatest enemy of all, and warned against governments that preyed on terror in order to subdue the least protest among their own citizens. "Surely we cannot be so stupid as to let ourselves become shackled by senseless fears . . . For the leading democracy in the world to indulge in them is a very great danger, not to us alone but to the world."

Eleanor traveled widely, on semiofficial visits, meeting world leaders, giving talks, easing cold war tensions between the United States and other countries. Trude Lash accompanied Eleanor on a trip to Italy and Israel in 1955, and found it hard going. "Somehow it is impossible for her to just sit and enjoy the sun and the view from her room or her balcony, even for half an hour," she complained to Joe from Rome. "I like to look at some things more than a minute and so I often look up and find her gone."

Many people felt sorry for Tommy, who wore herself out trying to keep up with Eleanor's work pace. Anna Roosevelt recalled:

I used to just cringe sometimes when I'd hear Mother at eleven thirty at night say to Tommy, "I've still got a column to do." And this weary, weary woman who didn't have Mother's stamina would sit down at a typewriter and Mother would dictate to her. And both of them so tired. I remember one time when Tommy with asperity said, "You'll have to speak louder. I can't hear you." And Mother's response was, "If you will listen, you can hear *perfectly* well."

Tommy became ill in the spring of 1951, and Eleanor hired Maureen Corr, a young, Irish-born secretary, to act as Tommy's assistant. By this time Eleanor was aware that she had asked too much of Tommy, who had sacrificed her personal life to the Roosevelt cause. She did not want to make the same mistake again. "I want you to have your own life," she told Maureen Corr. "I want you to be free and not completely overwhelmed by my life."

April 12, 1953, was the eighth anniversary of FDR's death. Tommy, who had just turned sixty, was unconscious in a New York hospital after a stroke. Eleanor did not want to miss the annual ceremony by Franklin's grave in the rose garden at Hyde Park. She decided to drive up in the morning—a two-hour drive—and come straight back after lunch. As she walked back into the hospital in the late afternoon, Tommy drew her last breath. She had been Eleanor's secretary for almost thirty years. "In many, many ways she not only made my life easier but gave me a reason for living," Eleanor wrote.

For the first time in her life, Eleanor was truly on her own.

As FDR's widow, Eleanor Roosevelt remained a highly influential political figure. Over the years she offered advice to presidents Truman,

Eisenhower, and Kennedy. John Kenneth Galbraith, the noted economist, observed: "Throughout the 1950s Eleanor Roosevelt was one of the less visible but most important people in the Democratic party . . . She was a force behind the scenes. It would have been impossible for any Democrat to run for high office without her support, and certainly not if he had had her opposition."

In 1952, Eleanor came out for the governor of Illinois, Adlai Stevenson, though she knew he had little hope against the Republican candidate, Dwight D. Eisenhower. She was right. It was the end of a twenty-year period of continuous Democratic rule and the beginning of eight years of hard-line Republicanism. The anticommunist scourge—the gavel-pounding red-baiting of Senator Joe McCarthy and his colleagues in HUAC, the subpoenas, "loyalty oaths," whole-scale firings, imprisonment of the famous "Hollywood Ten" directors and screenwriters who had once been, or still were, members of the Communist Party—had all but gagged free speech in the United States.

By 1956, Eleanor, now seventy-two, could stand it no more. This time, she threw herself energetically into the Stevenson campaign. Once again, she knew that the Democrats had almost no chance of winning. The nation was prosperous, and the cold war had the United States caught up in another arms race. Eisenhower won again. "When it was all over, I was glad to be out of politics," Eleanor wrote. "I couldn't forget that sometimes my feet hurt during that campaign and that I seldom got enough sleep."

In 1960, she pushed for Adlai Stevenson a third time. But Stevenson was now viewed as a loser, and it was John F. Kennedy, the handsome young senator from Massachusetts, who won the presidential nomination at the Democratic National Convention. Eleanor did not believe a Catholic could win the election. She vehemently disliked JFK's wheeler-dealer father, and thought JFK young and arrogant. Kennedy, knowing how important it was to get Eleanor Roosevelt's support, pursued her like a suitor. Finally she agreed to his visiting her at Val-Kill. On Saturday, August 13, the day before his visit, Eleanor's granddaughter, Sally—John's daughter—was killed in a horse-riding accident. Kennedy proposed canceling their meeting. Eleanor said she would see him nevertheless.

They talked for an hour, alone, over lunch. Eleanor wrote to a Democrat friend: "My final judgment now is that . . . he really is interested in helping the people of his own country and mankind in general. I will be surer of this as time goes on, but I think I am not mistaken in feeling that he would make a good President if elected."

Eleanor detested the Republican presidential candidate, Vice President Richard Nixon, who had been a member of HUAC, and whom she thought of as a "dangerous opportunist." For the next few months, she spoke out for Kennedy. The election was frighteningly close, but Kennedy emerged triumphant. John Kenneth Galbraith believed it could well have been Eleanor's support that swung it.

Eleanor was delighted to see the Democrats back in power, but still worried that President Kennedy, the Bostonian, came across to many people as cold and aloof. In July 1961, at the age of seventy-six, she wrote to him:

Dear Mr. President:

I hope you will forgive me if I seem presumptuous, but I am concerned because I feel there is not as yet established a real feeling among the people that you are consulting them. I listened during a rather long drive . . . to your last press conference and decided that it did not take the place of fireside chats. The questions asked were asked by men and women of good background and were much too sophisticated for the average person to understand . . . I wish you could get someone like my old teacher (probably her daughter) to help you deepen and strengthen your voice on radio and TV. It would give you more warmth and personality in your voice. It can be learned, and I think it would make a tremendous difference . . . I apologize for taking up your time, and I feel I should also apologize to all your many advisers who probably understand the whole situation far better than I do, but I do get the reaction, and have the reaction, of the ordinary man in the street, and I think this may be one of the things which it is hard for you to get.

There was one last romantic friendship in Eleanor's life, and in many ways she was reliving aspects of her relationship with Franklin. Dr. David Gurewitsch was a friend of Trude Lash's. When Eleanor first met him, shortly before Franklin's death, she was drawn to him immediately. When she moved out of the White House and settled in New

York, she asked David Gurewitsch whether he would take her on as a patient. He readily agreed.

For two years they rarely saw each other. Eleanor, as it happened, was a great deal healthier than her doctor. In November 1947 they sat next to each other on a plane to Switzerland. Eleanor was going to a UN meeting in Geneva to work on the Universal Declaration of Human Rights. David Gurewitsch was going to a sanatorium in the mountains of Davos for a tuberculosis cure. She was sixty-three; he was forty-five. David was the son of Russian Jewish parents; his father had died before David was born. They discovered, as they traveled through the clouds, that they had both spent their childhood fantasizing about their lost fathers.

David Gurewitsch was handsome, cultured, and charming. He loved people, and wanted nothing more than to help them. From Geneva, Eleanor wrote to him almost daily. Back in New York, she could not see enough of him. He was flattered by her attention, liked the glamour of her company, and enjoyed the intimacy of their conversations, but he felt a little stifled by Eleanor, and was distracted by younger, more beautiful women. Eleanor suffered agonies of rejection:

> David my dearest—
> I've been sitting here thinking of you to-night and wondering why I make you feel shy. I want you to feel at home with me as you would with a member of your family and I can't achieve it! Something wrong with me! I'd love to hear you call me by my first name but you can't. Perhaps it is my age! I do love you and you are always in my thoughts and if that bothers you I could hide it. I'm good at that . . . In the meantime love me a little, and show it if you can and remember to take care of yourself for you are the most precious person in the world.

David Gurewitsch was Eleanor's favorite escort to the theater and official functions. They were traveling companions—to Germany, the Soviet Union, Yugoslavia, Morocco, Russia, India, other places. Wherever Eleanor went, she was happiest if David went with her. Joe Lash was jealous. Eleanor's children were jealous. She was critical of her children, particularly her sons (their broken marriages, heavy drinking, and political opportunism), but David could do no wrong.

Eleanor was devastated in February 1958, when David Gurewitsch announced that he was marrying his young girlfriend, Edna Perkel. She brooded for weeks. Although she was terrified of losing him, she insisted that the wedding ceremony take place in her New York apartment. Edna Perkel, who was at first thoroughly tongue-tied in Eleanor's presence, wrote to her tentatively: "I know how much you mean to David and what your feelings and opinions mean to him. I can repay you in part only by doing all I can to make David happy."

In the fall of 1960, the three moved into a house together—a five-story limestone-fronted townhouse at 55 East Seventy-fourth Street. Eleanor lived downstairs; the Gurewitsches lived upstairs. Eleanor had always been happiest living with others. By now she was seventy-six and ailing, and felt reassured to know that David, her personal physician, was close. She was as sociable as ever. On November 8, 1960, election night, the front door to the house was open—so was the door to Eleanor's apartment—and as it became clear that John F. Kennedy had won, more and more friends streamed in with champagne.

Eleanor was careful not to intrude on David and Edna's privacy. She knew how easily David felt "claustrophobic," as she put it, if she tried to pin him down to social appointments too far in advance. She phoned before going upstairs. She tried not to play too large a role in their lives. But there must have been times when she felt just like her mother-in-law.

The Salk polio vaccine, which would almost eradicate the dreaded disease in the United States within a few years, was introduced in April 1955. Dr. Jonas Salk told Eleanor how often, in his work, he had thought of FDR. "I know that would have meant a great deal to my husband," Eleanor wrote in her column. "Though he accepted the blow of the crippling attack of polio and went forward with never a complaint, still anyone remembering him as a young athletic and strong man could not fail to realize what a terrific battle must have gone on within before this acceptance was possible."

In 1960, soon after she moved into her new apartment, Eleanor was diagnosed with aplastic anemia, an incurable bone marrow disease. She was tired. Nevertheless, she kept up her travels, her column, her public appearances. Her health rapidly declined in the summer of 1962. She was in and out of the hospital. In mid-August, ignoring David Gurewitsch's protests, she insisted on going to Campobello for the dedication of the Franklin D. Roosevelt Memorial Bridge, which linked the island to the mainland. "Now there will be a bridge from Lubec to the island instead of the little ferry which always took our cars across in the later years," she wrote in her column. "Still, those of us who remember the past will have a nostalgic feeling for the days when you could spend a month or six weeks, virtually cut off from the world and all its troubles, enjoying to the full the 'beloved island.'"

She had already handed over the Little White House in Warm Springs to the state of Georgia. It was to be open to the public, maintained exactly as it was in FDR's lifetime. "I hope it will serve as a reminder of what a gallant spirit can accomplish in spite of physical handicaps," she said.

While staying in their sprawling red house on Campobello, she was negotiating with John F. Kennedy for the U.S. government to buy the house and donate it to the Canadian government as a memorial to FDR. She was ill, too weak to do more than totter for a few steps in front of the house, and she told David one morning that in the night she had thought she was going to die there. She wished she could have. She was about to turn seventy-eight, and she no longer had any stamina. She was ready to go.

"Our dear Mrs. Roosevelt died last evening," Edna Gurewitsch wrote in her journal on November 8, 1962. "Around a quarter of nine, I saw from my bedroom window the simple casket leaving the house, it being placed into the hearse, and Mrs. Roosevelt alone with David driving away from 74th Street for the last time."

The sky was leaden on November 11, the day of the funeral. More than two hundred people were crammed into the tiny gray edifice, St. James Episcopal Church, in the village of Hyde Park. Then the funeral cortege made its way two miles down the Albany Post Road to the Roosevelt estate. When the oak coffin, covered with pine boughs from the surrounding woods, arrived in the rose garden, it began to drizzle with rain. Among the mourners were the three presidents who followed FDR in office, Harry S. Truman, Dwight D. Eisenhower, and John F. Kennedy; the secretary-general of the United Nations, U Thant; the singer Marian Anderson; and hundreds of lesser-known people from all races, classes, and creeds. They were there to pay tribute to Eleanor

Roosevelt not because she had been married to FDR, not because she lived in the White House longer than any other first lady, not because she held an elected public office—she never did—but because she had never ceased to advance the cause of freedom, peace, and justice for all people, and she had won the hearts of millions.

FDR had stipulated in his will that a plain white-marble monument be placed over his grave—eight feet long, four feet wide, three feet high. "It is my hope that my dear wife will on her death be buried there also." He wanted the monument to bear no inscription—just their names and dates:

FRANKLIN DELANO ROOSEVELT
1882–1945
ANNA ELEANOR ROOSEVELT
1884–1962

It felt right, somehow, when Eleanor's casket was lowered into the plot next to Franklin's. They had stood by each other in life, and they lay together in death. Married under a rose arbor, they were buried in the rose garden—the "field of roses" in the old Dutch family name. The two Roosevelt cousins had loved each other as they had lived—generously, courageously, without fear.

NOTES

Unless otherwise stated, the correspondence refers to papers held at the FDR Library at Hyde Park. Most of the letters from FDR are also published in the four volumes entitled *F.D.R.: His Personal Letters*.

ABBREVIATIONS
ER   Eleanor Roosevelt
FDR   Franklin Delano Roosevelt
FDRL   FDR Library
PL   *F.D.R.: His Personal Letters, Early Years, 1947*, vol. 1 (New York: Duell, Sloan and Pearce, 1947)
PL   *F.D.R.: His Personal Letters, 1905–1928*, vol. 2 (New York: Duell, Sloan and Pearce, 1948)
PL   *F.D.R.: His Personal Letters, 1928–1945*, vol. 3 (New York: Duell, Sloan and Pearce, 1950)
SDR   Sara Delano Roosevelt
TIMS   Eleanor Roosevelt, *This Is My Story* (New York: Harper & Bros., 1937)
TIR   Eleanor Roosevelt, *This I Remember* (New York: Harper & Bros., 1949)
TR   Theodore Roosevelt

PREFACE
xvi   "I never liked": Gellhorn to Adlai Stevenson, Nov. 8, 1962, *Selected Letters of Martha Gellhorn*, ed. Caroline Moorehead (New York: Henry Holt, 2006), 296.

ONE: COUSINS IN LOVE
7   "James Roosevelt is": "Roosevelt-Delano," *New York World*, Oct. 8, 1880, in Jan Pottker, *Sara and Eleanor* (New York: St. Martin's Press, 2004), 48.
8   "We have had such": SDR diary, July 6, 1881, FDRL.
8   "dear old boy": TR to Anna (Bye) Roosevelt, TR papers, Houghton Library, Harvard.
8   "one of the most": *New York Herald*, Dec. 2, 1883.

10   "He came back convinced": TR to Bye Roosevelt, July 12, 1891, TR papers, Houghton Library, Harvard.

10   "Elliott Roosevelt Demented": *New York Herald*, Aug. 18, 1891.

10   "He was in a mood": TR to Bye Roosevelt, Jan. 21, 1892, TR papers, Houghton Library, Harvard.

10   "Do not come": Elliott Roosevelt quotes Mary Hall in his letter back to her, Nov. 26, 1892.

10   "Can I not win forgiveness?": Elliott Roosevelt to Mrs. Hall, Nov. 26, 1892.

10   "I ought to be with her": Elliott Roosevelt to Mrs. Hall, Dec. 7, 1892.

11   "Many people will be pained": *The World*, Aug. 16, 1894.

12   "My mother made": ER, *TIMS*, 17.

12   "With my father I was": Ibid., 6.

12   "After we were installed": Ibid., 20.

13   "I do not think that": ER, "Insuring Democracy," in *Collier's* 105 (June 15, 1940), reprinted in Allida M. Black, *Courage in a Dangerous World* (New York: Columbia University Press, 1999), 71.

13   "We must remember": Lash, *Eleanor and Franklin*, 49.

13   "all those *little* things": Ibid., 52.

13, 14   "Dear Father" . . . "don't you think": ER to Elliott Roosevelt, July 30, 1894, FDRL.

14   "I have after all": Lash, *Eleanor and Franklin*, 55.

14   "Poor child has had": Mary Hall to Corinne Robinson, Aug. 25, 1894, FDRL.

15   "My dear mamma": FDR to SDR, May 18, 1888.

15   "Mama left this morning": FDR to James Roosevelt, June 7, 1890.

15   "We never tried": SDR, *My Boy Franklin*, as told to Isabel Leighton and Gabrielle Forbush (New York: Ray Long and Richard R. Smith, 1933), 4–5.

17   "We used to call him": Michael Teague, *Mrs. L: Conversations with Alice Roosevelt Longworth* (New York: Doubleday, 1981), 156.

18   "I am getting on": FDR to his parents, Sept. 20, 1896.

18   "The Biddle boy is": FDR to his parents, Sept. 27, 1896.

18   "You will be pleased": FDR to his parents, Oct. 3, 1897.

19   "splendid talk on his adventures": FDR to his parents, June 4, 1897.

19   "I am sorry you didn't": FDR to his parents, June 11, 1897.

19   "I wish you would think": FDR to SDR, Dec. 4, 1898.

20   "As you know very few": SDR to FDR, Dec. 6, 1898.

20   "My darling Mama": FDR to his parents, June 25, 1900.

20   "Whereas she responded": Teague, *Mrs. L*, 151–55.

21   "Poor Auntie Pussie": ER diary, Nov. 18, 1898, FDRL.

21   "Poor little soul": Edith Roosevelt to Gertrude Carow, Nov. 4, 1893, TR papers, Houghton Library, Harvard.

22   "It may seem strange": Lash, *Eleanor and Franklin*, 70.

22   "She is full of sympathy": Marie Souvestre to Mary Hall, Feb. 18, 1901, FDRL.

23   "eagle eye which penetrated": ER, *TIMS*, 65.

23   "It is impossible to wish": Marie Souvestre to Mary Hall, June 24, 1902, FDRL.

24   "Never again would I": ER, *TIMS*, 84.

24   "She was beloved by": Joseph Lash interview with Corinne Cole, in Joseph Lash, *Eleanor and Franklin* (New York: W. W. Norton, 1971), 84.

24   "This was the first time": ER, *TIMS*, 65.

25 "When does the big season": Marie Souvestre to ER, Oct. 5, 1902, FDRL. This is a translation. Souvestre wrote to ER in French.

25 "Protect yourself to some extent": Marie Souvestre to ER, July 7, 1902, FDRL.

25 "Interesting-looking": *Town Topics*, Dec. 18, 1902, in Lash, *Eleanor and Franklin*, 93.

25 "I do not think": ER, *TIMS*, 100.

26 "That first winter": Ibid., 101.

26 All that ended when: ER once told her friend Edna Gurewitsch that she'd had a marriage proposal, before Franklin's, from her Scottish friend, Robert Ferguson. Edna had been taken aback. "Why, if you had married Robert Ferguson, you wouldn't be Mrs. Roosevelt!" Edna Gurewitsch, *Kindred Souls: The Friendship of Eleanor Roosevelt and David Gurewitsch* (New York: St. Martin's Press, 2002), 238.

26 "Do you realize that": James Roosevelt to FDR, Jan. 29, 1899.

27 "Boy millionaire weds": Geoffrey Ward, *Before the Trumpet*, 219.

27 "Your father cannot get": SDR to FDR, Oct. 20, 1900.

27 "The disgusting business": FDR to SDR, Oct. 31, 1900.

27 "darling father's spirit": SDR to FDR, Jan. 5, 1901.

28 "Spend evening on lawn": FDR diary, July 8, 1902.

29 "In a day and age": Geoffrey Ward, *Before the Trumpet* (New York: Harper & Row, 1985), 253, and note, 363.

29 "I did not wish": Ibid., 254.

30 "I really want you": FDR to SDR, April 27, 1903.

30 "I am perfectly willing": SDR to FDR, April 29, 1903.

31 "handsome at the tiller": Corinne Robinson, unpublished memoir, Alsop family papers, Houghton Library, Harvard, in Ward, *Before the Trumpet*, 308.

31 "I *meant* to be": SDR to FDR, July 25, 1903.

32 "I never want her": ER to FDR, Nov. 24, 1903.

32 "Franklin gave me": SDR diary, Nov. 26, 1903, FDRL.

33 "I love you dearest": ER to FDR, Dec. 1, 1903.

33 "a long talk": SDR diary, Dec. 1, 1903, FDRL.

34 "Dearest Cousin Sally": ER to SDR, Dec. 2, 1903.

34 "Dearest Mama": FDR to SDR, Dec. 4, 1903.

35 "My dearest Franklin": SDR to FDR, Dec. 6, 1903.

35 "I am so glad": FDR to SDR, Dec. 6, 1903.

35 "You know how grateful": ER to FDR, Dec. 14, 1903.

36 "It is hard for her": ER to FDR, Dec. 9, 1903.

36 "the nicest part of the day": ER to FDR, Jan. 6, 1904.

37 "Darling Franklin": SDR to FDR, March 1904, undated.

37 "I know how much": ER to FDR, Dec. 19, 1903.

37 "I pray that my precious Franklin": SDR to ER, Oct. 11, 1904.

37 "Mrs. Roosevelt has more claims": *Town Topics*, March 9, 1905.

37 "We are greatly rejoiced": TR to FDR, Nov. 29, 1904, FDRL.

TWO: A VICTORIAN MARRIAGE

40 "laughing gaily at his stories": ER, *TIMS*, 126.

40 "My father . . . lived": Michael Teague, *Mrs. L: Conversations with Alice Roosevelt Longworth* (New York: Doubleday, 1981), 156.

40 "the lion of the afternoon": ER, *TIMS*, 126.

41 "I almost came to grief": Teague, *Mrs. L*, 57.

42 "the dreadful day after": ER, "Fear—the Great Enemy," *You Learn by Living* (New York: Harper & Row, 1960), 29.

42 "The event was characterized": *Town Topics*, March 23, 1905. It was no doubt true that the Hall family had been careful with costs. There was no photographer at the wedding—merely studio photos of the bride, taken on January 20, 1905.

42 "Thank you so much": ER to SDR, June 7, 1905.

42 "Yesterday a.m.": FDR and ER to SDR, June 22, 1905.

43 "Your letters are so nice": ER to SDR, July 19, 1905.

43 "We are having": FDR to SDR, Aug. 14, 1905.

43 "How terrible to be seasick": ER, *TIMS*, 127.

43 "I will say nothing": SDR to FDR, July 31, 1907.

44 "It took us nearly": FDR to SDR, July 15, 1905.

44 "My husband climbed": ER, *TIMS*, 130.

44 "Griselda moods": Ibid., 149.

44 "We are so glad": FDR to SDR, July 22, 1905.

44 "Franklin and I had tea": ER to SDR, July 19, 1905.

44 "You are an angel": ER and FDR to SDR, Aug. 1, 1905.

45 "Don't you see": ER, *TIMS*, 135.

45 "I cannot tell you": FDR to SDR, Sept. 7, 1905.

45 "Eleanor very tired": SDR diary, Sept. 30, 1905, FDRL.

45 "fourteen foot mansion": FDR to SDR, Aug. 22, 1905.

46 "I was growing very dependent": ER, *TIMS*, 152–53.

46 "the size of the Great Pyramid": Edith Roosevelt to Isabella Ferguson, Jan. 10, 1906, Ferguson Collection, Arizona Historical Society.

47 "The pain was considerable": ER, *TIMS*, 146–47.

47 "This was rather": Ibid., 151.

48 "bent on being the head": ER, *TIR*, 11–13.

48 "far better": ER to SDR, Aug. 12, 1907.

48 *Half Moon*: The sixty-foot schooner, bought by James Roosevelt just before his death, was the second family yacht with that name.

49 "I must get it": ER to SDR, July 19, 1907.

49 "Two fat volumes": ER to SDR, July 22, 1907.

49 "I see Franklin": ER to SDR, Aug. 5, 1907.

49 "Just think": FDR to SDR, Sept. 6, 1907.

49 "relief and joy": ER, *TIMS*, 150.

50 "My own dear Babs": FDR to ER, June 12, 1908.

50 "In some places": Ibid.

50 "The path was": FDR to ER, June 15, 1908.

50 They were going: FDR to ER, June 15, 1908.

50 "My one regret": Ibid.

51 "That autumn I did not": ER, *TIMS*, 162.

51 "Sometimes I think I cannot": ER to Isabella Ferguson, Oct. 26, 1909, Ferguson Collection, Arizona Historical Society.

52 "I made myself": ER, *TIMS*, 165.

52 "an ordeal to be borne": Anna Roosevelt recalled this comment in an interview with Bernard Asbell. See Asbell, *The FDR Memoirs* (New York: Doubleday, 1973), 222.

52 "entirely reasonable": The colleague who recalled this conversation was Grenville Clark. See Kenneth S. Davis, *FDR: The Beckoning of Destiny* (New York: G. P. Putnam's Sons, 1971), 214.

54 "In the coming campaign": *Daily Eagle*, Oct. 7, 1910, in *PL*, vol. 2, 154.

55 "I think I knew that": ER, *TIMS*, 171.

55 "It seems like": SDR to ER and FDR, Jan. 5, 1910.

56 "Roosevelt is tall": W. A. Warn, *The New York Times*, Jan. 22, 1911, in John Gunther, *Roosevelt in Retrospect* (New York: Harper, 1950), 206.

57 "I took an interest": ER, *TIMS*, 173.

57 "I realized that": Ibid., 180–81.

57 "It is hard enough": FDR to ER, April 14, 1912.

58 "much stronger and keener": Isabella Ferguson to Olivia Cutting, May 13, 1912, Greenway Collection, Arizona Historical Society, in Kristie Miller, *Isabella Greenway: An Enterprising Woman* (Tucson: University of Arizona Press, 2004).

58 "At this wedding": ER, *TIMS*, 187.

58 "keen interest": Ibid., 188.

58 "WILSON NOMINATED": FDR to ER, July 2, 1912.

58 "I wish Franklin": ER to the Fergusons, July 1912, Greenway Collection, Arizona Historical Society.

60 "Here is your first ad": Lela Stiles, *The Man Behind Roosevelt* (Cleveland, OH, and New York: World Publishing, 1954), 37.

60 "that dirty little man": Joseph Lash, *Eleanor and Franklin*, 274.

60 "Nice fat ladies": ER to Isabella Ferguson, March 12, 1913, Greenway Collection, Arizona Historical Society.

61 "love at first sight": Josephus Daniels, *The Wilson Era* (Chapel Hill: University of North Carolina Press, 1944), 125.

61 "I'd like it bully well": Josephus Daniels, *The Wilson Era* (Chapel Hill: University of North Carolina Press, 1946), 124–25.

61 "His distinguished cousin": Josephus Daniels, March 15, 1913, in Edmund David Cronon, editor, *The Cabinet Diaries of Josephus Daniels, 1913–1921* (Lincoln: University of Nebraska Press, 1963), 10.

THREE: SOMEWHAT AT SEA

63 "My dearest Franklin": SDR to FDR, March 14, 1913.

64 "I am game": Louis Howe to FDR, March 23, 1913.

64 "provide the toe weights": *The Washington Post*, obituary of Louis Howe, April 20, 1936.

64 "It would have been": ER, *TIR*, 23.

65 "Always keeping himself": Josephus Daniels, *The Wilson Era* (Chapel Hill: University of North Carolina Press, 1946), 128.

66 "one long afternoon" . . . "last night a big": ER to Maude Waterbury, May 27, 1913, in Joseph Lash, *Eleanor and Franklin* (New York: W. W. Norton, 1971), 185.

66 "I'm trying to keep": ER to Bye Cowles, April 1913, in Joseph Lash, *Love, Eleanor* (New York: Doubleday, 1982), 64.

66 "the terror of displeasing": ER, "Fear—the Great Enemy," *You Learn by Living* (Louisville, KY: Westminster John Knox Press, 1960), 29.

66 "She was a wonderful": ER, *TIMS*, 113–15.

67 "I learned a liberating": ER, *You Learn by Living*, 32.

67 "whether I went ahead": ER, *TIMS*, 211.

68 "Miss Mercer is here": SDR to ER, March 15, 1915.

68 "small army": ER, *TIMS*, 227.

68 "Up to yesterday": FDR to ER, July 19, 1914.

69 "A complete smash up": FDR to ER, Aug. 1, 1914.

69 "They really believe": FDR to ER, Aug. 2, 1914.

69 "The heat has come": FDR to ER, Aug. 10, 1914.

69 "The Belgians are putting": FDR to ER, Aug. 7, 1914.

69 "All one's thoughts": ER to FDR, Aug. 7, 1914.

70 "a more or less uncomfortable": SDR to Isabella Ferguson, Aug. 23, 1914, Ferguson Collection, Arizona Historical Society.

70 "Eleanor had a harder time": FDR to Isabella Ferguson, Aug. 19, 1914, Ferguson Collection, Arizona Historical Society.

70 "with a keen sense": ER, "Insuring Democracy," in *Collier's* 105 (June 15, 1940), in Allida M. Black, *What I Hope to Leave Behind* (New York: Carlson Publishing, 1995), 91.

71 "enforced celibacy": This is FDR biographer Ted Morgan's term; see Morgan, *FDR: A Biography* (New York: Simon & Schuster, 1985), 202.

71 "inexorably drawn": Elizabeth Shoumatoff, *FDR's Unfinished Portrait* (Pittsburgh: University of Pittsburgh Press, 1990), 109.

72 "Mr. Roosevelt is a beautifully": Walter Camp to FDR, July 25, 1917. FDR had presumably asked for a physical reference from his coach.

72 "His face is long": *New York Tribune*, July 4, 1918, quoted in Jonathan Daniels, *Washington Quadrille* (New York: Doubleday, 1968), 146.

72 "Kiss the chicks": FDR to ER, July 10, 1916.

72 "The heat in Washington": FDR to ER, July 16, 1916.

73 "I am too sorry": FDR to ER, Aug. 5, 1916.

73 "*Please* kill all the flies": FDR to ER, July 7, 1916.

73 "Various villages are keeping": FDR to ER, Aug. 18 and Aug. 22, 1916.

73 "Be careful of the sparks": FDR to ER, Sept. 24, 1916.

74 "Not laying that barrage": Josephus Daniels, *Our Navy at War* (New York: George H. Doran Company, 1922), 130.

74 "a gentleman was no different": ER, *TIMS*, 251–52.

75 "I'm going home": ER, *You Learn by Living*, 80–81.

75 "I didn't want to wake": Joseph Alsop, *FDR: A Centenary Remembrance* (New York: Viking, 1982), 67.

76 "Dearest Babs": FDR to ER, July 16, 1917.

76 "Dearest Honey": ER to FDR, July 18, 1917.

76 "Mrs. Roosevelt on her pledge": *The New York Times*, July 17, 1917.

77 "All I can say is that": FDR to ER, July 18, 1917.

77 "I feel dreadfully": ER to FDR, July 20, 1917.

77 "By the way": FDR to ER, July 19, 1917.

77 "We had a bully" . . . "Since I got back": FDR to ER, July 23 and July 25, 1917.

77 "I'm glad you": ER to FDR, July 24, 1917.

77 "I do miss you": FDR to ER, July 26, 1917.

78 "Dearest son": SDR to FDR, Aug. 10, 1917.

78 "I hated to leave you": ER to FDR, Aug. 15, 1917.

78 "Lucy Mercer went": FDR to ER, Aug. 20, 1917.

78   "heavy blast of gossip": Mrs. Charles Sumner Hamlin to Jonathan Daniels, Feb. 19, 1955, in Daniels, *Washington Quadrille*, 141.

78   "Often. I used to think": Alsop, *FDR*, 69.

78   "I saw you twenty miles": Joseph Lash interview with Alice Longworth, Feb. 6, 1967, in Lash, *Eleanor and Franklin*, 225–26.

78   "He *deserved* a good time": Henry Brandon, "A Talk with an 83 year old enfant terrible," *The New York Times Magazine*, Aug. 6, 1967.

79   "This afternoon": ER to FDR, 1918, undated.

79   "It is going to mean": ER to SDR, March 6, 1918.

79   "It is quite a temptation": ER to FDR, July 20, 1918, and ER to SDR, July 22, 1918.

79   "We must come over": FDR to ER, July 20, 1918.

79   "It was very dreadful": TR to Frank McCoy, Sept. 12, 1918, in Stacy A. Cordery, *Alice* (New York: Viking, 2007), 270.

80   "Think if it were our John": ER to FDR, July 20, 1918.

80   "He is surely making": ER to SDR, July 1918.

80   "men, women and children": FDR to ER, diary and letters, in *PL*, vol. 2, 397.

80   "I've come to the conclusion": ER to FDR, summer 1918, undated.

80   "I do not need to tell": FDR to Josephus Daniels, Sept. 4, 1918, in Carroll Kilpatrick, editor, *Roosevelt and Daniels: A Friendship in Politics* (Chapel Hill: University of North Carolina Press, 1952), 50.

80   "Somehow I don't believe": FDR to ER, Aug. 20, 1918.

80   "It has practically been decided": Louis Howe to ER, Aug. 23, 1918.

80   "I hate not being": ER to FDR, Aug. 1, 1918.

80   "I do long for letters": ER to FDR, Aug. 17, 1918.

82   "rather well-kept secret": James Roosevelt with James Libby, *My Parents: A Differing View* (Chicago: Playboy Press, 1976), 101.

82   "She and Franklin were": Elizabeth Lyman Cotten to Jonathan Daniels, in Daniels, *Washington Quadrille*, 145.

82   "sat up for first time": SDR diary, Sept. 1918, FDRL.

83   "Washington, like every other": ER, *TIMS*, 272.

83   "horrid time": ER to Bob Ferguson, Nov. 13, 1917, Ferguson Collection, Arizona Historical Society.

84   "Decidedly we are growing": ER to SDR, Jan. 1919.

84   "All the women": ER to SDR, Jan. 11, 1919, in *PL*, vol. 2, 452.

84   "It is no place": ER to SDR, Feb. 11, 1919, ibid., 469.

84   "Greeted by chicks": ER diary, Feb. 1919, FDRL.

85   "During the war": ER, *TIMS*, 260.

85   "Franklin nervous": ER diary, April 1919, FDRL.

85   "I feel as though": ER to FDR, July 23, 1919.

85   "My mother-in-law": ER, "Facing Responsibility," *You Learn by Living*, 155.

86   "Mama and I have had": ER to FDR, Oct. 3, 1919.

86   "I know, Mummy dear": ER to SDR, Oct. 6, 1919.

86   "absolute judgments on people": ER to FDR, Dec. 3, 1920.

86   "Now we are roped off": ER to SDR, June 3, 1919.

87   "With darkies one": ER to SDR, March 13, 1919.

87   "Still no letter or telegram": ER to FDR, July 24, 1919.

87   "Your telegram came": FDR to ER, July 23 and July 25, 1919, in *PL*, vol. 2, 479–81.

87 "It has been so full": ER to Isabella Ferguson, July 11, 1919, Greenway Collection, Arizona Historical Society.

87 "I do not think I have": ER diary, Oct. 5, 1919, FDRL.

88 "It was one of": ER, *TIMS*, 308.

88 "If she had had": Ibid., 300.

89 "Did you know": ER to SDR, Feb. 14, 1920.

FOUR: TRAGEDY AT CAMPOBELLO

92 "Franklin Roosevelt was": Frances Perkins, *The Roosevelt I Knew* (New York: Viking Press, 1946), 27.

92 "I was delighted": Emil Ludwig, *Roosevelt: A Study in Fortune and Power* (New York: Viking, 1938), 80.

93 "America's opportunity is": FDR's acceptance speech, in *PL*, vol. 2, 499–508.

94 "first of all a domestic woman": *Poughkeepsie Eagle News*, July 16, 1920.

94 "for the umpty-umpth time": ER, *TIMS*, 318.

95 "rather extraordinary eyes": Ibid., 314.

95 "a darned good sail": Linda Lotridge Levin, *The Making of FDR* (New York: Prometheus Books, 2008), 59.

95 "I confidently expect": Stephen Early to FDR, Nov. 8, 1920, FDRL.

96 "If you can get off": FDR to Stephen Early, Dec. 21, 1920, in *PL*, vol. 2, 514.

97 "I've had a very interesting": ER to FDR, April 11, 1921.

97 "My mother-in-law": ER, *TIMS*, 325–26.

97 "Franklin took us": Joseph Lash interview with Esther Lape, March 3, 1970, Lash papers, FDRL.

98 "most deplorable, disgraceful": Geoffrey Ward, *A First-Class Temperament* (New York: Harper & Row, 1989), 571.

98 "As I expected": FDR to ER, July 21, 1921, in *PL*, vol. 2, 517.

98 "Tell Louis I expect": Ibid., 518.

99 "When Father was mad": James Roosevelt and Sidney Shalett, *Affectionately, FDR* (New York: Harcourt, Brace, 1959), 141.

99 "I'd never felt anything": Earle Looker, *This Man Roosevelt* (New York: Brewer, Warren & Putnam, 1932), 111.

100 "I don't know what's": Ward, *A First-Class Temperament*, 586.

101 "He thinks a clot": ER to Rosy Roosevelt, Aug. 14, 1921, in *PL*, vol. 2, 524.

101 "Yesterday and today": ER to Rosy Roosevelt, Aug. 18, 1921, in ibid., 525.

101 "I am telling everybody": Rosy Roosevelt to FDR, Aug. 20 and Sept. 2, 1921.

102 "unquestionably Infantile Paralysis": Frederic Delano to ER, Aug. 20, 1921.

102 "a fine old chap" . . . "Pardon my being": Frederic Delano to ER, Aug. 20, 1921.

103 "His reaction to any": Ward, *A First-Class Temperament*, 591.

103 "studied quality": Frances Perkins interview, Columbia University Oral History Collection.

103 "not in a sneaking way": Robert Lovett to George Draper, Sept. 12, 1921, Robert W. Lovett papers, Francis A. Countway Library of Medicine, Harvard.

104 "There is nothing" . . . "mental depression": Robert Lovett to Eben Bennet, Sept. 3, 1921, ibid.

104 "I took breakfast with": Louis Howe to FDR, Sept. 1, 1921, FDRL.

105 "Dear Boss": Ibid.

106 "Dear Mrs. Roosevelt": Marguerite LeHand to ER, Aug. 23, 1921.

107 "Dearest Mama": ER to SDR, Aug. 27, 1921, in *PL*, vol. 2, 529.

107 "such a splendid young life": SDR to Dora Forbes, Sept. 3, 1921.

107 "Laura flashed down": Algonac diaries, Delano family papers, FDRL, in Geoffrey Ward, *Before the Trumpet* (New York: Harper & Row, 1985), 118–19.

108 "I got here yesterday": SDR to Frederic Delano, Sept. 2, 1921.

108 "My thoughts are with you": SDR to ER, Sept. 4, 1921.

109 "F. D. ROOSEVELT ILL": *The New York Times*, Sept. 16, 1921.

110 "While the doctors were": FDR to Adolph S. Ochs, Sept. 16, 1921, in Ward, *A First-Class Temperament*, 603.

110 "cheerful thing": FDR to Langdon Marvin, Sept. 1921, in Ward, *A First-Class Temperament*, 630.

110 "somewhat rebellious legs" . . . "temporarily out of commission" . . . "most encouraging": FDR to Walter Camp, Sept. 28, 1921, in *PL*, vol. 2, 530.

110 "I can keep up with everything": This is repeated in various letters to F&D clients, actually written by Howe. "Family Business and Personal Papers," FDRL.

111 "I am much concerned": George Draper to Robert Lovett, Sept. 24, 1921, Robert W. Lovett papers, Francis A. Countway Library of Medicine, Harvard.

111 The bad news was: George Draper to Robert Lovett, Oct. 11, 1921, ibid.

112 "trial by fire": FDR and ER both used this term. ER, *TIMS*, 328.

113 "He is exceedingly": George Draper to Robert Lovett, Nov. 19, 1921, Robert W. Lovett papers, Francis A. Countway Library of Medicine, Harvard.

113 Franklin's full-time nurse: FDR to Robert Lovett, April 27, 1923, ibid.

113 "You thought you were": Josephus Daniels, *The Wilson Era* (Chapel Hill: University of North Carolina Press, 1946), 131.

113 "We cannot realize": Isabella Ferguson to FDR, 1921, undated, FDRL.

113 "When I came home": James Roosevelt, *My Parents: A Differing View* (Chicago: Playboy Press, 1976), 73–74.

114 "He is a wonderful patient": Kathleen Lake to Robert Lovett, Dec. 17, 1921, Robert W. Lovett papers, Francis A. Countway Library of Medicine, Harvard.

115 "dirty little man": Lash, *Eleanor and Franklin*, 274.

115 "much more openly": Joseph Lash interview with Anna Roosevelt Halsted, June 22, 1966, and Oct. 29, 1968, Lash papers, FDRL.

115 "I know that Mrs. Roosevelt": Frances Perkins, Columbia University Oral History Collection.

115 "I was intrigued": Joseph Lash interview with Corinne Robinson Cole, April 1967, in Joseph Lash, *Love, Eleanor* (New York: Doubleday, 1982), 81.

116 "Dearest wife of mine": Louis Howe to Grace Howe, July 10, 1922, Howe papers, FDRL.

116 "the most trying winter": ER, *TIMS*, 336.

116 "Elliott came in from school": Ibid., 339.

117 "My mother-in-law thought": Ibid., 335–36.

117 "the intense and devastating": George Draper to Robert Lovett, June 9, 1922, Robert W. Lovett papers, Francis A. Countway Library of Medicine, Harvard.

117 "If only his wife": Kathleen Lake to Robert Lovett, May 24, 1923, ibid.

118 "Mrs. R is pretty much": George Draper to Robert Lovett, March 25, 1922, ibid.

118 "I am sorrier for you": Lash, *Eleanor and Franklin*, 274.

118 "superb courage" . . . "Ours are the years": Isabella Ferguson to ER, Dec. 1921, FDRL.

FIVE: THE WILDERNESS YEARS

119 "Who had ever heard": Ted Morgan, *FDR: A Biography* (New York: Simon & Schuster, 1985), 257–58.

120 "He has all sorts": Kathleen Lake to Robert Lovett, March 17, 1922, Robert W. Lovett papers, Francis A. Countway Library of Medicine, Harvard.

120 "I must get": Anna Roosevelt Halsted interview, Columbia Oral History Collection, Columbia University.

121 "I am so thankful": SDR to Robert Lovett, June 8, 1922, ibid.

121 "I think it is very important": Robert Lovett to FDR, Aug. 14, 1922, ibid.

121 "the strenuous life": FDR to George Draper, Aug. 14, 1922.

122 In addition to the four-man: The arrangements for Leroy Jones were always awkward, whether in the South or North. This time, the crew members had agreed to share their sleeping quarters with a "darkie," as they called him, providing he caused no trouble.

122 "I am sunburned": FDR to SDR, March 5, 1923.

123 Eleanor went down for a week: Esther Lape wrote to one of their political-activist friends: "I was happy to be with Eleanor Roosevelt when there was nothing for either of us to do. She is an utterly splendid person." Esther Lape to Narcissa Vanderlip, March 1, 1923, Frank Vanderlip Collection, Columbia University.

123 "When we anchored": ER *TIMS*, 345–46.

123 *"Colder, colder grew the night"*: *Weona II* log, FDRL.

123 This time, Franklin: Franklin bought the boat with a Harvard friend, John Lawrence. *Larooco* was made up of the first syllables of Lawrence, Roosevelt, and Co.

123 "I haven't told Mama": ER to FDR, Feb. 24, 1924.

124 "There were days": Marguerite LeHand told this to Frances Perkins, in Frank Freidel, *A Rendezvous with Destiny* (Boston: Little Brown, 1990), 191.

126 "He stood there": Joseph Lash interview with Emma Bugbee, May 25, 1970, Lash papers, FDRL.

126 "delightful and very comfortable": FDR to SDR, Oct. 1924.

126 "It may be monkey glands": FDR to George Draper, Feb. 1923, FDRL.

127 "Dollar and a half": Theo Lippman Jr., *The Squire of Warm Springs: FDR in Georgia, 1924–1945* (Chicago: Playboy Press, 1977), 85.

127 "It is too bad that": FDR to SDR, Oct. 1924.

128 "I just hate to have": Bye Cowles to Corinne Alsop, Oct. 1924, Alsop family papers, Houghton Library, Harvard, in Geoffrey Ward, *A First-Class Temperament* (New York: Harper & Row, 1989), 701.

128 "deep in politics": Isabella Ferguson to John Greenway, July 28, 1923, Greenway Collection, Arizona Historical Society.

128 "The weight of the tragedy": Isabella Ferguson to John Greenway, Aug. 5, 1923, ibid.

129 "so utterly charming a man": Marion Dickerman, quoted in Kenneth S. Davis, *Invincible Summer* (New York: Atheneum, 1974), p. 17.

129 "Eleanor's parlor pinks": Ward, *A First-Class Temperament*, 631.

130 "But aren't you girls": This is Dickerman's memory of FDR's words, in Davis, *Invincible Summer*, 35.

130 "I walk around": FDR to Abram I. Elkus, Oct. 24, 1924, in Lash, *Eleanor and Franklin*, 296.

130 "I like him ever so much": FDR to ER, Oct. 24, 1924.

131 "Franklin D. Roosevelt": Cleburne Gregory, "Franklin Roosevelt Will Swim to Health," *The Atlanta Journal*, Sunday magazine, Oct. 26, 1924.

131 "You need not be proud": ER to FDR, Feb. 6, 1924.

132 "Courage is more exhilarating": ER, "Fear—the Great Enemy," *You Learn by Living* (New York: Harper & Row, 1960), 41.

133 "Don't worry about": ER to FDR, March 26, 1925.

133 "more and more lonesome": Franklin Roosevelt Jr. to Anna Roosevelt, Feb. 1925, Halstead papers, FDRL.

133 "That's up to Granny": John R. Boettiger, *A Love in Shadow* (New York: Norton, 1978), 96.

133 "Mama has done nothing": ER to FDR, 1926 and 1927, in Lash, *Eleanor and Franklin*, 303.

134 "Two people have been carried off": FDR talk, Warm Springs, Georgia, Nov. 29, 1934, in *Public Papers and Addresses of Franklin D. Roosevelt*, vol. 3, 485.

135 "If you build it": FDR to Nancy Cook and Marion Dickerman, March 6, 1925, Dickerman papers, FDRL.

135 "If you three girls": Davis, *Invincible Summer*, 44.

135 "Last Saturday and Sunday": FDR to ER in various letters written in the summer of 1925, in ibid., 46–47.

135 "I knew you three": FDR to ER, Sept. 1925, ibid., 48.

136 "For my little pilgrim": Ibid., 50.

136 "Sometimes I think": ER to FDR, March 28, 1926.

136 "Eleanor dear": SDR to ER, March 30, 1925.

137 "They came over here": SDR to FDR, April 2, 1926.

137 "Don't let yourself in": ER to FDR, April 6, 1926.

137 "He feels . . . that he's": ER to Marion Dickerman, April 24, 1926, in Davis, *Invincible Summer*, 61.

138 "Your Missus is gaining": Louis Howe to FDR, March 21, 1927.

138 "a definite attraction": Joseph Lash interview with Marion Dickerman, Jan. 30, 1967, Lash papers, FDRL.

138 "belittling emotion of jealousy": Davis, *Invincible Summer*, 60.

139 "I hate to think": ER to Marion Dickerman, May 18, 1926.

139 "Do you know that": FDR to Marion Dickerman, in Davis, *Invincible Summer*, 59.

139 "I miss you very much": ER to FDR, Feb. 24, 1924.

139 "You must learn to": ER, *You Learn by Living*, 66–67.

140 "By illness or accident": Hugh Gregory Gallagher, *FDR's Splendid Deception* (New York: Dodd, Mead, 1985), 138–39.

141 "I'm going to be": Marguerite LeHand to FDR, undated.

143 "FDR is walking": Helena Mahoney to ER, April 23, 1927, FDRL.

143 "Dear Mr. Roosevelt": Helena Mahoney to FDR, May 15, 1927.

144 "a long weary time": Helena Mahoney to ER, May 27, 1928.

144 "I hope you know": Marguerite LeHand to ER, undated, FDRL.

145 "Between now and the 16th": FDR to Lucy Rutherfurd, May 22, 1926, FDRL.

145 "I hope you have a happy": Lucy Rutherfurd to FDR, July 2, 1927.

145 "well—really well": FDR to Lucy Rutherfurd, Sept. 15, 1927, FDRL.

146 "It is going to be": ER to Marion Dickerman, Feb. 9, 1927.

146 "I'm telling everyone": ER to FDR, April 1928.

146 "a figure tall and proud": Will Durant, *New York World*, June 28, 1928.

146 "Unemployment in the sense of distress": Herbert Hoover speech accepting the Republican nomination, Palo Alto, California, Aug. 11, 1928.

147 "My doctors are very definite": FDR telegram to Al Smith, Oct. 1, 1928, FDRL.

148 "I hope your spine": Louis Howe to FDR, Sept. 1928, Howe papers, FDRL.

148 "I have to go to Rochester": ER to FDR, Sept. 30, 1928.

148 "Go ahead and take it": FDR and Anna Roosevelt exchange, in *PL*, vol. 2, 645.

148 "Mess is no name": Louis Howe to FDR, Oct. 2, 1928. That same day, ER sent FDR a telegram: "Regret that you had to accept." But this was probably for the political record. Howe might have asked her to do it.

149 "A Governor does not have": *PL*, vol. 2, 647.

149 He set up his team: The Biltmore Hotel, designed by Whitney Warren and Charles Wetmore, the same architects who designed Grand Central Terminal, was torn down in the early 1980s.

149 "No movies of me": Frank Freidel, *Franklin D. Roosevelt: The Ordeal* (Boston: Little Brown, 1954), 267.

149 "I had quite a detached": Samuel I. Rosenman, *Working with Roosevelt* (New York: Harper & Brothers, 1952), 16.

150 "I am horribly afraid": Louis Howe to FDR, Oct. 1928, in Elliott Roosevelt and James Brough, *Untold Story* (New York: G. P. Putnam's Sons, 1973), 274.

150 "The conversation revolved": Grace Tully, *F.D.R., My Boss* (New York: Charles Scribner's Sons, 1949), 32.

SIX: IN THE GOVERNOR'S MANSION

153 "Mrs. Roosevelt to Keep": *The New York Times*, Nov. 10, 1928.

153 "It is one thing": Helena Huntington Smith, "Noblesse Oblige," *The New Yorker*, April 5, 1930, in Blanche Wiesen Cook, *Eleanor Roosevelt, Volume One: 1884–1933* (New York: Viking Penguin, 1992), 399.

153 "I know if I take": ER to Elinor Morgenthau, Nov. 13, 1928, Morgenthau papers, FDRL.

154 "to develop, one must": ER, *TIR*, 17.

154 "Besides, I'd like you": Samuel I. Rosenman, *Working with Roosevelt* (New York: Harper & Brothers, 1952), 27.

155 "You have to decide": Frances Perkins, Columbia University Oral History Collection.

155 "I hope you will": ER to FDR, Nov. 22, 1928, FDRL.

155 "You see, Al's a good": Frances Perkins, *The Roosevelt I Knew* (New York: Viking Press, 1946), 55.

156 "Six hundred letters": Louis Howe to FDR, Nov. 12, 1928.

156 "I had never met Missy": Grace Tully, *F.D.R., My Boss* (New York: Charles Scribner's Sons, 1949), 39–40, 339.

157 "Sam, I shall want you": Rosenman, *Working with Roosevelt*, 30–31.

157 "For many the most difficult": Alfred B. Rollins Jr., *Roosevelt and Howe* (New York: Alfred A. Knopf, 1962), 254–55.

158 "the official taste": This was what ER told Frances Perkins, Columbia University Oral History Collection.

158 "not really decent": ER to FDR, Dec. 1–2, 1928.

159 "Now what follows is": SDR to FDR, Oct. 2, 1928.

160 "Mrs. Roosevelt that day": Lorena A. Hickok, *Eleanor Roosevelt: Reluctant First Lady* (New York: Dodd, Mead & Company, 1962), 10–11.

160 "I can see her now riding": Ibid., 23.

160 "We don't envy you": Joseph Lash, *Love, Eleanor* (New York: Doubleday, 1982), 117.

161 "My dear, if you haven't": Hickok, *Eleanor Roosevelt*, 86.

161 It was Earl Miller who taught her: Joseph Lash interview with Earl Miller, in Lash, *Love, Eleanor*, 117.

162 "He used to annoy me": Joseph Lash interview with Marion Dickerman, ibid., 116.

162 "I believe there may have been": James Roosevelt, *My Parents: A Differing View* (Chicago: Playboy Press, 1976), 111. This was the same Playboy Press book in which James Roosevelt claimed to have seen a Virginia Beach motel register showing that FDR and Lucy Mercer had spent a night together.

163 FDR believed that: FDR pointed out that this had nothing to do with "socialism"; his Republican cousin, Theodore Roosevelt, had always advocated regulation.

165 "I'm sorry": Rosenman, *Working with Roosevelt*, 32, 37.

165 "Albany was the hardest": Elliott Roosevelt and James Brough, *An Untold Story* (New York: G. P. Putnam's Sons, 1973), 279.

166 "Mrs. Caroline O'Day of Westchester": *New York Evening Journal*, "Women to Begin Roosevelt Fight for Re-Election," by a staff correspondent, June 16, 1930.

166 "No woman has a better": Smith, "Noblesse Oblige."

166 "I have my hands full": FDR to E. L. Riley, Dec. 4, 1931; in Ted Morgan, *FDR: A Biography* (New York: Simon & Schuster, 1985), 327.

167 "Roosevelt is recognized": Ernest Lindley, *Franklin D. Roosevelt: A Career in Progressive Democracy* (Indianapolis, IN: Bobbs-Merrill, 1931), 35.

167 "Franklin, you damned": Lela Stiles, *The Man Behind Roosevelt: The Story of Lewis McHenry Howe* (Cleveland, OH, and New York: World Publishing, 1954), 160–61.

167 "Dorothy and I knew": Joseph Lash interview with Samuel Rosenman, Dec. 3, 1969, Lash papers, FDRL.

168 "Oh no," Elinor insisted: Joseph Lash interview with Agnes Leach, Lash papers, FDRL, in Joseph Lash, *Eleanor and Franklin* (New York: W. W. Norton, 1971), 342.

168 "Glad Earl told Missy": ER to FDR, May 18, 1932.

168 "That's why I got married": Lash, *Love, Eleanor*, 119.

170 "The Governor, his wife": Rosenman, *Working with Roosevelt*, 70.

170 "Of course he'll last": Stiles, *The Man Behind Roosevelt*, 185–86.

170 "I hope we get a chance": Rosenman, *Working with Roosevelt*, 67.

170 "Effdee, you look just like": Ibid., 72.

171 "I regret that I am late": FDR's nomination address to the Democratic National Convention, July 2, 1932. Reprinted in *The Public Papers and Addresses of Franklin D. Roosevelt*, vol. 1, 1928–32 (New York: Random House, 1938), 647.

172 "I did not go to the funeral": Hickok, *Eleanor Roosevelt*, 48–49.

173 "It's good to have you": Ibid., 58.

173 "I want to say just a word": FDR acceptance speech, Nov. 2, 1932.

174 "Of course I'm pleased": Lash, *Eleanor and Franklin*, 354.

174 "When we land": FDR to SDR, Feb. 6, 1933, in *PL*, vol. 1, 328.

175 "I have had": *The New York Times*, Feb. 16, 1933.

175 In New York, when the news: Hickok, *Eleanor Roosevelt*, 82.

175 "There was nothing": Raymond Moley, *After Seven Years* (Lincoln: University of Nebraska Press, 1971), 139.

175 "That's apt to happen": Hickok, *Eleanor Roosevelt*, 82. Anton Cermak died from the bullet that was meant for the president-elect; Zangara went to the electric chair.

175 "They've all left": Hickok, *Eleanor Roosevelt*, 96.

175 "There I was": Ibid., 95–96.

175 "A reporter": Ibid., 96.

176 "And so you think they gossip": ER to Lorena Hickok, Nov. 27, 1933, in Rodger Streitmatter, editor, *Empty Without You* (New York: Free Press, 1998), 45. The surviving ER/Hickok correspondence in its entirety is in the FDRL, and unless otherwise stated, my quotations from this correspondence can be seen in Streitmatter's selection.

SEVEN: GRAND HOTEL

179 "O Lord": Kenneth S. Davis, *FDR: The New Deal Years, 1933–1937*, vol. 3 (New York: Random House, 1986), 27.

180 "Her pale face": Emma Bugbee, *New York Herald Tribune*, March 5, 1933, in Blanche Wiesen Cook, *Eleanor Roosevelt, Volume Two: 1933–1938* (New York: Viking Penguin, 1990), 25.

180 "This great nation will endure": It is generally thought that Louis Howe added the famous line about fear, forever associated with FDR.

181 "He's taken the ship": Ted Morgan, *FDR: A Biography* (New York: Simon & Schuster, 1985), 375.

181 "It was . . . a little terrifying": Lorena A. Hickok interview with ER, March 4, 1933, in Lorena Hickok, *Eleanor Roosevelt: Reluctant First Lady* (New York: Dodd, Mead & Company, 1962), 103.

181 nearly all of whom were: To the family's astonishment, Corinne Robinson, the youngest and last surviving sibling of Theodore Roosevelt, had voted for FDR. She died in February 1933, just before the inauguration.

181 "deeply troubled": ER, *TIR*, 74.

182 "If I wanted to be selfish": Hickok, *Eleanor Roosevelt*, 1–2.

182 "I am doing all I can": ER to Lorena Hickok, Aug. 3, 1936, in Rodger Streitmatter, editor, *Empty Without You* (New York: Free Press, 1998), 192.

182 It's absurd, this myth: Jonathan Alter, *The Defining Moment: FDR's Hundred Days and the Triumph of Hope* (New York: Simon & Schuster, 2006). Alter actually has Eleanor crying in a corner on election night. He gives Eleanor's cousin, Corinne Alsop, as his source. Other sources tell quite different stories.

184 "Hick my dearest": ER to Hickok, March 5, 1933, in *Empty Without You*, 16.

184 "Hick darling": ER to Lorena Hickok, March 6, 1933, in Streitmatter, *Empty Without You*, 17.

184 "I can't kiss you": ER to Hickok, March 9, 1933, ibid., 22.

184 "Well here goes for the diary": ER to Hickok, March 7, 1933, ibid., 19.

184 "Oh, I'm bad, my dear": Lorena Hickok to ER, Aug. 15, 1934, ibid., 133.

185 "I've been trying today": Lorena Hickok to ER, Dec. 5, 1933, ibid., 52.

185 "dog tired": Harold L. Ickes, March 5, 1933, in Harold L. Ickes, *The Secret Diary of Harold L. Ickes: The First Thousand Days, 1933–1936* (New York: Simon & Schuster, 1952), 3.

186 "It seems queer to telephone": Anthony J. Badger, *FDR: The First Hundred Days* (New York: Hill and Wang, 2008), 47.

187 "Oh, spinach!": Hickok, *Eleanor Roosevelt*, 113.

188 "His mind was focused": Frances Perkins, *The Roosevelt I Knew* (New York: Viking Press, 1946), 72.

188 "I can assure you": FDR fireside chat, March 12, 1933, in *FDR's Fireside Chats*, eds. Russell D. Buhite and David W. Levy (Norman: University of Oklahoma Press, 1992).

189 "What was impressed": Alistair Cooke, *Memories of the Great and the Good* (New York: Arcade Publishing, 1999), 62–63.

190 "It's more than a New Deal": Ray Tucker, "Ickes—and No Fooling," in *Collier's* (Sept. 30, 1933), reprinted in Jean Edward Smith, *FDR* (New York: Random House, 2007), 332.

190 "Especially do I want": ER to Lorena Hickok, June 26, 1933, FDRL.

190 "The sun is out": ER to Lorena Hickok, June 27, 1933, FDRL.

191 "After speeches he came": ER to Lorena Hickok, June 29, 1933, FDRL.

191 "Are you any relation": ER, *TIR*, 123.

191 "You know how it was": Joseph Lash, *Eleanor and Franklin* (New York: W. W. Norton, 1971), 369.

192 "Take a seat": William D. Hassett, *Off the Record with FDR* (London: George Allen & Unwin, 1960), 65–67.

192 "The grandchildren were": ER, *TIR*, 84.

193 "It's strange to say now": Jon Meacham interview with George Elsey, in Jon Meacham, *Franklin and Winston* (New York: Random House, 2003), 163.

193 "I learned to save anything": ER, *TIR*, 99.

194 "Gosh, it will be good": Marguerite LeHand to FDR, Dec. 4, 1936, FDRL.

194 "She knows when he is bored": "Missy: Marguerite LeHand Is President's Super-Secretary," in *Newsweek* (Aug. 12, 1933), 15–16.

195 "Well, Russia is recognized": ER to Lorena Hickok, Nov. 17, 1933, in Streitmatter, *Empty Without You*, 36.

195 "Missy was young": ER, *TIR*, 114.

195 "We have been spending": Ickes, *The Secret Diary of Harold L. Ickes*, 152.

196 "I never pass": Cabell Phillips, *From the Crash to the Blitz, 1929–1939* (New York: Fordham University Press, 2000), 251.

197 "I don't want a professional": Henrietta Nesbitt, *White House Diary* (New York: Doubleday, 1948), 20, 5.

197 "Except for special occasions": Ibid., 66, 70.

198 "Whenever he became tense": Ibid., 184–85.

198 "The housekeeper was one expression": Cook, *Eleanor Roosevelt: The Destiny Years, 1933–1938*, vol. 2 (New York: Penguin, 1999), 55.

198 "The Lord only knows": FDR to ER, July 5, 1934.

198 "Everywhere they spoke": FDR to ER, July 10, 1934.

198 "As long as my husband": Emma Bugbee, "Puerto Ricans Hail Arrival of Mrs. Roosevelt," front-page article, *New York Herald Tribune*, March 9, 1934.

198 "a rotund lady": *Time* (Feb. 19, 1934), in Streitmatter, *Empty Without You*, 83.

198 "I'm glad you haven't": ER to Lorena Hickok, April 16, 1934, ibid., 99.

199 "in *droves*": Hickok, *Eleanor Roosevelt*, 170.

199 "If only you weren't": Lorena Hickok to ER, Oct. 12, 1938, FDRL.

199 "I'm afraid you & I": ER to Lorena Hickok, Aug. 11, 1934, in Streitmatter, *Empty Without You*, 130–31.

199 "I blow off to you": ER to Hickok, May 2, 1935, ibid., 150–51.

199 "How about another": Samuel I. Rosenman, *Working with Roosevelt* (New York: Harper & Brothers, 1952), 150.

199 "I will probably fly home": ER to Anna Roosevelt, Nov. 19, 1934, in Bernard Asbell, *Mother and Daughter* (New York: Fromm International, 1988), 67–68.

200 "telephone voice": James A. Farley, *Behind the Ballots* (New York: Harcourt Brace, 1938), 298.

201 "No hope beyond": Mary Howe Baker to Robert Baker, March 19, 1935, in Alfred B. Rollins Jr., *Roosevelt and Howe* (New York: Knopf, 1962), 443.

201 "Why in hell": Lela Stiles, *The Man Behind Roosevelt* (Cleveland, OH, and New York: World Publishing, 1954), 279.

201 "If he is not too 'fuzzy'": FDR to ER, March 31, 1935.

201 "Louis Howe is a New Deal": Stiles, *The Man Behind Roosevelt*, 278–79.

201 "He is no better": ER to Anna Roosevelt, Aug. 1935, in Joseph Lash, *Love, Eleanor* (New York: Doubleday, 1982), 227.

201 "What's the matter": Stiles, *The Man Behind Roosevelt*, 281.

202 "I want some plain rat cheese": Nesbitt, *White House Diary*, 126.

202 "Louis is feeling 'hurt'": Stephen Early to Marvin McIntyre, Sept. 10, 1935, Howe papers, FDRL.

202 "I wonder if anyone else glories": *My Day: The Best of Eleanor Roosevelt's Acclaimed Newspaper Columns, 1936–1962*, ed. David Emblidge (Cambridge, MA: Da Capo Press, 2001), 5.

204 "A Red Letter Day": Geoffrey C. Ward, editor, *Closest Companion* (Boston and New York: Houghton Mifflin, 1995), 4.

204 "The Pres. & I drive": Ibid., 5.

204 "I miss the River": FDR to Margaret Suckley, Oct. 28, 1933, ibid., 6. All quoted correspondence between FDR and Suckley, as well as the passages from Suckley's diary, are in Ward, *Closest Companion*.

204 "There is a hill": FDR to Margaret Suckley, March 6, 1935, ibid., 18.

204 "I love the desert": FDR to Margaret Suckley, Sept. 30, 1935, ibid., 41.

205 "Early this morning": Margaret Suckley to FDR, Oct. 1, 1935, ibid., 43.

205 "First of all": FDR to Margaret Suckley, Oct. 5, 1935, ibid., 44.

206 "historic for all time": FDR's address to Congress, Aug. 14, 1935, in Samuel I. Rosenman, editor, *Public Papers and Addresses*, vol. 4 (New York: Random House, 1938), 324–26.

206 "With each adverse decision": Grace Tully, *F.D.R., My Boss* (New York: Charles Scribner's Sons, 1949), 199.

206 "Louis is not doing too well" . . . "At heart I am a minstrel": Stiles, *The Man Behind Roosevelt*, 270.

207 "I have been as close": Ibid., 290.

207 "I got in from speaking": ER to Lorena Hickok, April 19, 1936, in Streitmatter, *Empty Without You*, 183.

207 "appeared oblivious to everything": *The New York Times*, April 23, 1936.

207 "This little man": ER, *TIR*, 65.

208 "It was the most frightful": Arthur Schlesinger, *Politics of Upheaval: 1935–1936* (New York: Houghton Mifflin, 1960), 583.

208 "We have won": FDR speech before the 1936 Democratic National Convention, Philadelphia, June 27, 1936.

208 "I think F *felt*": ER, "My Day," June 28, 1936. ER's "My Day" columns are readily found in George Washington University's comprehensive electronic edition of Eleanor Roosevelt's "My Day" columns: www.gwu.edu/~erpapers/myday.

209 "a terrible precedent": Linda Lotridge Levin, *The Making of FDR* (New York: Prometheus Press, 2008), 222.

209 "I might get myself": ER to Molly Dewson, June 22, 1936, FDRL.

209 "Hick dearest": ER to Lorena Hickok, Oct. 14, 1936, in Streitmatter, *Empty Without You*, 195.

209 "You could be a king": ER to FDR, Nov. 14, 1936.

EIGHT: EMBATTLED

211 "As President I have to be": FDR to William Dodd, March 16, 1936, in *PL*, vol. 1, 1928–1945, 571.

211 "Loads and loads of love": FDR to ER, Nov. 26, 1936.

211, 212 "I do wish" . . . "Three years ago": FDR to James Cox, Dec. 9, 1936.

212 "My heart sank": ER, "My Day," Dec. 2, 1936.

212 "That part of it accentuates": FDR to ER, Dec. 10, 1936.

212 "Tomorrow we go ashore": FDR to ER, Dec. 19, 1936.

212 "Pa has no time": ER to Anna Roosevelt Boettiger, Dec. 16, 1936, in Bernard Asbell, *Mother and Daughter* (New York: Fromm International, 1988), 74. Anna and John Boettiger were working as journalists/editors for a major Hearst newspaper, the *Seattle Post-Intelligencer*, hoping to make some impact on anti-Roosevelt readers.

213 "soaked through": ER, "My Day," Jan. 21, 1937.

213 Eleanor was "appalled": ER, *TIR*, 165.

213 "I think our young people": ER to Lorena Hickok, Jan. 1, 1938, FDRL.

214 "I was sensitive": Henrietta Nesbitt, *White House Diary* (New York: Doubleday, 1948), 185–86.

214 "Pa is both nervous": ER to Anna Roosevelt Boettiger, March 3, 1937, in Asbell, *Mother and Daughter*, 79.

215 "The three horses are": FDR fireside chat, March 9, 1937, in Russell D. Buhite and David W. Levy, editors, *FDR's Fireside Chats* (Norman: University of Oklahoma Press, 1992), 86–87.

215 "Here are these people": ER, "My Day," Feb. 13, 1937. ER claimed to be quoting one of the many letters she received. It is, of course, quite possible that the letter was written by FDR or one of his advisers.

216 "Once you've spent": Blanche Wiesen Cook, *Eleanor Roosevelt: The Defining Years, 1933–1938*, vol. 2 (New York: Viking Penguin, 1999), 555.

216 "After her hundreds": David Emblidge quotes this in *My Day: The Best of Eleanor Roosevelt's Acclaimed Newspaper Columns*, editor David Emblidge (Cambridge, MA: Da Capo Press, 2001), 34.

216 "There may be something": Malvina Thompson to Anna Roosevelt Boettiger, March 17, 1937, Halsted papers, FDRL.

217 "valued, tough-minded assessment": *The New York Times*, Jan. 2, 1938.

217 He wanted the "inner story": Bruce Gould, *An American Story* (New York: Harper & Brothers, 1968), 188.

218 "arresting in its combination": *The New York Times*, Nov. 21, 1937.

218 "I came to New York": ER, "My Day," Feb. 22, 1938.

218 "There is no doubt": ER, "My Day," Oct. 27, 1937.

218 "Like almost every other": ER, "My Day," Aug. 17, 1937.

218 "In the hundreds of thousands": Elliott Roosevelt and James Brough, *An Untold Story* (New York: G. P. Putnam's Sons, 1973), 281.

219 "He would tell anecdotes": Samuel I. Rosenman, *Working with Roosevelt* (New York: Harper & Brothers, 1952), 151.

219 "the wisdom of the serpent": Joseph Lash, *Eleanor and Franklin* (New York: W. W. Norton, 1971), 452.

220 "I never tried to exert": ER, *TIR*, 7.

220 "Dear Harry, Is it true": ER to Harry Hopkins, July 16, 1935, Hopkins papers, FDRL.

220 "Dear Harry, This family": ER to Harry Hopkins, Nov. 9, 1938, ibid.

220 "I hope you do not think": ER to Harold Ickes, April 4, 1939, in Lash, *Eleanor and Franklin*, 471.

220 "Dear Mr. Fischer": ER to Louis Fischer, Feb. 28, 1938, FDRL.

221 "My dear Mr. Fischer": ER to Louis Fischer, Dec. 16, 1944, FDRL.

221 "Every time Eleanor": *Alabama Sun*, April 28, 1944, Halsted papers, FDRL.

221 "My dear Mrs. Carey": ER to Esther Carey, April 20, 1937, in Cook, *Eleanor Roosevelt, Volume Two*, 439.

222 "FDR, I would like": Oct. 1934, in Lash, *Eleanor and Franklin*, 516.

222 "I feel a skunk": ER to Lorena Hickok, March 18, 1936, FDRL.

222 "The Marian Anderson concert": Walter White to ER, April 12, 1939, FDRL.

222 "sometimes serve as": ER, *TIR*, 164.

223 "I hate to see that place": FDR to Margaret Suckley, Dec. 5, 1936, in Geoffrey C. Ward, editor, *Closest Companion* (Boston and New York: Houghton Mifflin, 1995), 93.

223 "One weekend . . . [the President]": Rosenman, *Working with Roosevelt*, 193.

223 "You have made the wings": Margaret Suckley to FDR, Oct. 1937, in Ward, *Closest Companion*, 105.

224 "He loved driving recklessly": Dorothy Schiff papers, NYPL.

224 "If he had said": Ted Morgan, *FDR: A Biography* (New York: Simon & Schuster, 1985), 453.

224 "with all those other cripples": Jeffrey Potter, *Men, Money and Magic* (New York: Coward, McCann & Geoghegan, 1976), 156–70.

224 The year it was finished: The *New York Post* was progressive until Rupert Murdoch bought it in 1976.

225 "My house seems nicer": ER to Anna Roosevelt Boettiger, Oct. 16, 1937, in Asbell, *Mother and Daughter*, 94.

226 To Perkins's embarrassment: Frances Perkins interview, Columbia University Oral History Collection.

226 "As a peace negotiator": Nancy Cook to FDR, Nov. 14, 1938, in Cook, *Eleanor Roosevelt, Volume Two*, 534. It is striking that the language Nancy used was Eleanor's; it shows how symbiotic their relationship had become.

227 "Elizabeth, what you say": Joseph Lash interview with Esther Lape, in Lash, *Eleanor and Franklin*, 478.

227 "My boss is a very big person": Malvina Thompson to Lorena Hickok, in Joseph Lash, *Eleanor: The Years Alone* (New York: W. W. Norton, 1972), 237.

227 "You didn't do that": ER, *On My Own* (New York: Harper & Brothers, 1958), 107.

227 "Did she tell you that": Malvina Thompson to Anna Roosevelt Boettiger, Nov. 12, 1938, Halsted papers, FDRL.

228 "Did you hear Hitler": FDR to Margaret Suckley, Sept. 26, 1938, in Ward, *Closest Companion*, 125.

229 "In the dim distant past": A widely published statement by FDR, in Geoffrey Ward, *A First-Class Temperament* (New York: Harper & Row, 1989), 254. Ward writes that 15 percent of FDR's top executive appointments were Jewish, at a time when Jews represented 3 percent of the general population.

229 "My husband says": ER to Justine Polier, Jan. 4, 1939, in Robert N. Rosen, *Saving the Jews: Franklin D. Roosevelt and the Holocaust* (New York: Perseus, 2006), 84.

229 "twenty thousand charming children": Ibid., 85.

229 "You may": FDR to ER, Feb. 1939. From 1939 to 1945, the United States took in no more than a quarter of a million Jewish refugees, but this was more than any other nation.

229 "Democracy requires": ER, "My Day," Feb. 2, 1939.

230 "My dear King George": FDR to King George VI, Aug. 25, 1938, in *PL*, vol. 2, 806.

230 "Probably the official visit": FDR to King George VI, Nov. 2, 1938, ibid., 824.

230 "MY DAY, MAY 26, 1939": In *My Day*, ed. David Emblidge, 36.

231 "Mrs. James Roosevelt": Margaret Suckley diary, June 11, 1939, in Ward, *Closest Companion*, 130–31.

232 "was dashing about": Helen Robinson diaries, June 11, 1939, Lash papers, FDRL.

232 "My mother-in-law was": ER, *TIR*, 196–97.

233 "Well, Bill, it's come": Joseph Alsop and Robert Kintner, *American White Paper*, in Kenneth S. Davis, *FDR: Into the Storm, 1937–1940*, vol. 3 (New York: Random House, 1993), 461.

233 "My countrymen and my friends": FDR radio talk, Sept. 3, 1939, in *FDR's Fireside Chats*, 148–51.

233 "I hope that, in spite": ER, "My Day," Sept. 5, 1939.

233 "We must not reach": ER, "My Day," 1949, in Allida M. Black, *Casting Her Own Shadow* (New York: Columbia University Press, 1996), 148.

234 Eleanor found herself: In November 1940 ER wrote to Joseph Lash: "I think I knew we were going to be friends or rather that I wanted to be when I looked across the table at you about a year ago!" Joseph Lash, *Love, Eleanor* (New York: Doubleday, 1982), 323.

235 "She dove in" . . . "Let's accept the opinion": These quotes come from both the Lash papers, FDRL, and Joseph Lash, *Eleanor Roosevelt: A Friend's Memoir* (New York: Doubleday, 1964), 27.

236 "Perhaps I'll drop in": ER to Joseph Lash, Jan. 27, 1940, Lash papers, FDRL.

236 "I find the woods": Lash, *Love, Eleanor*, 289.

237 "I expect that the Battle of Britain": Winston Churchill's speech to the House of Commons, June 18, 1940, in *The Churchill War Papers*, vol. 2, compiled by Martin Gilbert (New York: Norton, 1993), 368.

238 "This is no ordinary time": Kenneth S. Davis, *FDR into the Storm, 1937–1940*, 600.

239 "You turned a rout": George Norris to ER, July 19, 1940, in Lash, *Eleanor and Franklin*, 624.

239 "I have said before": Rosenman, *Working with Roosevelt*, 242.

240 "Some of the things": ER, "My Day," Nov. 2, 1940.

240 "It was a narrow escape": FDR to Samuel Rosenman, Nov. 13, 1940, in Rosenman, *Working with Roosevelt*, 236.

NINE: "I AM A BIT EXHAUSTED . . ."

242 "Because he knew Franklin": ER, *TIR*, 167–68.

242 "If by any unfortunate chance": FDR to Crown Prince Olav, Jan. 4, 1940. FDR wrote a similar letter to the royal families of Belgium and Holland.

242 Martha (as she called herself . . .): The princess's name was spelled Märthe and pronounced *Mairta*. In the United States she wrote it as "Martha."

243 "Missy is very ill again": ER to Anna Roosevelt Boettiger, June 12, 1941, in Bernard Asbell, *Mother and Daughter* (New York: Fromm International, 1988), 132.

243 "They don't know what it is": ER to Anna Roosevelt Boettiger, June 22, 1941, in Asbell, *Mother and Daughter*, 133.

244 "Father has begun to forget": ER to Anna Roosevelt Boettiger, Sept. 10, 1941, in Asbell, *Mother and Daughter*, 136.

245 "It's such an unattractive death": ER to Anna Roosevelt Boettiger, Sept. 17, 1941, in ibid., 137.

245 "He sank down beside her": James Roosevelt, *My Parents: A Differing View* (Chicago: Playboy Press, 1976), 113.

245 "I left half my estate": Ibid., 108. FDR was not worried about his children, who had a substantial inheritance from their grandmother. According to his will, if Missy died before Eleanor, Missy's half would revert to Eleanor. In fact, Missy died during FDR's lifetime, but FDR did not change the wording of his will.

247 "that man who": Kenneth S. Davis, *FDR, the War President, 1940–1943* (New York: Random House, 2000), 352.

247 "The clouds of uncertainty": ER, "My Day," Dec. 8, 1941. Hitler had not yet declared war when ER wrote this.

247 "She knew they had to go": Joseph Lash, *Eleanor Roosevelt: A Friend's Memoir* (New York: Doubleday, 1964), 262.

248 "The house is full": ER to Joseph Lash, Dec. 24, 1941, in Lash, *Love, Eleanor*, 366.

248 "There is great danger": Davis, *FDR, the War President*, 354.

248 "the most important partnership": Samuel I. Rosenman, *Working with Roosevelt* (New York: Harper & Brothers, 1952), 318.

248 Eleanor tried to like Winston: FDR thought the same. He tried to push the cause of Indian independence with Churchill, who told him that the British Empire was not negotiable.

248 "siren suit" . . . "joy": Lash, *Eleanor Roosevelt*, 263.

248 "Looking back on it": ER, *On My Own* (New York: Harper & Brothers, 1958), 34.

249 "I'd like to very much": Lorena Hickok to ER, Jan. 29, 1940, in Rodger Streitmatter, editor, *Empty Without You* (New York: Free Press, 1998), 225.

249 "like a pea on a hot shovel": ER to Lorena Hickok, July 20, 1940, ibid., 230.

250 "I've grown to love you": ER to Joseph Lash, Aug. 1941, in Joseph Lash, *Love, Eleanor* (New York: Doubleday, 1982), 354.

250 "Do come up": ER to Joseph Lash, Dec. 2, 1941, ibid., 363.

250 "Why have you returned": ER to Joseph Lash, Aug. 1942, ibid., 400.

250 "With Earl and me": Ibid., 400.

250 "A little bit of my heart": ER to Joseph Lash, April 6, 1942, ibid., 381–82.

251 "That settled that": ER, *TIR*, 257.

251 "I met Louise occasionally": Ibid., 257–58.

251 "Gosh, I shouldn't think": Lorena Hickok to ER, July 6, 1942, in Streitmatter, *Empty Without You*, 243.

252 "Missy . . . started crying": Anna Rochon to FDR, undated, Roosevelt family papers, FDRL.

252 "a community of pleasure-seekers": Lucy Rutherfurd to FDR, undated (almost certainly early 1942).

253 "She is tall & good-looking": Margaret Suckley diary, Sept. 1, 1944, in Geoffrey C. Ward, editor, *Closest Companion* (Boston and New York: Houghton Mifflin, 1995), 323.

253 "This kind of letter": Lucy Rutherfurd to FDR, undated (same letter that was probably from early 1942).

253 "I *do* remember the times": FDR to Lucy Rutherfurd, Oct. 29, 1941.

253 "A small house would be": Lucy Rutherfurd to FDR, undated (same letter that was probably from early 1942).

253 "Save any problems": FDR to Margaret Suckley, Aug. 3, 1941, in Ward, *Closest Companion*, 139.

254 "I can see why FDR": Margaret Suckley diary, Sept. 29, 1943, ibid., 243.

254 She intended it for posterity: Margaret Suckley's diary entry for Jan. 14, 1945, reads: "I am writing about this just because this book will probably be published, & will inevitably be considered a 'source book' if it is." Ibid., 382.

254 "It is not even catty": Gertrude Pratt to Joseph Lash, March 1943, in Lash, *Love, Eleanor*, 437.

254 "Martha was there": Gertrude Pratt to Joseph Lash, summer 1942, ibid., 399.

254 "But Harald," Franklin said: William D. Hassett diary, July 3, 1942, in William D. Hassett, *Off the Record with FDR* (Warm Springs, GA: Warm Springs Foundation, 1958), 84.

255 "I think to hound someone": ER to Francis Biddle, Jan. 9, 1942, in Lash, *Love, Eleanor*, 370–71.

255 "About nine o'clock": Joseph Lash reproduces this and other significant pages of his FBI file in the appendix of *Love, Eleanor*.

256 "I'm sorry I was": Joseph Lash to ER, March 1943, in Lash, *Love, Eleanor*, 489.

256 "I watched you": ER to Joseph Lash, April 29, 1943, ibid., 500.

257 "I shall be praying": ER to Anna Roosevelt Boettiger, Dec. 21, 1942, in Asbell, *Mother and Daughter*, 152.

257 "I wake up": ER to Anna Roosevelt Boettiger, Jan. 2, 1943, ibid.

257 "We should remember": ER, "My Day," Feb. 12, 1942.

257 "the same Bill of Rights": ER, "The Democratic Effort," *Common Ground* 2, 3 (Spring 1942), in Allida M. Black, *What I Hope to Leave Behind* (New York: Carlson Publishing, 1995), 107–108.

257 "so much more German": Pearl Buck to ER, undated, in Leonard C. Schlup and Donald W. Whisenhunt, editors, *It Seems to Me: Selected Letters of Eleanor Roosevelt* (Lexington: University Press of Kentucky, 2001), 39.

257 "I regret the need": ER to Pearl Buck, May 29, 1942, in Schlup and Whisenhunt, editors, *It Seems to Me*, 39–40.

257 "It is not possible": ER to Mr. Arnum, July 20, 1940, Emergency Rescue Committee files, FDRL.

258 "If I were a Negro": ER, "If I Were a Negro," *Negro Digest* (Oct. 1943).

258 "It is one of the prices": FDR to Crown Prince Olav, Jan. 4, 1940, in *PL*, vol. 2, 984.

258 "The blackout here": ER to Joseph Lash, Oct. 29, 1942, in Lash, *Love, Eleanor*, 412.

259 "fifty miles through factories": *London Daily Mail*, Nov. 18, 1942.

259 "vile cold": Lash, *Eleanor and Franklin*, 667.

259 "You certainly have left": Joseph Lash, *Eleanor and Franklin* (New York: W. W. Norton, 1971), 668.

259 "More than anyone else": Lorena Hickok to ER, Nov. 1, 1942, in Streitmatter, *Empty Without You*, 246.

259 "I really think Franklin": Lash, *Eleanor and Franklin*, 668.

259 "he hates to be left": Margaret Suckley diary, Jan. 9, 1943, in Ward, *Closest Companion*, 195.

260 "I'm a bit tired": FDR to ER, Jan. 29, 1943.

260 "When I say that": William F. Halsey and J. Bryan III, *Admiral Halsey's Story* (New York: McGraw-Hill, 1947), 167.

261 "So this is": Joseph Lash diary, in Lash, *Eleanor and Franklin*, 690.

261 "We sat on a screen porch": Joseph Lash to Gertrude Pratt, Sept. 19, 1943, ibid.

261 Eleanor was not going: The GI Bill, signed into law on June 22, 1944, was pioneering legislation that had a major impact on postwar America. It involved one of FDR's bitterest fights with Congress.

262 "No lover ever studied": Jon Meacham, *Franklin and Winston* (New York: Random House, 2003), 245.

262 "I realized at Teheran": Ibid., 259.

263 "Father and I never had": Asbell, *Mother and Daughter*, 175.

263 "It was immaterial": Ibid., 176.

263 "Anna's presence was": ER, *TIR*, 319.

264 "Mother, can't you see": Grace Tully, *F.D.R., My Boss* (New York: Charles Scribner's Sons, 1949), 110.

264 "[Mother] came in": Asbell, *Mother and Daughter*, 177.

265 "I think she is": Margaret Suckley diary, March 4, 1944, in Ward, *Closest Companion*, 282.

265 He told Daisy: Margaret Suckley diary, March 25, 1944, ibid., 287.

266 "Mr. President, you may not": Robert H. Ferrell, *The Dying President* (Columbia: University of Missouri Press, 1998), 19.

266 "The P. called up": Margaret Suckley diary, March 28, 1944, in Ward, *Closest Companion*, 288–89.

267 "shake off": Frank Kelley, "Roosevelt Goes South for Two Weeks," *The New York Times*, April 10, 1944.

267 "The conversation was animated": Howard G. Bruenn, "Clinical Notes on the Illness and Death of President Franklin D. Roosevelt," in *Annals of Internal Medicine* 72, 4 (April 1970).

267 "Those newspapermen": Michael F. Reilly, *Reilly of the White House* (New York: Simon & Schuster, 1947), 197.

267 "He looked much better": James Roosevelt and Sidney Shalett, *Affectionately, FDR* (New York: Harcourt, Brace, 1959), 350.

267 "Under his tan": Margaret Suckley diary, May 4, 1944, in Ward, *Closest Companion*, 294.

268 "I think all of us": ER, *TIR*, 329.

268 "The doctors are very pleased": ER to James Roosevelt, May 29, 1944, in Roosevelt and Shalett, *Affectionately, FDR*, 350.

268 "I cannot think": Winston Churchill to FDR, June 23, 1944, in Warren F. Kimball, editor, *Churchill & Roosevelt, Complete Correspondence*, vol. 3 (Princeton, NJ: Princeton University Press, 1984), 203.

268 "His health is excellent": *The New York Times*, April 5, 1944.

269 "I don't know what": ER to Joseph Lash, April 30, 1944, in Lash, *Eleanor and Franklin*, 707–708.

269 "Reluctantly, but as a good soldier": FDR to Robert E. Hannigan, July 11, 1944, in Samuel I. Rosenman, editor, *Public Papers and Addresses*, vol. 13 (New York: Random House, 1933–50), 197–99.

269 "Dearest Babs": FDR to ER, July 21, 1944.

269 "It was grand": Roosevelt and Shalett, *Affectionately, FDR*, 352.

270 "All concerned": Early to FDR, July 31, 1944, FDRL.

270 "Miss LeHand was utterly selfless": Rosenman, *Public Papers and Addresses*, 212–13.

270 "His Dutch is up": Hassett, *Off the Record with FDR*, 282.

270 "These Republican leaders": FDR address to the International Brotherhood of Teamsters, Sept. 23, 1944, *Public Papers and Addresses*, 290.

272 "The little man": FDR to James Roosevelt, Nov. 13, 1944, in *PL*, vol. 2, 1553.

272 "a premonition": ER, *TIR*, 339.

272 "Darling, there won't be": Tully, *F.D.R., My Boss*, 108.

272 "I said Yalta, not Malta": Jon Meacham, *Franklin and Winston* (New York: Random House, 2003), 314–15.

273 "Dearest Babs": FDR to ER, Feb. 12, 1945, in *PL*, vol. 2, 1570.

273 "Your diplomatic abilities": ER to FDR, Feb. 13, 1945.

273 "I hope that you will pardon me": FDR, address to Congress, March 1, 1945, in Rosenman, *Public Papers and Addresses*, 570–86.

274 "Complete contrast": Hassett, *Off the Record with FDR*, 323–25.

274 "Thus another milestone": Ibid.

TEN: THE ROSE GARDEN

275 "A Big Day!": Margaret Suckley diary, March 25, 1945, in Geoffrey C. Ward, editor, *Closest Companion* (Boston and New York: Houghton Mifflin, 1995), 400–401.

276 "sleep and sleep": Margaret Suckley diary, March 14, 1945, ibid., 400.

276 It worried him: Michael F. Reilly, *Reilly of the White House* (New York: Simon & Schuster, 1947), 226–27.

276 "He is slipping away": William D. Hassett, *Off the Record with FDR* (London: George Allen & Unwin, 1960), 327.

277 "We said good night": William D. Hassett, March 30, 1945, in Hassett, *Off the Record* (Warm Springs, GA: Warm Springs Foundation, 1958), 329.

277 Bruenn was furious: Howard Bruenn recalled this phone call when talking to Dr. James Halsted, Anna Roosevelt's third husband, in March 1967, in Frank Freidel, *Rendezvous with Destiny* (Boston: Little Brown and Co., 1990), 604.

277 "You realize that": Margaret Suckley diary, March 31, 1945, in Ward, *Closest Companion*, 403.

277 "To be in a position": Margaret Suckley diary, Dec. 17, 1944, ibid., 366.

278 "I have been hoping": Lucy Rutherfurd to Margaret Suckley, Dec. 11, 1944, ibid., 360.

278 "We understand each other": Margaret Suckley diary, Dec. 3, 1944, ibid., 353.

278 "She & I have": Margaret Suckley diary, Jan. 12, 1945, ibid., 380.

278 "We went out": ER, "My Day," April 9, 1945.

279 "Lots of azaleas": Margaret Suckley diary, March 31 and April 3, 1945, in Ward, *Closest Companion*, 404–406.

279 "I sit on the edge": Margaret Suckley diary, April 4, 1945, ibid., 408.

280 "I felt badly": Lucy Rutherfurd to Margaret Suckley, Dec. 8, 1944, ibid., 358.

280 "Lucy is such a lovely": Margaret Suckley diary, April 11, 1945, ibid., 415.

281 "I was delegated": Margaret Suckley diary, April 11, 1945, ibid., 416.

281 "put an end to this": April 11, 1945, in Hassett, *Off the Record with FDR*, 333–34.

282 "I have a terrific pain": Margaret Suckley diary, April 12, 1945, in Ward, *Closest Companion*, 418.

282 "Steve Early, very much upset": ER, *TIR*, 344.

283 "Darlings": James Roosevelt, *My Parents*, 285.

283 "Harry, the President is dead" . . . "Is there anything": Lash, *Eleanor and Franklin*, 721.

283 "An air of complete demoralization": Gladstone Williams, *The Atlanta Constitution*, April 13, 1945.

283 "In Franklin Roosevelt": Winston Churchill, *The Second World War, 1948–1954*, vol. 6 (London: Cassell, 1953), 413.

283 ". . . I never saw him": Carl Carmer, "April 14, 1945," in Russell D. Buhite and David W. Levy, editors, *FDR's Fireside Chats* (Norman: University of Oklahoma Press, 1992), xx.

284 "His face was": Albert Camus, in *Combat*, April 14, 1945, in *Camus at Combat: Writings 1944–1947*, Jacqueline Lévi-Valensi, editor (Princeton, NJ: Princeton University Press, 2006), 192–93.

284 "Tully, dear": Grace Tully, *F.D.R., My Boss* (New York: Charles Scribner's Sons, 1949), 366.

284 "Were you here, Grace?": Ibid.

284 "grave but composed": Ibid.

284 "I guess I never realized": Lorena Hickok to ER, April 13, 1945, in Rodger Streitmatter, editor, *Empty Without You* (New York: Free Press, 1998), 267.

285 "I lay in my berth": ER, *TIR*, 345.

286 "We've had it too easy": Robert E. Sherwood, *Roosevelt and Hopkins: An Intimate History* (New York: Harper, 1950), 881.

286 "The funeral was very beautiful": Gertrude Pratt Lash to Joseph Lash, April 15, 1945, in Joseph P. Lash, *A World of Love* (New York: Doubleday, 1984), 184.

287 "Mrs. Roosevelt was": Gertrude Pratt Lash to Joseph Lash, [April 1945], Lash papers, FDRL.

287 "There was a big vacuum": ER, *On My Own* (New York: Harper & Brothers, 1958), 1–2.

287 "I have never known": ER, *TIR*, 68.

287 "Hick dearest": ER to Hickok, April 19, 1945.

288 "We walked tonight": ER, "My Day," April 26, 1945.

288 "Unconditional surrender": ER, "My Day," May 9, 1945.

288 "There is only one way": ER, "My Day," April 17, 1945.

289 "Are we learning nothing": ER, "My Day," April 30, 1945.

290 "Franklin had pictured": ER, *On My Own*, 9.

290 "I had an almost impersonal feeling": ER, *TIR*, 347–49.

292 "Dear Eleanor": Lucy Rutherfurd to ER, May 2, 1945, FDRL.

293 "Anna dear": Lucy Rutherfurd to Anna Roosevelt Boettiger, May 9, 1945, in Bernard Asbell, *Mother and Daughter* (New York: Fromm International, 1988), 188–89.

294 "Mrs. Winthrop Rutherfurd": Tully, *F.D.R., My Boss*, 360.

294 The extreme right-wing: "I am sorry for all the controversy it stirred up in the Pegler columns but if our friend, M.L.S. [Margaret Suckley] hadn't talked so much I wouldn't have been forced into mentioning the visit," Grace Tully wrote to Anna Roosevelt Boettiger on January 12, 1950. "Under the circumstances, I had no alternative as an eye witness." Halsted papers, FDRL. Westbrook Pegler apparently talked to Suckley.

294 "Miller got in a lather": Malvina Thompson to Anna Roosevelt Boettiger, March 20, 1950, in Lash, *A World of Love*, 317.

294 "The Russians seem to have": Pamela C. Harriman's introduction, David Emblidge, editor, *My Day 1945–1952* (New York: Pharos Books, 1990), 8.

296 "Somehow it is impossible": Gertrude Pratt Lash to Joseph Lash, March 23, 1955, in Lash papers, FDRL.

296 "I used to just cringe": Asbell, *Mother and Daughter*, 298.

296 "I want you to have": Emily Williams oral history interview with Maureen Corr, Oct. 28, 1972, FDRL.

296 "In many, many ways": ER, *On My Own*, 107.

297 "Throughout the 1950s": John Kenneth Galbraith, *Name-Dropping* (Boston and New York: Houghton Mifflin, 1999), 51.

297 "When it was all over": ER, *On My Own*, 175.

297 "My final judgment": ER to Mary Lasker, Aug. 15, 1960, in Leonard C. Schlup and Donald W. Whisenhunt, editors, *It Seems to Me: Selected Letters of Eleanor Roosevelt* (Lexington: University Press of Kentucky, 2001), 249–51.

298 "dangerous opportunist": ER, *On My Own*, 167.

298 "Dear Mr. President": ER to John F. Kennedy, July 22, 1961, in Schlup and Whisenhunt, *It Seems to Me*, 268–69.

299 "David my dearest": ER to David Gurewitsch, Feb. 8, 1956, in Edna P. Gurewitsch, *Kindred Souls: The Friendship of Eleanor Roosevelt and David Gurewitsch* (New York: St. Martin's Press, 2002), 91.

300 "I know how much": Edna Perkel to ER, Feb. 21, 1958, in Lash, *A World of Love*, 479.

300 "I know that would have": ER, "My Day," April 15, 1955.

301 "Now there will be": ER, "My Day," Aug. 10, 1962.

301 "I hope it will serve": ER to Jonathan Daniels, June 18, 1947, in Schlup and Whisenhunt, *It Seems to Me*, 81–82. Jonathan Daniels, son of Josephus Daniels, presided over the dedication ceremony.

301 "Our dear Mrs. Roosevelt": Gurewitsch, *Kindred Souls*, 285–86.

302 "It is my hope": Roosevelt and Shalett, *Affectionately, FDR*, 367–69.

ACKNOWLEDGMENTS

Among the many things they did to leave this world a better place than they found it, Franklin and Eleanor Roosevelt had the generosity and sense of history to leave to the public their Hyde Park estate, the cottage at Campobello, and the Little White House in Warm Springs, for future generations to enjoy. I was greatly inspired by my visits to these places, and they gave me invaluable insight into the Roosevelts' private lives.

I was also grateful to FDR for conceiving the idea, back in the late 1930s, of the Franklin Delano Roosevelt Library, the first presidential library in history. I spent many weeks there, at Hyde Park. Since there is no one still alive who knew the Roosevelt couple intimately, I relied entirely on existing primary sources—interviews, letters, diaries, memoirs, documents, audiovisual material. The FDR Library contains not only the FDR, Eleanor Roosevelt, and Roosevelt family papers but also the recently opened Howe papers and, indeed, those of almost everyone in the Roosevelt circle. The place is a treasure trove, and the archivists, knowledgeable and helpful, added to the pleasure of my research trips. My thanks to Alycia Vivona, Virginia Lewick, and especially to Bob Clark and Mark Renovitch for their warm and generous assistance.

When I say "relied on," I learned quickly that all sources, both primary and secondary, were unreliable. There was so much that could not be said, even in private letters. Most of the memoirs by friends, colleagues, and children were in fact ghostwritten, and always in the same jaunty tone. Eleanor Roosevelt's autobiography and "My Day" column, just like Lorena Hickok's memoir, *Reluctant First Lady*, were thick with mythmaking. But some sources were more reliable than others.

Lorena Hickok preserved most of the 3,500 letters she and Eleanor wrote each other from 1932 until Eleanor's death. (They were under embargo until 1978.) For me, these were precious letters. They show Eleanor close-up—vulnerable, funny, snide, and tender.

Daisy Suckley kept her secret to herself until the day she died, at the age of one hundred. Shortly after her death in 1991, a battered black suitcase was found under her bed in the tower at Wilderstein, containing thousands of pages of diaries and a playful, affectionate correspondence with FDR. Without that suitcase, this would have been a different book.

I am deeply indebted to Joseph Lash, who played something of a James Boswell role in relation to Eleanor Roosevelt. A close friend of hers, he kept their entire correspondence, wrote a journal about their meetings, got his future wife, Trude, to do the same, conducted dozens of interviews with Roosevelt children, friends, and acquaintances, and left all his notes, papers, and correspondence to the FDR Library. His published books also contain hundreds of letters from Eleanor to her friends.

My debt to the many Roosevelt scholars who have preceded me will be clear from my endnotes. I feel particular gratitude to Blanche Wiesen Cook, who in her biography of Eleanor Roosevelt (still in progress) dared to show Eleanor as a passionate woman, and to suggest that she might actually have had a physical relationship with Lorena Hickok—and, indeed, with Earl Miller. Cook took quite a bit of flak for turning the icon into a woman of flesh and blood. I come along, gratefully, in her shadow.

At the Roosevelt Institute in Warm Springs, F. Martin Harmon, Mike Shadix, Linda Creekbaum, and David Burke entered into the spirit of my quest with enthusiasm, and did all they could to help me clear up some mysteries. At Wilderstein, Duane and Linda Watson were most helpful and hospitable. Jack Eckert, at the Countway Library of Medicine, Boston, greatly facilitated my research. I thank the Arizona Historical Society, in Tucson, and the Oral History Project at Columbia University. I also thank Nancy Roosevelt Ireland, Eleanor Roosevelt's literary executor, for her kindness and generosity.

I am extremely grateful to the New York Public Library for providing me with the privilege of working in the Frederick Lewis Allen Room, with superb access to the NYPL's research collection. My thanks to Dave Smith and Jay Barksdale for making this possible.

My agents, Lane Zachary and Todd Shuster, have given me generous quantities of their time and energy. I am especially grateful to them for placing this book with Farrar, Straus and Giroux, a publishing house I have always regarded with awe, and which in these perilous times still exudes a love of good books over crass commercialism. It has been a privilege to work with my editor, Eric Chinski, whose fine mind and quiet enthusiasm I have greatly appreciated. I also thank Eugenie Cha, Karla Eoff, and Wah-Ming Chang for their careful attention to detail.

For their encouragement along the way, warm thanks to Jeannette Ambrose, Elaine Bernard, Andrea Bonotto, Lynn Buchanan, Dominique Desanti, Louise Fuller, Lucia Guimaraes, Odile Hellier, Isabel Hight, Carla Kaplan, Robert Klara, Christine Levecq, Rosemary Lloyd, Claire and Ed Margolies, Rudi Mayer, Alex Miller, Toril Moi, Louis Phillips, Dominique Ridou, Pamela and Richard Stanley, Will Swift, Julie Wark, Asa Zatz, and the late Howard Zinn.

I am deeply grateful to Ellen Feldman, whose novel, *Lucy*, about Lucy Mercer, was an inspiration to me, who provided soulmate support throughout the writing, and who read my final manuscript with great care. Finally, my sister, Della, is a marvel in more ways than I can say, and my mother, Betty, was behind me all the way, interested and encouraging.

INDEX

A

Alabama Sun, 221
Algonac, 7, 73, 107
Allenswood, 5, 22–24
Alsop, Corinne Douglas Robinson, 24, 82, 115, 128
Amberjack II, 190
American Communist Party, 234
American Federation of Labor (AFL), 190
American Legion, USS, 242
American Museum of Natural History, 16
American Youth Congress (AYC), 234–35, 236, 243
Anderson, Marian, 222, 301
anti-Semitism, 228–29, 240, 289
Arthurdale, 195–96, 217, 226
Asbell, Bernard, 263
Assembly Ball, 25
Astor, Helen Schermerhorn, 7
Astor, Vincent, 121, 174
Atlanta Journal, The, 130

B

Backer, George, 224
Baruch, Bernard, 229, 267

Belgenland, SS, 145
Bellinger, Ruth, 168
Bennet, Eben, 70; FDR's polio and, 100–104, 108
Biddle, Francis, 255
birth control, 52, 71
Black, Van Lear, 96, 98, 99, 105
blacks, 235; ER and, 87, 195, 208–209, 220, 221–22, 257–58; lynchings and, 87, 221–22, 234; Subsistence Homestead Program and, 195; women workers, 88; World War I veterans, 87; World War II and, 257–58
Boettiger, Anna Eleanor Roosevelt, 115, 122, 129, 133, 148, 168, 192, 199, 201, 212, 216, 227, 244, 272, 276, 278, 283, 294, 296; birth of, 46–47; childhood of, 47, 49–50, 54, 60, 85, 91; as FDR's assistant, 263–64, 291; FDR's polio and, 114–15; and FDR's relationship with Mercer, 290–93; marriage to Curtis Dall, 129, 136
Boettiger, Johnny, 276
Boettiger, John, 263
Botts, Fred, 134
Boy Scouts, 98
Brains Trust, 169
Braun, Eva, 288
Brown, Lathrop, 26, 32, 36, 39, 72
Bruenn, Howard, 266, 267, 276–77, 279, 281–82

Buck, Pearl, 257
Bugbee, Emma, 126, 180
Bullitt, William C., 194–95, 203, 233, 237
Bussy, Dorothy Strachey, 23
Bye, George, 217

C

Calder, Frank, 68, 100–101, 105–106, 108, 109
Camp, Walter, 72
Campobello, 17, 31, 53, 68, 71, 72, 91, 97–100, 135, 190–91, 301
Camus, Albert, 284
Care and Feeding of Children, The (Holt), 47
Carmer, Carl Lamson, 283–84
Carter, Ledyard and Milburn, 49, 52
Cermak, Anton, 175
Chevy Chase Club, 67, 68, 74
China, 216
Churchill, Sarah, 262
Churchill, Winston, 237, 248, 259, 259–60, 262–63, 265, 268, 272–73, 279, 288; FDR's death and, 283
Civilian Conservation Corps (CCC), 189–90
Columbia Law School, 32, 37, 45–46
Combat, 284
communism, 86–87, 88, 174, 196, 216, 233–34, 239, 256, 295, 297
Congress, 186, 189, 201, 206, 214–15, 228, 233, 235, 241, 258, 273
contraception, 52, 71
Cook, Blanche Wiesen, 12, 198
Cook, Nancy, 127–28, 129, 158, 185, 186, 190, 195, 199, 201; ER's falling out with, 225–27; ER's relationship with, 138–39; Miller and, 162; Todhunter School and, 145–46; at Val-Kill, 129–30, 134–35, 138, 145; *Women's Democratic News* and, 138
Cooke, Alistair, 189
Coolidge, Calvin, 131
Corr, Maureen, 296

Cowles, Anna Roosevelt ("Bye") (aunt of ER), 3, 5, 6–10, 26, 29, 36, 60, 65, 66–67, 74, 78, 79, 112, 127–28, 132; ER's emulation of, 66; women's suffrage and, 57, 66
Cowles, Sheffield, 65, 74, 78, 84
Cowles, William, 65
Cox, James, 92, 94
Crosby, Maunsell, 123
Cuff Links Gang, 95, 114, 200, 201
Curtin, John, 267

D

Dall, Anna Eleanor Roosevelt, *see* Boettiger, Anna Eleanor Roosevelt
Dall, Curtis, 136, 192
Daniels, Josephus, 60–61, 65, 66, 69, 71, 73, 74, 80, 82; FDR's polio and, 113
Daniels, Mrs. Josephus, 79
Daughters of the American Revolution (DAR), 222
Davis, Livingston, 123
De Lannoy, Philippe, 7
Delano, Frederic, 102, 104, 107, 108
Delano, Laura, 107
Delano, Laura Franklin ("Polly"), 276, 279–82, 284, 285
Delano, Louise, 107
Delano, Philippe, 107
Delano, Warren (brother of Sara), 50
Delano, Warren (father of Sara), 7, 41
Democratic National Committee, 249
Democratic National Conventions: of 1920, 92; of 1924, 125–26; of 1928, 146, 147–48; of 1932, 169–71; of 1936, 207–208; of 1940, 238–39; of 1944, 268, 269
Detroit, Mich., 258
Dewey, Thomas, 268, 270–72
Dewson, Molly, 156, 172, 185
Dickerman, Marion, 127, 129, 138, 161, 185, 190, 191, 199, 201; ER's falling out with, 225–27; ER's relationship with, 139; on labor relations

committee, 226; Miller and, 162; Todhunter School and, 145–46; at Val-Kill, 129–30, 135–36, 138, 145; *Women's Democratic News* and, 138

Dies, Martin, 216

Dolphin, 73

Douglas, Lewis, 186

Dowdell's Knob, 142

Draper, George, 81, 82, 105, 110–14, 117, 118, 127

Dreier, Mary, 185

E

Early, Stephen, 93, 95, 96, 98, 188, 192, 202, 208–209, 213, 214, 270, 271, 282–83, 291

Edward VIII, King, 212

Eisenhower, Dwight, 297, 301

Eleanor and Franklin (Lash), xiv

Eleanor Roosevelt: Reluctant First Lady (Hickok), 176, 182, 184

Eleanor Roosevelt's Weekly Forum, 295

Elizabeth, Queen, 229–32, 258

Ely, Albert, 69

Emergency Rescue Committee, 257

F

Fair Employment Practices Act, 289

Fala, 247–48, 271, 275, 276, 281; FDR's speech about, 270–71

Farley, James, 169, 170, 173, 174, 200

FBI (Federal Bureau of Investigation), 255–56

FDR: A Biography (Morgan), 119

F.D.R., My Boss (Tully), 294

Federal Arts Project, 205

Federal Emergency Relief Administration (FERA), 189, 194, 195, 198, 205

Federal Theatre Project, 206, 234

Federal Writers' Project, 205–206

Ferguson, Hector, 45

Ferguson, Isabella Selmes, 45, 46, 51, 57–58, 60, 67, 70, 83, 87, 118, 128; FDR's polio and, 113

Ferguson, Robert Munro, 26, 41, 45, 52, 57–58, 67, 83, 118

Fidelity and Deposit Company of Maryland, 96, 105, 115, 117, 120, 123, 159

Fischer, Louis, 220–21

flappers, 128–29

Forbes, Dora, 84, 107

Ford, Edsel, 141–42

Fox, George, 193, 267, 276, 279

France, 233

Franco, Francisco, 211, 216, 249

Frankfurter, Felix, 229

Franklin D. Roosevelt: A Career in Progressive Democracy (Lindley), 167

Franklin D. Roosevelt Memorial Bridge, 301

Franklin D. Roosevelt Presidential Library and Museum, xiii–xiv, xv, xvii, 223, 244–45, 253, 275, 289–90

Franklin-Eleanor relationship: courtship and engagement, 29–38, 41; divorce considered, 82, 294; European trip (1919), 83–84; FDR's death and, 287; fortieth anniversary, 274; honeymoon, 41, 42–45; independence in, 132, 136, 175–76; mystery and secrecy surrounding, xv; Nesbitt and, 198; political nature of, xvi; Sara and, 30, 31, 32–37, 38; scandalous stories about, 294; sex in, 52, 71; side-taking in views of, xi–xii; train meeting, 3, 5–6, 29; twentieth anniversary, 132; Val-Kill and, 139; Warm Springs and, 139; wedding, 38, 39–42

Freud, Sigmund, 194–95

Friends of Roosevelt, 167

G

Galbraith, John Kenneth, 297, 298

Gallagher, Hugh Gregory, 140

Gandy, Kitty, 44

Garner, John, 170, 207
Gellhorn, Martha, xv–xvi
Gennerich, August Adolph ("Gus"), 164, 171, 175, 193, 208, 223, 224; death of, 212, 213, 223
George VI, King, 229–32, 258
George Washington, 83
Germany, Nazi, xviii, 189, 211, 216, 228, 233, 237, 239, 242, 248, 257, 260, 272, 278, 283, 288, 289; *Kristallnacht* in, 228; Lindbergh and, 240; Soviet pact with, 233, 234, 235
GI Bill of Rights, 261–62
Goodwin, Doris Kearns, xiv
Gould, Bruce, 217
Grayson, Cary, 77, 78
Great Britain: ER's visit to, 258–59; visit of King George and Queen Elizabeth, 229–32; in World War II, 233, 237, 248, 268
Great Depression, xviii, 141, 146, 163–64, 169, 172, 179, 194, 195, 216; end of, 256; FDR's economic policies, 180–81, 185–86, 188, 189
Gregory, Cleburne, 130–31
Gridiron dinner, 187, 219
Groton School, 32, 49, 65, 179; Elliott Roosevelt at, 133; FDR at, 17–20, 26; James Roosevelt at, 91, 94, 113, 125; John Roosevelt at, 129
Guadalcanal, 261
Gugler, Eric, 196
Gurewitsch, David, 298–301
Gurewitsch, Edna Perkel, 300, 301

H

Hackmeister, Louise, 212
Half Moon, 16, 28, 31, 48, 49, 70, 91
Hall, Mary, 10–11, 21–23, 25, 26, 30, 31, 74; death of, 88
Hall, Valentine, 21
Halsey, William F., 260–61
Harald V, 254
Harding, Warren, 93, 124, 127
Harvard Crimson, 6, 30, 37, 186

Harvard University, 58, 237; FDR at, 5–6, 26–27, 30, 37
Hassett, Bill, 274, 276–77, 279, 281–82
Hawkey, Harry, 54, 59
Helm, Edith, 255
Hemingway, Ernest, xvi
Hickok, Lorena, 159–60, 172–73, 175, 187, 190, 191, 207, 209, 213, 222, 225, 227, 249, 251, 259, 284–85, 287–88; *Eleanor Roosevelt: Reluctant First Lady*, 176, 182, 184; and ER's becoming first lady, 183, 184, 185; ER's relationship with, 160, 172–73, 176–77, 183–85, 193–94, 198–99; ER's trip to California with, 198–99; ER's trip to French Canada with, 191–92; at FERA, 194, 195, 198; in Puerto Rico, 198; resignation from Associated Press, 193
Hitler, Adolf, xviii, 189, 211, 228–29, 233, 237, 240, 247, 257, 283, 288
Hobcaw Barony, 267
Holt, L. Emmett, 47
Hooker, Harry, 273–74
Hoover, Herbert, 146, 147, 163–64, 169, 173, 174, 176, 179, 215, 216
Hoover, J. Edgar, 255, 256
Hoovervilles, 169
Hopkins, Diana, 242, 247–48, 251, 271
Hopkins, Harry, 189, 194, 198, 201, 205, 220, 223, 241–42, 246, 249, 251, 262, 263, 273, 285–86; marriage of, 251
Hopkins, Louise Macy, 251, 263
Hopkins, Robert, 262
Houghteling, Laura, 229
House Un-American Activities Committee (HUAC), 216, 234, 255, 295, 297, 298
Houston, USS, 198
Howe, Grace, 56, 59, 91, 98, 99, 115–16, 157, 190, 192, 201–202
Howe, Hartley, 98, 103, 116, 157, 190, 192
Howe, Louis McHenry, 91, 98, 99, 115, 132, 165; Arthurdale and, 196; death and funeral of, 207, 213; ER and, xvii, 80, 82–83, 95, 96, 104, 115, 116, 128, 138, 153, 155, 187, 203, 208,

216, 277; ER on, 64–65; ER's friends and, 129; FDR and, xvii, 59–60, 64–65, 93, 95, 96, 115–17, 120, 122, 123, 132, 156, 157, 159, 200, 241, 244; FDR interviewed by, 56; FDR-Mercer affair and, 82–83; FDR's gubernatorial campaign and, 147–49, 151; FDR's polio and, 100–102, 104–106, 108–15, 124; FDR's political comeback and, 124–25; FDR's presidential campaign and, 166–67, 169, 170, 171, 173–74; on Florida trip, 122–23; health problems of, 192, 200–202, 206–207; Hickok and, 172, 176; Miller and, 162; New Deal and, 190; Newport affair and, 92, 97; Sara Roosevelt and, 60, 115, 117, 133; at White House, 181, 192; *Women's Democratic News* and, 138

Howe, Mary, 99, 115–16

Hubbard, LeRoy, 142

Hunting Big Game in the Eighties (Roosevelt), 11

Hurst, Fannie, 206

Hyde Park, 14; farming land at, 141; FDR Library and Museum at, xiii–xiv, xv, xvii, 223, 244–45, 253, 275, 289–90; Roosevelt friends' land and homes at, 212, 223, 224; royal visit to, 230, 231–32; Springwood estate, *see* Springwood estate, Hyde Park; Top Cottage, x, 223–24, 228, 232, 236, 254; Val-Kill, xiii–xiv, 129–30, 134–39, 145, 162, 168

I

Ickes, Harold, 189, 190, 195, 196, 220, 222

Indianapolis, 211, 212

Indiscreet Letters from Peking (Weale), 49

infantile paralysis, *see* polio

International Congress of Working Women, 88

International Rescue and Relief Committee, 257

International Student Service, 243, 244, 249

Italy, 211, 239

J

Jackson, Andrew, 187

James, Henry, 22

Japan, 216, 239, 246, 257, 260, 261, 272, 273, 278, 283; Pearl Harbor, 103, 246–47, 252

Japanese Americans, internment camps for, 257

Johnson, James, 143

Jones, Leroy, 113, 120, 122

K

Keen, W. W., 101, 102

Kennedy, John F., xiv, 297–98, 300, 301

Kuhn, Mrs. Hartman, 31

L

labor, 64–65, 226, 234

Labor, Department of, 155

Ladies' Home Journal, 217, 218

Lahey, Frank, 266, 267

Lake, Kathleen, 114, 117–18, 120, 121

Landon, Alf, 208, 209

Lape, Esther, 97, 123, 185, 225

Larooco, 123, 132, 134

Lash, Gertrude ("Trude"), 249, 254, 256, 261, 286–87, 295–96, 298

Lash, Joseph, 138, 168, 234–37, 243, 247, 254, 258, 286, 299; book written by, xiv; ER's relationship with, 249–50, 255–56; ER's visit to, in Guadalcanal, 261; FBI and, 255–56; in military, 250, 255, 256, 261; Pratt and, 249

Law, Nigel, 74, 75, 77

Leach, Agnes, 168
League of Nations, 92, 93
League of Women Voters, 128, 168
LeHand, Bernard, 144, 190
LeHand, Marguerite ("Missy"), xvii, 94,
    96, 98, 121–22, 124, 137, 157, 158,
    164, 165, 167–68, 170, 171, 172,
    190, 192, 193, 209, 224, 235–37;
    Betsey Roosevelt and, 213; breakdown
    suffered by, 142–44; Bullitt and,
    194–95, 203; death of, 269–70; ER
    and, 122, 144; and FDR as governor,
    154–55; FDR's estate and, 245; FDR's
    polio and, 105, 106, 110, 117; FDR's
    relationship with, 129, 130, 132–35,
    139–41, 144–45, 148, 154–55,
    162–63, 168, 194, 217, 243–44,
    251–52, 270; on Florida trip, 122–23;
    move to Boston, 251; profile of, 194;
    stroke suffered by, 243–46, 251–52,
    263; Tully and, 156–57; World War II
    and, 233
Lend-Lease, 241, 247, 248
Leviathan, 81
Levine, Samuel, 102
Lincoln, Abraham, 4
Lincoln Memorial, 222
Lindbergh, Charles, 171, 240
Lindley, Ernest, 167
Longworth, Alice Roosevelt, 17, 20–21,
    29, 30, 39–40, 41, 75, 82; affair of,
    78, 81; debut of, 5, 25; and FDR's
    affair with Mercer, 78–79
Longworth, Nicholas, 78
Lovett, Robert, 102–105, 111, 113, 114,
    117–18, 120–21, 134
Low, George Cabot Ward, 18–19
Loyless, Tom, 127, 130, 134
Ludwig, Emil, 93
Lynch, Tom, 93–94

M

MacArthur, Douglas, 269
Macy, Louise, *see* Hopkins, Louise Macy
Mahoney, Helena, 142–43, 144

Mann, Katy, 10, 11
Martha, Princess, 242, 254, 272
McCarthy, Charles, 94
McCarthy, Joe, 295, 297
McDonald, William, 135
McDuffie, Irwin, 164, 165, 192
McEachern, Elespie, 41
McIntire, Ross, 193, 201, 207, 237, 243,
    266–68, 276, 282–83
McIntyre, Marvin, 93, 192, 202, 213
McKinley, William, 4, 6
Mercer, Carroll, 67, 68
Mercer, Lucy, *see* Rutherfurd, Lucy
    Mercer
Mercer, Minnie, 67, 68
Mercer, Violetta, 75
Meriwether Inn, 126, 134
Metropolitan Club, 67
Miller, Earl, 160–63, 165, 168, 171,
    199, 223, 225, 236, 250, 294
Miller, Simone, 294
miners, 195
Moley, Raymond, 169, 175, 181
Morestin, Hippolyte, 84
Morgan, Ted, 119, 224
Morgenthau, Elinor, 138, 168, 192
Morgenthau, Henry, Jr., 192–93, 229
Moskowitz, Belle, 155
Munn, Charlie, 77
Mussolini, Benito, 205, 211, 288
My Boy Franklin (Roosevelt), 15
My Parents: A Differing View (Roosevelt),
    82

N

National Association for the
    Advancement of Colored People
    (NAACP), 221
National Progressive Party (Bull
    Moosers), 58
National Recovery Administration
    (NRA), 189
Naval Bill, 72
Negro Digest, 258
Nehru, Pandit, xiv

Nesbitt, Henrietta, 197–98, 202, 213, 264
Newboldt, Mary, 20
New Deal, 171, 189–90, 196, 205–206, 208, 209, 213–16, 226, 229, 235, 239
Newport affair, 92, 97–98, 99
Newsweek, 194
New Woman, 128–29
New York, 92
New York Boy Scouts, 98
New Yorker, The, 166
New York Evening Journal, 166
New York Herald, 56
New York Herald Tribune, 180
New York League of Women Voters, 96–97
New York Post, 149, 224
New York State Democratic Committee, 169; Women's Division of, 128, 139, 145, 156, 166, 172, 192, 226
New York Times, The, 56, 76, 98, 153, 207, 216, 217, 218, 294; FDR's polio reported in, 109–10
New York Tribune, 72
New York World Telegram, 56
Nixon, Richard, 298
No Ordinary Time: Franklin and Eleanor Roosevelt: The Home Front in World War II (Goodwin), xiv
Norris, George, 239
Norway, 242

Ochs, Adolph S., 110
O'Day, Caroline, 138, 166, 172
Olav, Prince, 242
Olivia (Bussy), 23
Olmsted, Frederick Law, Jr., 196
Osthagen, Henry, 227

Palmer, A. Mitchell, 86–87
Parish, Susan, 30, 36, 38, 291

Peabody, Endicott, 18, 32, 39, 179, 285
Peabody, George Foster, 126, 137
Pearl Harbor, 103, 246–47, 252
Pegler, Westbrook, 294
Perkins, Frances, 92, 103, 115, 155–56, 181, 185, 188, 190, 206, 226, 238
Phillips, Caroline Drayton, 118
Pine Mountain, 142; FDR's farm at, 141
Platt, Charles A., 46
polio (infantile paralysis), 72–73; of FDR, xvi–xvii, xviii, 98, 100–18, 119–27, 130–33, 135, 140, 142, 143, 147, 149, 150, 188–89, 193, 217–19, 224, 300; of FDR, public perception of, xvii, 124–26, 131, 132, 146, 149, 150, 188–89, 232; fund-raising for, 213; Salk vaccine for, 300; Warm Springs and, 126, 134
Pooks Hill, 242
Poughkeepsie Eagle News, 94
Pratt, Gertrude ("Trude"), *see* Lash, Gertrude
Presidential Special, 204
Prettyman, Arthur, 279
Prohibition, 147, 164, 186
Proust, Marcel, 22
Public Works Administration (PWA), 189
Puerto Rico, 198

Q

Quincy, 272, 273

R

Read, Elizabeth, 96–97, 185, 215, 225, 227
Red Cross, 79, 80, 129, 260
Reed, John, 195
Reed, Louise Bryant, 195
Reilly, Mike, 208, 240, 267, 276, 281
Robbins, Irene, 74–75
Robbins, Kassie, 32, 107, 176

Robbins, Muriel, 32

Robbins, Warren Delano, 74–75

Robinson, Corinne Douglas (cousin of ER), *see* Alsop, Corinne Douglas Robinson

Robinson, Corinne Roosevelt (aunt of ER), 3, 6, 7, 14, 31

Robinson, Douglas, 10

Rochon, Anna, 251, 269, 270

Rockey, Edna, 104, 113, 117–18, 120, 121

Rollins, Alfred B., 157–58

Roosevelt, Alice (daughter of TR), *see* Longworth, Alice Roosevelt

Roosevelt, Alice Hathaway Lee (first wife of TR), 20

Roosevelt, Anna ("Bye") (aunt of ER), *see* Cowles, Anna Roosevelt

Roosevelt, Anna Eleanor (daughter of ER and FDR), *see* Boettiger, Anna Eleanor Roosevelt

Roosevelt, Anna Hall (mother of ER), 8–11, 88; death of, 10–11, 12, 20, 21; ER's relationship with, 11–12, 21, 46

Roosevelt, Betsey Cushing, 179, 213–14

Roosevelt, Edith, 21, 39, 84

Roosevelt, Eleanor: alcohol and, 199–200; ambition of, 182–83; Anna (mother) and, 11–12, 21, 46; on Anna (daughter) as FDR's assistant, 263–64; Anna born to, 46–47; Arthurdale project of, 195–96, 217, 226; assertiveness gained by, 74; autobiography of, xvii, 3, 8, 11, 12, 23, 24, 43, 44, 48, 51, 58, 117, 181–83, 217–222, 248, 251, 263–64, 290; birth of, 9; at boarding school, 5, 22–24; Bullitt and, 195; character of, 20–21, 29–30; childhood of, 3, 11–14, 20–24; Churchill and, 248, 259, 265; communal living enjoyed by, 191–92, 300; Communists and, 233–34, 256; Cook's relationship with, 138–39; courage of, xviii, 132; daily schedule at White House, 192–93; death of, 295, 301–302; debut of, 24, 25–16; at Democratic convention of 1940, 238; depression suffered by, 51, 54; diary

of, 184; Dickerman's relationship with, 139; Elliott (father) and, 11–14, 21; Elliott born to, 54; FBI file on, 255–56; and FDR as governor, 153–54, 159–60; FDR's death and, 282–84, 287, 288, 290; FDR's failing health and, 277; FDR's funeral and, 284–87; FDR's inauguration and, 179, 180, 181; FDR's polio and, 100–104, 107–109, 112–14, 116–18, 120–22, 124; FDR's relationship with, *see* Franklin-Eleanor relationship; FDR's vice-presidential campaign and, 93, 94–95; Ferguson and, 26; as first lady, 175, 181–82, 185, 219; Franklin Jr. born to (1914), 70; and Franklin Jr.'s birth and death (1909), 51–52, 54; funeral of, 301–302; governor's mansion and, 158; grave of, xiii, 302; Greenwich Village apartment of, 225; Griselda moods of, 44, 74–75; Gurewitsch's relationship with, 298–300; Hall's death and, 245; health decline of, 300–301; hemorrhoid operation of, 47; Hickok's memoir of, 176, 182, 184; Hickok's relationship with, 160, 172–73, 176–77, 183–85, 193–94, 198–99; Hickok's trip to California with, 198–99; Hickok's trip to French Canada with, 191; Hopkins and, 241–42, 251; as hostess, 67; houses of, 44, 45–46, 48, 51, 53, 55, 65, 96, 129–30; on Howe, 64–65; Howe and, xvii, 80, 82–83, 95, 96, 104, 115, 116, 128, 138, 153, 155, 187, 203, 208, 216, 277; International Congress of Working Women attended by, 88; interviewed on household management, 76–77; James born to, 49; John born to, 71; Kennedy and, 297–98, 301; Lash's relationship with, 249–50, 255–56; LeHand and, 122, 144; lesbian friends of, 97, 129, 185; as liberal voice, 295; Martha and, 254; Miller's relationship with, 160–63, 168, 250; motherhood as viewed by, 46–47, 70; "My Day" columns of,

202–203, 208, 212, 214, 215, 218, 227, 230–31, 232, 247, 258, 259, 260, 288, 295; New Deal projects and, 209; on New York League of Women Voters board, 96–97; photographs of, 161; physical appearance of, 9, 21, 159–60, 161, 173; pleurisy of, 84; political activities of, 128, 133, 150, 153–54, 155, 166, 172, 183, 209, 296–97; political influence of, 219–22; as political wife, 56–57, 65–66, 94–95, 153–54, 159–60, 175, 181–83; popularity of, xviii, 216; pregnancies of, 45–46, 48, 49, 52, 53, 54, 67, 68; 69–70, 71; press conferences of, 187, 208–209; in Puerto Rico, 198; race consciousness of, 87, 195, 208–209, 220, 221–22, 257–58; Red Cross work of, 79, 80, 260; on Sara, 48, 85–86, 117; Sara's relationship with, 45–46, 47–48, 51, 55, 56, 85–86, 91, 96, 130, 132, 133, 136, 217–18, 244, 264, 277; servants and, 76–77, 87, 158; in settlement movement, 36; sex and, 41, 52, 71; shyness of, 67; socializing of, 65–66, 67; Southern attitudes and, 208, 213, 221; South Pacific trip of, 260–61; Souvestre and, 5, 22–24, 25, 29–30, 42, 46, 66, 97, 165, 185; Stevenson and, 297; as teacher at Todhunter School, 145–46, 150, 153, 165–66; Thompson's friendship with, 227; *This Troubled World*, 217; trust fund of, 46; United Nations work of, 294–95, 299; Val-Kill cottage of, *see* Val-Kill; visits to hospitals and military posts in World War II, 260–61, 265; visits to prisons, hospitals, and asylums, 161; White House and, 186–87; as *Women's Democratic News* editor, 138, 145, 153, 166; women's suffrage and, 57; World War II and, 256–62, 265; *You Learn by Living*, 139

Roosevelt, Elliott (father of ER), 3, 4, 6, 8–11, 20, 225; death of, 11, 14, 21; ER's relationship with, 11–14, 21

Roosevelt, Elliott (son of ER and FDR), 168, 170, 171, 262, 286; birth of, 54; childhood of, 55, 83, 85, 91; on ER's writings, 218–19; FDR's polio and, 146; at Groton, 133; in World War II, 247

Roosevelt, Elliott, Jr. ("Ellie") (brother of ER), 9–13

Roosevelt, Franklin Delano: advisers and colleagues of, 156, 157–58, 165, 169, 219; airplane trips of, 171, 259–60; Anna as assistant to, 263–64, 291; anti-Semitism and, 229; assassination attempt on, 174–75; as assistant secretary of the navy, 61, 63–69, 73–74, 79–80, 83–84, 91, 92, 93, 97–98; automobiles of, 141, 224; in Big Three meetings, 262–63, 272–73; bird collection of, xiii, 16, 41, 290; birth of, 8, 15; Brains Trust organized by, 169; Bullitt and, 194–95; calmness of, 103, 216; childhood of, 14–20; Churchill and, 248, 259–60, 262–63, 268, 272–73, 279; cocktails of, 164, 199–200; code devised by, 28; communal living enjoyed by, 132, 191–92; Congress and, 186, 189, 201, 206, 214–15, 228, 233, 235, 241, 258, 273; daily schedule of, 164–65, 193; death of, xv, 266, 282–84, 287, 288, 290, 291; at Democratic convention of 1920, 92; at Democratic convention of 1924, 125–26; at Democratic convention of, 1928, 146; at Democratic convention of 1932, 171; economic crisis and, 180–81, 185–86, 188, 189; elected president, xvii, 173–74, 179; ER's political influence on, 219–22; ER's relationship with, *see* Franklin-Eleanor relationship; Fala speech of, 270–71; Fidelity and Deposit Company and, 96, 105, 115, 117, 120, 123, 159; fifty-fifth birthday of, 213; fireside chats of, 187–88, 215, 233; first hundred days of presidency, 186, 189–90; flirtatiousness of, 44, 79, 224, 243, 254; in Florida, 122–23;

Roosevelt, Franklin Delano (*cont.*)
food and, 197, 198, 214; funeral of, 284–87, 290; Gennerich's death and, 212, 213; good looks and athleticism of, 71–72, 92, 94, 97, 167; as governor of New York, xvii, 148–49, 151, 153–59, 164–67; grave of, ix, 302; at Groton, 17–20, 26; gubernatorial campaign of, 147–49, 151; at Harvard, 5–6, 26–27, 30, 37; health decline of, 263, 265–69, 271, 273, 275–77, 279–82; heart attack of, 237; Hopkins and, 241–42, 286–87; houses of, 44, 45–46, 48, 51, 53, 55, 65, 96; Howe and, *see* Howe, Louis; inauguration as governor, 158–59; inaugurations as president, xviii, 179–81, 213, 244, 272; James as secretary to, 213, 26; law practice of, 49, 52, 96, 115; in law school, 32, 37, 45–46; LeHand's relationship with, 129, 130, 132–35, 139–41, 144–45, 148, 154–55, 162–63, 168, 194, 217, 243–44, 251–52, 270; *see also* LeHand, Marguerite; Lend-Lease program of, 241, 247, 248; Lindley's biography of, 167; Martha and, 242, 254; Mercer's affair with, xv, xvi, 71, 72, 75, 78–79, 81–83, 144–45, 217, 252–53, 280, 284, 290–94; Miller and, 162; naval collection of, ix, 64, 289; New Deal of, 171, 189–90, 196, 205–206, 208, 209, 213–16, 226, 229, 235, 239; Newport affair and, 92, 97–98, 99; night episodes of, 43, 45, 48–49; photographs of, 130–31, 149, 188–89, 271; pneumonia of, 81; polio of, xvi–xvii, xviii, 98, 100–18, 119–27, 130–33, 135, 140, 142, 143, 147, 149, 150, 188–89, 193, 217–19, 224, 300; political ambitions of, 28, 29, 52, 53, 84, 122, 131, 149, 166, 169, 182; political comeback of, 124–26, 133, 145, 147; political views of, 163–64; as presidential candidate, 166–67, 169, 170–73, 182; press conferences of, 186; privacy and secrecy of, xvii, 219; Prohibition ended by, 186; public perception of disability of, xvii, 124–26, 131, 132, 146, 149, 150, 188–89, 232; radio addresses of, 40, 164, 169, 187–88, 215, 233; rare books of, 42, 43; reelected governor, 166; reelected president in 1936, 207–208, 209, 214; reelected president in 1940, 237–40; reelected president in 1944, 265–66, 268–72; retirement planned by, 222–23; salary as governor, 159; salary as president, 217; Sara's relationship with, xvii, 15–16, 17, 27, 28, 30, 32–37, 38, 44, 117, 159, 244–45, 264; Schiff and, 224; second presidential term of, 215–16, 222; Smith's nomination addresses by, 125–26; Social Security Bill of, 201, 206; Sohier and, 28–29; South American trip of, 211–12; stamp collection of, 16, 49, 290; as state senator, 52–57, 59–60, 182; storytelling of, 219, 224, 232; Suckley and, 203–205, 223–24, 253–54; Supreme Court and, 206, 212, 214–15; Tammany Hall and, 56, 59, 70; throat infection of, 78; TR and, 5, 66, 93, 237; trip to Virginia, Kentucky, and Tennessee, 50; trust fund of, 33, 46, 159; tutors of, 17; typhoid fever contracted by, 59, 60; U.S. Senate campaign of, 70; vice-presidential campaign, 92–95; at Warm Springs, 126–27, 130–31, 134, 139, 141, 154–57, 161, 199–200, 224, 245–46, 276–78, 280; Warm Springs purchased by, 134, 137, 141–42, 145; will and estate of, 245, 302; World War I and, 69, 71, 74, 79–80, 83

Roosevelt, Franklin, Jr. (son of ER and FDR, born and died 1909), 51–52, 54, 244

Roosevelt, Franklin, Jr. (son of ER and FDR, born 1914), 133, 135, 190; birth of, 70; childhood of, 83, 85, 91; in World War II, 247

Roosevelt, Hall (brother of ER), 10–12, 21, 13–14, 32, 49, 50, 60, 199, 223; death of, 245; marriage of, 58

Roosevelt, James (son of ER and FDR), 172, 176, 179, 180, 190, 211, 245, 267, 268, 269, 272, 287; birth of, 49; childhood of, 49–50, 54, 85, 86, 91; on FDR-Mercer affair, 82; FDR's polio and, 113–15, 125–26, 150, 208; at Groton, 91, 94, 113, 125; on Miller, 162; as presidential secretary, 213, 263; in World War II, 247

Roosevelt, James, Jr. ("Rosy") (half brother of FDR), 7, 16, 19, 27, 29, 30, 129

Roosevelt, James, Sr. (father of FDR), 6–8, 14–15, 16, 17, 26, 244; death of, 6, 27; fortune of, 33; heart problems of, 17, 27, 117

Roosevelt, John Aspinwall (son of ER and FDR), 133, 171, 190, 218; birth of, 71; childhood of, 72–73, 83, 85, 91; at Groton, 129; in World War II, 247

Roosevelt, Margaret Richardson (wife of Hall Roosevelt), 58, 60

Roosevelt, Martha, 7

Roosevelt, Quentin, 79–80

Roosevelt, Sally, 297

Roosevelt, Sara Delano ("Sallie"), 6, 8, 27, 34, 47, 176, 278, 289; Anna's marriage and, 136; Cook and, 129; death of, 244; ER on, 48, 85–86, 117; ER's autobiography and, 217–18; ER's relationship with, 45–46, 47–48, 51, 55, 56, 85–86, 91, 96, 130, 132, 133, 136, 217–18, 244, 277; FDR and ER's honeymoon and, 41, 42–43, 45; and FDR as assistant secretary of the navy, 63; and FDR as governor, 159; and FDR's affair with Mercer, 82–83; FDR's birth and, 15; FDR's courtship with ER and, 30, 31, 32–37, 38; FDR's polio and, 104, 106–108, 114, 117, 119–22, 133; FDR's relationship with, xvii, 15–16, 17, 27, 28, 30, 32–37, 38, 44, 117, 159, 244–45; and FDR's schooling at Groton, 17, 19–20; fortune of, 33, 46, 47–48, 159; houses procured for FDR and ER by, 44, 46, 48, 51, 53; Howe and, 60, 115, 117, 133; husband's heart attack and, 17; marriage of, 6–8; Miller and, 161–62;

royal visit and, 231, 232; Top Cottage and, 223; Val-Kill and, 136, 138

Roosevelt, Taddy, 19, 26–27, 28

Roosevelt, Theodore, xi, 6, 20, 26, 53, 55, 57, 58, 61, 67, 171, 191, 274; becomes president, 4, 182; death of, 83–84; Elliott Roosevelt and, 9, 10; FDR and, 5, 66, 93, 237; FDR's marriage to ER and, 37–38, 39, 40; as governor, 4, 158–59; Groton talk of, 19; political rise of, 3–4; political views of, 4, 5, 18; presidential election won by, 38; on Quentin's death, 79–80; World War I and, 69, 74

Roosevelt, Theodore, Jr., 127

Roosevelt Special, 172

Rosenman, Sam, 149–50, 154, 157, 165, 167, 170, 171, 199, 219, 223, 224, 229, 239, 248

Rosenvelt, Claes van, 3

Roser, Mr., 22

Russian Revolution, 86–87, 195

Rutherfurd, Barbara, 280

Rutherfurd, Lucy Mercer, 67–68, 77, 78, 252, 265, 267, 278, 280–81; death of, 293; ER's hiring of, 67; FDR's affair with, xv, xvi, 71, 72, 75, 78–79, 81–83, 144–45, 217, 252–53, 280, 284, 290–94; FDR's death and, 282, 284, 291; Law and, 74, 75; marriage of, 89; navy assignment of, 75; Shoumatoff and, 280, 291–92, 294

Rutherfurd, Winthrop, 89, 252, 292; death of, 265

S

Sabalo, 98, 99, 105

Salk, Jonas, 300

Sanger, Margaret, 52

Schiff, Dorothy, 224

Schwartz, Nell, 155

Secret Service, 249, 253, 259, 267, 280, 281, 285

Selassie, Haile, xiv

settlement houses, 36

sex and birth control, 52, 71
Shaw, Alice Sohier, 28–29
Sheehan, William F., 56
Shoumatoff, Elizabeth, 280–82, 291–92, 294
Simpson, Wallis, 212
Smith, Alfred E., 124, 127, 131, 146–49, 150–51, 155, 158, 160, 169; FDR's nomination speeches for, 125–26, 146
Social Security Act, 201, 206
Sohier, Alice, 28–29
South America, 211–12
Souvestre, Marie, 5, 22–24, 25, 29–30, 46, 66, 97, 128, 165, 185; death of, 42
Soviet Union, 195, 234, 260, 294; Big Three meetings, 262–63; Germany's pact with, 233, 234, 235
Spain, 211, 216, 220, 249
Spanish influenza, 81, 83
Springwood estate, Hyde Park, xiii, 6, 7, 15, 96, 130, 139, 165, 222–23; extension of, 70; FDR and ER's honeymoon at, 41–42; FDR's convalescence at, 119–20; FDR's will and, 289
Staff Officer's Scrap-book During the Russo-Japanese War, A (Hamilton), 49
Stalin, Joseph, 259, 262–63, 265, 266, 272–73, 279
State Department, 257
Stephen, Leslie, 22
Stevenson, Adlai, xv–xvi, 297
stock market, 163, 216
Strachey, Lytton, 23
Subsistence Homestead Program, 195–96
Suckley, Margaret ("Daisy"), 203–205, 223–24, 228, 231, 253–54, 259, 265, 266–68, 272, 275–82, 284, 285, 292
Supreme Court, 206, 212, 214–15
Suspect, The, 274
Sylph, 75, 77

Teamsters Union, 270
Teapot Dome scandal, 127
Tennessee Valley Authority (TVA), 189
Thant, U, 301
Thiel, Seline, 91
This Troubled World (Roosevelt), 217
Thompson, Malvina ("Tommy"), 150, 165, 193, 199, 203, 211, 216, 225, 226, 227, 233, 255, 258–61, 265, 278, 282, 287, 288, 294, 296; death of, 296; ER's friendship with, 227
Time, 198
Tito, Marshal, xiv
Todhunter, Winifred, 145
Todhunter School for Girls, 129, 145–46, 150, 153, 165–66, 226
Toombs, Henry, 134
Top Cottage, xiv, 223–24, 228, 232, 236, 254
Town Topic, 25, 37, 42
Tripartite Pact, 239
Truman, Harry S., 269, 283, 288, 289, 294, 296, 301
Tully, Grace, 150, 156, 157, 158, 165, 170, 171, 206, 243, 246, 265, 279, 284, 284; LeHand and, 156–57; memorabilia and, 244–45
Tuscaloosa, 241

U

United Nations, 273, 278, 281, 282; ER's work for, 294–95, 299
United States Committee for the Care of European Children, 257
Universal Declaration of Human Rights, 295, 299
University Settlement House, 36

V

Val-Kill, xiii–xiv, 129–30, 134–39, 162, 168, 224–26, 227, 232, 236, 288

T

Taft, William Howard, 53, 58
Tammany Hall, 56, 59, 70

Val-Kill Industries, 138, 141, 145, 225, 226
Vanderbilt family, 14
Vanderlip, Mrs. Frank, 96
Vireo, 91

W

Wagner-Rogers Bill, 229
Wallace, Henry, 238, 269
Washington, D.C.: race riots in, 87; social life in, 65–66
Warm Springs, 126–27, 130–31, 134, 139, 141, 148, 154–57, 161, 199–200, 224, 244, 245–46, 276–78, 280; FDR's purchase of, 134, 137, 141–42, 145; opened to public, 301
Washington *Evening Star*, 201
Washington Post, The, 80, 89
Watson, Edwin ("Pa"), 262, 273
Webb, Beatrice, 22
Webb, Sidney, 22
Weona II, 122
Westboro, 93, 94
White, Walter, 221, 222
White House, 186–87, 191–92; cooking in, 196–98, 214; renovation of, 196, 201, 202; World War II and, 247
White House Diary (Nesbitt), 197
Wilderstein, 275
Willkie, Wendell, 239, 240, 242
Wilson, Woodrow, 58, 60–61, 69, 72, 73, 74, 80, 83, 84, 86, 92
Wiltwyck School for Boys, xiv
Women's Democratic News, 138, 145, 153, 166
Women's Division of the New York State Democratic Committee, 128, 139, 145, 156, 166, 172, 192, 226

women's suffrage, 57, 66, 93, 96
Women's Trade Union League, 128
women workers, 88
Woolf, Virginia, 22
Works Progress Administration (WPA), 205–206, 220
World, The, 11
World War I, 69, 71, 72, 79–80, 81, 84–85, 129, 217; black soldiers in, 87; end of, 83, 92; FDR and, 69, 71, 74, 79–80, 83; U.S. entry into, 73–74, 76, 92
World War II, xviii, 228–29, 232, 235, 237, 239, 247, 248, 250, 251, 254, 256–57, 268, 269, 278, 279, 283, 288, 289; Anglo-American relations and, 229–30, 258; Big Three meetings, 262–63, 272–73, 279; end of, 277, 288; ER and, 256–62, 265; FDR's fourth term and, 265–66; FDR's meeting with Churchill, 259–60; Japanese Americans and, 257; Jewish immigrants and, 228–29; Lend-Lease in, 241, 247, 248; Pearl Harbor, 103, 246–47, 252; outbreak of, 233; preparedness for, 216, 217, 228; U.S. entry into, xviii, 246, 247, 256, 257, 265; veterans of, 261–62

Y

Yalta, 272–73, 279
You Learn by Living (Roosevelt), 139

Z

Zangara, Giuseppe, 175